MYTH AND LAW AMONG THE INDO-EUROPEANS

PUBLISHED UNDER THE AUSPICES OF THE CENTER FOR THE STUDY OF COMPARATIVE FOLKLORE AND MYTHOLOGY, UNIVERSITY OF CALIFORNIA, LOS ANGELES

PUBLICATIONS OF THE UCLA CENTER FOR THE STUDY OF COMPARATIVE FOLKLORE AND MYTHOLOGY

1. Jaan Puhvel (ed.), *Myth and Law among the Indo-Europeans.* 1970.

Myth and Law Among the Indo-Europeans

Studies in Indo-European Comparative Mythology

edited by JAAN PUHVEL

UNIVERSITY OF CALIFORNIA PRESS
Berkeley Los Angeles London 1970

UCLA CENTER FOR THE STUDY OF
COMPARATIVE FOLKLORE AND MYTHOLOGY

Publications: I

University of California Press
Berkeley and Los Angeles, California

University of California Press, Ltd.
London, England

ISBN: 0-520-01587-8
Library of Congress Catalog Card Number: 75-627781
Designed by David Pauly
Printed in the United States of America

Preface

Research activity in Indo-European comparative mythology has been regularly pursued at the University of California, Los Angeles, since the academic year 1959–60, when the Seminar in Indo-European Mythology was held for the first time. Other organizational milestones have been the creation of the Center for the Study of Comparative Folklore and Mythology in 1961 and of the Section of Indo-European Studies as an autonomous part of the Department of Classics in 1964.

Workers from many fields—anthropology, classical languages, English, folklore, Germanic languages, Indo-European studies, Slavic languages—have participated in these endeavors. Numerous research papers have been written and discussed over the years. A succession of research assistants (Anastasia Demetriades, C. Scott Littleton, Robert Gartman, Eleanor Long, Antoinette Botsford) have helped lay an exhaustive bibliographical and documentary groundwork under the auspices of the mythology section of the Center. At least two published doctoral dissertations have drawn their inspiration and inception from these efforts (C. Scott Littleton, *The New Comparative Mythology: An Anthropological Assessment of the Theories of Georges Dumézil* [Berkeley and Los Angeles, 1966], and Donald Ward, *The Divine Twins: An Indo-European Myth in Germanic Tradition* [Berkeley and Los Angeles, 1968]).

In a purely historical sense, the activity has centered on discovering and understanding the mythic, religious, social, and legal underpinnings of the ancient Indo-European-speaking continuum in terms of their oldest or most archaic manifestations. In a comparativistic vein, these materials have been used as starting points for prehistoric reconstruction. The theoretical viability of such attempts is enhanced by the renascence of the discipline of Indo-European comparative mythology during the past several decades through the efforts of such scholars as Georges Dumézil, Jan de Vries, Stig Wikander, and others. Thereby the long lacuna that ensued upon the largely abortive theoretical beginnings by F. Max Müller, Adalbert Kuhn, and others in the nineteenth century can securely be declared closed, and a present-day comparative mythology proclaimed as firmly established, fortified by the material gains and theoretical lessons of an entire century.

Most of the works gathered into this volume were originally presented at a symposium held under the joint auspices of the Center and of the Section of Indo-European Studies on March 17–18, 1967. Postfixed to their printed versions is a bibliographical inventory of scholarly works that constitute the documentation of the new Indo-European comparative mythology.

Thanks are due the Chancellor of the University of California, Los Angeles, for a subsidy toward the cost of publication, Wayland D. Hand, the director of the Center for the Study of Comparative Folklore and Mythology, Antoinette Botsford for editorial assistance, and Anne-Marie Virgint for help with the index.

JAAN PUHVEL

Contents

ABBREVIATIONS viii
CALVERT WATKINS Language of Gods and Language of Men: Remarks on Some Indo-European Metalinguistic Traditions 1
KEES W. BOLLE In Defense of Euhemerus 19
STEPHEN P. SCHWARTZ Comparative Legal Reconstruction in Germanic 39
EDGAR POLOMÉ The Indo-European Component in Germanic Religion 55
C. SCOTT LITTLETON The "Kingship in Heaven" Theme 83
DONALD J. WARD The Threefold Death: An Indo-European Trifunctional Sacrifice? 123
JEANNINE E. TALLEY The Threefold Death in Finnish Lore 143
ROBERT L. FISHER, JR. Indo-European Elements in Baltic and Slavic Chronicles 147
JAAN PUHVEL Aspects of Equine Functionality 159
JAMES L. SAUVÉ The Divine Victim: Aspects of Human Sacrifice in Viking Scandinavia and Vedic India 173
DONALD J. WARD The Separate Functions of the Indo-European Divine Twins 193
JACQUES DUCHESNE-GUILLEMIN Reflections on *yaoždā*, with a Digression on *xvaētvadaθa* 203
UDO STRUTYNSKI The Three Functions of Indo-European Tradition in the *Eumenides* of Aeschylus 211
C. SCOTT LITTLETON Some Possible Indo-European Themes in the *Iliad* 229
BIBLIOGRAPHY 247
INDEX 269

Abbreviations

AAHG	*Anzeiger für die Altertumwissenschaft*
ABSA	*Annual of the British School at Athens*
AC	*L'antiquité classique*
AESC	*Annales économies, sociétés, civilisations*
AHES	*Annales d'histoire économique et sociale*
AIPhO	*Annuaire, Institut de philologie et d'histoire orientales et slaves, Brussels*
AJA	*American Journal of Archaeology*
AJPh	*American Journal of Philology*
ANF	*Arkiv för nordisk filologi*
AO	*Archiv Orientální*
APhS	*Acta Philologica Scandinavica*
ArchClass	*Archeologia Classica*
ASNP	*Annali della Scuola normale superiore di Pisa.*
ASoc	*L'année sociologique*
AsS	*Asiatische Studien*
BAClLg	*Bulletin, Association des classiques, Université de Liège*
BARB	*Bulletin, Académie royale de Belgique (Classe des lettres)*
BFS	*Bulletin, Faculté des lettres, Strasbourg*
BO	*Bibliotheca orientalis*
BSL	*Bulletin, Société de linguistique de Paris*
BSO(A)S	*Bulletin, School of Oriental (and African) Studies, University of London*
CPh	*Classical Philology*
CR	*Classical Review*
CS	*Cahiers du Sud*
DLZ	*Deutsche Literatur-Zeitung*

EC	*Études celtiques*
ECl	*Les études classiques*
EG	*Études germaniques*
FFC	Folklore Fellows Communications
GIF	*Giornale italiano di filologia*
GRM	*Germanisch-romanische Monatsschrift*
GUÅ	Göteborgs Universitets Årsskrift
Hum (RES)	*Humanités: Revue d'enseignement secondaire et d'éducation*
HZnMTL	*Handelingen der Zuidnederlandse Maatschappij voor Taal- en Letterkunde en Geschiedenis*
IF	*Indogermanische Forschungen*
IH	*L'information historique*
IIJ	*Indo-Iranian Journal*
IL	*L'information littéraire*
JA	*Journal asiatique*
JAF	*Journal of American Folklore*
JAOS	*Journal of the American Oriental Society*
JCS	*Journal of Cuneiform Studies*
JEGP	*Journal of English and Germanic Philology*
JFI	*Journal of the Folklore Institute*
JPsych	*Journal de psychologie normale et pathologique*
JRAI	*Journal of the Royal Anthropological Institute*
JRASB	*Journal of the Bombay Branch of the Royal Asiatic Society*
JRS	*Journal of Roman Studies*
JThS	*Journal of Theological Studies*
MARB	Mémoires, Académie royale de Belgique (Classe des lettres)
MF	*Midwest Folklore*
NClio	*La nouvelle Clio*
NNRF	*La nouvelle nouvelle revue française*
NRF	*La nouvelle revue française*
OS	*Orientalia Suecana*
PBA	*Proceedings of the British Academy*
PBB(T)	(Paul-Braunes) *Beiträge zur Geschichte der deutschen Sprache und Literatur* (Tübingen).
PICO	*Proceedings of the International Congress of Orientalists*
PMLA	*Publications of the Modern Language Association*
RA	*Revue archéologique*
RBPh	*Revue belge de philologie et d'histoire*

RC	*Revue celtique*
REA	*Revue des études anciennes*
REArm	*Revue des études arméniennes*
RecSR	*Recherches de science religieuse*
REG	*Revue des études grecques*
REL	*Revue des études latines*
RESl	*Revue des études slaves*
RevP	*Revue de Paris*
RH	*Revue historique*
RHA	*Revue hittite et asianique*
RHPh	*Revue d'histoire de la philosophie et d'histoire générale de la civilisation*
RHPhR	*Revue d'histoire et de philosophie religieuses*
RHR	*Revue de l'histoire des religions*
RHSE	*Revue historique du Sud-Est européen*
RoB	*Religion och Bibel*
RPh	*Revue de philologie*
RPhilos	*Revue philosophique*
RSPT	*Revue des sciences philosophiques et théologiques*
RSR	*Revue des sciences religieuses*
RSyn	*Revue de synthèse*
RU	*Revue universitaire*
SL	*Studia linguistica*
SMSR	*Studi e materiali di storia delle religioni*
SS	*Scandinavian Studies*
TCAAS	Transactions of the Connecticut Academy of Arts and Sciences
TPhS	*Transactions of the Philological Society*
TR	*La table ronde*
UUÅ	Uppsala Universitets Årsskrift
VDI	*Vestnik drevnej istorii* (Akademii Nauk SSSR)
VIJ	*Visveshvaranand Indological Journal*
VSLÅ	*Vetenskaps-societen i Lund, Årsbok*
VSLS	Vetenskaps-societen i Lund, Skrifter
WF	*Western Folklore*
ZDA	*Zeitschrift für deutsches Altertum*
ZDMG	*Zeitschrift der Deutschen morgenländischen Gesellschaft*
ZDPh	*Zeitschrift für deutsche Philologie*
ZEthn	*Zeitschrift für Ethnologie*
ZRGG	*Zeitschrift für Religions- und Geistesgeschichte*

Language of Gods and Language of Men: Remarks on Some Indo-European Metalinguistic Traditions

CALVERT WATKINS, *Harvard University*

The fundamental work on "language of men" and "language of gods" is Hermann Güntert's *Von der Sprache der Götter und Geister*[1] which presents a detailed examination of this figure in two Indo-European traditions: the Homeric poems and the *Alvissmǫl* of the Old Norse *Poetic Edda*. More recently, the figure has been analyzed by R. Lazzeroni.[2]

In Homer we have a total of six instances of the figure. Four of these contrast two lexical items, as belonging to the language of men and gods, respectively; the typical formula is (*Iliad* 14. 290–291)

> ὄρνιθι λιγυρῇ ἐναλίγκιος, ἥν τ' ἐν ὄρεσσι
> χαλκίδα κικλήσκουσι θεοί, ἄνδρες δὲ κύμινδιν.

Here we have the contrast between two appellations for the same bird: κύμινδις (men) and χαλκίς (gods). In the other three, we have personal and local names. Thus, giving first the name in the language of men,

a hill Βατίεια: σῆμα πολυσκάρθμοιο Μυρίνης (*Iliad* 2.813–814);
the river Σκάμανδρος: Ξάνθος (*Iliad* 20.74);
a giant Αἰγαίων: Βριάρεως (*Iliad* 1.403, etc.).

---

1 Halle, 1921.
2 *ASNP*, ser. 2, 26:1–25 (1957), with intervening literature.

In two instances we have only the "gods' word": μῶλυ δέ μιν καλέουσι θεοί (*Odyssey* 10.305) and Πλαγκτὰς δή τοι τάς γε θεοὶ μάκαρες καλέουσιν (*Odyssey* 12.61).

In all the cases where there is an opposition, as Güntert recognized, the term attributed to the language of men is the normal Greek designation of the object, place, or being, and that attributed to the language of the gods is a "poetische Umschreibung allgemeiner Art." Thus χαλκίς, 'the χαλκός-colored'; Βριάρεως, 'the strong' (βριαρός; note that the synizesis in the line of -εω- from -ηο- is generally a mark of recentness).[3] In σῆμα Μυρίνης (following the scholia) we have a "scholarly" reference to a heroine cult which is quite Hellenistic in effect.

In these cases we have a metalinguistic poetic figure setting forth explicitly a hierarchy in the lexicon: the relation between the designations of the same entity on two levels of discourse. The lower level, that of ordinary language, is figured as the "language of men," while the higher and more restricted level of formal, poetic, or otherwise exotic language is figured in this ancient metaphor as the "language of the gods." This metaphor represents a conscious signalization of an opposition existing in the lexicon, between the common, *semantically unmarked term*, and a rarer, more "charged," *semantically marked term*. On the plane of discourse the opposition is most commonly (and clearly in the *Edda*, as we shall see below) that between ordinary and poetic language in the widest sense.

There are words in the lexicon which for reasons having to do with the culture have an immanent semantic charge or mark, without there necessarily existing any semantically unmarked equivalent. Such a form is μῶλυ, with its aura of black magic and taboo comparable with that of *mandrake, mandragora,* and the like. It is a semantically marked term, and as such is assigned to the language of the gods; there simply is no unmarked equivalent designation, hence the absence of a term for men. It is characteristic of the Greek examples that they are precisely *not* common ordinary lexical items, in contrast with the Old Norse material. We do not have, for example, a putative opposition between a "human" term αἷμα and a "divine" εἶαρ as the word for "blood." For this reason it is well not to insist too much on the Homeric examples, which are complex in character. There are particular reasons in the Homeric poems why the paired designations appear when they do (only six times in some 25,000 lines); these are connected with the metaphor itself and

---

[3] Cf. P. Chantraine, *Grammaire homérique*, I (Paris, 1942), 37.

the "divine association" of the entity or personage in question. They have been quite well analyzed by Lazzeroni, and there is no need to go into them here. What is basic is the possibility of the contrast itself; Lazzeroni when separating entirely the Greek facts from those of Old Norse and other traditions goes too far in ignoring the basic fact that the human term in both traditions is the neutral, semantically unmarked member.

This system is far clearer in the verses of the *Alvíssmǫl,* where there are thirteen stanzas of the following typical configuration; the translation of the terms merely aims at being diacritical:

Stanza 9 [Thor:] segđu mér þat, Alvíss . . .
hvé sú iǫrđ heitir . . .
Stanza 10 [Alvíss:] iǫrđ heitir međ mǫnnum enn međ ásom fold

kalla vega vanir
ígrœn iǫtnar álfar gróandi
kalla aur upregin

[Thor:] tell me that, Alvíss . . .
how the earth is called . . .
[Alvíss:] *earth* it is called by men and by the Aesir *land*
the vanir call it *way*
green the giants the elves *growing*
the upregin call it *sandy soil.*

Despite the superficial proliferation of synonyms and associate divine beings, we have in reality merely the elaboration of a poetic figure opposing a single genuine pair of lexical items as "human" and "divine." The greater complexity of the "divine" set is a reflex of a more complicated pantheon of divine and otherworld beings and of the necessity of filling out the system.

In all cases but two ("sea" and "grain") the word used by Thor in his question "how is *x* called" is the ordinary, unmarked "human" word; the exceptions are introduced for the sake of alliteration. That the poet saw no contradiction in Thor's using the human word is to be expected, and shows that the metaphor was indeed just a metaphor. Similarly in Homer, where the gods speak men's Greek.

In all thirteen cases the word attributed to men is still the normal word for the object in Modern Norwegian, as Einar Haugen informs me. By contrast, in nine cases the word attributed to the gods is a genuine, semantically marked poetic word, as we know from other texts, whereas the words assigned to the other beings are of drastically lower frequency.

Perhaps the greatest merit of Güntert's work was to point out the role of alliteration in the distribution of the synonyms and the beings assigned them. The verse scheme requires a bridge of alliteration between the two hemistichs of the first line, which always begins with the men's word in the first hemistich. We may in fact set up two basic ordered rules: (1) if the men's word begins with a vowel, the gods are called *ǽsir* for alliteration and the choice of the god's word is free; (2) if the men's word does not begin with a vowel, the gods are called *gođ* and the god's word must alliterate with the men's word.

When rule 1 applies, we get a genuine opposition between the unmarked term and the rarer, poetic term:

earth	(st. 10)	*iǫrđ* : *fold*
fire	(st. 26)	*eldr* : *funi*

The case of *ǫl*, 'ale' : *biórr*, 'beer' (34) is apart, for technological reasons; the hierarchy is there, but it is an economic or gastronomic one rather than a semantic one, the opposition being apparently between the old native brew without hops (*ǫl*) and the new, more expensive, and better-tasting brew with hops (*biórr*).

In the remaining cases, where rule 2 applies, there may be a genuine opposition, if the existing poetic synonym happens to alliterate:

heaven	(st. 12)	*himinn* : *hlýrnir*
moon	(st. 14)	*máni* : *mýlinn*
sun	(st. 16)	*sól* : *sunna*
calm	(st. 22)	*logn* : *lœgi*
night	(st. 30)	*nǫtt* : *niól*
grain	(st. 32)	*bygg* : *barr*

But if the poetic word does not alliterate with the normal word, it is assigned to a group other than the *gođ*, and an alliterative word is invented for the designation by the *gođ*.

sea (st. 24) *sǽr* : *marr* (*dvergar*)

and probably

wood (st. 28) *viđr* : *eldi* 'firewood' (*iǫtnar*)

In the remaining two cases, *ský*, 'cloud,' and *vindr*, 'wind,' no genuine opposed term existed which could be brought into the system of alliteration, and the terms in the whole series are simply inventions of the poet, as Güntert showed.

The remaining terms attributed to other beings are in a large measure ἅπαξ λεγόμενα; they are all kennings, transferred meanings, or other poetic creations, doubtless the work of the author of the *Alvíssmǫl* himself. Their repartition among the remaining divine or otherworld beings is to a large extent governed by alliteration, as is the occasional permutation of one divine group for another. Compare the constant of words in initial *v-* for the *vanir,* in *h-* for the beings *i helio.* The whole is, as H. Gering termed it[4] "ein versifiziertes Kapitel aus der skaldischen Poetik," and indeed a quite artificial literary showpiece and tour de force.

It is thus clear that in the *Alvíssmǫl* text what is basic is the binary opposition "human : divine," the poetic figuration of an opposition in the lexicon *semantically unmarked term* : *semantically marked term.* There may be genuinely more than one of the latter, as probably in Old Norse *bygg* : *barr, sáð,* and more can always be freely created, as the rest of the *Alvíssmǫl* shows, but this does not alter the fundamental structural set; an English equivalent would be *horse* : *steed, mount, charger,* and so on. As E. Benveniste has so well expressed it,[5] "Il est dans la nature des faits linguistiques, puisqu'ils sont des signes, de se réaliser en oppositions, et de ne signifier que par là," and this is equally valid for the lexicon of a language.

Güntert further pointed out the existence of the same poetic figure in early Sanskrit literature, in the *Śatapatha-Brāhmaṇa* (10.4.6.1). Since he cites only the translation, I give the passage here:

> háyo bhutvā́ devā́n avahad vājī́ gandharvā́n
> árvā ásurān áśvo manuṣyā̀n
>
> as *háya* he carried the gods, as *vājín* the gandharvas,
> as *árvan* the asuras, as *áśva* men.

The semantic opposition is *áśva* : *háya, vājín, árvan*; the unmarked term is the normal inherited Indo-European word for "horse" (Lat. *equos*).

It is important to note, as Güntert did not, that all three of the semantically marked, noble, poetic terms are also found as such in earlier Vedic literature, in the *Rig-Veda* passim. The choice of one or the other of them is indifferent; what is relevant is only the semantic opposition of each to *áśva* as *marked* to *unmarked.*

In the hymn to the sacrificial horse (1.163) we find *vājín* and *árvan* several times as terms of direct address (vocatives) to the horse about to be sacrificed, whereas in this hymn *áśva* is used only in neutral, declarative context.

---

4 Cf. Güntert, *op. cit.,* p. 132.

5 *JPsych* 43:129 (1950), republished in *Problèmes de linguistique générale* (Paris, 1966), p. 175.

In another hymn (7.74.4) we find *áśva* and *háya* coexisting in the same mantra:

áśvāso yé vām úpa dāśúṣo gṛhám
yuvā́ṃ dī́yanti bíbhrataḥ
makṣūyúbhir narā háyebhir aśvinā
ā́ devā yātam asmayū́

Your horses which fly, bringing you to the house of the sacrificer, with [these] swift horses come here for us, O heroes, O gods Aśvin.

The relative sentence is worth noting, for it shows a sentence of an archaic paratactic Indo-European type which recurs most clearly in Hittite: the antecedent of the relative clause appears both in the relative clause and in the succeeding main clause. (This type is also of interest for the general syntactic theory of the relative sentence.) Thus in Hittite:

nu-mu É-ir kuit ešta
nu-kán *IŠTU* É-*YA* d*IŠTAR* URUŠamuḫa ḫantiyanun

and the house which I had,
and with my house I was true to Ištar of Šamuḫa.[6]

and

INIM.MEŠ-ar-ta (= uddār-ta) kue memiškimi
nu-mu uddanaš GEŠTUK-an parā lagān ḫark

the words which I speak to thee,
to my words [thine] ear hold inclined.[7]

and

nu-za KUR URUTapāpanuwa kuit dān EGIR-pa ešat
nu KUR URUTapāpanuwa arḫa warnuir

and the land of Tapāpanuwa which was seditious a second time,
and they burned the land of Tapāpanuwa.[8]

Such Hittite relative sentences have an evident structural similarity to the Vedic relative sentence quoted above. But there is an interesting stylistic difference. The noun *áśva* modified by the relative clause is not simply repeated in the following main clause; rather it is there replaced by the equivalent but more semantically marked noun *háya*. Thus for an underlying relative sentence of the Indo-European type:

áśvāso yé dī́yanti	the horses that fly,
*áśvebhir ā́ yātam	come with the horses

[6] A. Götze, *Ḫattušiliš* (Leipzig, 1925), p. 46.
[7] *Song of Ullikummi*, First Tablet, A III 38'–39'; see H. G. Güterbock, *JCS* 5:154 (1951).
[8] A. Götze, *Die Annalen des Muršiliš* (Leipzig, 1933), p. 174.

is substituted as a stylistic figure

áśvāso yé dī́yanti
háyebhir ā́ yātam

It is clear that such a particular stylistic "transformation"—of lexical substitution in a determined syntactic position—is explicable only in terms of a semantic hierarchy in the lexicon: unmarked *áśva* → marked *háya*. It is equally evident that this hierarchical relation between the terms *áśva* and *háya* existed in Indic prior to Rig-Vedic times, and was continued intact until the time of its different poetic configuration as "language of men" and "language of gods" in the *Śatapatha-Brāhmaṇa*. It is the semantic hierarchy that is basic, and the metaphor of "language of men" and "language of gods" is derived from it; for this reason I would hesitate to ascribe the metaphor itself to a putative Indo-European poetic "doctrine" as some have done; I prefer to regard it as an independent (and quite natural) creation in the traditions that show it.

It may be that the semantic hierarchy of *áśva* and *háya* is older still. As noted, *áśva* is the well-known IE **ékwo-*. The word *háya*, alone among the semantically marked words for "horse," has a cognate in Armenian, *ji* (gen. *jioy*), the normal (semantically unmarked) word for horse; vis-à-vis Sanskrit it has moved down a step in semantic mark. But Sanskrit *áśva* has also an exact cognate in Armenian (*fide* R. Godel): the word is *ēš* (gen. *išoy*) and the meaning is 'donkey.' We know from Iranian tradition (*Vidēvdāt* 7.42) that the donkey (Avestan *xara-*) was considered the least worthy of the *staora*, 'Grossvieh,' below the horse, and it is not unlikely that a similar view prevailed among the Iranianized Armenians. But the semantic shift from "horse" to "donkey" would be difficult to understand except in the context of such a semantic hierarchy between *ji* and *ēš* in preclassical Armenian as we can observe between *háya* and *áśva* in Vedic.

Since Güntert's time the figure of language of men and language of gods has been reported for one other tradition: ancient Anatolian, by J. Friedrich.[9] Here we have such passages in Hittite as

tandukešni Tašimmetiš, DINGIR.MEŠ-naš-a ištarna
ᵈ*IŠTAR*-iš SAL.LUGAL-aš zik

to mankind you are Tašimmetiš, but among the gods
you are Ištar the queen.[10]

[9] *Sprachgeschichte und Wortbedeutung: Festschrift A. Debrunner* (Bern, 1954), pp. 135–139.

[10] *Keilschrifturkunden aus Boghazköi*, VIII 41 II 8–9.

Such passages in fact come from bilingual texts in Hittite and Hattic; they are edited by E. Laroche.[11] Some of the tablets are in the archaic cuneiform ductus of the Old Kingdom, as noted by H. Otten.[12] The tradition is thus old; but it is likely that this figure is a Hattic one borrowed by translation into Hittite.

All the examples of this figure concern the names or epithets of deities; we never have any reference to an ordinary lexical item being assigned to the language of men or to the language of gods. For this reason the Anatolian figure is not really comparable with that in Greek, and particularly Old Norse or Indic. Rather it reflects a specific Anatolian cultic practice; it is basically more akin to the Greek hymnic tradition of invoking a divinity by a number of different names or epithets than it is to the Homeric language of gods and language of men.

To my knowledge it has never before been noted that there exists in early Irish an analogue to the figure of language of gods and language of men. It is found in one of the most curious of all Irish texts, the *Auraicept na n-Éces*, the "Scholar's Primer" or "Handbook of the Learned," as it is called by its editor and translator George Calder.[13] It is a treatise on grammar and poetics, *Filidecht*, and compiled out of elements of variable antiquity; the language is in the main Middle Irish, but has numerous traits requiring the supposition of antecedent Old Irish material. Whereas the text shows considerable influence of Isidore and the grammarian Virgilius Maro, this element clearly represents an overlay upon a basic purely native Irish doctrine of poetic learning which is of enormous interest. The text and its doctrine have been virtually untouched in Irish scholarship since Calder's (scarcely definitive) edition of 1917, and it remains a fertile field for investigation of Irish poetical and grammatical theory.

At a certain point in the text (1457, cf. 1236 *et passim*), the compilator is discussing the principle *dialt didiu bunad cacha Gaedelge acht mod 7 tod 7 troth*, 'syllable [*dialt*] however, is the origin of all Gaelic except *moth, toth,* and *traeth* [the verbal symbols for masculine, feminine, and neuter gender].' Calder correctly saw (pp. xlvi–xlvii) that this curious asseveration actually means that while the grammatical categories of number, case, person, degree, tense, and mood are all expressed by overt morphemes (prefixes, suffixes, endings), thus "syllables," gender alone is not; it has no formal correlate

11 *JCS* 1:187–216 (1947).

12 *Religionsgeschichte des alten Orients*, Handbuch der Orientalistik, Abt. 1, Bd. 8, Abschn. 1, p. 100.

13 Edinburgh, 1917.

in Irish substantives, but is simply an inherent, immanent property. It is a remarkable observation for the native Irish grammarians to have made.

Continuing the discussion of *moth, toth, traeth,* the compilator adds (1493–1496): *secundum quosdam cumad etarscarad indsci: isse, issi, issed iar Macaib Miled; uindius, uindsi, ondor iar Feraib Bolg; mod, tod, traeth iar Tuathaib De Danand,* 'according to some, it is a distinction of speech: *is é* [it is he] *is sí* [it is she] *is ed* [it is it] according to the Sons of Milesius; *uindse* [voilà (the man)], *uindsi* [voilà (the woman)], *ondar* [voilà (the thing)] according to the Fir Bolg, *moth* [everything male or masculine], *toth* [everything female or feminine], *traeth* [everything neuter] according to the Túatha Dé Danann.'

In the long version of the *Yellow Book of Lecan* the passage reads (4554–4556): *etargairi a n-innsgib: is e, is i, is eudh iar Macaib Miled; masgoul, feimin, neutor lasin Laitneoir; uindse, uindsi, oundar iar bFeraib Bolg; moth, touth, traothad la Tuaith De Danaan,* thus adding: "masculine, feminine, neuter with the Latinist." In view of the late character of these loan words, whose Latin origin was of course well known to the compilator of *Auraicept,* this passage is probably an interpolation.

The three ways of specifying gender are thus attributed to successive "legendary races" of men and gods which occupied Ireland: the Milesians (Sons of Mil), ancestors of the Gaels; the Fir Bolg invaders; and the ancient Celtic pagan gods, the Túatha Dé Danann.[14]

Of the terms themselves, the most "normal" and semantically unmarked is that of the syntagm of copula plus pronoun, *is é/sí/ed.* That the Irish in fact regarded these forms as giving the "key" to the gender of a word is clear from *Auraicept* 617–620 where the phenomenon is discussed, under the technical term *erlonn* (*aurlann, airlann*), 'preceding word, leading word [lit. butt end, handle]': *nasdefrigidar a tri urlundinnsci* .i. *a iii remslonnudh* .i. *slointi rempu* .i. *riasna hinscibh* .i. *ise isi ised,* 'their three leading words of gender distinguish them, i.e., their three antedenotations, i.e. denotations before them, i.e., before the genders, i.e., *is é, is sí, is ed.*' The notion is naturally derived from the normal sentence pattern beginning *is é in fer* (*as*), *is sí in ben* (*as*), 'he is the man/she is the woman (who is).' On the term *erlonn* (*aurlann*) see the *Contributions to a Dictionary of the Irish language* (Royal Irish Academy), *s.v.* 2 *airlann*; the editors suggest it

[14] The legendary history may be found in the *Lebor Gabálach* "Book of Invasions."

may be the same word as 3 *airlann*, 'correspondence, analogy.' One wonders whether it may not also be ultimately connected with 1 *airlann*, 'forecourt, open space before a residence, fort, or city,' despite the variation in declension.

The forms *uindse, uindsi, ondar* are doubtless artificially introduced here; they have nothing to do with gender, and the repartition of the three forms as 'voilà' implying a masculine, feminine, or neuter object to be looked at (cf. *Auraicept* 648–649) finds no confirmation whatsoever in other texts. Probably the reason for their introduction is the earlier section of the *Auraicept* (705 ff.), where there is discussion of the difference between *uinse*, 'voici, voilà,' and *is é*, 'it is he, he is.' There *is é* is specifically called a "denotation of gender" (*sluind ceniuil*, 712), in contrast with *uindse*. For the forms *uindse, uindsi, ondar* see M. A. O'Brien, *Ériu* 11:163 (1932); *uind* is doubtless imperative 2 sing. active of the rare verb *uindim*, meaning 'see, behold,' and *-se/-si* are simply variant later spellings of the Old Irish 2 sing. suffixed subject pronoun *-siu*. The "neuter" *ondar* would be the imperative 3 sing. passive of the same verb. If the inclusion of these terms for gender is thus artificial, it follows that its attribution to the Fir Bolg is likewise artificial. The real opposing member is the following one.

In *moth, toth, traeth*, particularly in view of the often repeated maxim that "syllable is the root of all Gaelic save *moth, toth, traeth*" discussed above, we have a genuine and archaic designation of masculine, feminine, neuter. The terms are glossed respectively as *cach ferda*, 'everything masculine,' *cach mbanda*, 'everything feminine,' *cach neoturda*, 'everything neuter'; specifically the first two are also used for the male and female sexual organs as well. As R. Thurneysen once said of another form, the terms *moth* and *toth* can "beliebig alt sein"; they were compared by O'Brien and Thurneysen with the Latin divine name Mūtūnus Tutūnus,[15] which shows the suffix *-ūnus* occurring in other ancient Latin divine names like Neptūnus.[16]

The origin of *traeth* is obscure; but it seems to be connected with the weak verb *traethaid*, 'subdues, abates' (verbal noun *traethad*, a variant of *traeth* in *Auraicept* 4568), and certainly was by the Irish themselves (cf. *Auraicept* 1485). If so, we would have a noun meaning 'abatement, suspension [of the categories masculine and feminine, or

15 Cf. the discussion and references in A. Ernout and A. Meillet, *Dictionnaire étymologique de la langue latine* (4th ed.), *s.v. muto*; also the skeptical remarks of A. Walde and J. B. Hofmann, *Lateinisches etymologisches Wörterbuch* (3d ed.) *s.v.*, likewise with references.

16 Neptūnus has plausible connections with Ireland; see G. Dumézil, "Le puits de Nechtan," *Celtica* 6:50–61 (1963).

the difference between them]' and a concept akin to the modern linguistic one of "neutralization."

We may venture the speculation that in the system *moth, toth, traeth* were also *erlonn* (*aurlann, airlann*), 'leading word,' but belonging to a grammatical doctrine of gender on a more theoretical plane and/or older chronological level than the purely empirical system *is é, is sí, is ed*; the latter system can of course be only as old as the emphasizing construction *is é in fer* (*as*), which is a Celtic innovation. But in any case, however complex the legends involved, the two sets are fundamentally opposed in the metaphorical figure of language of men (Gaels, the Sons of Mil) and language of gods (the Túatha Dé Danann), the two basic opposing groups in the Irish invasion legend.

Such a figure as this is to my knowledge unique in Irish literature. That the compilator of the *Auraicept* introduced the figure by *secundum quosdam* indicates that there was some sort of tradition; but in view of the artificial character of some of the forms so contrasted, and their attribution to vaguely historical or pseudohistorical as well as divine figures, all unique to Ireland, it is scarcely likely that the figure or metaphor can be in any way considered an inheritance. Rather it would indicate the naturalness of the figure of attributing variant forms in the lexicon to whatever contrastable groups exist in the traditional lore; Maicc Miled, Fir Bolg, and Túatha Dé Danann in Ireland; *manuṣyāḥ, devāḥ, gandharvāḥ* and *asurāḥ* in India; *menn, gođ, ǽsir, vanir, iǫtnar, alfar, dvergar,* or cover terms like *upregin* in Iceland. From these examples it should be clear that the social groups can be multiplied to fit the number of synonyms or quasisynonyms in the lexicon to be contrasted. By the same token, as is quite clear in the *Alvíssmǫl*, the number of "synonyms" can be arbitrarily increased (by the invention of kennings and the like) to correspond to the number of groups of divine or semidivine beings.

But however high the number of synonyms, it can always be reduced to a basically binary opposition between the neutral, semantically unmarked member and one or more charged, semantically marked members. It is this basic opposition, a synchronic hierarchy existing in the lexicon, which is metaphorically figured in the contrast of the language of men (= unmarked member) and the language of gods (= marked member), as in Greece and Anatolia (both Indo-European Hittite and non-Indo-European Hattic). If more than one marked member exists, it is a simple matter to multiply (or subdivide) the divine or semidivine groups, as in India and Iceland.

In Christian Ireland, the attribution of the opposition directly to *men: (pagan) gods* would scarcely have been a natural one; hence we find here the opposition correlated with successive legendary races invading and populating Ireland. The unmarked member is that of the language of the Sons of Mil, ancestors of the Gaels, whereas the marked member is attributed to the historically antecedent divine figures of the Túatha Dé Danann.

Yet this unique and isolated figure is not really the basic opposition in the semantic hierarchy of the lexicon in native Irish tradition. For this we must consider another passage in the *Auraicept* (1302) and scrutinize the technical terms which it employs:

> it e coic gne berla tobaidi .i. berla Fene 7 fasaige na filed 7 berla etarsgarta 7 berla fortchide na filed triasa n-agallit cach dib a chele 7 iarmberla

> These are five species of the Selected Language, viz.: Language of the Irish, Maxims of the Poets, Separated Language, Obscure Language of the Poets through which each of them addresses his fellow, and Unaccented Language.

It is probable here that *berla Fene*, 'Language of the Irish,' is to be taken to mean 'Ordinary Language,' mentioned some time later (1336) as the fifth category: *iss e in coiced gne in gnat[h]berla fogni do c[h]ac[h]*, 'the fifth kind is the ordinary language that serves for everyone.' Compare from the *Book of Ballymote* (300^{b}2) *in gnathberla fogni do chach is e in berla bunaid no is berla topaide*, 'ordinary language which serves for everyone, that is the foundation language; or it is the Selected Language.' Note especially that in Cormac's glossary *gnáthbérla* is opposed to *senbérla*.[17]

Bérla tobaide is the normal term for Gaelic in the *Auraicept* and related glossatorial texts: *tóbaithe* (in Old Irish form), 'cut; defined, selected,' is the past participle of *to-fo-ben*. An alternate form is *bérla teipide* (in Old Irish form *bélre teipithe*), 'cut, excised, fashioned, selected,' from *to-ess-ben*. These participial formations are particularly interesting in that they form a perfect pendant to the Indic terms *saṃskr̥ta-*, 'perfected; Sanskrit,' beside *prakr̥ta-* from *prakr̥ti*, 'la matière brute du langage,' as L. Renou defines it in his brief but characteristically illuminating discussion of these terms.[18]

The compilator of the *Auraicept* goes on to report that some authorities equate *bérla Féine*, 'Language of the Irish,' with *Fásaige*

[17] Cf. *Contributions to a Dictionary of the Irish Language*, Royal Irish Academy (Dublin), *s.v. nairne*.

[18] *Histoire de la langue sanskrite* (Lyon, 1956), pp. 5–6.

na filed, 'Maxims of The Poets.' On this basis, the expression *fásaige na filed* probably means 'poetic language' as opposed to *gnáthbérla,* 'ordinary language.' *Bérla Féine,* insofar as different, refers to poetico-juridical, "professional" language.

The third term *bérla etarscartha,* 'separated language,' refers to the common Irish glossatorial practice of making fanciful etymologies by segmenting and "stretching" words to form phrases, for example (*Auraicept* 1319), *ros,* 'wood' .i. *roi oiss,* 'plain of deer.' It is probable that the "separation" of words in this manner reflected not merely glossatorial practice for purposes of etymology, but also a genuine practice of artificial deformation of words for poetic purposes. The existence of archaic (presyncope) poetic technical terms like *díchned,* lit. 'beheading,' which means "aphaeresis of the initial or apocope of the final consonant," points to the existence of a doctrine of word deformation going back to early times. Note that in the curious poems at the end of the *Auraicept* (1962 ff.) *díchned* is one of the twelve "faces of defense" (*gnúis díten*) of poetry against *anocht,* 'error, incorrect form'; the latter is itself a form of Indo-European antiquity, identical with Sanskrit *an-ukta-,* 'unsaid, unsayable,' as Thurneysen saw. *Díchned* is also used in early Irish to describe the synchronic formal relation between an ordinary, semantically unmarked word and a rarer, semantically marked word that can be synchronically derived from the former by aphaeresis or apocope. Thus in *Auraicept* 390–391 the form *epe,* 'cutting,' is cited as the *díchned* of *tepe,* 'id.' Here *te(i)pe,* verbal noun of *to-ess-ben,* is a very common early Irish form (both verb and noun), whereas *e(i)pe,* verbal noun of *ess-ben* without the second preverb *to,* is an archaism occurring (outside *Auraicept*) only in the Laws, and quotations from the Laws in O'Davoren's glossary; the finite verb *ess-ben* is scarcely attested.[19]

Even more striking is the case of the normal Irish word for "woman" at all periods of the language, *ben* < **g^w^enā,* whose *díchned* is given in *Auraicept* 1852 as *bé.* The latter is a neuter noun, well attested in archaic or archaising early Irish poetry and rhetorics, and clearly a part of *bérla na filed,* 'language of the poets' (on which see below). I find that my interpretation of this word as an ancient consonant stem **g^w^en-* has been anticipated by W. Meid, and indeed both of us by H. Pedersen.[20] Meid and I differ in that he sees an old

---

19 Cf. R. Thurneysen, *A Grammar of Old Irish* (Dublin, 1946), pp. 507–510, and *Contributions to a Dictionary of the Irish Language, s. vv. eipe, eipit.*

20 See Meid, *Zeitschrift für vergleichende Sprachforschung* 80:271–272 (1966); Pedersen, *Vergleichende Grammatik der keltichen Sprachen,* II (Göttingen, 1913), 113.

neuter nom. **g^{w}en,* gen. **g^{w}en-s,* whereas I prefer an animate (or feminine) nom. **g^{w}én-s,* acc. **g^{w}en-m̥* (whence archaic Old Irish *bein,* acc. of *ben*), gen. **g^{w}(e)n-ós.* The latter paradigm is, I suggest, also indirectly attested in Hittite nom. SAL-*za* (once SAL-*anza*), acc. SAL-*nan,* gen. SAL-*naš*.[21] The form *bein* in the word for "woman" may well have served as an important channel for the spread of **-m̥* (**-en*) as the accusative of feminine *ā*-stems. The nom. *túath* < **teutā,* acc. *túaith* < **teutm̥* would thus imitate nom. **g^{w}enā* (replacing **g^{w}ens*), acc. **g^{w}enm̥.* It is more likely that the word was originally animate (feminine) gender, as in Hittite. The transfer of a monosyllabic consonant-stem noun to neuter gender in Irish may be observed also in the neuter *dét,* 'tooth,' beside the animate (masculine) gender of the cognates in all other Indo-European languages.

The term *íarmbérla* in Irish grammatical tradition always means 'unstressed word,' and it is a remarkable tribute to the Irish grammarians that they registered this feature of sentence phonetics: *focul,* 'word' = "stressed word." The list of forms in *íarmbérla* includes such categories as prepositions (*iar,* 'after,' *ar,* 'for'), particles, conjunctions, and some adverbs (*dano,* 'then,' *immorro,* 'moreover') including conjugated prepositions functioning as adverbs (*iarum,* 'then'; lit. 'after it'), preposition plus article (*forsna,* 'on the'), the substantive verb *atat,* 'there are,' and constructs like *edon,* 'id est,' *cisne,* 'how many are.' All these are termed *dialt n-etarlemmi,* 'interloping syllable' for the poet, that is, they constitute the *temps faible* of the verse line, between *temps forts* of stressed words. This state of affairs represents, of course, a linguistic feature equally characteristic of ordinary language.

The final term is *bérla fortchide na filed,* 'Obscure language of the poets': *fortchide* is another past participle, 'covered, concealed,' from *for·tuigethar.* It is more commonly referred to in Irish tradition as simply *bérla na filed,* 'language of the poets.' *Bérla na filed* represents a higher, more elevated, and more obscure form of poetic language than the "straightforward" poetic language termed *fásaige na filed,* 'maxims of poets,' although the difference is merely one of degree. It is the language of the "rhetorics" in Old Irish sagas, passages of verse or rhythmical prose clearly valued for precisely their obscurantism and their bold contrast with the surrounding and transparent prose narrative.

Bérla na filed relied for its effect partly on poetic devices like alliteration, partly on perturbations of normal Irish word order, but

[21] Cf. already A. Götze and H. Pedersen, *Muršilis Sprachlähmung* (Copenhagen, 1934), p. 65.

mostly on obscure lexical items that were otherwise lost in the ordinary language; in other words, archaisms. Compare *senbérla* opposed to *gnáthbérla* above.

The five categories of language enumerated by the compilator of *Auraicept na n-Éces* as such represent only a conventional pentad; compare the five provinces of Ireland, the five banqueting halls of Ireland, or the Five Ways to Judgment. We may at once exclude *íarmbérla* (unaccented words), as referring to a ubiquitous feature of the language. Similarly *bérla etarscartha* (separated language) may be excluded, as referring to a particular technique, of native exegesis, rather than to a type of discourse. Of the remaining terms, the first, *bérla Féine* ('language of the Irish') is equated by the Irish tradition with either *gnáthbérla* ('ordinary language') or *fásaige na filed* ('pronouncements of poets'): a genuine ambiguity or ambivalence that requires explanation.

As Binchy informs me, we know from the statements of later jurists that certain rules are found *isin bérla*, a phrase sometimes expanded to *isin bérla Féine*. We can thus equate *bérla* alone with *bérla Féine* (the "professional" language). The fact that *bérla* is used alone shows that it must be the unmarked member of any semantic opposition to a contrasting term. We may note also that *bérla Féine* (= *bérla*) appears first in the list of the five sorts of language, another indication that it is the unmarked member. Compare in grammar the Latin *first* declension, *first* conjugation, or the *first* class of verbs of the Hindu grammarians.

The hesitation of the Irish tradition on the position of *bérla Féine* is genuine, and reflects the relative position of the same element on two levels of discourse; it is marked, poetic language by opposition to ordinary language, but it is unmarked, ordinary "professional" (gnomic-poetic-legal) language by opposition to the particular and specialized poetic form of speech known technically as *bérla na filed*.

Following the lead of grammatical parallelism, we can establish three oppositions:

compound:	
gnáthbérla : *senbérla*	ordinary : old
genitival:	
bérla (*b. Féine*) : *bérla na filed*	professional : poetic
participial:	
bérla tóbaide : *bérla fortchuide*	fashioned, selected : concealed.

Thus the most highly marked form of discourse in Irish is that which is archaic, uniquely poetic, and obscure: precisely the characteristic of the so-called "rhetorics" in Irish saga. It is in these oppositions that we find the genuine Irish counterpart of the opposition of language of men and language of gods in the metalinguistic traditions of other Indo-European languages.

It is possible to make a further comparison, this time with Indic, which might suggest that we have to deal here in Irish with a genuine inheritance from an Indo-European poetic doctrine, a doctrine of the nature of poetic language and its relation to ordinary language. Consider the following mantras from the *Rig-Veda* (7. 87.4):

> uvā́ca me váruṇo mé̄dhirāya
> tríḥ saptá nā́mā́ ághnyā bibharti
> vidvā́n padásya gúhyā ná vocad
> yugā́ya vípra úparāya śíkṣan
>
> Varuṇa said to me, the wise one:
> "The cow bears thrice seven names.
> He who knows the spoor should tell them like secrets
> if he wishes to serve as poet to the later generation."

Let us note at once that the speaker of the quotation in the hymn is Varuṇa and the hymn is addressed to him, one of the principal deities of Dumézil's first function and one associated here with the patronage of poetry. R. Jakobson points out to me the poet who is *Velesovŭ vnukŭ*, 'grandson of Veles' (root **wel-* as in Old Irish *fili*, 'poet') in the *Slovo o Polku Igoreve.*

Yet the Vedic poet is in fact calling to mind the same set of oppositions between ordinary and poetic language as the Irish tradition.

The opposition between *ordinary* and *old* (Irish *gnáthbérla* : *senbérla*) is figured in the *yugā́ya vípra úparāya*: the poet is old vis-à-vis the later generation.

The opposition between the simply *professional* and specifically *poetic* (OIr. *bérla Féine* : *bérla na filed*) is precisely figured in the contrast of the poet (the ego of the hymn) who is *médhira* before Varuṇa speaks to him, and becomes *vípra* after the intervention of the deity.

Finally, just as in Ireland, one of the characteristics of this *archaic, poetic* language is its *obscurity* (Irish *fortchuide*). Just so the thrice seven names of the cow are *gúhyā*, 'secret.' And in *Rig-Veda* 4.5.3 *padáṃ na gór ápagūḷham vividvā́n* (*guh-*, 'hide') we have a participle in *-tá-*, 'hidden,' comparable both with the formation of *saṃskṛta, prakṛta* and with OIr. *forchuide*, 'hidden.'

Indeed in the *Rig-Veda* the "secret name" or "word" (*pada*) (of the cows, gods, and so on) is a quite common figure (some nine examples.). Note especially *gúhyam nā́ma gónām*, 'the secret names of the cows,' a formula occupying the same metrical position (from caesura to verse end) in both *Rig-Veda* 5.3.3 and 9.87.3. This metrical feature is in itself an index of archaism. The figure of the "secret name" or "word" frequently plays on the basic meaning of *pada* which is 'spoor,' as in the preceding example. Probably it had something to do with the semantic development of *pada*, for example, originally "secret word."

Another typical example is *Rig-Veda* 8.41.5.

yó usrā́nām apīcyā́
véda nā́māni gúhyā
sá kavíḥ kā́vyā purú
rūpáṃ dyáur iva puṣyati

He who knows the secret hidden names of the cows,
as a poet/seer he greatly prospers poetic art
as the bright sky its color

The message is virtually identical to that of 7.87.4 above: knowledge of the secret names establishes the poet in his prerogative. And I further suspect that when the Vedic poet uses *ághnyā*, 'she not to be harmed,' or *usrā́*, 'she the gleaming one,' for 'cow' here, instead of the neutral *go-* as in other passages, he is consciously utilizing one of these "secret" names for the cow. We have to deal with a versified "synonymy," in a fashion similar to that of the *Alvíssmǫl* in Old Norse.

Specifically the technique is the introduction of a semantically marked synonym in place of the unmarked, "normal" variant, that is, *go-*. We noted earlier the replacement of unmarked *áśva* by marked *háya* in a determined syntactic context. Here we have another instance of the same poetic process. We have a formula *gúhyam nā́ma gónām*, which on metrical grounds may well be old. The version in 8.41.5 *usrā́ṇām . . . nā́māni gúhyā* is just such a stylistic transformation of this formula, by means of the semantic hierarchy *gó* ⟶ *usrā́, ághnyā, . . .* plus other trivial transformations of word order, grammatical number, and so on, which may be discounted here.

In Defense of Euhemerus

KEES W. BOLLE, *University of California, Los Angeles*

EUHEMERISM

It may be best to admit[1] that my reflections on Euhemerus were motivated by the Wikander-Dumézilian interpretation of the *Mahābhārata.*[2] It is one of the contexts in which the words "euhemerism" and "euhemerization" come up. Certain gods, functioning in an early Indo-European mythical structure are "transposed," so it is said, into heroic figures. And as we know, Indo-Europeanists have to deal with a number of such "euhemerizing" transpositions. Next to the *Mahābhārata,* there are the first books of Livy, the saga of Hadding in Saxo Grammaticus, and several themes and narrations in Snorri Sturluson, to name some of the best-known euhemerizing texts.

If anything is clear, it is the variety of these documents, and indubitably, the "transposition" remains an enigmatic procedure. Since the name of the Greek Euhemerus is linked with the discussions, euhemerism as a Western intellectual fashion deserves some reflections. Thus I venture on this excursus in defense of Euhemerus with the hope that in the eyes of specialists it will not be a raid on his behalf.

It is a curious manner of reading and explaining myths which is

---

1 I am indebted to Professor Jacques Duchesne-Guillemin and to Professor Truesdell S. Brown for their counsel in bibliographical matters.

2 For convenient references and bibliography see C. S. Littleton, *The New Comparative Mythology: An Anthropological Assessment of the Theories of Georges Dumézil* (Berkeley and Los Angeles, 1966).

generally, and somewhat too easily, attributed to this *romancier* Euhemerus (*ca.* 340–260 B.C.). This method can be summed up in two words: historization and humanization. The information we have about Euhemerus is scanty.[3] The most important fragment of his work, the most unmistakable one, we owe to the famous early Christian church historian Eusebius (*ca.* A.D. 300), who in turn owed his information to Diodorus (first century B.C.), who quoted Euhemerus. (Book 6 where Diodorus begins to speak explicitly about Euhemerus is among the lost books of his history.) This information, given to us in such a roundabout way, is nevertheless most important. The story is well known and needs no elaborate rendering here. Euhemerus narrates how he once traveled to some islands in the East and visited the people named the Panchaeans. The story is rather fantastic. Euhemerus would have us believe for instance—assuming, as is generally done, that this information given by Diodorus elsewhere also comes from Euhemerus—that from one of these islands, at least from a promontory on it, on a clear day one could see India. On the principal island a temple of Zeus is situated, Zeus Triphylios, to be exact. There is a large golden pillar in this temple on which Zeus himself had made inscriptions. In these inscriptions were recorded the deeds of Zeus, of his father Kronos, and of his grandfather Ouranos. For Zeus, like his grandfather and father, at one time was king of the inhabited earth. Like his ancestors, he received the honor of divinity because of the great tasks he performed for mankind. The nucleus of the theory, then, is simply that the gods at the time were human beings, who came to be worshiped as gods because of their acts on behalf of men. Admittedly, as a scholarly theory on the origin of myth Euhemerus' romance is hardly worth considering. But the reason why a specific method of interpretation became associated with his name was perhaps precisely that he wrote not a learned treatise but something with a more popular appeal. And it seems to me that there are two very important reasons why euhemerism is worth considering from the point of view of the historian of religions. The most conspicuous point of interest in euhemerism is its tenacity in intellectual circles in the West; unabated it survived in eighteenth-century scholarship and lingered even in the nineteenth century. Related to this is the fact I already mentioned that several documents informing us on Indo-European mythology are somehow euhemer-

---

3 The texts of ancient authors by and concerning Euhemerus have been collected by Felix Jacoby, *Die Fragmente der griechischen Historiker,* I (Berlin, 1923), 300–313.

istic. It is necessary to understand the nature of euhemerism to make use of such documents. An additional reason for looking closely at euhemerism is the general, perhaps not too well-qualified depreciation of it in modern scholarship.

It is highly unlikely that the ideas generated by Euhemerus were totally original. Generally critical evaluations of the ancient traditions were not novel. Two centuries before Euhemerus another Greek, the famous philosopher Xenophanes of Colophon, spoke words that testify to the occurrence of more or less "euhemeristic" tendencies even then. These words have been quoted many times since: "But the mortals think that the gods are born and dress, speak, and look just like they themselves do."[4] And "the Ethiopians imagine that their gods are black and have snub noses, but the Tracians think of *their* gods as blue-eyed and having red hair."[5] "If cows, horses and lions had hands and could use them to paint and make artifacts, as people do, then the horses would paint divine images like horses, the cows like cows; they would create images appearing like themselves."[6] It may be useful, though, to remind ourselves that this is not the irony of some modern demythologizer. Another fragment of Xenophanes adds: "[For there is] only one single God, the supreme one among gods and people, unlike the mortals both in appearance and in thought."[7] For every good and severe criticism or serious doubt has another, positive side to it. In this context we may think also of that philosophical giant Aristotle (384–322 B.C.), an older contemporary of Euhemerus. Aristotle can hardly pass as an adherent to traditional religion. Yet he was most impressed by perpetual, regular motion. This he found in the cyclical course of the heavenly bodies, as stated in *De Caelo* (e.g., 285a29, 292a20, 292b1). Corresponding statements are made by Aristotle in his *Metaphysics* (see 1074a30). He makes a sharp distinction between traditional beliefs and the divine nature of the heavens, and even speaks of the celestial bodies as "divine" (θεῖος) bodies (*Metaphysics* 1074a30). One passage is so revealing that I like to quote it in full:

> A tradition has been handed down by the ancient thinkers of very early times, and bequeathed to posterity in the form of a myth, to the effect that these heavenly bodies are gods, and that the Divine pervades the whole of nature. The rest of their tradition has been added later in a

---

4 Hermann Diels, ed., *Die Fragmente der Vorsokratiker* (5th ed.; Berlin, 1934), fr. 14.

5 *Ibid.*, fr. 16.

6 *Ibid.*, fr. 15.

7 *Ibid.*, fr. 23.

mythological form to influence the vulgar and as a constitutional and utilitarian expedient; they say that these gods are human in shape or are like certain other animals, and make other statements consequent upon and similar to those which we have mentioned. Now if we separate these statements and accept only the first, that they supposed the primary substances to be gods, we must regard it as an inspired saying; and reflect that whereas every art and philosophy has probably been repeatedly developed to the utmost and has perished again, these beliefs of theirs have been preserved as a relic of former knowledge. To this extent only, then, are the views of our forefathers and of the earliest thinkers intelligible to us. [*Metaphysics* 1074b1–14].[8]

In the same context in which Diodorus quotes Euhemerus a distinction is made that is not without analogy to Aristotle's exposition. Certain of the gods are said to be eternal and imperishable. It is interesting to note that Diodorus expressly mentions that the ancients have always known that. Such gods are, for instance, "the sun and the moon and the other stars of the heavens" ("Fragmenta Libri VI," 1.2).[9] And further "for each of these the genesis and duration are from everlasting to everlasting."[10] The appeal to tradition may be invalid in terms of modern scholarship, both here and in the case of Aristotle, but this question does not concern us here. The Dutch scholar Schippers has shown convincingly that this type of distinction must have been part of Euhemerus' world of ideas;[11] evidently it was a distinction of a sort that was already accepted in intellectual circles. We learn from Diodorus that Euhemerus' theory deals with the second type of deity, and it is worth mentioning that here too Diodorus, and presumably also Euhemerus, makes a reference to tradition: "But the other gods, *we are told,* were terrestrial beings, who attained to immortal honor and fame because of their benefactions to mankind" ("Fragmenta Libri VI," 1.2).[12] This is the group to which Zeus belongs, and the other deities who play a role in Euhemerus' story.

Certainly the existence of critical evaluations like those by Xenophanes and Aristotle should not lead us to believe that Euhemerus was equally sharp in his criticism; if anything, he was conservative in comparison. The distinction between natural gods and divinized

---

[8] Hugh Tredennick, trans., *Aristotle, Metaphysics X–XIV,* Loeb Classical Library (London, 1952), p. 163.

[9] C. H. Oldfather, trans., *Diodorus of Sicily,* Loeb Classical Library (London, 1952), III, 331.

[10] *Ibid.*

[11] J. W. Schippers, *De ontwikkeling der Euhemeristische godencritiek in de Christelijke Latijnse literatuur* (Groningen, 1952), esp. pp. 23–24.

[12] Oldfather, *op. cit.,* p. 331.

human beings, as recorded in the text of Diodorus, is much less radical and jibes well with the one certain knowledge we have of Euhemerus: that he attributed the divinization of certain people to the vast positive value their exploits had for mankind.

The fair account we owe to Eusebius (taken from Diodorus about Euhemerus) contrasts favorably with the uses other early Christians made of "Euhemerism." Evidently Euhemerus knew himself that the ideas he unfolded were not new. Also, his treatment of the gods could not have been as offensive as we might think for the simple reason that the Greek gods were very unlike the God of the Old Testament and New Testament. Rightly, this point has been stressed by Professor Truesdell Brown.[13] After all, the sacred traditions of the Greeks were given in the form of stories, in which the gods act among people and in many ways like them.

The theory attributed to Euhemerus changed considerably under the impact of growing Christianity. This change was neither abrupt nor revolutionary, for in many quarters Imperial Rome saw the growth of new multiform religious cults and ideas, and not in the last place demonologies.[14] More and more the pagan gods were seen and explained as people elevated not because of their benefactions and virtue but through their tremendous immorality. In fact, they were demonic. Next to Euhemerism proper, a type of theorizing becomes customary that is hardly worthy of the same name. It is a *euhemerismus inversus*, an improper euhemerism. Yet, as I hope to show, another name for this other theory would also be misleading. For the moment let me just recall the difficulty we have in assessing Euhemerus' own intentions. We do not know enough of him or of the spirit of his time to answer the question to what extent for instance irony played a role in his romance, and if it played a role, what sort of role it was.[15]

---

13 Truesdell S. Brown, "Euhemerus and the Historians," *Harvard Theological Review* 39:263 (1946).

14 Jean Bayet, *Histoire politique et psychologique de la religion romaine* (Paris, 1957), pp. 255–266.

15 The diversity in scholarly interpretations of Euhemerus' own intentions is indeed baffling. An elaborate discussion is given by Frank Susemihl, *Geschichte der griechischen Litteratur in der Alexandrinerzeit* (Leipzig, 1891), I, 316–322. On the one hand, Susemihl sees Euhemerus as one depicting to some extent his own ideals (p. 318), but he reproaches him also of "Plattheit" (p. 319), follows in the scholarly tradition to classify Euhemerus in more or less the same category as Lucian and Voltaire (p. 320), and concludes by saying: "thatsächlich war er ohne Zweifel ein unbedingter Atheist und ward denn auch vielfach als ein solcher angesehen" (p. 322). To add to the puzzle of Euhemerus' intentions, cf. Robert von Pohlmann, *Geschichte der sozialen Frage und des Sozialismus in der antiken Welt*

When it comes to the divinization of people, ideas of a biblical origin are much easier to fathom. Such divinization is a sinful affair. The idea itself that the gods were glorified men is not limited to the world of Greek intellectuals. The Wisdom of Solomon (*ca.* 80 B.C.) is one of the apocryphal books. It was written in Greek but formed part of the Septuagint. One passage clearly condemns the divinization of people and contemptuously attributes it to human need for consolation.

In the Wisdom of Solomon 14:15–17 we read:

> For a father afflicted by untimely grief made a likeness of his child that had been quickly taken from him, and presently honored as a god him who was once a dead man, and handed down to his subjects mysteries and rites. Then the ungodly practice, strengthened by time, came to be observed as law, and by the orders of monarchs carved images were worshipped. And when men could not honor them in their presence because they lived far away, they imagined how they looked, far away, and made a visible image of the king they honored, so as by their zeal to flatter the absent one as though he were present."[16]

Ideas like these, nourished by the biblical tradition spreading in the process of European Christianization, helped to form a matrix for improper Euhemerism. An important religious role in late Antiquity was played by the oracular writings known as the Sibylline Books. The third book begins with a biblical story (the Tower of

(Munich, 1925), II, 293–305. For Heinrich Dörrie (*Der Königskult des Antiochos von Kommagene im Lichte neuer Inschriften-Funde* [Göttingen, 1964], pp. 218–224) Euhemerus' romance is the support of an ideology *enabling* kings to enhance their own political prestige. In fact, Euhemerus becomes much like a blueprint for apotheosis. Granted that "divine kingship" in late antiquity, beginning with Alexander, is a problem for scholars, this thesis—like the one that sees in Euhemerus some modern blasphemer or atheist—begs the question. It ignores the enigma of existing traditions that made the very process of divinization possible and acceptable. Giovanna Vallauri (*Evemero di Messene, testimonianze e frammenti, con introduzione e commento* and *Origine e diffusione dell'evemerismo nel pensiero classico*, Pubblicazioni della Facultà di Lettere e Filosofia [Torino: Università di Torino, 1956 and 1960]) is very important in this context, because she addresses herself in the first essay precisely to the question what Euhemerus himself might have had in mind. Her writings are also noteworthy because of the scrupulous textual references. But this author, too, is mesmerized by sociopolitical views. There is little consideration for the fact that Euhemerus *told a story*. Euhemerus' text becomes the crystallization of a sociopolitical ideology accelerating a process of religious decay (see especially *Evemero di Messene*, p. 23). All these diverse explanations of Euhemerus—personal crudeness, atheism, antireligious irony, utopianism, commitment to one political ideology—have in common that they are intent on taking away the strangeness of the data by substituting something familiar to the modern author.

[16] J. M. Powis Smith and Edgar J. Goodspeed, *The Complete Bible* (Chicago, 1948).

Babel) and a euhemeristic narration of a motif in Greek religion, whereby euhemerism serves to show the inferiority of paganism.[17] Euhemerizations provided with a new edge by the biblical tradition occur frequently in the Church Fathers and the medieval bishops.[18]

By the fourth century A.D. euhemerism, albeit of an amalgamated nature, has become so widespread that Saint Augustine devotes some lengthy reasonings to it. Specifically he feels that it is necessary to discuss the honor paid by Christians to their martyrs in order to point out that such worship, such honor, differs from paganism. Many reasonings of Saint Augustine are clearly euhemeristic. (In some passages he shows himself familiar with the name of Euhemerus.) Thus in *The City of God* (8.26) it is said: "with such blindness do impious men, as it were, stumble over mountains, and will not see the things which strike their own eyes, that they do not attend to the fact that in all the literature of the pagans there are not found any, or scarcely any gods, who have not been men to whom, when dead, divine honours have been paid."[19] But for Augustine the pagan customs are also an affair of demons. He concludes in the same section with a peroration that clearly shows the amalgamation I mentioned before: "it was the grief of the demons which was expressing itself through his [Hermes Trismegistus'] mouth, who were sorrowing on account of the punishments which were about to fall upon them at the tombs of the martyrs. For in many such places they were tortured and compelled to confess, and were cast out of the bodies of men, of which they had taken possession."

Considering the strength of Christianity and its spokesmen, it is astonishing that euhemerizations could continue to flourish which were not totally improper and could indeed serve as vehicles for mythical motifs, for example, in Saxo Grammaticus. It would seem sometimes as if the negative potential of euhemerism provided the framework within which a "proper" euhemeristic construction could go on, preserving the mythological material.

THE POWER OF PRESERVATION

There is indeed one exceedingly important point in all those euhemerizing reasonings which a modern man is inclined to overlook. It is simply this: that the historization and humanization, which, in

---

17 M. P. Nilsson, *Geschichte der griechischen Religion*, II (2d ed.; Munich, 1961), 112.

18 See Schippers (*op. cit.*) on Cyprian, pp. 84, 85, and on others (*passim*).

19 Marcus Dods, trans., *The City of God by Saint Augustine* (New York, 1948), I, p. 348.

our terms, involve the *making up* of stories, do not rob a god of his reality. In this respect euhemerism differs fundamentally from all nineteenth- and twentieth-century popular intellectualism that declares gods and spirits nonexistent. The Christian apologist Lactantius is one of our sources for Euhemerus; he does not quote Euhemerus but provides a little treatise about him,[20] and even this militant Christian says that it is *Jupiter* who in the way he went about things, constituting his own worship, was very clever ("quod ille astutissime excogitavit, ut et sibi honorem divinum et hospitibus suis perpetuum nomen adquireret cum religione coniunctum."[21] Schippers, in discussing this passage, adds a footnote to the effect that actually it should have been Euhemerus who had thought these things out so cleverly.[22] It is revealing that Lactantius did not see it that way and apparently saw in Euhemerus an authoritative interpreter. He found no reason at all to make a point that the very figure of Jupiter was a figment of the imagination.

Euhemerism's power to preserve may well serve as a point of departure in reflecting on some Indo-European fragments, on the curious tenacity of the theory in intellectual circles and on its rejection by modern scholars.

Even though it is difficult to establish Euhemerus' own psychological attitude, it is obvious that he did not sneer at the gods. Certainly no one would accuse Diodorus, that storehouse of facts, of an overgrown sense of irony. Now it is interesting to note the manner in which Diodorus (in one of the preserved books: Book 5) speaks of the gods in the fabulous land of Panchaea (for the information drawing on Euhemerus in all likelihood). For example, in 5.44 he renders the local tradition concerning Ouranos. In this record the relationship of Ouranos and the sky—of course, well established in traditional lore—is perfectly preserved under the new euhemeristic garb. There is a lofty mountain, he says, which is made sacred to the gods and is called the "Throne of Ouranos" (Οὐρανοῦ δίφρος); and he continues: "For the myth relates that in ancient times, when Ouranos was king of the inhabited earth, he took pleasure in tarrying in that place and in surveying from its lofty top both the heavens and the stars therein . . ." (5.44.6).[23]

Apparently the mythical narrative traditions were too strong either

---

20 Schippers, *op. cit.*, pp. 19–25.
21 Jacoby, *op. cit.*, p. 312.
22 Schippers, *op. cit.*, p. 22, fr. 2.
23 Oldfather, *op. cit.*, p. 221.

for Diodorus or for his spokesmen to simply transfer Ouranos into the realm of "natural deities," in spite of the fashionable fascination for the heavens. Instead, Ouranos is presented humanly—not, however, *just* humanly but as some ancient king-astronomer. Thus a theme constitutive of the Ouranos myth is preserved. In the fragments of Book 6 the image of Ouranos is completed with explicit reference to Euhemerus: ". . . that Ouranos was the first to be king, that he was an honorable (ἐπιεικής) man and beneficent (εὐεργετικός), who was versed in the movement of the stars, and that he was also the first to honour the gods of the heavens with sacrifices, whence he was called Ouranos or Heaven" (6.1.8).[24] Clearly the words "historization" and "humanization" to sum up euhemeristic procedure must be used cautiously. The euhemeristic wordings contain much more than a reduction to mere human conditionings. Ouranos' primary kingship, his knowledge of the stars, and his institution of sacrificial ceremonies for the gods of the heavens give Euhemerus' account itself the flavor of a *myth of origins.*

Traits of a positive evaluation of ancient mythological tradition can be pointed out in later Western texts. Not only were certain themes of myths preserved, but I think we can see evidence of this positive attitude itself, in spite of the increased interest in demonology, in spite of changes brought by Christianity. Most eloquent is a certain inner contradiction in Saxo Grammaticus (*ca.* 1200) and in Snorri: on the one hand the traditional gods are not gods, on the other hand the author cannot be silent concerning their divinity.

In the first book of Saxo's *Danish History* a well-known curious passage occurs about Odin, much like an interlude in the historical account. It begins as follows: "At this time there was one Odin, who was credited all over Europe with the honour, *which was false,* of godhead (*falso divinitatis titulo censeretur*) . . ." (1.7.1).[25] This introduction hardly sets the tone for a sympathetic exposition of devotion to Odin, and the next couple of pages certainly strengthen that impression. But one soon begins to wonder about the astonishing abilities of this "false" godhead. The kings of the North are eager to worship Odin and make a golden image for him in his likeness, much to his pleasure. Then Frigga, Odin's wife, enters the story. She is portrayed as a most wanton woman. She has the image stripped

---

24 *Ibid.*, p. 335.

25 Text in J. Olrik and H. Raeder, *Saxonis Gesta Danorum*, vol. 1 (Copenhagen, 1931). Translation in Oliver Elton, *The First Nine Books of the Danish History of Saxo Grammaticus* (London, 1905), p. 110. The italics are mine.

by smiths, to use the gold for her own splendor. Odin hangs the smiths and then Saxo tells us that he "mounted the statue upon a pedestal, which by the marvellous skill of his art he made to speak when a mortal touched it" *(ibid.)*.[62] Still this famous magic of Odin as reported does not conflict with Saxo's personal reserves. He elaborates on Frigga's low morals and greed, who even goes so far as to submit herself "to the embraces of one of her servants" and to break the image. And Saxo sighs: ". . . but what should I here add, save that such a godhead was worthy of such a wife?" (*ibid.*).[27] Yet Odin is not depicted as deprived of a sense of honor. Filled with shame, he goes into exile. In his absence another person, Mit-Othin, "famous for his juggling tricks . . . was likewise quickened, as though by inspiration from on high to seize the opportunity of feigning to be a god" (1.7.2).[28] The period of his reign is described as a catastrophe. He upsets the cultic practices and must finally flee to Finland, where he is slain. His evil power is so uncanny that even his death does not immediately put an end to it: ". . . he spread such pestilence that he seemed almost to leave a filthier record in his death than in his life" (*ibid.*).[29]

After this episode of Mit-Othin one is inclined to overlook the curious change in style with which Saxo narrates in conclusion the return of Odin. (This return apparently became possible after Frigga's death):

> The death of Odin's wife revived the ancient splendor of his name, and seemed to wipe out the disgrace upon *his deity* (coniugis fato pristinae claritatis opinione recuperata ac veluti expiata divinitatis infamia), so, returning from exile, he forced all those who had used his absence to assume the honors of divine rank to resign them as usurped; and the gangs of sorcerers that had arisen he scattered like a darkness before the advancing glory of his *godhead* (superveniente numinis sui fulgore). And he forced them by his power not only to lay down their divinity, but further he quit the country, deeming that they, who tried to foist themselves so iniquitously into the skies, ought to be outcasts from the earth.[30]

One wonders about this conclusion: It seems that after all Odin was not "foisting himself into the sky so iniquitously" like the others. And certainly in the Latin in which Saxo so solemnly wrought his history the references to Odin's divinity could not be a slip of the pen.

---

26 Elton, *op. cit.*
27 *Ibid.*
28 *Ibid.*, p. 111.
29 *Ibid.*
30 *Ibid.*, p. 112.

The only sensible conclusion is that the inner contradiction that strikes us did not disturb Saxo. And why should this be so amazing? His "sense of history" was different from ours. It allowed him to include a story like this one in a book dealing with the history of kings. Somewhat in anticipation of some final problems it may be useful to remember that we ourselves had to wait for a nineteenth-century German scholar to be told that the work of a historian is to find out "wie es eigentlich gewesen . . . ," and even then that historian did not mean it in that emaciated manner in which we as a rule have heard it quoted. However this may be, the euhemerizations of a Saxo Grammaticus must not be taken as a cut-and-dried theory of explaining myth. That systematic notion is of a much later date. When we speak of Saxo's euhemerism—chances are that Saxo did not even know the name of Euhemerus—we should understand it in a disconcertingly less definable way: as a broad popular and intellectual movement in which storytelling meant something; it was less a matter of elaborating on one sweeping causal explanation than a matter of recording what had already been experienced in previous narrations.

Whatever the merits are of Saxo Grammaticus, the works of Snorri Sturluson, his younger contemporary, show a much greater artistic balance. His narratives are also known so much more widely that a few observations suffice to indicate that he too shows the same fascinating "inner contradiction" in his euhemerizations. As we know from the prologue of his *Prose Edda,* he has the god Thor travel from ancient Troy in a northern direction, making a deep impression wherever he passes through. The whole narration gradually fills the Nordic pantheon, and it is as if Snorri applies a most "orthodox" euhemerism, making use—like Euhemerus in the case of Uranos—of striking etymologies (to which all modern scholarship hastens to add that they are fanciful). Thor, of course, is of royal descent. He is the son of a king in the area of Troy. His mother was a daughter of King Priam himself. Priam was called Tróán, and Thor's original name was Trór. Thor's character is in no way changed in the euhemerizing process. At the age of twelve he has attained his brutal strength, kills his foster parents, to whose care he had been entrusted, and afterward on his journeys through the world kills beserkers, giants, a huge dragon, and wild beasts left and right. Among his descendants is Odin, who with his wife Frigg likewise travels north and finally settles in Sweden. Odin and his companions bring blessings wherever they go. They were called Aesir which, Snorri assures us, meant "men of Asia." "Their travels were attended by such prosperity that wherever they stayed in a country, that region enjoyed good harvests and peace, and everyone believed that they caused this, since the native inhabitants had never seen any other people like them for good looks and intelligence."[31]

But was all this a matter of make-believe? Was Odin, were the gods, really human or were they really divine? This question is not raised. It is our question, and perhaps not a very good one. If we ask Snorri's text and insist on an answer, the cumulative thematic evidence points to mythical structures and not to a theory of historical facts: "Odin, and also his wife, had the gift of prophecy, and by means of this magic art he discovered that his name would be famous in the northern part of the world and honoured above that of all kings. For this reason he set out on a journey from Turkey."[32]

The very beginning of this whole passage is revealing, for Snorri underlines that the place where Troy is situated, "where what we call Turkey lies," is "near the centre of the world."[33] It could not be put more mythologically.

There is no one-way explanation of the gods for Snorri; there is very little resembling the sort of thing that is nowadays called the "genetic approach." Instead we find a great concern for relating the traditions in the midst of which Snorri as a man of his time had to orient himself. It implied a mythological integration and the means for it was the narrative. It is well known that the history of Troy was a constant inspiration for many medieval poetic historians, not least in the time of Snorri (e.g., the poet Jacob van Maerlant in the Low Countries). And as if linking up Nordic and classical traditions were not enough, Snorri's endeavors of integration are prefaced by a summary discussion of the biblical creation account and the story of Adam and Eve. If this manner of presentation is called "pseudohistory," we are jumping to conclusions. This manner of integration in narrative form is rooted in myth; it is itself truly mythological. It is easy to see that the euhemerism of a Snorri is a powerful mythological tool. Its characteristic is precisely its built-in ambiguity. It makes it possible to relate where a later generation could only insist on a rather dogmatic choice. In other words, there is a reason for the suggestion I made before: not to be too hasty in separating a "proper"

---

[31] Jean J. Young, trans., *The Prose Edda of Snorri Sturluson* (Berkeley and Los Angeles, 1965). p. 27.

[32] *Ibid.*, p. 26.

[33] *Ibid.*, p. 25.

from an "improper" euhemerism. The two are aspects of the same power to preserve old themes in a new clash of traditions, each of which is irrefutably valid.

Of course, the question can be raised—and is hard to repress in the study of the Indo-European materials of which we should like to have so much more than we have: How much was lost of the earlier tradition in these euhemerizing processes? It is a moot question. It is somewhat like asking: How much more history is there than the history of which we have documents? Yet, I think that we have enough data to reflect on euhemerism by making a distinction different from that between "proper" and "improper": I have in mind the simple distinction between earlier and later euhemerism. The former is the intellectual tradition characterized by narration, integrating existing traditions and for that reason able to preserve earlier mythological motifs; it shows a structural kinship with the procedure of Euhemerus himself, even when its negative propensities stand out too (as in the case of Saxo). These historizations, although the work of artistic individuals, thus show themselves a specific religious structure of which the popular appeal is noteworthy. They relate to other well-known historizing efforts of the time; I think of the devout descriptions of the life of the Lord (especially in Christmas songs with miraculous and almost romantic details)[34] and of the Mary-legends. In fact these historizations and humanizations should be considered a religious structure worthy of attention as much as "mysticism" and "gnosticism." Because of its popular appeal and inner relation to widespread devotional forms this type of euhemerism is especially worthy of attention, much more worthy of attention than would appear from such general labels as "pseudo-history." Narration occurs as a *vehicle of the sacred.*

Later euhemerism is of an entirely different nature. It has played such an uncritically accepted role in scholarship that this alone can explain why earlier euhemerism has often been explained on its terms. Scholars have been so preoccupied with the question of *origins*

---

[34] I think of some lines in a traditional Dutch song about the Lord's childhood:

> 't At pap uit een pannetje, 't en maakt hem niet vuil,
> 't Viel op de aarde, t' en had er geen buil. . . .
>
> He ate porridge from a bowl, but did not make himself dirty,
> He fell on the ground, and he did not get a bruise. . . .

This type of literature, in the form in which it was given in the Netherlands in the Middle Ages, has been described by M. H. v.d. Zeyde, "De letterkunde in de Lage Landen," in J. S. Bartstra and W. Banning, *Nederland tussen de natien* (Amsterdam, 1946), I, 218–225.

of myths that all attention was given to the thematic *causes* of existing euhemeristic documents. It was taken for granted that these documents were not the real myths—justifiably so, but a genetic obsession too easily leads to a methodological reductionism.

LATER EUHEMERISM

The watershed between early and later euhemerism is the Enlightenment period.[35] To be sure, many eighteenth-century scholars dealing with religion had as "naïve" an idea of history as Saxo and Snorri. It was not unusual to begin the discussion of man's religion, as Fontenelle (d. 1757) did, with the question if and how the original (biblical) revelation was lost in the history of the other nations. Perhaps in some cases—with scholars taking all the bible as history, just as Herodotus took Homer—we might think of reverential bows made in the direction of the clergy. We can think of a man, however, who did not make a habit of reverential bows, David Hume, and we shall see in him at the same time a reflection of the old and the new, more clearly than in anyone else at the time of transition. On the one hand, there is an acceptance of the naïve, pseudohistorical side of the euhemeristic procedure. On the other hand there is an unmistakable interest in general theories concerning the causes of the mythical world. If with some caution we may use the words historization and humanization for early euhemerism, we are here justified in speaking of system and reduction. The *Natural History of Religion* is a small treatise, not interested in rendering or preserving mythical themes but devoted to a general analysis of religion.

Polytheism is for Hume principally a matter of "uninstructed mankind." With this idea Hume is very much a child of his age. Speaking of this uninstructed mankind, incapable as yet of conceiving one supreme creator, Hume says: "They suppose their deities, however potent and invisible, to be nothing but a species of human creatures, perhaps raised from among mankind, and retaining all human passions and appetites, together with corporeal limbs and organs."[36] Although this euhemerism of the search for general causes is quite different from early euhemerism, it is of a negative sort that is strangely reminiscent of the Church Fathers. The negative factor of fear is

[35] An interesting general discussion of euhemerism in the Enlightenment period is given by Frank E. Manuel, *The Eighteenth Century Confronts the Gods* (New York, 1967), chap. iii.

[36] David Hume, *The Natural History of Religion* (1757), ed. H. E. Root (London, 1956), pp. 30–31.

much more effective in the making of gods than hope in Hume's estimation. Generally, "men are much oftener thrown on their knees by the melancholy than by the agreeable passions."[37]

The search for sufficient explanations makes one question indeed inevitable: how precisely can human beings be raised to a superhuman status? This question was not an urgent one for the early euhemerists, for somehow they were convinced of the more than human qualities from the outset. It did not even disturb the Church Fathers very much in their reasonings, for the image of demons for them was a reality. Hume makes an attempt to answer the question, for he seems to realize that a general psychological observation about man's fear will not do. Fear and the lower passions by themselves are not creative and could hardly be credited with a good many stories about the gods. It is surprising to see that Hume's critical mind did not penetrate into these questions more profoundly than it did. This is what Hume's euhemerism sounds like:

> The deities of the vulgar are so little superior to human creatures, that, where men are affected with strong sentiments of veneration or gratitude for any hero or public benefactor, nothing can be more natural than to convert him into a god, and fill the heavens, after this manner, with continual recruits from among mankind. Most of the divinities of the ancient world are supposed to have once been men, and to have been beholden for their *apotheosis* to the admiration and affection of the people. The real history of their adventures, corrupted by tradition, and elevated by the marvellous, became a plentiful source of fable; especially in passing through the hands of poets, allegorists, and priests, who successively improved upon the wonder and astonishment of the ignorant multitude.[38]

It is really surprising that Hume, who took no philosophical idea from the ancient philosophers for granted but reexamined every single one of them critically, did not judge euhemerism. He simply accepted it in its negative, "improper" form, embellished only with some features (allegory, priestly and poetical changes) that were as traditional as this euhemerism itself. The overriding concern for a general explanation of religious materials as expressed here sets the tone for nineteenth-century scholarship. It is leaning on euhemerism without critically examining it. Exactly for that reason it distorts it. By its very nature, this new concern can view euhemerism as nothing but a theory on the causes of polytheism.

Later euhemerism actually did not deal with myth as early euhem-

---

37 *Ibid.*, p. 31.
38 *Ibid.*, p. 39.

erism did. The typical nineteenth-century students of religion, particularly under the influence of the budding science of anthropology, dealt with religion in general. It has been rightly observed that Herbert Spencer's theory on the evolution of religion was flavored by euhemerism[39]—"later euhemerism" I should like to say. Spencer wanted to see in ancestor worship the first form of religion. This theory implied the raise in status of humans upon their death. E. B. Tylor's theory of animism as the first and basic form of all religion can be understood perfectly as a theory fermented with later euhemerism. Its principal content is the ghosts of the dead. Myths figured only on the fringes of these new scientific undertakings, and it is not hard to understand that the narration that played the central part in early euhemerism and had grown on the basis of mythology was a closed book for that scholarship.

Now the same question raised before may be raised again in an intensified manner: Does not euhemerism leave out elements that were important in the traditions it pretends to deal with, and does it not distort those traditions? The answer must be: Later euhemerism stands guilty in many respects. In terms of a philosophy of culture it can and perhaps must be argued that destruction of myth is always an optical illusion. Is not the scientific search for origins by nineteenth-century evolutionists itself a rejuvenated myth of the utmost value?[40] Within the small scope of the present topic, however, it must be said that later euhemerism by its very nature was very much more destructive than early euhemerism. We may remember that the Church Fathers were able to transform gods into demons; they did not have to deny their existence. By comparison, many missionaries of the nineteenth and twentieth centuries were thoroughly modern, post-Enlightenment men. They did not have that peculiar power. They could only say of the gods, of this, that, or the other people in the wide world, that they did not really exist. Later euhemerism has indeed been destructive in its reductionism. Endeavors to establish a worthwhile contact with people whose life was oriented toward those gods have often failed. They only helped in creating a vacuum, the very vacuum in which many of our academic doings in the study of man are going on today. Clearly, euhemerism in a Snorri text is not reductionistic any more than in Euhemerus himself (for all we know).

[39] Jan de Vries, *The Study of Religion: A Historical Approach* (New York, 1967), p. 104.

[40] See Mircea Eliade, "The Quest for the 'Origins' of Religion," *History of Religions* 4:154–169 (1964).

It has a preserving power that does not show any resemblance to the "break" or "vacuum" associated with later euhemerism in its blanket explanation of tradition.

CONCLUSIONS

In this paper I have contented myself with a comparison and articulation of lines of thought evident in euhemerism in the widest sense. We have found major differences between a euhemerism that made up stories after the patterns and themes of myths, and a reductionistic theorizing, and have seen the crucial period of transition in the Enlightenment. These findings admittedly are of a very general nature, but it is in order to state some reflective conclusions that bear on the nature of our dealings with myth. The first conclusion relates to an indiscriminate depreciation of euhemerism in modern scholarship. The second has to do with the nature of mythical documents.

Jan de Vries is perhaps the most general depreciator of all euhemerism. He speaks of a rationalistic trend in Herodotus, who precisely for that reason can be regarded as a "precursor of Euhemerus,"[41] whereby it must be noted that for de Vries "rationalistic" is always an adjective of condemnation. Wherever euhemerism occurs, it smacks of causalistic obsessions for de Vries, in spite of the fact that for him as a Germanist historizing materials were among his documents; he had to deal with euhemerizations in the sense of documents "transposing" gods into humans. The bugaboo of what I have called "later euhemerism" clouds the discussion. The romantic historian Karl Otfried Müller has de Vries's greatest sympathy. Yet Müller's suggestion that some myths can be understood somehow as memory of historical events meets with de Vries's critical reaction.[42] This reaction too is not wholly just. After all, there are myths of which we cannot doubt that historical events codetermined their form. The foundation myth of the ancient empire of Fu-nan in Southeast Asia celebrated the marriage of an Indian immigrant and a local princess; it is impossible to separate the myth from the actual cultural historical origin of Fu-nan (and Cambodia).[43] Historical causes deserve some scholarly consideration in some cases, even though they can never explain the whole myth and all its themes. Above all, one should

---

41 Jan de Vries, *Forschungsgeschichte der Mythologie* (Munich, 1961), p. 8.

42 de Vries, *The Study of Religion*, p. 58.

43 See G. Coedès, *Les états hindouisés d'Indochine et d'Indonésie* (Paris, 1948), pp. 69–70. For euhemerizations in China, see Derk Bodde, "Myths of Ancient China," in S. N. Kramer, ed., *Mythologies of the Ancient World* (New York, 1961), pp. 372–376.

not confuse an interest in historical *causes* of certain myths with the euhemerizations of earlier centuries that did not "explain" myth but transferred it *into history*. De Vries's aversion to euhemerism obliterates the distinction. The Church Fathers come to resemble the "philosophes" of the eighteenth century.

This sort of fuzziness is by no means an individual's affair. It is given with our scholarly inheritance that is much more interested in causes, in finding the "original" mythical themes, than in the structure of given documents of an age that in comparison cannot be the supposedly original mythopoeic age. There is a widespread tendency to speak of euhemerization and degeneration, or at least chances of decay, in one breath. Even our esteemed friend Littleton, in his excellent exposition of Dumézil's work, gives in to this pattern: "*despite* the presence of Christian symbolism and euhemerization, the tripartite ideology persisted."[44] Bayet, whose sympathy for Dumézil's work is quite evident, speaks outright of "ce processus de désintégration religieuse et d'historisation des mythes."[45] The examples he gives of historization of myths on the same page, however, are principally inventions of new etiologies for taboos that were no longer understood. Hence here also, the modern theory of explanation forms the telescope through which all euhemerism is viewed. I want to underline that these views cannot be easily refuted, for there obviously are phases in Roman history on which we are so abundantly and diversely documented that the impression of a religious confusion is hard to avoid. Historizing explanations in the texts seem to be presented at random. Bayet adds: "de telles actions ne s'expliqueraient pas sur un capital mythique assuré ni en un milieu ou l'esprit mythique aurait été vivant."[46] And quite consistent in his views of a certain process of decay, Bayet continues to say: "And when it occurs that fundamental Indo-European myths, like those studied by G. Dumézil, are included in the historical fabric with a national and ethical value, certainly we have in that case the completion of a desacralization that began long before then."[47]

I am not competent to present an alternative arrangement of historical details. But a discussion of euhemerism requires an open eye for more nuances than are perceived in these quotations. It is justifiable to repeat that euhemerizations are not all explanations of old

---

44 Littleton, *op. cit.*, p. 18.
45 Bayet, *op. cit.*, p. 48.
46 *Ibid.*
47 *Ibid.*

and obscure traditions, but are also new orientations, in narratives based on myth, when necessitated by the clash of various traditions. It is not necessary to link such a new orientation per se with decay. Indeed, the greatest puzzle is hidden in words like "fundamental myths" and "milieux in which there was at one time an 'esprit mythique . . . vivant.' "

This leads to the second concluding reflection. The "genetic approach" is valid, of course, in the study of euhemerizing documents, but its limit becomes visible when it disregards the form and structure of the document under discussion by focusing only on what may have been left of the "original" myth. The genetic approach, unless used with the greatest caution and self-criticism, is prone to the same weaknesses as a bygone evolutionism. The question must be raised: When does a document stop being an original mythical document and when does it become a secondary, derived piece of work? Chances are that neither Snorri nor Saxo could have offered any of their treatises to a nineteenth-century, or for that matter many a twentieth-century, professor, as a doctoral dissertation. And why? Not because these modern learned men would not accept euhemerism as a method, but because they would sense that those old euhemerizations were too fanciful.

Times have changed. We still should not accept the *History of the Danish Kings* or the *Heimskringla* as Ph.D. dissertations. But we would no longer reject them because of their inadequate euhemerizations. They are mythical documents, as such subject to historical causalities and vicissitudes, but in this respect too like all other mythical documents.

Thus the findings I have submitted to you, general though they are, include a warning that at least for myself, in my own type of work, is not misplaced. The very first step in the study of euhemeristic texts, the step of tracing traditional themes, although exceedingly important, must not be the only step. Otherwise, we harm the materials in a way *as if* they were reductionistic. The euhemerizing materials of a Snorri or a Saxo—and I may add by extending the line: the *Mahābhārata*—remain mythical. The type of myth they represent in each case can be formulated in a manner I have tried to indicate. Even if one wants to limit himself to the discovery of an "original structure," one must pay careful attention to the structure of the euhemerizing text in order to make a legitimate separation between a specific more original tradition and the new "narrational myth." We ourselves have reached a place in history of such "secularity" that we can recognize the mythical character of early euhemerism. From a certain point of view the present paper is a case study in secularization. There is a definite break between the myth of euhemerism and, if you allow me to put it this way, the myth of finding origins characteristic of post-Enlightenment scholarship. It would be wrong to go on confusing the two. I am far from saying that no effort is necessary to avoid the confusion. There is, however, a constant and useful reminder with us in the fact that in all specialized areas of study the problem of finding an original myth, a "mythe fondamental," causes difficulties that we cannot ignore. They are not only philosophical problems, but above all problems for a sound historiography. From a philosophical point of view it may be true that myth is given with human existence and that there is no human life without myth. It may even be defensible to do what Claude Lévi-Strauss so brilliantly proposed: to study all versions of a myth regardless, and therefore, by way of example, to consider Freud's version of the Oedipus myth on a par with the Greek versions.[48] Indubitably, it is a radical solution of the problem of how to transcend evolutionism. But to me, it seems an inadmissible procedure for the historian of religions. It is a manner of confusing a mythical story with a reductionism, or one mythical structure with a very different one; in other words, adding apples and pears.

---

48 Claude Lévi-Strauss, *Anthropologie structurale* (Paris, 1958), p. 242.

Comparative Legal Reconstruction in Germanic

STEPHEN P. SCHWARTZ, *University of California, Los Angeles*

The Romantic movement in German literature, which began in the first few decades of the nineteenth century, was responsible for a new surge of interest in the semilegendary (if not wholly legendary) world of pre-Christian, agricultural Germany. Essentially and often avowedly anti-intellectual, it substituted emotion for reason and intuition for systematic investigation. It attempted to recapture an age that was in almost total opposition to the very real situation of an ununited Germany then undergoing the painful transition into the urbanized, cosmopolitan world.

The social problems engendered by the rather rapid change from an agricultural to an industrial economy, plus a massive migration from rural areas into cities, were viewed as constants of a system regarded *ab initio* as evil; industrialized, urbanized society. The chronological coincidence of Romanticism with the industrial revolution had the effect of neither solving nor significantly ameliorating these problems. Rather, it would produce a reaction, more appropriately a revulsion to them and substitute, for programs that might lessen the social consequences of a changed society, a yearning for bygone centuries, when Germany was by definition rural and agricultural, untouched by the contaminating effects of contemporary society. Parallel to this would occur a burgeoning nationalism that glorified things German and rejected things international, such as the exchange of ideas and past and present foreign influence. Since the present was not good, the past *must* have been better. If the past had been so much better, why had it not survived? Because of external, foreign influences upon a Germany politically divided into territorial states, city-states and cities, and thus divided unable to withstand external forces upon her.

It would fall to Romanticism, when it had discarded the bonds of creative literature and moved into the arena of social comment, to venerate the past as a means of escaping the present. This veneration of the pagan, heroic Germanic past led to an upsurge of antiquarian research into such areas as archaeology, ethnography, literature, and folklore. Prior to this time interest in the Germanic past had been negligible. We are reminded of the reaction of Frederick the Great to an edition of the *Nibelungenlied* by Christoph Heinrich Müller. Frederick wrote, ". . . dass dieser miserable Plunder kein Schuss Pulvers wert sei."[1] Although we are admonished that a general's opinion of a work of literature may not be especially worthy of serious consideration, de Vries comments that this evaluation of one of the cornerstones of Middle High German literature is representative of the climate of cultural opinion during the age of German Classicism, and that the Romantics would evaluate such literature differently.

The Age of Romanticism was the time of an energetic search of monastery cellars, of monastery and cathedral libraries, to unearth the literary remains of medieval Germany. By 1830 (the end of the Romantic Period), such representative works as the Old High German *Hildebrandslied*, the Middle High German *Kudrun*, the Old English *Beowulf*, and the Old Saxon *Heliand* were rediscovered. With passing decades still more manuscripts would come to light, be edited, published, and integrated, where possible, into Germanic historical, cultural, and literary evolution. From a conscious rejection by the intelligentsia of the Germanic past, the pendulum had swung to the opposite extreme, and the momentum generated by the Romantic Period would keep the pendulum extended long after Romanticism had faded into the twilight world of literary history. Romanticism as a cultural *idée fixe* would continue to affect future antiquarian scholarship for years to come, and although it would never actually become a bar to such scholarship (the many nineteenth-century editions of folk literature, medieval literature, and legal documents bear witness to this), it did produce a certain uniformity of critical consideration of the data under investigation and attempted to draw more substantive conclusions from these data than

---

[1] Cited in Jan de Vries, *Heldenlied und Heldensage* (Bern, 1961), p. 84.

a purely analytic approach would have done. What I have been intimating in a somewhat roundabout fashion is that there has been an inherent bias in the critical apparatus used to investigate Germanic legal antiquities. Bias is a strong word, and I use it with a certain hesitation in this instance; less argumentative terms such as "lack of perspective," "too limited a scope," or "a tendency to generalize" might be more charitable. Yet charity is not warranted in this case; rather, if anything, Occam's razor.

Let me elaborate this point. The study of Germanic legal antiquities was not the only field of scholarship in Europe that received its impetus in the first few decades of the nineteenth century, nor the only field that grew and flourished under the banner of Romanticism. Yet it is probably the only one that still, in large measure, operates according to preconceived and foreordained ideas that shape both a scholarly *modus operandi* and the conclusions that must inevitably be drawn therefrom. It is a contradiction for any field of scholarly investigation that purports even to the slightest degree to be operating according to scientific principles, to rely upon emotion instead of reason and intuition instead of analysis and systematic investigation (or to rely upon works that do). Unfortunately for the status of comparative Germanic law such has all too frequently been the case, and present-day scholarship shows few encouraging signs of change.

As an example, one may contrast the present status of comparative and historical Indo-European linguistics, whose origin and development *chronologically* and *geographically* coincided with the first studies in the more restricted field of Germanic law, with the present status of Germanic legal antiquities as an area of scholarship. Once men realized that language was neither of divine origin nor mystical, but an aspect of human behavior, it could be investigated without the implied or admitted obligation to confirm traditional prescientific theories. Rather, its goal was, after the collection of data and their description, analysis, and subsequent comparison with other data, to set up guidelines, postulates, or rules for the inclusion of later evidence. This method was open-ended, geared to receive additional evidence, and free to modify its structures if new evidence so warranted. It was characterized as an evolutionary process by increasing thoroughness and rigor and ever more systematic treatment. In our day Rousseau's and Herder's *Essays on the Origin of Language* are of little more than antiquarian interest, or, when cited, serve to point up the futility of an intuitive treatment of language.

The rejection by linguistics of a Romantic approach to the phenomenon of language should have served, if not as a warning, at least as an indication, that to retain this Romantic approach to legal antiquities in an age that was becoming more and more scientific in its handling of data, would at best reduce comparative Germanic law to the purview of dilettantes (although commentators would not regard their work as dilettantish), at worst make comparative Germanic law an impossibility. In this case I am not referring to occasional excellent works on individual laws themselves or on specific topics, but to the broader subject which *is* comparative Germanic law. A much-awaited event in the study of Germanic law is a reissue (rather than an updating or reediting) of Jakob Grimm's *Deutsche Rechtsaltertümer*, first published in 1828. Benjamin Thorpe's *Ancient Laws and Institutes of England,* published in 1840, is still considered "highly useful." The major improvement on Thorpe's work is considered to be Felix Liebermann's *Die Gesetze der Angelsachsen,* published in 1898. Yet this work is a collation of laws, with some grammatical commentary, nothing more. In a more recent book containing several Old English laws and a modern English translation, it is stated that it is an advance in utility over Liebermann's book because those who cannot read German now have an English translation provided.[2] Surely the twentieth century deserves more than yet another publication of early legal codes and their translation.[3]

It cannot be denied that the comparative grammars of Indo-European of the nineteenth century are still "highly useful," but these were, as their description states, comparative, not merely reproductions of texts in the various languages. Above all, conclusions were drawn from the comparative evidence. It is reasonable to say that we await the appearance in print of advances in a field, far more than a reprinting of a very early contribution, however highly it may be regarded. The large number of nineteenth-century works ostensibly dealing with Germanic law which are still considered "highly useful" bear witness to a state of stagnation, or perhaps inertia, and not to the fact that all required research has been done. Real comparison cannot begin until all the data to be compared are in usable form, and at this time they are not.

---

2 F. N. Attenborough, *The Laws of the Earliest English Kings* (Cambridge, 1922), p. v.

3. The only truly comparative study of the laws of the Germanic peoples is the two-volume work by Garabed Artin Davoud-Oghlou, *Histoire de la législation des Anciens Germains* (Berlin, 1845), a work apparently unknown (or if known, inaccessible) to scholars in this field.

I have omitted in this account a statement and/or definition of what constitutes Germanic law. But before this can be answered, a distinction must be made between Germanic law (that is, the law of the Germanic people) and later laws applicable only to individual tribes. A while ago, during an investigation of a more restricted problem of Germanic law, I attempted to resolve this distinction, but could not. I began in the usual manner, by consulting the relevant commentaries on the laws themselves, and traditional handbooks, especially those that synthesized the data provided by the laws and provided from this synthesis a picture of what was posited as the customary law of the pre-*Völkerwanderung*, pre-Christian, ethnographically undifferentiated Germanic people. I was trying to do in law what Germanists do when they compare the earliest written records of the Germanic languages in order to reconstruct Proto-Germanic, an evolutionary offshoot of late Indo-European, prior to dialect differentiation into the various Germanic languages. As a point of departure I intended to see if one could apply the methods of comparative and historical linguistics to law. I wanted to ascertain whether, by comparing similarities and differences in the earliest laws of ethnographically (and linguistically) differentiated tribes, one could reconstruct a Proto-Germanic law: an "Urrecht" on the same basis as an "Ursprache." Working forward in time, I might then discover whether legal differences and similarities paralleled linguistic differentiation. It was at this still theoretical level that new problems arose. The first was the result of handbook treatments of comparative legal evidence. Instead of attempting to reconstruct this "Urrecht" (I had thought that nineteenth-century commentators had already done this, and that I would merely have the opportunity to modify, emend, or otherwise offer suggestions), this stage had been omitted. Despite such omission, conclusions had been drawn about social behavior based upon sanctions and prohibitions of the laws themselves. This procedure seemed, in a word, unscientific. I could not imagine that it would be possible to generalize from evidence as fragmentary as laws whole patterns of behavior for a period when no direct written evidence was available. It appeared as if we knew more about the life and customs of the pre-*Völkerwanderung* Germanic people than we knew about their language. This was and is a fundamental inconsistency. At first I thought that I was on the wrong track; that my ideas about the reconstruction of proto-laws were a vestige of linguistic training and unsuited to the legal data at hand; that conclusions drawn from legal citations were overwhelming, and that as early as 120 years ago Wilda, in *Das Strafrecht der Germanen,* had provided as complete a picture as one could wish for. I felt as one might after reading massive tomes of virtually any given subject; that the field is closed, and that one had better set about investigating other areas.

In this connection I found that one aspect of comparative Germanic law is not restricted to the laws themselves and merits comment because of the place it still has in legal research and in folkloristic studies. This is something that for want of a better term, and because no other term is known to me, I call "law in literature." This is the extraction from works of literature of accounts of the actions of individuals either in their relationship to other characters or in response to events, actions that are interpreted as a reflection of behavior in conformity with or in rejection of some aspect of Germanic customary law. There is surely no lack of these citations which may be found in the literature of any of the older Germanic dialects. The best examples, and those most frequently cited, are found in Icelandic saga literature. To what extent citations found in rather late medieval literature may be taken as reflections of *Germanic* law will remain moot until it has been determined what constitutes Germanic law and what are later developments of the legal systems of particular cultures. It is tempting to use such literary citations to build up an impressive case for dogmatic statements about the customary law of the Germanic people, but they should be used with care at this stage of investigation.

Another topic included in studies of Germanic law is worthy of mention especially for the reason that in this case linguistic methods *are* used to provide answers. This is the extraction from texts of the medieval period of lexical items which, because of their etymological meaning, are assumed to be survivals of Germanic law, although they are not found in legal documents. To cite but two examples in passing: Gothic *unsibjáim* (in the dative plural) occurring in Mark 15:28, where the crucifixion is described: *jah miþ unsibjáim rahniþs was,* "and he was reckoned among criminals." Etymologically *unsibjáim* would mean "with the 'de-clanned' " and has cognates in Old English and Old High German. In the Old High German version of Tatian's *Gospel Harmony,* the phrase *mit harmu* is used. Translated it would mean "harmfully" or "with injury," yet the Old English cognate phrase *mid hearme,* occurring in legal texts, is generally translated as "with hue and cry," because of the uncertainty of the legal practice to which *mid hearme* applies. The Gothic word was early identified as a likely survival of Germanic legal antiquity, although used in a strictly Christian environment and with an obvious change in meaning. To my knowledge the Old High German citation has escaped notice. "Harm" has a satisfactory etymology and has cognates in the Slavic languages, but interestingly is not found in Gothic. Whether this owes to the limited number of Gothic texts and their predominantly religious nature, or is a case of legal practices following linguistic lines, must also remain moot. Like the citations under the heading "law in literature," the place in Germanic law of petrified items of legal vocabulary awaits the determination of what constitutes Germanic law. Isolated, although numerous, examples of the survival of legal vocabulary in nonlegal texts should be placed in the framework of Germanic law and not used to build up its structure.

In the early part of this report I emphasized at some length the importance of understanding the climate of cultural opinion at the time when many of the basic works on Germanic law were being written. At the heart of this opinion was a belief in the innate superiority of the pagan Germanic past, when the Germanic people, prior to their dissolution into tribes, were untouched by non-German influences. Of course, one might raise the question whether or not such a state of affairs actually existed. But this was not a question one would have raised. It was considered axiomatic by social critics and others writing under the aegis of Romanticism, and as an axiom needed neither proof nor verification. Indeed, to attempt to verify it by sound methods of scholarship would have brought the countercharge that these methods were themselves outworn and the product of non-German cultural influences, and that only emotion and intuition would enable one to capture the *Geist* of the Germanic past. To demonstrate the effect of the Romantic worship of the past, I comment upon what was considered to be the basis for the origin and development of law among the Germanic people by nineteenth-century legal scholarship. This was the "peace theory," and what was considered its legal by-product, namely outlawry. The "peace theory" conceived of peace as a positive state and not merely the absence of war or other hostilities; peace was considered to be a reflection of normal, harmonious, pre-*Völkerwanderung*, undifferentiated Germanic society. But for the purposes of legal scholarship, it is not the state of peace that is of primary importance, but rather the opposite of peace which was *peacelessness*. According to nineteenth-century handbooks, the essential tenet of the "peace theory" as the foundation of Germanic law was that a man who broke the peace was subject to violent counterreaction by members of his community. This assumption is supported by ascribing to the Germanic people a belief that an injury to one man is an injury to all men. This view is rather sophisticated for Common Germanic times and reflects more an idealized conception than actual conditions; incidentally, it is incompatible with the next stage of the "peace theory," which attempted to equate peacelessness with outlawry.

This equation was facilely made in the past century and is so entrenched that the one major effort to disprove it in the twentieth century, by Gobel in *Felony and Misdemeanor,* produced a spate of unfavorable reviews and, it would seem, no reappraisal.[4] But the equation of peacelessness with outlawry can be questioned on grounds which take into account the assumed social organization of the period. Even if we accept the social organization assumed by commentators of both classical antiquity and the Romantic period, this very type of social organization itself would prevent the equation of peacelessness with outlawry. The basis of Germanic organization was the *sib,* in extended form the clan (that is for the period when the "peace theory" was assumed to be operative). We find that the earliest form of punishment for an act of wrongdoing against a person or persons was not a declaration of peacelessness but a revenge in blood. Clearly, the equation peacelessness = outlawry cannot be posited for a time when vengeance and the blood feud were the sole forms of punishment for commission of a major wrong. In addition, vengeance and feud were by nature personal or familial; outlawry was by its nature territorial. I think that one is unlikely to have a punishment territorial in nature before the establishment of clearly demarcated territories, a development that no one will posit for pre-*Völkerwanderung* Germanic times. To equate peacelessness with outlawry is an attempt to solve one unknown by means of another. We also have no evidence to show how the peace of the *sib* or clan evolved into the peace of the later, greater unit, the tribe thus yielding the so-called "folk peace." Those who claim that the post-*Völkerwanderung* tribe was governed by the "folk peace" must explain how the peace of the *sib* evolved into the "folk peace." If it did, the surest way to demonstrate it is by comparative legal reconstruction, not by etymological citation, which is the common practice.

There are later peaces that are historically verifiable. These are the "peace" or "truce" of God at the end of the tenth century, and

---

4 Julius Gobel, Jr., *Felony and Misdemeanor: A Study in the History of English Criminal Procedure* (New York, 1937).

the "king's peace" of the eleventh century. Was the concept of "folk peace," postulated for Germanic tribes, a result of these later, historically attested forms of peace and of nineteenth-ceutury belief in the continuity of the Germanic past, plus wish-fulfillment about cherished notions of the past? Since we cannot equate peacelessness with outlawry, nor the peaceless man with the outlaw, how may we account for the existence in law of both outlawry and the outlaw? The evidence of the laws themselves provides a partial answer, as do later literary citations. It appears that outlawry was not a part of the customary law of the undifferentiated Germanic past. Outlawry as a punishment for specific offenses occurs in medieval Scandinavian laws and some laws of Anglo-Saxon England. On the other hand, the *Leges Barbarorum,* the laws of the continental West Germanic tribes of the early Middle Ages, do not treat outlawry explicitly. Since peacelessness = outlawry is assumed for the undifferentiated Germanic past, its absence in the earliest laws of continental West Germanic tribes is a major weakness of that theory. Interestingly, the term "outlaw" itself is restricted to the Scandinavian languages and to Old English and its descendants, and did not appear in Anglo-Saxon law until 922 in the *Laws of Edward and Guthrum,* which appeared after the Danish invasions; and Guthrum was a Dane.

Outlaws, as heroes, are not infrequent in Icelandic saga literature, but far less frequent numerically in medieval English literature. The flourishing of outlaw heroes in saga literature, the dearth of outlaw heroes in English literature for a comparable period, and the absence of outlawry in the *Leges Barbarorum* seem to indicate that outlawry was a secondary phenomenon in law; that it was not to be equated with peacelessness and was not an aspect of Germanic customary law, but constituted a later example of statutory law originating in Scandinavia, which was brought to England during the Danish invasions. I have included outlawry as a topic in order to demonstrate the unsystematic methodology used to reconstruct a part of the Germanic legal past, and to put it into proper perspective. One question remains unanswered, however, and that is, why was outlawry (after being equated with peacelessness) seized upon by early commentators as being the basis for all Germanic customary law that was to follow?

I suggest that one of the reasons (perhaps the main reason) was the cultural climate of the early Romantic period and its reflection in creative literature, literature that would precede in time the works of scholarship dealing with Germanic legal antiquity. To illustrate this point I have selected a *Novelle* by Ludwig Tieck, entitled *Der Runenberg*. The title itself is of course more than suggestive of Germanic antiquity (especially of the culturally isolated North). The story concerns a young hunter named Christian, who leaves his village to go into the deepest part of the mountains, ". . . um sich aus dem Kreise der wiederkehrenden Gewöhnlichkeit zu enfernen." This is of course mirrored in later social criticism that rejected urbanization. The choice of the name "Christian" is symbolic, as is his profession, that of hunter. The nineteenth-century Christian reverted to his pagan past as a hunter. Christian in the forest imagines that the waters are speaking to him, but he cannot understand them. Loudly, he sings a song about the joys of the hunt, of going through the forest with hunting-horn resounding, and recalls "die schöne Jägerzeit." "Seine Heimat sind die Klüfte,/Alle Bäume grüßen ihn" begins another verse. The poem concludes with a statement of the joys of the chase, the forest, and of the blissful hunter in his new "Heimat." His old "Heimat" was, of course, a village. Tieck's choice of vocabulary, his inclusion of an episode with a screaming mandrake root, the use of the name "Christian" for a man who rejects the oppressive nature of his ordered existence as a gardener's son to go off into the unspoiled wilderness, are conscious attempts to resolve the conflict between present and past. I have given but a few examples of what upon reading strikes one as being almost hyper-Romantic, until one realizes that the romantic elements in *Der Runenberg* are not the exception but the rule. From this literary interlude I again raise the question why outlawry was selected as the basis for Germanic law, despite the fact that close analysis militates against this choice.

Observe the legendary outlaw, who leaves home, hearth, and family, because he has committed an offense against the established order of his society, to flee into the mountains and forests to evade capture. There he becomes a changed man, both in the eyes of the law and by his own actions, and gains new strength by being in communion with unspoiled nature. Contrast this prototypical outlaw of medieval literature with Christian of *Der Runenberg*, who calls his existence "das Ebene" and is more at home in "das Gebirge," and who flees from his family and village not because of the external pressure which forced the flight of the outlaw, but is driven by some internal compulsion to escape the restrictions of early nineteenth-century society in order to return to the world of the past represented by untouched natural forces rather than the manmade ones, which are always ordered (his father was a gardener). Christian's actions are not rational, as we know the term, they cannot be explained but only felt. This Romantic approach serves literature quite well, but, extended into the realm of scientific analysis and investigation, it postulated that the desire to escape the present was a manifestation of a Germanic longing for the unspoiled wilderness. It generalized from the internal pressures of an unstable individual, which produced an emotional rejection of his present existence, to a theory that these pressures and subsequent rejection are analogous to the sociolegal pressures leading to outlawry; it thus derived later laws from outlawry and biased forever the question of the origin and genesis of Germanic law.

It would be simplistic to state that one *Novelle* by a German Romanticist could produce this effect on later scholarship. *Der Runenberg* was used merely as an example to show the literary climate of the times, a climate that stressed nature above man-made things; the unspoiled wilderness above the cosmopolitan city (or even village); rejection of society rather than attempts to modify it; and a feeling that somehow Germanic civilization had been corrupted by external non-German pressures. To this would be added the almost universal belief in the outlaw as a romantic figure, who had been made to suffer unjustly for something that was beyond his control, but which, nevertheless, was also a constant of his society. Outlawry, as the basis for Germanic law, may now tentatively be rejected and systematic investigation begun.

But where? Classically we should begin with the earliest written laws of the Germanic tribes and/or kingdoms which are extant. And it is at this point that our first stumbling block appears. Calvert Watkins has previously demonstrated the inherent archaism and conservatism of legal language, and its value in both linguistic and cultural research. That this is true for many of the Indo-European languages is not in doubt. But for the Germanic languages the earliest laws are so "archaic" that they are not written in a Germanic language at all, but in Latin, and it would seem not very good Latin at that. To be sure, there are German words in most of the earliest laws, in instances where there is no equivalent in Roman law, as in the case of minor public officials, or for certain offenses. These latter are often given in both the Latin and the vernacular form. There are also a certain number of Latinized vernacular words. Writing, except for Runic characters and the Gothic alphabet, reached the Germanic peoples rather late. The dependence of Germanists upon works of classical antiquity for the earliest recorded information about their subject is testimony to this. This, coupled with the cultural advancement of Greece and Rome, meant that our earliest information took the form of citations of items of material culture absent in the classical world, personal and divine names, and, most importantly for our purposes, social behavior and quasi-legal proscription when they differed from those of Greece or Rome. To this void of information may be added the earliest laws themselves. We must determine to what extent Germanic law has been retained, despite being written in a foreign language, and to what extent these recorded laws of Germanic tribes are influenced by Roman law in addition to the Latin language. That is, to what extent did the medium determine the message?

We are a little more fortunate in Anglo-Saxon law, most of which is recorded in Old English and/or Latin, but this material is of later date and reflects a society far more changed, and in far greater cultural isolation than those tribes that remained on the continent. After the tenth century it is also subject to Scandinavian influence. In addition we must assume that the adoption of Christianity by the Germanic peoples also wrought changes in the laws. This is easiest to see in laws pertaining to members of the clergy, punishments for breaking into a church, working on religious holidays, and so on. But we cannot assume that Christian influence is reflected in the laws only when some aspect of Christianity is referred to. Drawing a parallel from early Germanic vernacular literature, it is quite possible to have Christian influence in such areas as choice of theme, of vocabulary, of treatment of events, and generally of *Weltanschauung*, although direct references to Christianity do not appear. Students of early Germanic vernacular literature are aware of the many long controversies about whether or not certain aspects of a given work of literature are of pagan origin, show Christian influence, were rewritten to conform to the new religion, and the like.

Still, references in a law to some aspect of Christianity are late developments. But this of course does not solve the problem, for references to the clergy or to Christianity itself may have been either added to the existing pre-Christian part of the law or merely transferred to those portions dealing with pagan religious practices. One thing may be said with certainty, however: by the time we have laws of a Germanic people written in Latin, the society affected by these laws had undergone great changes, not only in relation to undifferentiated Germanic times, but also to early tribal organization, and was evolving or had already evolved into a territorial state.

Extracting "the Germanic component" from laws written in Latin means more than collecting the vernacular words found therein. One possible means is to follow the lead of Grimm in contrasting such items as paired Latin expressions with their attested equivalents in a Germanic language.[5] He found some instances where a translation of the Latin yielded an alliterating sequence of two nominal or verbal forms. This does not mean that, to determine the entire Germanic component, all one has to do is translate the laws and compare them to laws in a vernacular language. I have done this as a mechanical exercise and found many of the results unrewarding. Alliteration as a stylistic device is the characteristic of early Germanic poetry, and handbooks on Germanic law list numerous examples of alliterating pairs of nominal and verbal forms that occur in the laws. Alliteration was most likely begun as a mnemonic device of a preliterate people, and its original purpose was functional or pragmatic rather than stylistic or ornamental. When the society became literate, alliteration became formulaic rather than functional. With the passage of time the formulaic nature of alliteration predominated and obscured the original meaning of those terms that alliterated. So much so, that although there is an abundance of alliterating forms in the laws, we often cannot determine what is meant. Thus the mere collection of alliteration proves nothing more than the retention (Grimm calls them *eingewurzelt* in the laws) in legal documents of a traditional Germanic literary device whose origins lay in a desire to bring speedy recall to memory. If it is doubted that survivals of alliteration are formulaic rather than functional, or ornamental rather than descriptive, consider what alliteration is doing in legal prose at all. It is a testimony to the conservatism of legal codices and to the likely connection between poetry and oral legal tradition, but may not bear testimony to contemporary customs, behavior, or proscriptions.

In this connection I would like to propose that the traditional distinction between customary law and statutory law be abandoned as providing no useful parameters for purposes of research. Customary law, common law, or folk law (it goes by all these designations) we take to be the unwritten expression of popular custom and belief (that is, "consensus law") in contrast with statutory law, which is "learned law" found in statutes and *imposed.* In perpetuating this distinction in Germanic law we are perpetuating an essential con-

[5] Jakob Grimm, *Deutsche Rechtsaltertümer* (Leipzig, 1922), I, 8.

tradition, for the earliest written laws of a Germanic people are still designated as "Volksrechte," that is, the setting down in print of the popular beliefs and customs of the people to whom they applied. To continue to use the term "Volksrechte" implies that at a later period other laws would be imposed upon people who got along very well with laws arrived at by consensus, if not by consent. That other, later laws were set down cannot be denied, but the process of evolution from clan to tribe to nation brings with it the concomitant change in law to cope with a new social situation. The expansion, revision, or imposition of new laws does not magically create statutory law. I feel that this distinction between customary law and statutory law should be given up, except in instances where a conflict of laws can be attested or surmised. The distinction just mentioned is illusory: as a society becomes more complex, there is an ever greater specialization of function. In the legal sphere this means that ever fewer members of that society have a direct say in the formulation of laws affecting them. Furthermore, there is enough secondary literature (albeit disputed) to prove that specialization of function in the form of the law-speaker (in Old Icelandic literature) existed prior to the period of written statutory law.

Up to this point I have stated in what ways I feel that studies of Germanic law have been based upon erroneous premises and have proceeded intuitively rather than systematically, and above all have treated fragments of the legal past, rather than the whole. I recommend abandoning such an approach in favor of using the methodology of comparative and historical linguistics (the "genetic" approach) to reconstruct a proto-law in the same manner (but obviously with the same limitations and difficulties) that a protolanguage is reconstructed. I am aware of the fact that the "genetic" approach to legal evolution and reconstruction is open to some question, but this owes in large measure to a lack of appreciation of the nature of the information desired. What we are after is not a miscellaneous grab-bag of proto-words, nor the *Geist*, but a series of statements about belief, prohibitions, and social behavior, to mention but a few. The only way to see if reconstruction of a proto-law will work is to begin to set it up. To get the best possible picture one must use all the data at hand. This is a difficulty, because of the lack of adequate, up-to-date editions of the relevant laws. This is a time-consuming, but not insurmountable difficulty, except in terms of accessibility in university and other libraries. A second difficulty is the question of language. Unlike the laws of many of the individual Indo-European languages, Germanic law is found written in many languages such as Latin, Old English, Old Icelandic, Norwegian, Swedish, Danish, Old Frisian, Old Low Franconian, Old High German, Middle Low German, Middle High German, and Norman French. To attempt to reconstruct this proto-law, one must have a knowledge of these languages. But this in itself is not enough, else it might have been tried before.

I recommend a new approach. First, collect all laws of the Germanic peoples, with a tentative cut-off date at the time of the *Sachsenspiegel* around 1230. The laws should then be carefully translated into one uniform language and broken down in a form suitable for computerized analysis, for the purposes of determining similarities and differences.[6] Of course the search for similarities and differences could be done without mechanical assistance, but it would be a tremendous advantage to subsequent interpretation. The data could be further augmented by the addition of material from the area of "law in literature," if this appears warranted. The question of time-depth will have to be resolved, but it can be handled in the same way that an Indo-Europeanist handles the time-depth question in comparing Hittite with Old Prussian and Lithuanian. Computerized analysis might provide an answer to the question of whether legal evolution follows ethnographic and linguistic lines. This was the question that got me started in legal antiquities and the question that led me to begin work in reconstructing something I call a proto-law. The result will determine the validity of this idea. Reconstruction should not cease because of the bias induced by Romanticism, but should proceed in the same manner as does paleontology, anthropology, linguistics, and philology. If this approach does not work, then so be it. It will at least have had the merit of being tried.

[6] On January 25, 1968, the *Lex Thuringorum* was the first of the laws subjected to computerized analysis.

The Indo-European Component in Germanic Religion

EDGAR POLOMÉ, *University of Texas*

Any scientific study and interpretation of ancient religion is closely dependent on the available source material. In the study of Germanic religion, the value and reliability of the sources appear to be a particularly important problem, since our information is scanty and desultory. What is at our disposal consists, indeed, mainly of circumstantial evidence and external testimony; we do not have any specific original ritual text, or any genuine Germanic writing witnessing the relationship between man and god in ancient times, and all we claim to know is what we can infer from the scattered remnants of Germanic religious life according to the prevailing views of our time, combined with our personal prejudices. This rather discouraging situation had led Vilhelm Grönbech half a century ago to concentrate his attention on the perception of the genuinely Germanic spiritual, intellectual, and cultural aspects of Old Germanic individual and social life, thus paving the way for a better insight into Germanic *Lebensgefühl* and basic religious concepts. His identification of some ethical concepts such as honor with a kind of magical vital force introduced the concept of a rather strict creed of predestination into the Old Germanic world, which led to far-fetched conclusions about the so-called *germanischer Schicksalglaube*.

In recent years, the idea that man shapes his gods according to his own being has received repeated confirmation in the study of exotic cultures; various efforts to apply this new knowledge to Germanic religion have led to careful reexamination of the scanty reliable evidence available in this field. But instead of carrying out minute historical research on the detailed development of the individual deities by patching up a ragged image composed of aimless bits of evidence, the new trends focused their attention on pattern and structure in Germanic religion, mainly according to three different approaches: (*a*) the Vienna school of anthropology; (*b*) the typological analysis of Mircea Eliade, based on the concept of archetypes coined by C. G. Jung and applied to religious studies by Karl Kerényi and Erich Neumann; (*c*) the sociological approach, mainly developed in the works of Georges Dumézil.

The basic idea of the Vienna school is that religious patterns develop in conformity with levels of culture. An illustration of this view is given by Alois Closs in his contribution "Die Religion des Semnonenstammes" to the volume *Die Indogermanen- und Germanenfrage,*[1] in which he analyzes the ritual implied in the human sacrifice described by Tacitus in chapter 39 of his *Germania,* and supplies rich comparative material to elucidate its motivation. Similarly, in his study "Das Versenkungsopfer," published in the volume *Kultur und Sprache,*[2] numerous parallels to the Germanic sacrifice by immersion occurring, for example, at the end of the Nerthus ritual (Tacitus, *Germania,* chap. 40), are listed in correlation with their Indo-European and general cultural background. A more comprehensive survey of his views is given by Closs in his contribution "Die Religion der Germanen in ethnologischer Sicht" to the second volume of *Christus und die Religionen der Erde,*[3] where he explains the main phenomena and trends of development in Germanic religion in connection with his views on Germanic ethnogenesis on the basis of Wilhelm Schmidt's somewhat subjective theories on original monotheism and on the prehistory of Indo-European tribes. His conclusion is typical of the Vienna school approach:

> Die mannigfachen Keime zur späteren intensiven Ausbildung von Stammesreligionen schon in der urgermanischen Anfangszeit lassen sich vielmehr in Erwägung der prähistorischen Verhältnisse am Ende der Steinzeit am besten als Ergebnis einer Völkermischung verstehen, wobei ins Dunkel gehüllt ist, wodurch aus verschiedenen Bestandteilen, alteuropäischen wie eurasiatischen, diese sehr wohl mit näheren Beziehungen zur turanischen Gruppe, ein neues Volk wurde. Ein besonderer religiöser Antrieb

---

1 Wiener Beiträge zur Kulturgeschichte und Linguistik 4, ed. W. Koppers (Salzburg and Leipzig, 1936), pp. 549–674.

2 Wiener Beiträge zur Kulturgeschichte und Linguistik 9, ed. W. Koppers, R. Heine-Geldern, and J. Haekel (Vienna, 1952), pp. 66–107.

3 Ed. Franz König (Vienna, 1952), pp. 271–366.

> zu dieser ersten Volkwerdung ist nicht scheinbar, wohl aber zeigt sich später, im Zuge der Zusammenballung der Stämme zu grösseren Kultverbänden, bereits im Zeitalter der Entstehung von Weltreligionen im ostindogermanischen und vorderasiatisch mediterranen Völkerkreise, bei den Suebogermanen ein amphiktyonischer Typ, der in einer Weise, wie dies weder bei den griechischen noch bei den polynesischen Amphiktyonien, wohl aber bei der latinischen . . . der Fall ist, in der Art der Zusammenkünfte, wie ein Haften an urtümlicher Verwandtschaft zwischen den Stämmen, wie eine Erinnerung an eine frühere Zusammengehörigkeit anmutet.[4]

Reformulated here, rather subjectively, in ethnological jargon are actually not very original views: (*a*) the theory of H. Güntert of the mixture of two populations—the "megalithic" pre-Indo-European agriculturalists and the Indo-European invaders—as the origin of the Germanic people; (*b*) the intimation of a parallelism between Germanic and Italic religious traditions.

Mircea Eliade's stress on patterns of rituals for archetypal deities is reflected in the study on the Germanic mother goddess which I published more than a decade ago.[5] In this article I tried essentially to reject the common interpretation of the Nerthus ritual as symbolic of a hierogamy between the skygod and the earth goddess, since there was no overt trace of a masculine element playing the part of the former. I indicated that, at an older stage, the archetypal *Terra mater* did not imply the coexistence of the phallic elements that appear in a later development; agriculture was still a typically feminine activity in the days of Tacitus, and only with its masculinization do the agrarian gods Ing and Freyr appear and does Nerthus change into the male god Njördr. Therefore, I preferred to interpret the Nerthus ritual as the celebration of a cosmic event—the advent of spring—along the lines described by M. Eliade:[6]

> For a moment, the life of the whole human group is concentrated into a tree or some effigy of vegetation, some symbol intended to represent and consecrate the thing that is happening to the universe: spring. . . . The presence of nature is indicated by a single object (or symbol). It is no pantheist adoration of nature or sense of being at one with it, but a feeling induced by the presence of the symbol (branch, tree or whatever it may be), and stimulated by the performing of the rite (processions, con-

---

[4] *Ibid.*, p. 363.

[5] E. Polomé, "À propos de la déesse Nerthus," *Latomus* 5:167–200 (1954); cf. also, on the same subject: "Nerthus-Njord," *HZnMTL* 5:99–124 (1951).

[6] *Patterns in Comparative Religion* (Cleveland and New York, 1963), pp. 321–322; for the French text, see *Traité d'histoire des religions* (Paris, 1949), p. 277.

> tests, fights, and the rest). The ceremonial is based on a comprehensive notion of the sacredness of all living force as expressed at every level of life, growing, wearing itself out and being regularly regenerated. This "bio-cosmic sacredness" is personified in many different forms, changing, it would seem to suit mood or circumstance. . . . What remains, what is basic and lasting, is the "power" of vegetation, which can be felt and manipulated equally well in a branch, an effigy or a mythological figure.

The symbol involved in the Nerthus ritual, which indicated to the priest the presence of the "power" of vegetation in its mobile shrine, was presumably the appearance of a definite plant or flower. This would complete the pattern "goddess-vegetation-sacred animals-priests" so characteristic of the Great Goddess,[7] since the Germanic Earth-Mother would then be associated with a vegetal symbol as well as with the heifers drawing her chariot and the priest and slaves attending her. The celebration of the ritual involves a *circumambulatio agrorum,* to effect the irradiating of her power; during this ceremonial procession there is general peace and all weapons are locked up; there is joy everywhere (*laeti tunc dies*), and presumably the community as a whole participates in the orgiastic frenzy that sets flowing the sacred energy of life. But to regenerate the sacred force of the goddess exhausted by irradiation, it is necessary to ritually restore it to her by immersion and compensatory human sacrifice. Accordingly, "le rituel de Nerthus apparaît . . . comme un réactualisation symbolique du renouveau, destinée à promouvoir la fertilité agricole par une procession solennelle et à régénérer la force vitale de la Terre Mère, symboliquement par l'immersion de son emblème et concrètement par la noyade des officiants."[8]

Thus, by applying Eliade's approach, I have ultimately reinterpreted a Germanic ritual as the enactment of a scenario *sui generis,* based on patterns whose variations abound in the most diverse cultures. This, however, excludes any close relationship with the cult of Cybele or any other mother goddess in the Western world.

Quite different is the situation with Dumézil's approach based on the functional tripartition of social life: (1) sovereignty, with its double aspect—juridical and magical; (2) physical force, mainly for military purposes; (3) fecundity, with its correlates: prosperity, health, long life, peace, and so on. Here Nerthus appears clearly as the representative of the third function in the *interpretatio Romana* of Tacitus, beside Mercurius and Mars as correspondents to Odin and

[7] *Ibid.*, p. 230; French ed., p. 244.

[8] Polomé, *op. cit.*, p. 199.

Týr on the level of the first function,[9] and Hercules—and partly also Jupiter, on account of lightning—as correspondent to Thor on the level of the second function. In the Scandinavian world, the position of Nerthus, whose name **nerþuz* literally means 'power,' has been taken over by Freyr because she has been reshaped into the male god Njördr with a shift in function in the Eddic mythology. The application of the Dumézilian tripartite system to the Germanic pantheon has, however, given rise to many objections. It has been pointed out that there were considerable differences in the social structure of the Germanic world, depending on which area of it was being considered: along the borders of the Roman Empire an undoubtedly more bellicose type of society prevailed, characterized by the totalitarian system of agriculture described by Caesar (*De Bello Gallico* 6.22) and the predominance of the gods of the first and second function, whereas on the shores of the Baltic a much more peaceful and stable society could safely practice a strictly distributive economy and give special reverence to the gods of the third function like the Ingaevones, constituting the amphictyony of Nerthus, or the Naharvali. While instability and insecurity tend to favor a kind of heroic unanimity with focus on the cult of first- and second-function gods, a completely different mood prevails when conditions are less fluid and property can be safely transferred from generation to generation. This duality of attitude depending on the state of the community fits perfectly into the Dumézilian system, as he has shown eloquently in his *Mitra-Varuna*.[10] Even those who, like R. Derolez, utterly reject Dumézil's

---

[9] Whereas the identification of Mercurius with *Wōðanaz owes to a rather secondary parallelism between the functions of Mercurius as conductor of the souls and the association of *Wōðanaz with the dead warriors (Old Norse *einherjar*), the link between Mars and Týr rests on the Germanic concept of war as a judgment by arms (ON *vápnadómr*), which puts it into the domain of the juridical functions of Tyr, whose association with the judicial and legislative assembly (ON *þing*) is also evidenced by the votive inscriptions to *Mars Thincsus*. While the identification of *Wōðanaz with Mercurius seems rather constant, as shown by inscriptions like *Mercurius Rex* (Nijmegen) and the sacrifice of prisoners of war to him by hanging them with a noose on trees, the sacrifice of horses to Mars, e.g., after the victory of the Hermunduri over the Chatti (A.D. 58), points rather to a specifically second-function god in the case of the Germanic correspondent to Mars. The text of chapter 9 of Tacitus' *Germania*, "Deorum maxime Mercurium colunt, cui certis diebus humanis quoque hostiis litare fas habent. Herculem et Martem concessis animalibus placant; pars Sueborum et Isidi sacrificat," is particularly significant in this regard, since it closely associates Mars with Hercules, while mentioning the third-function cult of "Isis" among the Suebians immediately thereafter.

[10] (2d ed.; Paris, 1948), pp. 152–159; cf. also my article "La religion germanique primitive, reflet d'une structure sociale," *Le Flambeau* 37:452–463 (1954).

views must admit that the structure of Germanic society agreed by and large with his postulated social pattern:

> At the head of every tribe was a king or a group of heads of smaller tribal units, but in the latter case, a suitable commander was chosen among them in time of war. Various religious elements appeared in the direction of the state: the king was "sacred," the priests kept order and peace in the "thing" assemblies and punished all crimes. . . . Political power belonged in principle to the "thing"; all important decisions were taken in those assemblies, in which all free men appeared in arms, but among these free men a smaller group of influential families controlled in fact the direction of public affairs, tending to make this situation permanent by isolating themselves from the lower classes and claiming they were born noblemen. Below the free men were the half-free taxpayers, and on the lowest level, the slaves. . . .[11]

It is obvious that Dumézil's approach involves a number of postulates. It implies (1) that the same event can be present as a myth in one group and as history in another, for example, when Dumézil compares the struggle and reconciliation between the Aesir and the Vanir with the Sabine War in ancient Rome as the reflex of an Indo-European mythologem about the shift to peaceful development in a warlike Indo-European people through a symbiosis with prosperous opponents; (2) that the tripartite system survives changes in society; only the functional attributes of the gods, not their names and specific personalities, are of vital importance. Accordingly, for Dumézil, Germanic religion is the religion of the Indo-Europeans in its transformation by the Germanic tribes. This assumption is utterly rejected by Karl Helm[12] who claims: "Die germanische Religion ist zum kleinsten Teil indogermanische Religion; ihre Grundlage ist die Religion des in den später germanischen Ländern beheimateten und hier vielleicht seit Urzeiten, d.h. schon vor der Bildung des Indogermanentums siedelnden völkischen Subtrates, wie sie sich im Laufe der Jahrhunderte unter den verschiedensten Einflüssen herausgebildet hat."[13] He accordingly emphasizes "Vanic" religion as the pre-Germanic religion of the neolithic farmers and considers, for example, the spread of the cult of Odin as a late development.[14] But if the Vanir and Aesir reflect the two constituents of the Germanic people in prehistoric times—the neolithic farmers and the Indo-

---

[11] Freely translated from R. Derolez, *De godsdienst der Germanen* (Roermond and Maaseik, 1959), pp. 28–29.

[12] "Mythologie auf alten und neuen Wegen," *PBB(T)* 77:347–365 (1955).

[13] *Ibid.*, p. 365.

[14] *Wodan: Ausbreitung und Wanderung seines Kultes* (Giessen, 1946), p. 85.

European invaders—[15] the structure of society in those days as assumed on archaeological grounds perfectly fits the Indo-European pattern;[16] moreover, the story of their struggle as compared with similar situations after the foundation of Rome reflects a general pattern of conflict and compromise which conforms to Indo-European tradition.

What actually opposes Helm and Dumézil is their basic attitude to the problem of Germanic religion: Helm wants to evaluate the scanty facts from a strictly historical point of view and to reach his conclusions about the individual gods by inductive reasoning; Dumézil has recognized a definite structure as basic to and specific of Indo-European society and, by comparison of the various attested systems, tries to back up his deductions on the survival of the original tripartition in the most disparate traditions of the Indo-European peoples. As Werner Betz[17] indicates: "Beide Wege sind notwendig. Der Germanist wird versuchen, die Gefahren beider zu vermeiden: geschichtsloses Strukturieren oder historisierendes Auflösen in auseinanderfallende Details—und dafür sich bemühen, die Vorteile beider fruchtbar zu machen: Herausarbeiten der grossen Zusammenhänge und Überprüfung des Beschlossenen am geschichtlichen Bezeugten."

Actually, when we want to evaluate the Indo-European component in Germanic religion we have to determine its varying impact on the available material and the precise type of correspondence it reflects.[18] Too often links have been assumed in the past on the basis of sheer etymological speculations: if one prefers to connect Sanskrit *ásuraḥ*, 'lord,' with Hittite *ḫaššuš*, 'king,' and Germanic **ansuz*, 'Ase,' instead of preserving the traditional interpretation of *ásuraḥ* as a derivation of **n̥su-* (reflected by *ásuḥ*, 'vital strength'), meaning 'gesteigerte Lebenskraft, *orenda*,' as Güntert puts it,[19] he will do so only with reference to the specific functions of the Germanic Aesir and the original Indo-Iranian Asuras as "sovereign gods," especially Odin

15 As pointed out by Hermann Güntert, *Der Ursprung der Germanen*, Kultur und Sprache 9 (Heidelberg, 1934), p. 148; cf. also my remarks in "La religion germanique primitive, reflet d'une structure sociale," pp. 451–452 (see n. 10).

16 Cf., e.g., *ibid.*, pp. 438–441.

17 "Die altgermanische Religion," in W. Stammler, ed., *Deutsche Philologie im Aufriss* (Berlin, 1957), III, col. 2476; 2d ed. (1962), col. 1558.

18 The virulent criticism of the "indogermanische Erbgutthese" by prominent Germanists like Ernst A. Philippson, e.g., in his article "Phänomenologie, Vergleichende Mythologie und Germanische Religionsgeschichte," *PMLA* 87:187–193 (1962), makes special care and prudence in this procedure particularly imperative.

19 *Der arische Weltkönig und Heiland* (Halle, 1923), pp. 101–102.

and Varuṇa as "masters of the bonds,"[20] since the etymon, IE *H_2*onsus*, is further connected with words like Greek ἡνία, 'bridle,' Middle Irish *ē(i)si-* (pl.) 'reins,' Old Norse *ǿs* < **ansjō*, 'threadhole in a shoe,' and so on.

More significant, however, are correspondences involving (*a*) typical gods of definite functions, (*b*) rituals, and (*c*) myths. Dumézil has been compiling impressive files of correspondences of the first type, pointing out, for example, the striking parallel between the functional mutilations of Odin and Týr and those of the Roman heroes of the Etruscan wars, Horatius Cocles and Mucius Scaevola.[21] Particularly instructive is his analysis of the saga of Hadingus[22] whose two lives reflect, on the one hand, an epical rehash of the myths of the Scandinavian Njördr and, on the other, his new career as an Odinic hero. Another pre-Germanic myth retrieved by careful comparison of Eddic sources and early Latin history is the already mentioned episode of the war of the Aesir and Vanir,[23] with which the Irish tale of the two battles of Mag Tured has also been compared. There are, indeed, obvious correspondences in the process by which gods and men with conflicting interests and ambitions as the king, the warrior, and the agriculturist-producer manage to come to an understanding after an initial strife. When one examines the development of the script in detail, however, one is struck by the superficiality of some correspondences. Take, for instance, the myth of Njördr's marriage. It is undoubtedly true, as Dumézil points out, that "tout ce qui est essentiel dans le récit du mariage de *Njǫrðr* et de *Skaði*—

[20] Cf. my study "L'étymologie du terme germanique **ansuz*, 'dieu souverain,'" *EG* 8:36–44 (1953), esp. pp. 41 ff. The objection of C. Scott Littleton, that the "binding" aspect of this etymology was obsolete, because the "binder god" thesis had already been largely rejected by Dumézil himself, rests on a tendentious interpretation (*The New Comparative Mythology* [Berkeley and Los Angeles, 1966], pp. 83–84, 135) of the views of Dumézil in the second edition of *Mitra-Varuna*, where the binding function of the "fearful sovereign" is explicitly emphasized (pp. 113–116; 202–203). This control of Varuṇa over the "bonds" is again restated in Dumézil's *L'idéologie tripartie des Indo-européens* (Brussels, 1958), p. 63, and compared with Odin's power to "bind" his enemies in *Les dieux des Germains* (Paris, 1959), p. 62.

[21] *Mitra-Varuna*, chap. ix, "Le borgne et le manchot," pp. 163–177; *L'héritage indo-européen à Rome* (Paris, 1949), pp. 159–169; *Les dieux des Germains*, pp. 71–74; *La religion romaine archaïque* (Paris, 1966), p. 86.

[22] *La Saga de Hadingus (Saxo Grammaticus I, v–viii): Du mythe au roman* (Paris, 1953).

[23] "La guerre des Sabines," *Jupiter Mars Quirinus* (Paris, 1940), pp. 155–166; *Tarpeia* (Paris, 1947), pp. 249–291; *L'héritage indo-européen à Rome*, pp. 125–142 (reproduced in *La religion romaine archaïque*, pp. 81–84); *La Saga de Hadingus*, pp. 105–111. Cf. also Jan de Vries, "Der Krieg der Asen und der Wanen," *Altgermanische Religionsgeschichte* (2d ed.; Berlin, 1957), II, 208–214. A divergent view is expressed by the same author in *ANF* 77:42–47 (1962).

svayaṃvara dans des conditions truquées, choix du mari d'après ses pieds nus, rire provoqué par une obscénité grotesque—est constitutivement lié à la nature du dieu";[24] yet if these motifs have not been gathered at random, they are nevertheless a scenario *sui generis* in the Germanic tradition. It requires, indeed, a stretch of the imagination to compare the *svayaṃvara* as described, for example, in the Nala episode of the *Mahābhārata,* with the kind of marriage lottery to which Skadi agrees; besides, the criterion of choice is without any actual parallel in Indo-European tradition.[25] The importance of footmarks in prehistoric symbolism points rather to the prevailing local association with fertility gods. As for the obscene interlude with the goat, devised by Loki to make Skadi laugh, again no direct parallel can be adduced, although obscene gestures designed to provoke laughter are common stock among the tales associated with fertility gods. Thus, if a definite scenario fits into the pattern of the social functions of a Germanic god, it does not imply pre-Germanic origins and can very well be a purely Germanic development motivated by local conditions.

In this respect, it might be advisable to reexamine Dumézil's discussion of one of the principal Germanic myths, the myth of Baldr. In a fresco of wide range, he depicts this mythological drama as the "keystone of world history."[26] Whereas the blind, otherwise unknown Hödr appears as the instrument of blind fate, the wise and generous Baldr who fathered the god of conciliation but whose decisions remained without effect, is the Scandinavian reflex of the minor sovereign gods Aryaman and Bhaga, whose epical transposition Dumézil recognizes, with Wikander, in Vidura and Dhr̥tarāṣṭra in the *Mahābhārata.*[27] Loki uses Hödr to eliminate Baldr in a fatal game that

---

24 *La Saga de Hadingus,* p. 35.

25 The resemblance to the *Sukanyā* episode in the *Mahābhārata* remains very superficial, in spite of Dumézil's efforts to correlate the stories (cf. *Naissance d'archanges* [Paris, 1945], pp. 159–162, 177–180).

26 *Les dieux des Germains,* p. 95. For Dumézil's discussion of the Baldr myth, cf. *Loki* (Paris, 1948), pp. 133–158, German ed. (Darmstadt, 1959), pp. 96–115; *Les dieux des Germains,* pp. 93–105, with the comments of de Vries in *PBB(T)* 81: 218–220 (1959).

27 The original contribution of Stig Wikander, "Pāṇḍava-sagan och Mahābhāratas mystika förutsättningar," published in *RoB* 6:27–39 (1947), was translated by Dumézil with extensive comments in *Jupiter Mars Quirinus IV* (Paris, 1948), pp. 37–85. Among the numerous further elaborations of the thesis that the Indian epic reflects, in a literary transposition, a set of myths relative to the Vedic and pre-Vedic gods, the article of Dumézil, "La transposition des dieux souverains mineurs en héros dans le *Mahābhārata*" *(IIJ* 3:1–16 [1959]), is especially relevant to the problem of Baldr, though he merely refers in footnote 39 (p. 15) to the figures of Baldr and Hödr as the ultimate Germanic outcome of the Indo-European minor sovereign gods.

spells disaster for the present world, since it opens a long dark age that ends in an ultimate battle between the forces of Evil and the gods, after which a new, regenerated world will arise. The parallelism with the *Mahābhārata* episode consists mainly in the following facts: (1) an apparently dangerless game compels Yudhiṣṭhira to exile on account of his partner's cheating; (2) after years of exile during which the evildoer Duryodhana prevails, Yudhiṣṭhira and his brothers return to claim their rights; the murderous battle of Kurukṣetra marks the victory of Good over Evil, after which Vidura and Dhṛtarāṣṭra, who did not take part in the fight, assume new functions in the reconciled society of heroes. Apart from the fact that, in both instances, a fateful game involving a blind partner is the decisive event in the drama, the two stories are quite different: Hödr in Snorri's tale is a mere instrument of the schemer Loki, whereas the blind Dhṛtarāṣṭra is more directly implicated, since he consented to the cheating through weakness and was aware of the consequences for Yudhiṣṭhira. Besides, the link of the death of Baldr with Ragnarök is extremely tenuous; before drawing such far-reaching conclusions it would be advisable to reexamine the whole Germanic tradition. It is indeed obvious that Loki, who is the keystone of Dumézil's eschatological interpretation of the episode, does not at all play the part that Snorri assigns to him. In the Eddic lay of "Baldr's Dreams," the seeress answers Odin's question about the name of Baldr's murderer as follows:

> Hödr will the hero hitherward send,
> He will Baldr slay, the blameless god,
> and end the life of Odin's son,[28]

a statement that the "Prophecy of the Seeress" (*Vǫluspá*, sts. 31–32) confirms:

> I saw for Baldr, the blessèd god,
> Ygg's dearest son, what doom is hidden:
> green and glossy there grew aloft,
> the trees among, the mistletoe.
>
> The slender-seeming sapling became
> a fell weapon when flung by Hödr
> but Baldr's brother was born full soon:
> but one night old slew him Odin's son.[29]

---

[28] Translation of L. M. Hollander, *The Poetic Edda* (Austin [Texas], 1962), p. 118.

[29] *Ibid.*, pp. 6–7. On the relation between *Baldrs draumar* and *Vǫluspá* cf. F. R. Schröder, "Die eddischen 'Balders Träume,'" *GRM* 45 (N.F.4):329–337 (1964).

This avenger is Váli, the son of the giantess Rind and Odin, who had forced her by magic spells to bear him this son. In the lay of "Baldr's Dreams" as well as in the "Prophecy of the Seeress," this Váli refuses to wash his hands and to comb his hair so long as Hödr has not paid with his life for the evil deed. There is no question of punishing Loki, and in the "Prophecy of the Seeress" the stanza about the atonement for Baldr's death ends with a reference to Frigg's lament over the "fateful deed." Since Baldr's death appears to be the prelude to world destruction, the immediately following question applies to the fettering of Loki. The latter's breaking loose is another prelude to Ragnarök, as is pointed out in the last stanza of "Baldr's Dreams": "Loki is loose from his bonds and the day will come of the doom of the gods."[30] The motif of Loki's fettering is accordingly only secondarily linked with Baldr's myth, and that this is also true of the whole intervention of Loki appears from the tale of Saxo Grammaticus, whose euhemeristic account reads as follows:

> Hotherus—i.e., Hödr—comes from Sweden; he is the son of Hodbroddus. Nanna, the daughter of the Norse king Gevarus, falls in love with him, but Balderus, the son of Othinus, after seeing her at her bath, is madly in love with her, and decides to get rid of Hotherus. The latter is warned by three nymphs, who also tell him that Balderus is half divine. When Hotherus sues for Nanna's hand, Gevarus flatly refuses to agree

30 Hollander, *op. cit.*, p. 119. There is no explicit mention of Loki's fettering in the Eddic sources as being specifically his punishment for participating in the murder of Baldr. There is no doubt, however, that Loki was somehow involved in it, since he brags about his being responsible for the absence of Baldr at the gathering of the gods in Aegir's hall (*Lokasenna*, st. 28):

> Be mindful, Frigg, what further I tell
>   of wicked works of mine:
> my rede wrought it that rides nevermore
>   hitherward Baldr to hall.

The phrase *ec þvi ræð* has, indeed, to be translated 'it is my fault' *(ich bin daran schuld)* according to H. Gering, *Kommentar zu den Liedern der Edda* [Halle, 1927], I, 291. E. Mogk thought that this applied to Loki's preventing Baldr from returning from Hell by refusing to bewail him under the shape of Thökk, but this is improbable (cf. F. R. Schröder, *Germanentum und Hellenismus* [Heidelberg, 1926], pp. 109–110; J. de Vries, *The Problem of Loki*, FFC 110 [Helsinki, 1933], pp. 163–171). This passage alludes rather to Loki's having been the *ráðbani* of Baldr, i.e., 'the contriver' of his murder, but he may very well have done this merely by supplying Hödr with the only weapon that could harm Baldr, the mistletoe: this would be in keeping with his function as "trickster" and parallel with his forging the only weapon that can slay the rooster Víðófnir on Mímameið (cf. *Fjǫlsvinnsmál*, st. 26)—a sword that is called Lœvateinn, literally 'the guileful twig.' Maybe his trick in the case of the *mistilteinn* was to harden it into a lethal weapon? Cf. the connection A. B. Rooth (*Loki in Scandinavian Mythology* [Lund, 1961], pp. 136–139) tries to establish with the "hardened holly" as a weapon in West European medieval tradition.

> to this marriage, because he is afraid of Balderus who is invulnerable. He advises Hotherus to try to obtain a sword from the forest-demon Mimingus, with which he would be able to strike Balderus mortally. Hotherus succeeds in securing the sword and a miraculous ring to boot, which causes the riches of its owner to increase constantly. After Hotherus has vanquished a certain Gelderus, while Nanna has rejected Balderus under the pretence that a marriage between a demigod and a mortal is unadvisable, both suitors wage a ruthless fight, in which the gods intervene. Balderus has to flee and Hotherus marries Nanna. Soon, however, Balderus attacks his land and Hotherus has to run away with his father-in-law. The struggle continues with varying success for both parties until Hotherus succeeds in secretly getting hold of the miraculous food from which Balderus derives his strength. When Hotherus meets with him shortly after, he runs his sword through him. In the meantime, heavy fighting goes on between their two armies, and in an alarming dream Balderus learns that he will soon stay with Proserpina. Three days later, his fate is sealed; his remains are buried under a barrow.[31]

Then follows the tale of Odin's revenge.

It would be hopeless to try to harmonize this account with Snorri's.[32] Saxo's source must have been a Danish tale, in which Hödr played the foremost part, whereas Snorri was using Icelandic traditions in which Baldr was the prominent character. Only a few details correspond in both versions, namely Baldr's premonitory dream and the mention of a miraculous ring, but even these parallel features appear in a basically different context: in the Eddic tradition, Baldr's dream is the point of departure for the whole chain of events, whereas in Saxo it is nothing but an anticipation of his imminent death after receiving a fatal wound. As for Draupnir, the "Lay of Skírnir" states that the ring "with Baldr, was burned" and that "eight rings as dear will drop from it every ninth night"; yet in Saxo it is nothing but an *armilla mirā quādam arcanāque virtute possessoris opes augere solita* ('an arm ring that, through a wonderful and mysterious power, used

---

[31] Cf., e.g., *Saxonis Gesta Danorum*, ed. J. Olrik and H. Raeder (Copenhagen, 1931), I, 63–69.

[32] For a comparison between the two versions of the Baldr myth cf., e.g., E. O. G. Turville-Petre, *Myth and Religion of the North* (New York, 1964), pp. 113–116. Dumézil, who considers Snorri's account as representing the Scandinavian vulgate, in a letter to Otto Höfler, published under the title "Høtherus et Balderus" (*PBB(T)* 83:259–270 [1961]), has tried to account for the differences by assuming a transfer of some of the attributes of Baldr to Hödr by Saxo when he reshaped the myth into a romantic story focused on Hotherus. Whatever new features Balderus has acquired are ascribed to borrowing from the myths of Freyr. Although the saga of Hadingus illustrates such adaptations of myth, it certainly does not give evidence of shifts so thoroughgoing as to confirm the assumption made here (p. 261) by Dumézil: "indifférent et sans doute fermé à l'ancienne valeur théologique des récits qu'il utilisait et des dieux qu'il transposait en héros, l'écrivain danois les a désarticulés sans scrupule et recomposés à sa façon."

to increase the riches of its owner'). Its owner is no longer Odin but the forest demon who supplies Hödr with the weapon with which to kill Baldr.

But let us not preoccupy ourselves with such details: they merely show the widespread *Entmythisierung*, the total recasting of the mythological data into the plot of a romantic tale, as commonly occurs in the first part of Saxo's *Gesta Danorum*. Apparently the Danish historian has no personal grasp of pagan religious thinking and shows a lack of involvement which Snorri does not share. Nevertheless, his story is not completely worthless as a source of information about the original form of the Baldr myth. On the contrary, whereas Snorri modifies the myth with ethical intentions, in order to make Loki the demonic opponent of the gods and assign to him the main role in opposition to the holy victim and the blind instrument Hödr, Saxo shows these latter two figures to better advantage and also indicates the reason for their enmity, namely their vying with each other for the hand of Nanna (who, by the way, totally disappears in the background in Snorri's tale). Moreover, in Saxo's tale Baldr and Hödr justify their respective names by their heroic behavior: *Hǫđr* is the Old Norse reflex of Germanic **haþu-*, 'combat,' which also appears as first component of the name of Hildebrand's father, *Hadubrand*. The word is cognate with Celtic **katu-*, 'combat,' which also appears in the names of Germanic chieftains like Catumerus, head of the Chatti, according to Tacitus, or Catualda, head of the Marcomanni at the end of the first century. It also occurs in the name of the Danish hero Starkadr, which reflects a compound **stark-hǫđr*, 'strong warrior,' whose meaning particularly fits with the character of Starkadr as an "Odinic warrior."[33]

[33] Cf. de Vries, "Die Starkadsage," *GRM* 36 (N.F. 5): 281–297 (1955). Dumézil, however, contrasts Starcatherus with Sigurdr, Helgi and Haraldr in his *Aspects de la fonction guerrière chez les Indo-européens* (Paris, 1956), pp. 80–93, and points out that his ugliness, grim courage, and brutal strength characterize him as a second-function figure—"une être dont on n'a pas beaucoup d'exemples dans la littérature scandinave: un héros de *Þórr*" (p. 88). Without denying his association with Odin, especially in the episode with Víkar, Dumézil considers "l'intervention d'Othinus dans sa vie . . . telle qu'on l'attend d'un dieu souverain; il fixe librement et seul le destin des individus et leur distribue les dons de nature" (*ibid.*). He therefore objects (*ibid.*, pp. 107–111) to the arguments of de Vries, who rightly points out, "Wie man sich das Verhältnis der Odin- und Thormotive in der Starkadsage zu denken hat, bleibt ungewiss" (*op. cit.*, p. 296). Dumézil's interpretation is based on Saxo's story, which he considers as closer to the original version than that of the *Gautrekssaga*; but as de Vries points out, "Nur die dänische Überlieferung zeigt Ansätze zu einem Starkadbild, das den Gegensatz zu Thor weniger betont" (*ibid.*). For an extensive discussion of the problem, cf. Turville-Petre, *op. cit.*, pp. 205–211.

As for the name Baldr, two etymologies are usually advanced: one is connected with the no longer accepted interpretation of Baldr as a sun-god and derives his name from the IE root **bhel-*, 'shining, white.' In the *Gylfaginning*, he is described as having a face so beautiful and bright that rays seemed to beam from him. This argument does not weigh very much, however, in view of the fact that such an earthbound divine figure as the vegetation god Freyr is also called "shining" and that his servant—actually a hypostasis of his—is called Skírnir, 'the bright one.' Therefore this etymology is usually abandoned in favor of the comparison with the Old English noun *bealdor* which is supposed to mean 'lord, prince.' The name would then belong to the same semantic area as Freyr, which also originally means 'lord.' Upon closer examination of the Old English sources, however, it is obvious that the ascription of the meaning 'lord, prince' to *bealdor* is unjustified, so that a third etymology may be considered. There is, indeed, another IE root **bhel-*, which refers mainly to bursting with vital strength.[34] Derived from it is the German adjective **bald-*, 'brave, hardy' (English *bold*), and connecting the name Baldr with it becomes even more plausible when one remembers that the name of his wife Nanna can reflect an older form **nanþō*, which is related to the Old High German words *nand*, 'audacity,' and *nendan*, 'dare,' with which the Old Irish word for 'combat,' *nēit*, is also akin. Thus, the names of the three main characters of the Baldr myth belong to the same conceptual sphere of "combat." Since the kennings always connect the name Baldr with the concept of "warrior,"[35] we could be tempted to consider Saxo's tale as a reflex of the oldest form of the myth, the more so since Snorri does not say a word about this "courageous" aspect of Baldr's personality.

The mythologem of fratricide for the possession of a woman is a common motif in the sphere of the cult of the divine twins, where male twins are usually associated with a female personage. In the oldest form of the myth this woman appears as their common wife; accordingly, Sūryā is the wife of both Aśvins, the originally horse-shaped sons of the Sky-god in the Vedic sources.[36] The social situation

---

34 F. R. Schröder, "Balder und der zweite Merseburger Spruch," *GRM* 34 (N.F.3):166–169 (1953). On Old English *bealdor* cf. H. Kuhn, "Es gibt kein balder 'Herr,'" *Erbe der Vergangenheit: Germanistische Beiträge. Festgabe für Karl Helm* (Tübingen, 1951), pp. 37–45.

35 Cf. de Vries, *Altgermanische Religionsgeschichte* (2d ed.), II, 214. For a list of the kennings cf. R. Meissner, *Die Kenningar der Skalden: Ein Beitrag zur skaldischen Poetik* (Bonn and Leipzig, 1921), p. 260.

36 Cf. A. H. Krappe, *Mythologie universelle* (Paris, 1930), pp. 82–84.

implicit in this common possession of one wife by two brothers is known as "phratrogamy" and seems to have been known among the Indo-Europeans. There is a tale in Pausanias according to which, on an evening, the Spartan Dioscuri requested the owner of the house in which they had spent their earthly life to put them up for the night. The man accepted, but refused to let them use their former room, as his own daughter slept there. The following morning the latter has disappeared with all her garments, and in her room the owner of the house found a bust of the Dioscuri with a laserwort twig in her stead.[37]

This common wife can obviously easily become a source of conflict between her two spouses, and at a later period we find numerous examples of twins who quarrel about a woman.[38] In Old Indic epic literature, for example, we hear about two brothers, Bālin and Sugrīva, sons of the Sun, who resemble each other so much that people cannot tell them apart; they are very close to each other until they grow into archenemies because of their rivalry for the hand of Rūma.[39]

It is not out of the question to consider Baldr and Hödr hypostases of the Indo-European divine twins who vie for the possession of the same woman—but, in that case, Snorri's account would have to be totally disregarded. This approach has been attempted by those who hold that Snorri had combined three originally separate elements into one continuous tale, the components being Baldr's death, the incineration, and Hermodr's descent to the world of the dead. The first and the third would have been taken over by Snorri from existing lays, whereas the second would be based on a description of the fresco that depicted Baldr's funeral ceremonies in the hall of the Icelandic prince Óláfr paí. The motif of the incineration would accordingly have been inserted between the two originally independent alliterative poems, after the model of the *Húsdrápa* of the Skald Úlfr Uggason.[40] Yet at the end of Snorri's account the dispatching of mes-

37 On the symbolic meaning of the laserwort (σίλφιον) in this context, cf. F. Chapouthier, *Les Dioscures au service d'une déesse* (Paris, 1935), pp. 88–89.

38 Krappe, *op. cit.*, pp. 87–89.

39 This was the conclusion de Vries reached after his analysis of the evidence on Baldr in the first edition of his *Altgermanische Religionsgeschichte* (Berlin and Leipzig, 1937), II, 252–253, a view shared by Güntert in his commentary on the *Vǫluspá: Die Schau der Seherin* (Heidelberg, 1944), p. 53.

40 G. Neckel, *Die Überlieferungen vom Gotte Balder* (Dortmund, 1920), pp. 65–66, who considers that the contents of two lays have been combined in Snorri's story and claims that the lay of Baldr's death, composed around 900, must have included a description of the funeral and incineration, "woher der Schnitzer des

sengers and their meeting with the giantess Thökk are completely independent of the descent to Hell of Hermodr, but nevertheless are based on an older lay on account of the literal quotation of a stanza by Snorri; one therefore wonders whether the efforts of the philologists to distinguish two different lays in the tale are justified —the more so since the prose text itself reminds us of the rhythm of the stanza of Thökk in the passage about the meeting of the Thing of the gods.

Before fragmenting Snorri's account, it would have been wiser to examine carefully whether there was any organic coherence among the three components of the mythologem. Partiality for explanations relating to fertility rites seems to have covered up the truth in this matter. On the basis of Frigg's intervention and of the universal dismay at his death, efforts have been made to transplant Baldr from the world of the Aesir (i.e., the warlike, ruling gods) into that of the Vanir (i.e., the protectors of agriculture and vegetation growth). He was, accordingly, brought into closer association with Freyr, the principal vegetation god: as already pointed out, it was thought that both names meant 'lord'; besides, Baldr was occasionally referred to as 'most favorable' and as 'reconciling men,' so that he could also be considered a god of peace and welfare. Like Freyr, he was an excellent horse rider; both excel in wisdom and bright appearance, and, like Freyr, Baldr even has a ship.[41]

But how is one to explain Baldr's death in this context? To do so, parallels from the world of the sagas have been adduced. In the stories about the hero Starkadr, a remarkable event took place during a simulated sacrifice to Odin: the lot had fallen upon King Víkar to serve as mock victim, and he was strung up, as it were, on a holy tree; people were supposed to poke him in the side with a reed, but, in the hands of Starkadr, the harmless cane became a spear by fateful

---

Olaf Pfau and Ulfr Uggason dies Motiv gekannt haben." With reference to Snorri's text, however, Schröder states more accurately in *Germanentum und Hellenismus,* p. 96: "Zwischen beide [Lieder] ist eine ausführliche Schilderung von Balders Leichenfeier eingeschoben. Diese hat Snorri der Húsdrápa des Skalden Úlfr Uggason entlehnt, der in diesem Gedichte bildliche Darstellungen der Baldersage besingt, die die Halle des vornehmen Isländers, Olaf Pfau schmückten." More recently, after pointing to the possibility of either woodcarvings (cf. Neckel, *op. cit.,* pp. 45 ff.) or wall hangings of tapestry (cf. Rooth, *op. cit.,* p. 140) as the source of Snorri's description, he remarks ("Balder-Probleme," *PBB(T)* 84:320 n. 1 [1962]): "Aber auch das Lied von Balders Tod kann den Aufzug der Götter schon gebracht haben, vgl. etwa die Aufzählung von Rossen und Reitern in der Kálfsvisa (*Dagr reið Drǫsli . . . , reið bani Belia* [Freyr] *Blóðughofa* usw.); Grímnismál 30, u.a."

41 On the correspondences between Baldr and Freyr, cf. especially Schröder, *Germanentum und Hellenismus,* pp. 122–123.

witchcraft and pierced Víkar's heart, so that he died then and there. The similarity between the reed and the mistletoe that caused Baldr's death is obvious, and the correspondence between the two episodes becomes even more striking when one thinks that the murderous blows are struck by characters who have actually the same name, since Starkadr means 'strong Hödr.' It is, accordingly, plausible to recognize originally a simulated sacrifice in the Baldr myth. But of what kind?

According to Snorri's account, the gods indulge in a kind of "game" on the "peace ground" at the Thing meeting. Since Baldr is supposed to be invulnerable, their sport is a symbolic "killing," comparable with the numerous usages on which folklore gives us ample information: simulated fights to celebrate the spring festival, in which the symbol of winter is fought against and vanquished; carrying around a kind of doll or manikin, which is beaten with rods, pierced with sticks, and finally cast into the water or burned on a bonfire. There are dozens of such descriptions of fertility rites on Germanic territory in the collections of W. Mannhardt, J. G. Frazer, and W. Liungman, which accounts for the fact that the Baldr myth was connected with them.

But there is more: specialists have always been struck by the resemblance of Baldr's story to the life of Siegfried.[42] The remarkable correspondences are, indeed, especially obvious if the Scandinavian traditions of Sigurdr are taken into consideration. Like Achilles, Siegfried is vulnerable in only one tiny spot, and a woman learns of it by deceit from another woman. Here the murderer, Hagen, is one-eyed, whereas Hödr is supposed to be blind. In both instances a woman is so inconsolably desperate that she ends up burning on the funeral pyre with her murdered husband: here Brünhilde gives Siegfried this proof of love; there Nanna dies of grief. Like Baldr and Freyr, Siegfried is "shiningly beautiful" and is considered a first-rate horse rider. Among the jewels that Siegfried has acquired with the hoard of the Niebelungen, there is a ring—Andvarinaut—which reminds us in a way of Draupnir.

This comparison between the Baldr myth and the Siegfried saga seems to be especially important with regard to the various assumed connections of the latter with fertility rites.[43] One thinks, for ex-

[42] Cf. especially Güntert, *Die Schau der Seherin*, pp. 50–51.

[43] Cf., e.g., H. W. J. Kroes, "Die Erweckung der Jungfrau hinter dem Flammenwall," *Neophilologus* 36:144–157 (1952), esp. pp. 145, 156; Schröder, "Mythos und Heldensage," *GRM* 36 (N.F.5):1–21 (1955), with revised version in *Zur Germanisch-Deutschen Heldensage*, ed. K. Hauck (Darmstadt, 1961), pp. 285–315.

ample, of the episode of the awakening of the Valkyrie in the *Edda*: when Sigurdr has crossed the flames to reach the sleeping Valkyrie and has awakened her by taking off her coat of mail, she says:

> Hail to you, gods! Hail, goddesses!
> Hail, earth, that gives to all!
> Goodly spells and speech bespeak we from you,
> and healing hands, in this life![44]

This invocation reminds us in some respects of the old hymn to the earth goddess which survives in the Old English charm:

> Hail to thee, earth, mother of men,
> may you be fruitful under God's protection,
> filled with food for the benefit of men.[45]

This would typify Siegfried as a young spring god—he would be a solar hero who performs hierogamy with the earth goddess for the sake of blessing Nature with prosperous crops. Such an association is, however, doomed to end fatefully with the summer solstice, and, therefore, the statement of the Middle High German *Nibelungenlied: ze einer sunnewenden der groze mord geschah*, 'the great murder took place at a solstice,' does not come unexpectedly.

Would this also be the case with Baldr's death? Such has been the assumption of some scholars, because the *fimbulvetr* ('the great and awful winter') to which the Eddic *Lay of Vafthrudnir* alludes might be its cosmic consequence.[46] Yet if this assumption were justified, one would expect that in accord with the usual scenario of fertility rites, after the death of the god and the lamentation he would rise from the dead. For Baldr there is no resurrection.

To this argument the defenders of the view just discussed would

---

[44] *Sigrdrífumál*, st. 3 (Hollander, *op. cit.*, p. 236).

[45] G. Storms, *Anglo-Saxon Magic* (The Hague, 1948), p. 177.

[46] As Schröder points out (*PBB(T)* 84:333 [1962]): "Im Mittelpunkt des kosmischen Geschehens steht die Gestalt Balders, mit dessen Sterben aller Segen auf Erden schwindet und der Niedergang unaufhaltsam einsetzt." The apparently endless winter need not be an Oriental motif, as has often been assumed (cf. against A. Olrik, *Ragnarök: Die Sagen vom Weltuntergang* [Berlin, 1922] pp. 15–19, 331–337; de Vries, *Altgermanische Religionsgeschichte* [2d ed], II, 399, 403; and Turville-Petre, *op. cit.*, p. 283). If Baldr is considered a "Vegetations- und Jahresgott . . . der in der Blüte der Jugend und der Fülle der Kraft dem finsteren feindlichen Gott, dem Dämon des Winters erliegt," it will be expected that he remain "während der langen Wintersnacht im unterirdischen Bereich, um erst im neuen Jahr zu neuem Leben zu erwachen." In the context of *Vǫluspá* "hat der Dichter . . . den Ablauf eines einzelnen Erdenjahres zum Weltjahr gesteigert und in dieses Balder mittenhineingestellt, den Fruchtbarkeitsgott zum kosmischen Gott erhöht" (Schröder, *op. cit.*).

oppose the "Prophecy of the Seeress," where the "new order" after *Ragnarök* is described:

> On unsown acres the ears will grow,
> all ill grow better; will Baldr come then.
> Both he and Hödr will in Hropt's hall dwell. . . .[47]

Therefore Dumézil concluded his research on Baldr's myth in his book *Loki* in 1948 with the following statement: "Baldr . . . ressuscitera à la fin du présent âge du monde pour un règne idyllique, complétant ainsi, au moins dans le temps cosmique, la séquence 'naissance-mort-résurrection' que d'autres religions expriment dans les mythes et dans les rites de l'alternance saisonnière."[48] But why would Odin, then, show such deep concern about Baldr's murder? And does one not forget, in this context, that Hermodr's descent to the world of the dead is a lost cause? Baldr ultimately has to remain in the underworld. Snorri's account actually points clearly to the fact: Hermodr comes back with the promise that Baldr will be allowed to leave the netherworld under one condition: the whole world must bewail him—but the giantess Thökk does not grieve for him! Why not? According to Snorri, because she is no one else but Loki himself—but this is merely a guess of his in connection with his dualistic interpretation of the myth as a symbol of the struggle between Good and Evil.[49]

---

47 *Vǫluspá*, st. 61 (Hollander, *op. cit.*, p. 12). With reference to F. Ström, *Nordisk hedendom: Tro och sed i förkristen tid* (Göteborg, 1961), p. 114, Schröder stresses (*op. cit.*, p. 334 n. 16) that the mention of crops growing on unsown fields would hardly make sense if it did not point to a fertility god.

48 *Loki*, p. 240. In *Les dieux des Germains*, p. 106, Dumézil rejects this Mannhardtian theory, with reference to the criticism of de Vries in "Der Mythos von Balders Tod," *ANF* 70:44–45 (1955). In the German edition of *Loki* (p. 195), he points out that Baldr must be considered, with de Vries, a first-function god, and not a third-function figure, as claimed by Schröder in his "Baldr und der zweite Merseburger Spruch," pp. 161–183, and by Ström in *Loki: Ein mythologisches Problem*, *GUÅ* 62.8 (1956), pp. 96–129. Dumézil emphasizes the striking parallel between the Baldr myth and the story of the Ossetic hero Soslan, but he carefully avoids postulating a common source (*op. cit.*, pp. 200–201), although he is tempted on account of the *Mahābhārata* episode (cf. above, p. 63) to assume an Indo-European heritage (cf. de Vries, "Loki und Kein Ende," *Festschrift für Franz Rolf Schröder* [Heidelberg, 1959], p. 2 n. 2).

49 The original extent of Loki's participation in Baldr's slaying has often been discussed: as Derolez points out, "his true nature becomes more difficult to understand when he pursues the apparently innocent Baldr with his hatred to the extreme limit" (*op. cit.*, p. 138). If he actually played the part assigned to him by Snorri, the other characters in the drama would be reduced to mere supernumeraries: Baldr is a martyr, Hödr a blind instrument (cf. de Vries, *Altgermanische Religionsgeschichte* [2d ed.], II, 218). This is the reason why, in spite of Dumézil (*Loki*, pp. 133–158; German ed., pp. 94–115), it is probable that the situation described by Snorri reflects a late development, as de Vries suggested (*The Problem of Loki*, pp. 177–179). The only element vouchsafing Loki's part in

The giantess who dwells in a cave is rather the goddess of death herself, and her very words give us a better idea of the real meaning of the Baldr myth: through his death, Baldr has entered the land of no return. There is no question of resurrection. The core of the theme of Hermodr's descent to Hell is accordingly the same as that of the Babylonian epic of Gilgamesh or of the Greek myth of Orpheus: nobody can escape death, and whoever thinks he has found a way out of it soon realizes his delusion. In Baldr's story Hermodr returns with joy: Who would not bewail Baldr's death? He is, accordingly, sure to be "wept out of Hell." But Hermodr has not understood the hidden meaning of Hel's remark: "It will have to be proved that Baldr is as much beloved by all as it is claimed." What she actually meant was: "The whole world may unanimously wish to revive the shining god, but Death herself will remain inexorable"; therefore, she says: "What Hel has, she may keep!" in the shape of Thökk. It accordingly seems to me that the Baldr myth deals with the problem of death, without the motif of the victorious resurrection of life from death.

What, then, is the significance of Baldr's death in the framework of Eddic cosmic history?

The "Prophecy of the Seeress" informs us about it: for the world of the gods, this death comes as a thunderclap out of a bright clear sky, and suddenly destroys the cosmic order painstakingly established after the war with the Vanir. The seeress describes Baldr explicitly as the "gory god" (*blóðgom tívur*), even before the murder is perpetrated, almost marking him as predestined to suffer that fateful death.[50] It can therefore be assumed that Baldr's death symbolizes the entry of death into the world. Besides, if we accept Bugge's interpretation of Old Norse *tívarr* as 'sacrifice' (as corresponding to Old English *tífer*, 'sacrifice,' and Old High German *zebar*, 'sacrificial animal'),[51] it could, moreover, be considered as the first sacrifice on the model of which later rituals developed.

The connection of the Boldr myth with a sacrificial rite has already been pointed out with reference to the death of King Víkar in the Starkadr saga. There, the dart that pierced the heart of the victim was a reed. Why?

This plant, which grows up from muddy puddles and pools, is

---

the murder in the Eddic poetic source is, indeed, the twenty-eighth stanza of the *Lokasenna* (cf. especially Schröder, "Das Symposion der Lokasenna," *ANF* 67:1–29 [1952]).

50 Turville-Petre, *op. cit.*, p. 108 (Hollander's translation 'blessed god,' quoted on p. 64, does not reflect the ON text accurately: *blóðugr* means 'bloodstained').

51 Cf. de Vries, *Altnordisches etymologisches Wörterbuch* (Leiden, 1960), p. 590.

often considered a symbol of the divine life that arises triumphantly from the primordial waters of chaos. This same motif is found in Old Indic cosmogonic symbolism, where the divinity reveals itself, together with the cosmos, by popping up out of a lotus floating on the waters.[52] Is mistletoe also such a symbolization of the divine principle of life? The numerous studies devoted to folk customs connected with this plant clearly indicate that it is actually considered a "plant of life";[53] but in the Baldr myth it appears as the plant of life that belongs to death, or better, of a life that is not granted to man —a kind of plant like the one that Gilgamesh wanted to acquire for man, but which ultimately had to remain in the netherworld.

Is Baldr, then, a man, to whom "divine" life has to be refused?

In this respect the parallelism with the Starkadr saga is particularly instructive: here the hero, acting as a warrior dedicated to Odin, becomes the instrument of a fate determined by the gods[54] and kills King Víkar during the ritual of a simulated sacrifice to Odin. The similarity of name between Starkadr and Baldr's killer has repeatedly been pointed out; the way both kill their victims is also the same. Yet Hödr is blind; he seems to be merely an instrument of Loki! Snorri, as we know, is constantly stressing the part of Loki in the light of his ethical interpretation of the myth. Eddic tradition, however, holds that Hödr is truly responsible for Baldr's death.[55] (Why would he, otherwise, have to "reconcile" himself with Baldr after Ragnarök?) This fact suggests another interpretation of his part in the drama: In the Germanic pantheon, some gods occur with significant bodily defects, for example, the one-handed Týr, the one-eyed Odin; it would be astonishing, to say the least, that a second Ase

---

52 Cf. Eliade, *op. cit.*, pp. 281–283; French text, pp. 245–267.

53 Cf. especially Neckel, *op. cit.*, pp. 175 ff.; J. G. Frazer, *The Golden Bough* (abridged ed.; London, 1950), pp. 658 ff.; T. H. Gaster, ed., *The New Golden Bough: A New Abridgement of the Classic Work by Sir James George Frazer* (New York, 1959), pp. 590 ff.; A. Kabell, *Balder and the Mistletoe*, FFC 196 (Helsinki, 1965).

54 This is evidenced by the words of Odin to Starkadr in the Gautrekssaga: *þá skalltu nú senda mér Víkar konung*, 'now then you shall dispatch to me King Víkar' (cf. de Vries, "Die Starkadsage," pp. 287–288).

55 According to the *Vǫluspá hin skamma* (the "Short Seeress' Prophecy" inserted in the *Hyndluljóð*)—Váli has avenged his brother Baldr by slaying his murderer—specifically designated as *handbani*, i.e., 'actual slayer' (cf. Old Saxon *handbano* [*Heliand* 5199], Old English *handbona* [*Beowulf* 460]). In the new world, where all disputes are settled, Hödr and Baldr can live together in Valhöll (designated in *Vǫluspá*, st. 62, as *Hrópts sigtoptir*, 'Hroptr's [i.e. Odin's] homes of victory,' and, according to a plausible emendation of Rasmus Rask, *vé* [instead of *vel*] *valtívar*, 'the shrine of the gods of the slain'). This is the reason why de Vries translated the second half of stanza 62: "Hödr and Baldr, both reconciled, live in Valhöll" (*Edda* [Amsterdam, 1966], p. 31; cf. also Derolez, *op. cit.*, p. 136).

would show the same defect as Odin—only to a worse degree, though, since he is totally blind![56] And even this difference is of little importance, since Odin himself is described as *Tvíblindi*, that is, 'blind with both eyes.' Is Hödr then a hypostasis of Odin himself?

If this possibility be admitted, it becomes clear why Odin does not intervene during the whole process, while, on the other hand, Hödr's appearance is restricted to the Baldr myth. But why would Odin, under the shape of Hödr, want to kill his son Baldr? Analyzing the motif of the struggle between father and son in the Hildebrandslied, de Vries[57] has indicated that it could very well be a mythologem belonging to an initiation rite. The myth, in which an unruly divine hero even dares to stand up against his father, but must finally be worsted on account of the latter's divine power, may be a symbolization of actual facts of life as well as a warning to presumptuous young warriors who would no longer feel due respect for paternal authority. With good reason, the best specialist of Germanic mythology surmised that the same mythological content underlay the Baldr myth, a hypothesis he worked out in his article "Der Mythos von Balders

---

[56] Hj. Falk, *Odensheite*, Videnskapsselskapets Skrifter II, Hist.-filos. Klasse (Christiania, 1924), p. 29; cf. also *ibid.*, p. 15. *Blindr inn bǫlvísi* (*Helgakviða Hundingsbana* 2, st. 2), to which de Vries (*Altgermanische Religionsgeschichte* [2d ed.], II, 82) adds *Svipdagr blindi*—"wohl eine Hypostase von Odin." But Schröder, *PBB(T)* 84:338 (1962), considers Svipdagr rather an "alten, früh verblassten Gott des Sommers, der lichten Jahreszeit, neben dem ganz urtümlich!—also sein negativer Pol *Svipdagr blindi* steht, der ebensowenig wie Höd darum nur eine Vermummung oder Hypostase Odins ist." He further compares the Irish tale of the death of Fergus mac Roig, whose characteristic correspondences with the Baldr myth he explicitly described in *Skadi und die Götter Skandinaviens* (Tübingen, 1941), pp. 141–144: Here, Ailill prompts his blind brother Lugaid to shoot Fergus whom he describes as a stag. Schröder connects these traditions with the "polarity of the vegetation god": "als Jahresgott [hat er], entsprechend den beiden Hälften des Jahres, seine lichte und seine dunkle Seite," which dark side then develops "als eigene Gottheit . . . zum Gegenspieler des Wachstumgottes, dem dieser erliegt" (cf. also O. Höfler, "Das Opfer in Semnonenhain," in *Edda, Skalden, Saga: Festschrift zum 70. Geburtstag von Felix Genzmer* [Heidelberg, 1952], pp. 38–41). This explanation, however, does not account for the fact that, as foster-father of the Swedish king Ingjaldr illráði, the blind Svipdagr gives him a wolf's heart to eat, which will give him a wolf's nature—a typical initiation motif, as de Vries points out (*ANF* 70.49 [1955]). Not convincing either is Dumézil's comparison of Hödr with the Vedic Bhaga (*Les dieux des Germains*, p. 99); although undoubtedly " 'aveugle' est tout autre chose que 'borgne' " (*IIJ* 3:9 n. 22 [1959]), Bhaga may accurately be described as a "répartiteur des biens et des destins ... indifférent aux mérites des hommes," parallel to the Latin Fortuna, even if Dumézil now (*La religion romaine archaïque*, p. 205) makes him preside more specifically over movable property (especially cattle)—a function that hardly corresponds to the episodic role played by Hödr in Eddic mythology.

[57] "Das Motiv des Vater-Sohn-Kampfes im Hildebrandslied," *GRM* 34 (N.F.3): 257–274 (1953).

Tod,"[58] the argument of which I reproduce here with slight modifications. According to de Vries, the kernel of the myth is the killing of a son begotten on a mortal by his divine father Odin. By implication Baldr is not a god: he does not die as a vegetation god only to rise from the dead and thus give proof of his irrepressible vital strength. Baldr dies and remains dead. Although he is called "the twelfth among the Aesir," he does not actually belong to their circle. Confirmation may be found in the Skaldic poem describing the arrival in Valhöll of Eiríkr blóðøx with a group of followers killed in combat: when they approach, Bragi thinks Baldr returns to the Hall with his retinue, but Odin immediately dismisses this suggestion as "nonsense."[59] Besides, the names Baldr, 'valiant,' and Hödr, 'warrior,' are by no means typically divine names, nor is Hermodr which means 'courageous in combat.' Thus the indications are that the main characters in the plot of the Baldr myth are not actually gods.

This conclusion is furthermore confirmed by the funeral rites. Obviously, Snorri has interwoven them with a few mythological incidents like the episode with the giantess Hyrrokkin, which he has presumably somewhat toned down, since it can be surmised from a Skaldic poem dedicated to Thor, which explicitly mentions her as dead, that in the original version her skull was crushed by Thor in anger.[60] The uncouth behavior of Thor is also evident in his treatment of the dwarf Litr. His kicking of the latter into the fire of the funeral pyre has a symbolic meaning as well; Old Norse *litr,* indeed, means 'nice complexion' and applies to the bloom of youth and health given by Lódur to the first human couple, Askr and Embla.[61] The typical attribute of youth characterizing Baldr is utterly destroyed by the flames—another hint that he will not rise from the dead.

As regards the ceremony itself, it is the typical funeral of heroes: he

---

58 Pp. 41–60; cf. also de Vries, *Altgermanische Religionsgeschichte* (2d ed.), II, 237–238.

59 *Heimsku mæla, Eiríksmál,* st. 4 (E. A. Kock, *Den norsk-isländska skaldediktningen* [Lund, 1946], I, 89).

60 Cf. Þorbjorn Dísarskáld, *Þórsdrapa,* st. 2: *Hyrrokkin dó fyrri,* 'Hyrrokkin died before [the other demons listed above]' (Kock, *op. cit.,* I, 74). Her name is also very significant in this context: **Hyrhrokkinn* means 'shrunk up by fire' (de Vries, *Altnordisches etymologisches Wörterbuch,* p. 276). A different tradition, however, is reported in Úlfr Uggason's *Húsdrápa* (st. 11), where the giantess (designated by the kenning *fjalla Hildr*), trudging with Baldr's ship Hringhorni, is ultimately killed by Odin's warriors (*Hrópts hjalmelda gildar*).

61 Cf. E. C. Polomé, "Some Comments on *Vǫluspá,* Stanzas 17 and 18," in E. C. Polomé, ed., *Old Norse Literature and Mythology* (Austin [Texas], 1969), pp. 265–290.

is burned in a ship, with his wife and presumably also his retinue, since Modgudr, meeting Hermodr on the bridge to Hell, tells him that "five throngs of dead men" rode over Giöll, the river of Hell, the day before; his horse is also put on the funeral pyre—all in conformity with Snorri's statement in the *Ynglingasaga* that Odin instituted the usage of cremation and determined that the dead should be burned with their earthly possessions in order to have them along in Valhöll.[62]

This, however, prompts a question: Why does Baldr not go to Valhöll after the "Odinic" sacrificial and funeral rites? Such a fate is excluded for two reasons: first of all, going to Valhöll would imply an unconditional resurrection in the society of the Aesir; second, as a symbol of man's fate, Baldr must go to the dark realms of Hel.

One more detail: Why is Draupnir returned to Hermodr?

As Dumézil pointed out,[63] this ring was the symbol of the regulation of time; it was accordingly out of place in the netherworld. But why, then, had Odin nevertheless placed it on the pyre? Two explanations are possible: from a cosmic angle, Baldr's death had disrupted the cosmic order, including the regulation of time; therefore it was foreboding the end of time in Eddic eschatology; from a strictly human point of view, the ring had to return to the world of the living, because, although death marks the end of all temporal activity for man, others will assume his temporal tasks.

Taking all these elements into consideration, it is possible to summarize the components of the mythologem of Baldr in Snorri's account; they consist of four motifs:

1. the first occurrence of death, which is henceforth the inescapable fate of man;
2. the establishment by Odin of human sacrifice, namely by means of a spear;
3. the introduction of cremation;
4. the failure of an effort to prevail over death for lack of fulfillment of one condition.[64]

Since de Vries considers the Baldr myth as the text of an initiation ritual, the problem is now to discover how these motifs are to be related to such religious practices.

The mythologem of death is the nucleus of such rituals: to be truly a man, one must have become fully conscious of the inevitability of

---

62 Snorri Sturluson, *Ynglingasaga*, ed. E. Wessén (Stockholm, 1952), p. 11.
63 *Tarpeia*, pp. 231–238.
64 de Vries, *ANF* 70:51 (1955).

death and accept it with calm resignation, with the understanding that the continually renewed existence of mankind is ensured only by the insertion of death in the cycle of life. This has been understood by the Old Norse: everywhere, death is considered as something unnatural; man cannot realize that it belonged to his original destiny, and he therefore ascribes it to the cunning intervention of a demonic being or to his own failure. A tiny plant was forgotten by Frigg when she received everyone's oath; this twig will become the instrument of man's fate. Snorri made Loki responsible, but against Dumézil and de Vries, I believe that he did so merely on the basis of his ethical concepts, in order to assign death definitely to the demonic element, as in the biblical cosmic drama. The heathen Germanic tribesman must have had a different outlook. He was not coddled as a child; "a parvulis labori et duritiae student," says Caesar;[65] only after proving their competence with pain and courage were they allowed to carry arms and to take their place in the social community, adds Tacitus.[66] This acceptance in the group, or rather, this passage from youth to the adult world of warriors was conditioned by particularly severe tests, as many tales show, for example, the *Vǫlsunga Saga*. Here, the mother of Sinfjötli, the future warrior dedicated to Odin, tests the courage of her children by sewing their shirts to their skins. All her sons cry with pain, but Sinfjötli bites his lips and does not breathe a word. Then she violently pulls the shirt from his body so that the skin of his arms is left hanging on the sleeves, but he remains silent. As she asks him if he does not feel anything, he simply answers: "For a Völsungr, this can merely be called insignificant pain." Then his father Sigmundr puts him through another test: he must knead a bag of flour in which a venomous snake is hidden, but he does not even notice it. Later, father and son put on wolfskins, and Sinfjötli now has to attack at least seven enemies at once. He, however, kills eleven of them. Seeing this, his father jumps at his throat and "kills" him, to revive him immediately afterward with a magic herb that a raven brought him.[67] After this strenuous "initiation" Sinfjötli is deemed capable of fulfilling his task, that is, avenging his grandfather's death.

The parallelism with Baldr's myth is obvious: Sinfjötli's mother

65 "From childhood up they stress toil and hardship" (*De Bello Gallico* 6:61).

66 *Germania*, chap. 13 (R. Much, *Die Germania des Tacitus erläutert* [Heidelberg, 1937], pp. 152–156, 203).

67 *Vǫlsunga Saga*, chap. 8. The appearance of Odin's bird is but one of the numerous "Odinic" features of this "ins Heroische gesteigerte Form alter Initiationsbräuche" (de Vries, *ANF* 70:55 [1955], with further reference to Höfler, *Kultische Geheimbünde der Germanen* [Frankfurt, 1934], pp. 190 ff.).

imposes difficult tests upon him in order to acquaint him with pain and fortify him against it. Is this not also the symbolic meaning of the oaths that Frigg receives? Owing to these preparatory steps taken by her, Baldr is apparently ready for any trial imposed upon him at the Thing. Then comes the ordeal of the initiation: this is a strictly manly affair; no women are allowed, a fact that excludes the possibility of a manifestation of a vegetation cult, which would not fit with the activity of the Aesir at the Thing meeting either. Frigg only hears what has happened from Loki who visits her, disguised as a woman. Otherwise, why would she have to ask: "Do you know what the Aesir did at the Thing meeting?" This clearly indicates that, like Sinfjötli's mother, she had to forfeit her son totally to the male community, quite in keeping with Tacitus' statement that before this transition rite the youths were members of the household, but that after it they belonged to the community.[68]

In both cases the final phase of the ritual is death, but Sinfjötli is immediately called back to life to fulfill his manly task. This is impossible in Baldr's case on account of the basic meaning of the mythologem, but Baldr is nevertheless reborn in another warrior, his own avenger, Váli, the son whom Odin begets for this very purpose and who, merely one night old, brings Baldr's slayer to the stake.

Several elements indicate that Váli represents the initiate who has become a "new man." First of all, his name does not reflect Germanic **wanilo*, 'little Vane,' that is, young vegetation god, as is usually assumed,[69] but rather Old Norse **waihalaR*, 'little warrior.' He is the youth who triumphantly sustained the hardships of the ordeal of initiation of an "Odinic" warrior and has just been accepted into the virile community where he is immediately expected to perform his first task as a warrior, that is, to kill his first enemy. This is explicitly indicated by the "Prophecy of the Seeress," according to which he "neither cleansed his hands nor combed his hair till Baldr's slayer he sent to Hel,"[70] a statement that reminds us of what Tacitus said about the typical "Odinic" warriors, the Chatti: "It has become a general usage among the Chatti that, as soon as they have reached puberty, they let their hair and beard grow and do not cut this facial adornment, vowed and pledged to courage, until they have killed an enemy. They then shave themselves on the bloody corpse and spoils,

---

68 *Germania*, chap. 13: *Ante hoc domus pars videntur, mox rei publicae.*

69 Cf., e.g., de Vries, *Altgermanische Religionsgeschichte* (2d ed.), II, 227; *Altnordisches etymologisches Wörterbuch*, p. 641; Schröder, *PBB(T)* 84:332 (1962).

70 *Vǫluspá*, st. 33 (Hollander, *op. cit.*).

and pretend that only then they have paid back the price of their birth. . . ."[71]

If, then, the Baldr myth is the mythologem of an initiation rite, how was it accomplished? Presumably the initiate stood in the middle of a circle of men; all kinds of weapons were thrown at him. Then "Odin" appeared under the shape of Hödr—the "warrior" par excellence; he cast the mistletoe. As struck by death, the initiate fell on the ground. This was probably enacted very realistically, so that the youth was really considered dead—hence the display of grief! The prior being was another man—reborn but not resurrected.[72]

The Baldr myth appears, accordingly, as a mythologic drama with a rich symbolism, in which the problem of man facing his destiny is solved in the framework of a typically Germanic social structure.

If this reexamination of the Baldr myth warns us to be careful about too hasty and far-reaching comparisons outside the Germanic social framework, other myths, on the contrary, give evidence of the elaboration of inherited Indo-European mythologems, for example, the cosmogonic episode about the creation of man in the "Prophecy of the Seeress," where the participating gods grant man attributes in keeping with their functional position in the Germanic pantheon.[73] Especially interesting in this context is the role of Lódur who endows man with "hair and beautiful complexion," his gifts relating to the physical aspect of man being perfectly in keeping with his probable Vanic origin; his name is, indeed, presumably closely connected with that of the Italic god Līber, who presides over growth and generation

71 *Germania*, chap. 31 (cf. Much, *op. cit.*, pp. 291–292).

72 As de Vries accurately points out (*ANF* 70:56 [1955]): "Die Initiation ist ja ein Durchgang durch den Tod. der zu der Geburt eines neuen, geschlechtsreifen, erwachsenen Mannes führt . . . Der junge Váli stellt also gewissermassen den wiedergeborenen Balder selber dar; fortan lebt er nur seiner Rachepflicht."

Another feature in the Baldr myth which clearly points to initiation practices is Odin's murmuring something into the ear of Baldr before he mounted the pyre (*Vafþrúðnismál*, st. 54–55): this act corresponds to the communication of a secret message, the magic password, that will give the initiate entrance and recognition in his new world. No wonder Vafthrudnir is defeated in the contest of wit by Odin's question about this message: only initiates know its content and, as a rule, they are strictly forbidden, under gravest penalties, to communicate it. Compare as a parallel Schröder, "Balder und der zweite Merseburger Spruch," p. 182: "Es ist zugleich die zentrale Szene des kultischen Spieles: Odin tritt zu Balder, murmelt ihm das geheimnisvolle Wort ins Ohr, das 'beseelende' Wort, bestreicht seine Lippen mit Honig—und Balder erwacht zu neuem Leben."

For further discussion of de Vries's illuminating interpretation of the Baldr myth as an initiation rite, cf. W. Betz, "Die altgermanische Religion," in W. Stammler, ed., *Deutsche Philologie im Aufriss* (Berlin, 1957), III, cols. 2506–2508, 2d ed. (1962), cols. 1592–1593.

73 Polomé, "Some Comments on *Vǫluspá*, Stanzas 17 and 18."

and protects the community. The analysis of such Eddic passages shows that careful reexamination of myth may still open valuable new avenues of research into the survival of Indo-European divine archetypes in Germanic.[74]

[74] Cf. the functional relationship between *Lóðurr* and the Italic Līber, assumed in conclusion, *ibid.*

The "Kingship in Heaven" Theme

C. SCOTT LITTLETON, *Occidental College*

INTRODUCTION

By all odds the most important single episode in Greek mythology is the one that begins with the emergence of Ouranos out of Chaos and ends with the final triumph of Zeus over Kronos and his fellow Titans; for on this account of how Zeus came to succeed to the "Kingship in Heaven" depend, directly or indirectly, almost all other Greek myths, sagas, and folktales, to say nothing of their associated rituals and ceremonies. It formed, in the Malinowskian sense, the "charter"[1] that legitimized the position of the Olympians relative to all other classes of natural and supernatural beings, and in so doing provided a firm foundation for the religious beliefs and practices of the ancient Greek-speaking community.

Yet, despite its fundamental importance to the whole structure of Greek myth and religion, the parenthood of these traditions relative to the "Kingship in Heaven" remains obscure. Through archaeological and linguistic research[2] it has become increasingly apparent that

---

1 According to B. Malinowski (*Magic, Science and Religion* [New York, 1955], p. 101), myth is ". . . a vital ingredient of human civilization; it is not an idle tale, but a hard-worked active force; it is not an intellectual explanation or an artistic imagery, but a pragmatic charter of primitive faith and moral wisdom."

2 The first to recognize the basic similarity between the Hittite-Hurrian and Greek versions of the "Kingship in Heaven" theme seems to have been E. O. Forrer; cf. his "Eine Geschichte des Götterkönigtums aus dem Hatti-Reiche," in *Mélanges Franz Cumont, AIPhO* 4 (Brussels, 1936), pp. 687–713. A second pioneer work in this area is H. G. Güterbock's *Kumarbi, Mythen vom churritischen Kronos, aus den hethitischen Fragmenten zusammengestellt, übersetzt und erklärt* (Istanbul, 1946). The Phoenician version was first put into its proper perspective by

the "Kingship in Heaven" theme,[3] as it has come to be called, was in fact quite widely distributed and that it generally served a legitimizing function similar to that served by it among the Greeks. Its presence can be documented in the Hittite and Hurrian "Kumarbi" myths, in the Phoenician "Theogony" of Philo of Byblos, in the Iranian *Shāhnāmeh* or "Book of Kings," as recorded by Firdausi, and, as I attempt to demonstrate, in two Bablyonian accounts of the Creation—the well-known *Enūma-Elish*[4] and the newly translated "Theogony of Dunnu"—and in the Norse traditions surrounding the ancestry and ascendance of Odin, as recorded in the *Edda*'s of Saemund and Snorri. In each instance a single pattern of events is present: an existing generation of gods was preceded by two (and in some cases three) earlier generations of supernatural beings, each succeeding generation being presided over by a "king in heaven" who has usurped (or at least assumed) the power of his predecessor. Moreover, there is generally a fourth figure, a monster of some sort, who, acting on behalf of the deposed "king" (in the Iranian and Babylonian versions, as we shall see, the monster became identified with the deposed "king" himself), presents a challenge to the final heavenly ruler and must be overcome before the latter can assert full and perpetual authority.

In considering the source of this "Kingship in Heaven" theme, one question necessarily looms large to the student of comparative Indo-European mythology: despite its apparent absence in the Indic, Balto-Slavic, Italic, and Celtic traditions (discussed later) and its occurrence in a variety of non-Indo-European speaking traditions, is there any possibility that the theme is ultimately derived from one that was present in the Indo-European *Urmythologie*? Perhaps the most ardent advocate of the Indo-European origin theory is the eminent Swedish Iranianist Stig Wikander,[5] who maintains that "l'histoire des Ouranides," as he terms it, reached the non-Indo-European peoples of Mesopotamia and Syria only *after* they had come into contact with the Hittites and Indo-Iranians who penetrated

C. Clemen (*Die phönikische Religion nach Philo von Byblos* [Leipzig, 1939]), and the Iranian version was discovered by S. Wikander, "Hethitiska myter hos greker och perser," *VSLÅ* (1951), pp. 35–56.

3 Cf. Güterbock's "Königtum im Himmel"; E. Laroche's "Royauté au Ciel." By *theme* I mean an expression of an idea or set of related ideas rather than a specific type of narrative or tale; cf. S. Thompson's definition of "tale-type:" ". . . a traditional tale that has an independent existence" (*The Folktale* [New York, 1946], p. 415). It should be noted, however, that in perhaps the majority of instances cognate expressions of a given theme will involve similar patterns of events and consequently may reflect a single tale-type.

4 Literally "When-on-High," from the opening words of the poem.

5 *Op. cit.*; "Histoire des Ouranides," *CS* 36 (314):9–17 (1952).

this region after 2000 B.C. This opinion is not shared, however, by most Orientalists. E. A. Speiser,[6] for example, although he suggests that the extant form of the *Enūma-Elish* seems to reflect an immediate Hittite or Hurrian origin, is nevertheless convinced that its roots lie deep in the early Babylonian and Sumerian traditions. A basically similar view has been advanced by the Hittitologist H. G. Güterbock,[7] who asserts that the Hittite version of the theme, from which the Phoenician and eventually the Greek versions appear to derive, is itself based upon Hurrian models, which in turn are probably derived from early Mesopotamian prototypes.

No one, however, has as yet attempted to resolve this question on the basis of a systematic, comparative survey of *all* the mythological materials relative to the "Kingship in Heaven."[8] The purposes of this paper[9] are thus (1) to put into evidence the salient points of similarity and difference between the several versions of the theme in question, among which I include two that heretofore have not generally been recognized as such, the Norse and Babylonian versions, and (2) to consider the question of Indo-European origin in light of the patterns revealed by this survey. I begin with the Greek version which, although it contains neither the oldest[10] nor necessarily the "purest" expression of the theme, is by far the most elaborate, best documented, and most familiar of the versions to be considered and thus can serve as a convenient point of departure.

THE GREEK VERSION

Inasmuch as the Homeric epics do not fully express the "Kingship in Heaven" theme and thus, for our purposes, cannot serve as pri-

---

6 "An Intrusive Hurro-Hittite Myth," *JAOS* 62:98–102(1942).

7 "The Hittite Version of the Hurrian Kumarbi Myths: Oriental Forerunners of Hesiod," *AJA* 42:123–134 (1948).

8 Note should be taken of a doctoral dissertation by Gerd Steiner, *Der Sukzessionmythos in Hesiods 'Theogonie' und ihre orientalischen Parallelen* (University of Hamburg, 1958), as yet unpublished, in which the *Enūma-Elish* is held to be the ultimate source of the theme, although the author does not consider the relevant Norse and Iranian traditions.

9 A shorter version of this paper, "Is the 'Kingship in Heaven' Theme Indo-European?", was delivered at the Third Indo-European Conference, held at the University of Pennsylvania on April 21–23, 1966, under the auspices of the American Council of Learned Societies, the National Science Foundation, and the University of Pennsylvania. It will appear in the proceedings (cf. p. 263, below). I should like to thank Professor Jaan Puhvel for his invaluable advice and encouragement not only as far as the present paper is concerned, but also throughout the entire course of the research upon which it is based. Special thanks are owing as well to Professor H. G. Güterbock of the Oriental Institute of the University of Chicago for his most helpful comments and suggestions.

10 The Hittite-Hurrian version (*ca.* 1400 B.C.) antedates Hesiod by at least 700 years, and the Babylonian versions may well be of much greater antiquity.

mary sources, the earliest and most important Greek source of data concerning the theme under discussion is to be found in the Hesiodic poems, especially the *Theogony*. Composed during the later part of the eighth century B.C.,[11] the *Theogony* is concerned primarily with the events surrounding and preceding the ascension of Zeus as "king" in heaven. It served as the major source of information about cosmogonic and theogonic matters for most Greek (and Roman) poets, essayists, and dramatists. A second source is to be found in the *Bibliotheca* of Apollodorus, which was composed sometime during the first or second centuries B.C.[12] While drawing heavily upon Hesiod, Apollodorus also includes certain data that are at variance with those contained in the *Theogony*, and therefore, as it may reflect an ongoing popular tradition that was either overlooked by or inaccessible to Hesiod, the *Bibliotheca* must be considered a primary source not only for the Greek version of the "Kingship in Heaven" but for Greek mythological data in general. Our third source is the *Dionysiaca* of Nonnos which, despite its fifth century A.D. date,[13] includes some original materials relevant to the theme not found elsewhere among classical works on myth. Nonnos, as we shall see, is especially concerned with the combat between Zeus and Typhon, and his description of this struggle may reflect a popular tradition unknown to either Hesiod or Apollodorus.

According to both the *Theogony* and the *Bibliotheca*[14] the first "king" in heaven is Ouranos ("Heaven" or "Sky"). In the *Theogony*, Heaven is born of Gaia ("Earth"), who is apparently autochthonous, although she is preceded by the nonpersonified state or condition termed Chaos: "Verily at first Chaos came to be, but next wide-bosomed Earth, the ever sure foundation of all. . . ." Earth or Gaia then gives birth to various beings (e.g., Hills; Pontos ["the Deep"]; *Theogony* 130) who are not specifically important to the theme under consideration. Next, she takes Heaven as a husband: "But afterwards she lay with Heaven . . ." (*Theogony* 135). Thus Hesiod defines the first generation.

In the *Bibliotheca*, these events are simplified: "Sky was the first who ruled over the whole world. And having wedded Earth . . ." (1.1.1). There is no hint of the incestuous situation described in the

---

11 Cf. H. G. Evelyn-White, *Hesiod, The Homeric Hymns and Homerica* (London, 1914), p. xxvi.

12 Cf. J. G. Frazer, *Apollodorus: The Library* (London, 1921), p. xvi.

13 Cf. W. H. D. Rouse, *Nonnos: Dionysiaca* (London, 1939), p. vii.

14 The numbers enclosed by parentheses refer to lines in the original texts of the *Theogony*, *Bibliotheca*, and *Dionysiaca*; the translations utilized are those, respectively, of H. G. Evelyn-White, J. G. Frazer, and W. H. D. Rouse.

Theogony. To Apollodorus, both Sky and Earth appear to be autochthonous.

At any event, with the marriage of Ouranos and Gaia we may proceed to the second generation, which includes the offspring of this primal pair, the youngest of whom is destined to become the second "king" in heaven. In the *Theogony* (135) Earth has intercourse with Heaven and brings forth first "Okeanos, Koios and Krios and Hyperion and Iapetos, Theia and Rhea, Themis and Mnemosyne . . . Phoibe and . . . Tethys." After these, she bears the so-called Hundred-handed: Kottos, Briareos, and Gyes, termed by Hesiod "presumptuous children" (*Theogony* 145). Then she bears the Cyclopes ("Orb-eyed"): Brontes, Steropes, and Arges;[15] finally, she bears Kronos.[16]

In the *Bibliotheca* these events are similarly reported (1.1.2–4).

15 Called, respectively, "Thunderer," "Lightener," and "Vivid One" (cf. Evelyn-White, *op. cit.*, p. 89.).

16 The etymology of Kronos (Κρόνος) is obscure (cf. H. Frisk, *Griechisches etymologisches Wörterbuch* [Heidelberg, 1961], II, 24–25; L. R. Farnell, *The Cults of the Greek States* [Oxford, 1896], I, 23). It has been suggested that the name was a variant form of Chronos (Χρόνος or 'Time'), though the shift from initial X to K would be difficult, if not impossible, to support philologically (cf. H. J. Rose, *A Handbook of Greek Mythology* [New York, 1959], p. 69). Another etymology has connected Kronos with κραίνω and has rendered the meaning as 'ripener' or 'completer.' While both Frisk (*op. cit.*) and Rose (*op. cit.*) consider this equally impossible philologically, the fact that Kronos was inevitably equated with Saturnus by most Latin authors (cf. Vergil, Ovid, Plutarch, *et al.*) should not be overlooked. Saturnus appears originally to have been a harvest god, a god who "ripened" or "completed" crops, and the early and consistent equation of this Roman deity with Kronos may well indicate that the latter once served a similar function. Finally, S. Janez ("Kronos und der Walfisch," *Linguistica* 2:54–56 [Supplement of *Slavistična Revija* 9, 1956] has proposed that the name Kronos be equated with Old English *hrān*, 'whale,' which, according to the first Germanic sound shift, would be philologically acceptable. He points out that the Greeks referred to Gibraltar as Κρόνου στῆλαι and compares this to Old English *Hronesnaess* (Beowulf 2805, 3136). Janez suggests that certain "popular superstitions" concerning emasculation of the whale during the sex act may yield a clue to the relationship between Kronos and whales; indeed, in a number of late traditions, especially in the younger Orphic theogonies, Kronos is represented as having been castrated by Zeus (cf. Pauly-Wissowa, *Realencyclopädie der Klassischen Altertumswissenschaft*, vol. 11, p. 2009 [33]: "Zeus den Kronos mit Honig trunken macht und ihn dann im Schlaf fesselt und entmannt"; W. H. Roscher, *Ausführliches Lexicon der griechischen und römischen Mythologie* [Leipzig, 1890], II, 1470–1471). It appears likely, however, that these late traditions were the result of conscious attempts by theologians to harmonize Zeus's overthrow of Kronos with the latter's overthrow of Ouranos, and it seems to me that, if Janez's equation Κρόνος = *hrān* be correct, the mere fact that the whale is an obvious symbol of bigness (cf. the English expression "a whale of a . . .") may explain the relationship more efficiently; perhaps the name Kronos itself is but the survival of an epithet once applied to a being (a harvest god?) whose proper name had disappeared before Homer's time.

Here, Apollodorus introduces the terms "Titan" (male) and "Titanide" (female) to refer to these offspring, terms Hesiod uses at a later point (see below).

Ouranos was jealous of his offspring, especially the Cyclopes and the giant Hundred-handed, and "used to hide them all away in a secret place of Earth . . . [Tartaros] . . . so soon as each was born, and would not suffer them to come up into the light . . ." (*Theogony* 155). Apollodorus (1.1.2–4) gives us a similar picture, locating Tartaros as a "gloomy place in Hades as far from earth as earth is distant from the sky." Here he follows Hesiod, who, in a later context (*Theogony* 725) describes Tartaros as so far below the earth that "a brazen anvil falling from earth nine nights and days would reach Tartaros upon the tenth."

Gaia, incensed over the treatment of her children by Ouranos, exhorts them to " '. . . punish the vile outrage of your father; for he first thought of doing shameful things' " (*Theogony* 165). None but Kronos, however, has the courage to take action (*Theogony* 165), and he tells her: " '. . . I will undertake to do this deed, for I reverence not our father of evil name. . . .' " The deed consists of an emasculation of Ouranos, performed with an "element of grey flint" made into a "jagged sickle" (*Theogony* 170), which Apollodorus (1.1.4) terms an "adamantine sickle."[17] Kronos ambushes his father, cuts off the latter's "members," and casts them into the sea. The blood so spilled impregnates Earth, who gives birth to the Giants (*Theogony* 180) and to the Furies (*Bibliotheca* 1.1.4). The seaborne "members" ultimately reach Cyprus and give birth to Aphrodite.[18]

With the emasculation of Ouranos his power has gone, and Kronos becomes "king in heaven." It is worth noting here for later comparative purposes that Ouranos is *not* killed by Kronos, merely rendered powerless. Kronos is a rebel, but not a parricide.

As regards the nature of this rebellion there seems to be a divergence between the two main sources. Hesiod, as we have seen, gives the impression that it was all accomplished—through guile—by Kronos himself, whereas Apollodorus implies that Kronos was merely the leader of a general attack against the father, one in which all

---

17 Cf. M. P. Nilsson, "The Sickle of Kronos," *ABSA* 46:122–124 (1939). Like Kronos, Saturnus is also associated with a sickle, Greek ἅρπη. This seems to be a proto-Indo-European term found also in Balto-Slavic (Lettish *sirpe*, Russian *serp*) and borrowed into Finno-Ugric (Finnish *sirppi*, 'sickle'). Perhaps the "adamantine" blade used by Kronos against Ouranos was originally a tool associated with an Indo-European harvest god ancestral to both Kronos and Saturnus (cf. n. 16, above).

18 Cf. Rose, *op. cit.*, p. 22.

save one of those siblings not previously consigned to Tartaros took part (*Bibliotheca* 1.1.4): "And they, all but Ocean, attacked him . . . and having dethroned their father, they brought up their brethren who had been hurled down to Tartaros, and committed the sovereignty to Kronos." In any case, after his ascension to power Kronos reconsigns all(?) these siblings to Tartaros (*Bibliotheca* 1.1.5): "But he again bound and shut them up in Tartaros. . . ."

Kronos, now firmly seated on the heavenly throne, marries his sister Rhea (*Theogony* 455; *Bibliotheca* 1.1.5). The children produced by this union suffer an unhappy fate, for Kronos, hearing from Heaven and Earth a prophecy that he is destined to be overthrown by his own son (*Theogony* 410, *Bibliotheca* 1.1.5), swallows his offspring as fast as they are born. Here, too, we have an episode that may be used for later comparative purposes: the swallowing of one's offspring.

The swallowed children include first (*Bibliotheca* 1.1.5) Hestia, "then Demeter and Hera, and after them Pluto (Hades) and Poseidon." Finally, pregnant with Zeus, Rhea decides to foil Kronos. As to the birth of Zeus our sources differ slightly. Both Apollodorus and Hesiod claim that the event took place in Crete; just where in Crete has long been a matter of some debate.[19]

A great deal of attention is given to the events surrounding the birth and upbringing of this youngest of Kronos' sons, an attention directed neither to the births of Zeus's siblings nor to those of the preceding generations of gods (or Titans), and several of these events must be mentioned as they have analogues in the versions to be discussed shortly. After hiding her son in Crete, Rhea gives Kronos (*Theogony* 485) "a great stone wrapped in swaddling clothes. Then he took it in his hands and thrust it down into his belly. . . ." Thus is Kronos deceived by his wife, an event that seems to parallel the duplicity of Gaia in the castration of Ouranos. Apollodorus gives us some information concerning the childhood of Zeus which may also have some comparative value (*Bibliotheca* 1.1.7): "She [Rhea] gave him to the Kouretes and to the nymphs Adrasteia and Ida,[20]

---

19 Frazer (*op. cit.*, p. 6) sums up this controversy rather succinctly: "According to Hesiod, Rhea gave birth to Zeus in Crete, and the infant god was hidden away in a cave of Mount Aegeum (*Theogony* 468–480). Diodorus Siculus (5.70) mentions the legend that Zeus was born at Dicte in Crete, and that the god afterwards founded a city on the site. But according to Diodorus, or his authorities, the child was brought up in a cave on Mount Ida. . . . The wavering of tradition on this point is indicated by Apollodorus who, while he calls the mountain Dicte, names one of the gods Ida."

20 Cf. *ibid.*

daughters of Melisseus, to nurse. So these nymphs fed the child on the milk of Amalthea." This last is apparently either a goat or a cow.[21] We shall have occasion to observe two other cases of this sort, that is, suckling by a goat or a cow, in the Iranian and in the Norse traditions.

Thus, Zeus matures to manhood, being one of the few Greek gods (or Titans) to have a defined childhood.[22] Both Apollodorus (1.2.1) and Hesiod (*Theogony* 490) indicate that this childhood lasted for a fair number of years.

Upon reaching adulthood, Zeus returns to heaven and sets about the overthrow of his father. According to the *Bibliotheca* (1.2.1) he "took Metis, daughter of Ocean, to help him, and she gave Kronos a drug to swallow, which forced him to disgorge first the stone and then the children whom he had swallowed. . . ." In the *Theogony* (495) Zeus is aided by Earth, who, apparently realizing that her son is evil, beguiles Kronos with "deep suggestions" and causes him to vomit up her grandchildren. This time, however, the older generation does not give up without a fight, and there ensues the famous "War of the Titans and Gods," (the latter term now used by both Hesiod and Apollodorus to distinguish the third generation [i.e., that of Zeus, Poseidon, Hera, *et al.*] from the two that preceded it). The war lasts ten years (*Bibliotheca* 1.2.1). On the one side are ranged Kronos and his siblings (save those still bound in Tartaros), and on the other Zeus, his mother,[23] and his siblings. Zeus enlists the aid of the Hundred-handed and the Cyclopes, whom he delivers from their subterranean prison. The latter forge thunderbolts for use against their Titan brethren, and for this they later escape the punishment of Kronos and the rest of the Titans (*Bibliotheca* 1.2.2). It is in this connection that we first see Zeus associated with the sky and with meteorological phenomena, for Zeus's chief weapon is the thunderbolt.

Having defeated the Titans, Zeus now becomes the third and perpetual "king in heaven." As Apollodorus puts it (1.2.2), Zeus "overcame the Titans, shut them up in Tartaros, and appointed the

21 Frazer (*ibid.*, p. 7) claims that "According to Callimachus, Amalthea was a goat. Aratus also reported, if he did not believe, the story that the supreme god had been suckled by a goat (Strabo, viii.7.5, p. 387). . . ."

22 Cf. that of Hermes (*Homeric Hymn* 4.17–19): "At dawn he [Hermes] was born, by noon he was playing on the lyre, and that evening he stole the cattle of Apollo Fardarter. . . ."

23 Although the extent to which Rhea is involved in the conspiracy to dislodge her offspring from Kronos' stomach is unclear, all accounts agree that she sides with Zeus in the ensuing struggle against her husband; cf. W. H. Roscher, "Rhea," in L. Preller, *Griechische Mythologie*, I (Berlin, 1894), 638 f.

Hundred-handed their guards.[24] According to the *Bibliotheca* (1.2.2), the gods cast lots for the sovereignty, and "Zeus was allotted the dominion of the sky, to Poseidon the dominion of the sea, and to Pluto the dominion in Hades." This lot-casting aspect is not included in the *Theogony*; apparently Hesiod merely assumed that Zeus succeeded to the position vacated by his father.

Thus the Olympians, a new breed of supernatural beings, have succeeded to power. But this power is not yet secure; it remains to be confirmed by the conflict between Zeus and a final challenger, the monster Typhon (or Typhoeus).[25]

According to Hesiod, "Typhoeus" is the youngest child of Earth, fathered by a personification of Tartaros at some point following the defeat of the Titans (*Theogony* 820). Apollodorus agrees as to the parentage of the monster, but locates his birth at a somewhat later point, that is, after a successful conclusion of the war of the Olympians against the Giants (offspring of Earth; see above). According to the *Bibliotheca* (1.4.2), "When the gods had overcome the giants, Earth, still more outraged, had intercourse with Tartaros and brought forth Typhon in Cilicia, a hybrid between man and beast." This reference to Cilicia has been used to claim an Oriental origin for the Typhon story; I return to this point shortly when I consider the Phoenician and Hittite traditions.

While there are some minor differences as to details, all three of

---

24 That Kronos and his fellow Titans escaped eternal punishment in Tartaros is reflected in a number of variant traditions, some of them quite early. In his *Works and Days* (169), Hesiod himself claims that Zeus gave Kronos and his fellows "a living and an abode apart from men, and made them dwell at the ends of the earth . . . untouched by sorrow in the islands of the blessed along the shore of deep swirling Ocean, happy heroes for whom the grain-giving earth bears honey and sweet fruit. . . ." Hesiod also claims (*ibid.*) that "Kronos rules over them; for the father of men and gods [i.e., Zeus] released him from his bonds." The idea that Kronos' ultimate fate is to rule over a group of western Elysian islands (i.e., the "islands of the blessed") is reflected in Pindar (*Olymp. Odes*, 2) and later in Plutarch (*De defectu oraculorum* 420), the latter claiming that Kronos, guarded by Briareos, sleeps peacefully on a sacred island near Britain. Vergil (*Aeneid* 8.319, 355–358) asserts that the defeated Titan fled by sea to Latium, where he founded a city, Saturnia, on the future site of Rome, and that the name of the district stems from Kronos' (i.e., Saturnus') hiding (*latere*) in it (cf. Rose, *op. cit.*, p. 45). The association of Kronos with the West, especially Italy, in the minds of later Greek and Roman writers can be seen in the assertion by Dionysius of Halicarnassus (1.36.1) that the Golden Age, which preceded the ascension of Zeus as "king in heaven," was in Italy under Kronos. It should also be noted that the element of escape or banishment resulting in a sea voyage has an interesting counterpart in the Norse version to be considered presently; cf. the fate of the giant Bergelmir.

25 Hesiod renders the monster's name as "Typhoeus"; Apollodorus and Nonnos render it as "Typhon."

our Greek sources agree upon one important aspect of Typhon's (or Typhoeus') physical appearance: snakes grow from his body. As Hesiod puts it (*Theogony* 823), "From his shoulders grew a hundred heads of a snake." This aspect of Typhon's appearance will be especially important when we turn to the Iranian version (cf. below, Firdausi's description of the monster Zohak). Also worthy of note here is Nonnos' description of Typhon advancing to battle (*Dionysiaca* 1.266–268), "There stood Typhon in the fish-giving sea, his feet firm on the weedy bottom, his belly in the air and (his head?) crushed in the clouds," which corresponds almost exactly to a similar description in the Hittite version (see below, the description of the monster Ullikummi before Mount Hazzi).

That Zeus defeats this monstrous challenger is agreed upon by all concerned. But between Hesiod and both Apollodorus and Nonnos there are some important divergences when it comes to the manner and location of this defeat. In the *Theogony* the defeat of Typhoeus is accomplished rapidly and apparently with little effort on Zeus's part; the latter merely "leaped from Olympus and struck him (i.e., Typhoeus), and burned all the marvelous heads of the monster about him." This accomplished, "Typhoeus was hurled down, a maimed wreck . . ."; finally, "in the bitterness of his anger Zeus cast him into wide Tartaros" (*Theogony* 850–869). Apollodorus, however, claims that Zeus uses an "adamantine sickle" to inflict a mortal wound upon Typhon, who flees to "Mount Kasios[26] which overhangs Syria." There, however, Typhon is able to wrest the sickle from Zeus and use it(?) to sever the sinews of the latter's hands and feet.[27] Then Typhon lifts Zeus to his shoulders (his power having briefly returned, apparently owing to Zeus's temporary physical incapacity) and carries him to the famous Corycian cave, again in Cilicia. Hiding the sinews, he leaves the "she-dragon Delphyne" to guard his prisoner. Hermes and Aigipan steal the sinews from their bearskin hiding place and, unobserved by the monster, fit them again to Zeus (*Bibliotheca* 1.3.2). There is also a tradition (Oppian, *Halieutica* 3.15–25) wherein Corycian Pan lures Typhon out of the cave with a

[26] The modern Kel Dag or "Bald Mountain," located just south of the mouth of the Orontes River in what is now Turkey.

[27] Nonnos also mentions the sinew-cutting episode (*Dionysiaca* 1.482–512). Here Kadmos comes to Zeus's aid instead of Hermes. In a note to his translation of the *Dionysiaca* (*op. cit.*, pp. 40–41) Rouse points out that "the story is obscurely told, and probably Nonnos did not understand it; it is obviously old. By some device or by a well-aimed blow, Typhon had evidently cut the sinews out of Zeus's arms, thus disabling him; Cadmos now gets them back by pretending that he wants them for harp strings." In this version there is no mention of a sickle, adamantine or other.

fish meal. In any event, Zeus regains his power. He pursues Typhon across Thrace and finally to Sicily, where he administers the coup de grâce by burying the monster inside Mount Etna (*Bibliotheca* 1.3.3).

It is clear that this final battle between the chief of the Olympians and the last and most monstrous representative of the old order involves more than is usually involved in most mythological monster slayings. Nonnos underscores this: "No herds of cattle were the cause of that struggle, no flocks of sheep, this was no quarrel for a beautiful woman, no fray for a petty town: *heaven itself was the stake in the fight* . . ." (*Dionysiaca* 2.359–363; italics mine). Thus, having defeated Typhon, Zeus has firmly consolidated the position of his revolutionary Olympian regime. Henceforth, he will rule as perpetual and unchallenged "king" in heaven.

Before leaving the Typhon episode, I should perhaps mention in passing that some years ago F. Vian suggested that it presents a number of interesting parallels to the widespread and quite probably Indo-European tradition wherein a hero (or a triad of heroes) slays a three-headed monster that is menacing the peace and security of the community (cf. the Indian account of the conflict between Indra and the tricephalic son of Tvaṣṭar and the Roman legend of a fight between the three Horatii and the three Curiatii).[28] I shall have more to say about this later on in the context of a general discussion of the possibility that the idea of the divine kingship is Indo-European in origin.

The myths concerning the later exploits of Zeus, his brethren, and his offspring, as well as those that concern the affairs of gods and mortals in subsequent generations (e.g., the Oedipus cycle, the siege of Troy) are not specifically germane to the theme in question, and therefore the delineation of the Greek version is concluded at this point. If I have dwelt here overlong, it is only because in the Greek tradition relative to the "Kingship in Heaven" there is a "model," so to speak, which can be utilized in making comparative statements as I consider the evidence from Anatolia, Phoenicia, Iran, Scandinavia, and Mesopotamia.

THE HURRIAN-HITTITE VERSION

Since the first study over thirty years ago[29] of the Hittite "Theogony" and the Hittite myth which H. G. Güterbock[30] has labeled the "Song

[28] F. Vian, "Le mythe de Typhée et le problème de ses origines orientales", *Éléments orientaux dans la religion grecque ancienne* (Paris, 1960), pp. 17–37. For a discussion of the Indo-European character of the tricephalic monster, see G. Dumézil, *Horace et les Curiaces* (Paris, 1942) and elsewhere.

[29] By Forrer, *op. cit.*

[30] "The Hittite Version of the Hurrian Kumarbi Myths," p. 124.

of Ullikummi," there has been a renewed interest in the argument —originally based on the presence of a Phoenician version of the theme under consideration—that the Greek "Kingship in Heaven" tradition just delineated is actually composed of myths having their origin somewhere in the ancient Near East. Indeed, I use the term "Hittite-Hurrian" here because of the indisputable evidence[31] that the Hurrians, who were well established in northern Syria and Mesopotamia by the middle of the second millennium B.C., and whose language appears to have been neither Indo-European nor Semitic, also possessed versions of the myths discussed below.

The texts containing the Hittite and/or Hurrian myths in question date approximately from the thirteenth century B.C. and were translated from a series of cuneiform tablets[32] found at Hattusha, the ancient Hittite capital, the site of which is located near the modern Turkish village of Bogazköy. These tablets are not well preserved and countless interpolations have had to be made in order to arrive at anything like a coherent narrative.[33] That which Güterbock terms the "Theogony"—the Hittite title is unfortunately missing—deals specifically with the "Kingship in Heaven." In it we see four generations of gods. The first is called Alalu, who reigns in heaven nine "years."[34] His future successor, Anu, is described as he who "bows down to his [Alalu's] feet and puts the cups for drinking into his hand" (i.10–11).[35] Although Anu (whose name derives from the Akkadianized form of the Sumerian god An, or 'Sky'[36]) is not specifically identified as Alalu's son, the fact that a god Alala is listed in a Babylonian god list as a father of Anu[37] leaves no doubt as to the filial relationship here. In the ninth "year" of Alalu's reign Anu rebels against him and either drives or hurls him "down to the dark earth" (1.12), the latter expression apparently referring to a subterranean region.[38]

---

31 Primarily in the form of Hurrian god names; cf. *ibid.*, p. 123 and H. G. Güterbock, "Hittite Mythology," in S. N. Kramer, ed., *Mythologies of the Ancient World* (New York, 1961); abbr.: *MAW*.

32 The texts are written in the Indo-European *Nesili* language, which was the official court language of the Hittite kingdom (cf. Güterbock, *MAW*, p. 142), but employ Akkadian cuneiform characters.

33 Güterbock, "The Hittite Version of the Hurrian Kumarbi Myths," p. 124; A. Goetze in J. B. Pritchard, ed., *Ancient Near Eastern Texts Relating to the Old Testament* (Princeton, 1955), p. 121; abbr.: *ANET*.

34 More likely "ages" or "eras" rather than calendar years; cf. Güterbock, "The Hittite Version of the Hurrian Kumarbi Myths," p. 124 n. 11.

35 The numbers enclosed by parentheses refer respectively to columns and lines in the original texts; cf. Güterbock, *Kumarbi*, pp. 6–10, 13–28.

36 Güterbock, *MAW*, p. 160.

37 *Ibid.*

38 Cf. Goetze, *ANET*, p. 120; Güterbock, "The Hittite Version of the Hurrian Kumarbi Myths," p. 134.

Thus, Anu becomes the second "king in heaven." But he, too, must cope with a rebellious offspring, the "mighty Kumarbi."[39] At first, Kumarbi is described as serving Anu in a manner identical to that in which the latter had served Alalu; however, like his father before him, Anu is only permitted to reign for nine "years," and in the ninth "year" Kumarbi rebels. This time the elder god flees, but Kumarbi "took Anu by the feet and pulled him down from heaven" (i.23–24). Then follows a most interesting passage in light of our Greek "model": "He [Kumarbi] bit his loins[40] [so that] his manhood was

---

39 The name Kumarbi is apparently Hurrian; cf. Güterbock, *MAW*, p. 160, who points out that Kumarbi is frequently, although not consistently, equated with the great Sumero-Akkadian god Enlil.

40 The approximate meaning "his loins" or "his thighs" seems to fit the reading *paršnuššuš* which various Hittite scholars, including Güterbock (personal communication, and *MAW*, p. 156), now prefer to the earlier emendational interpretation *genuššuš* "his knees" (cf. E. A. Hahn, *JAOS* 85:298–299 [1965]). In either case there is a euphemistic approximation for "male parts." On the widespread sexual connotations of the knee Professor Jaan Puhvel has contributed the following philological note:

Hittite *genu-* means both 'knee' and (secondarily) '[male] genitals' (sometimes combined in anatomical lists with *arraš* [= Old High German *ars*] 'anus'; cf. J. Friedrich, "Einige hethitische Namen von Körperteilen," *IF* 41:372–376 [1923]). This usage, however, is not a euphemism but has much more basic implications. Without having to delve deep into folkloristic and psychoanalytical records we find that "knee" is often an expression for sexual potency (cf., e.g., J. Laager, *Geburt und Kindheit des Gottes in der griechischen Mythologie* [Winterthur, 1957], p. 136). As random examples we may refer to the passage in the Old Norse *Flóamannasaga* where a man dreams of leeks (a well-known fertility symbol) growing from his knees (cf. W. P. Lehmann, *Germanic Review* 30:166 [1955]), and quote in translation these lines of Hesiod's *Works and Days* about the "dog days" (582–587; imitated in a drinking song of Alcaeus [*Oxford Book of Greek Verse*, p. 170]): "But when the artichoke blooms and the chirping grass-hopper sits in a tree and pours down his shrill song continually from under his wings in the season of wearisome heat, then goats are plumpest and wine sweetest; women are most wanton, but men are feeblest, because Sirius parches head and KNEES."

In various Semitic languages (e.g., Akkadian, Ethiopic) *b r k* (Akkadian *birku*) means both 'knee' and 'penis,' and then more widely 'strength,' 'family,' or 'tribe' (cf. M. Cohen, "Genou, famille, force dans le domaine chamito-sémitique," *Mémorial Henri Basset* [Paris, 1928], I, 203–210, and more generally W. Deonna, "Le genou, siège de force et de vie," *RA* 13:224–235 [1939]). 'Knee' in the sense of 'offspring,' 'family' is commonly found in Indo-European and Finno-Ugric languages: much as Akkadian *tarbit birkiya* means 'nurseling of my *birku*,' we have the synonymous Old Irish *glūn-daltae*, 'knee-nurseling' (cf. J. Loth, "Le mot désignant le genou au sense de génération chez les Celtes, les Germains, les Slaves, les Assyriens," *RC* 40:143–152 [1923]) and the Sogdian *z'nwk' z'tk*, 'knee-son' (see E. Benveniste, *BSL* 27:51–53 [1926]). Similarly Old English *cnéow*, Old Slavonic *kolěno*, and Finnish *polvi*, 'knee,' also mean 'offspring, generation.'

Some have claimed a connection between IE **ĝenu*, 'knee,' and the root **ĝen-* on the basis of ancient evidence for childbearing labor in a kneeling position (e.g., R. Back, "Medizinisch-Sprachliches," *IF* 40:162–167 [1922]; J. Klek, *IF* 44:79–80 [1927]; and S. Simonyi, "Knie und Geburt," *Zeitschrift für vergleichende Sprachforschung* 50:152–154 [1922]). Yet in spite of the Hittite *genzu*, 'lap,' 'female

absorbed in Kumarbi's interior . . ." (i.25); compare Kronos' emasculation of Ouranos. Indeed, the striking correspondences[41] here between Anu and Ouranos and between Kumarbi and Kronos have been noted frequently (see above).

Subsequent to his deposition and emasculation, Anu informs Kumarbi that by "absorbing" his "manhood" he has been impregnated with five "heavy" divinities: the Weather-god (i.e., the Hurrian Teshub),[42] the river goddess Aranzah (i.e., Tigris),[43] Tashmishu,[44] who is destined to be the vizier of the gods, and two others whose names are not mentioned by Anu.[45] Having thus addressed his successor, Anu "went up to heaven" and, after a visit to Nippur, perhaps to consult its chief deity Enlil about his pregnancy, Kumarbi becomes the third to occupy the heavenly throne.

From here on the text is too fragmentary for a consecutive nar-

---

genitals,' metonymically 'love,' the root of Latin *genus, gignō,* Greek γένος, γεννάω means primarily 'beget,' while other words are used for 'bear' (Latin *pariō,* Greek τίκτω). Others have argued that in patriarchal society formal recognition of a newborn child on the father's knee was the true means of legal affiliation or adoption, thus 'birth' in a juridical sense (cf., e.g., Old Norse *knēsetningr,* 'adopted son,' and Homeric and Roman practices, and see Benveniste, *op. cit.,* and M. Cahen, "'Genou', 'adoption', et 'parenté' en germanique," *BSL* 27:56–67 [1926]). In archaic Estonian the phrase *lapse põlvede peale tõstma,* 'lift a child on the knees,' is glossed with 'ein Kind gehörig zur Welt bringen' by F. Wiedemann, *Ehstnisch-deutsches Wörterbuch* (2d ed.; St. Petersburg, 1893), p. 864, and *põlwile sāma,* 'come on knees,' is rendered by 'geboren werden' (*ibid.*). Latin *genuīnus* was similarly connected with *genu,* 'knee,' by A. Meillet (*BSL* 27:54–55 [1926]), and IE **gnē-,* 'know, recognize,' was brought into play, including the vexed question of its possible original affinity with **ĝen-,* 'beget' (cf. γνήσιος 'genuine'). The semantic tangle was further aggravated by R. Meringer ("Spitze, Winkel, Knie im ursprünglichen Denken," *Wörter und Sachen* 11:118–123 [1928]) and H. Güntert (*ibid.,* pp. 124–142, esp. pp. 125–127), who tried to combine both Greek γόνυ, 'knee,' and γένυς, 'chin,' with γωνία, 'angle.'

Even without reference to such inconclusive root etymologies, however, we have unraveled the semantic ramifications of the notion of 'knee' in many languages as comprising 'genitals,' 'potency,' 'offspring,' 'family,' and 'filiation.'

41 Although both Ouranos and Anu are connected with the sky, we refer here of course to functional rather than linguistic correspondences.

42 Although the Hittite reading of the ideogram for weather-god is as yet unknown, it is highly probable that, given this and other contexts (cf. the Ullikummi texts), the Hittite deity in question can be none other than the Hurrian Weather- (or Storm-) god Teshub (cf. Goetze, *ANET,* p. 120; Güterbock, *Kumarbi,* p. 35; *id.,* "The Hittite Version of the Hurrian Kumarbi Myths," p. 124 n. 14; *id., MAW,* p. 158); thus I follow Güterbock and call the Hittite Weather-god by his Hurrian name.

43 Cf. Güterbock, "The Hittite Version of the Hurrian Kumarbi Myths," p. 124 n. 15.

44 *Ibid.,* n. 16.

45 From a reference in column ii it seems that these unmentioned divinities are Marduk (represented by a rare Sumerian name) and one whose name is written with the word sign KA.ZAL, 'lust'; cf. Güterbock, *MAW,* p. 158.

rative. It appears that Kumarbi attempts to avoid bearing these unwelcome offspring by spitting out Anu's seed (end of col. i);[46] nevertheless, a fragmentary reference to Kumarbi's failure to count months and the phrase "the ninth month came" clearly indicate that he carried Teshub *et al.* within him for a full term. Güterbock[47] points out that the theme of the mutilated first part of column ii is childbirth and that two of the gods in Kumarbi's "interior," Marduk and KA.ZAL (see n. 45, above), discuss with him several ways in which they might be born. Especially miraculous is the birth of the Weather-god or Teshub[48] (cf. the attention devoted by our Greek sources to the birth of Zeus,[49] to whom, as we shall see, Teshub corresponds in most respects). Then follows a passage that is especially interesting in view of the equivalence between Kumarbi and Kronos. In it someone (Kumarbi?) says "give me the child . . . I shall eat" (i.42); later there occurs the expression "Kumarbi begins to eat" (i.52), and prominent mention of the words "mouth" and "teeth" in connection with the Weather-god.

It seems that Teshub and his siblings are able to dethrone Kumarbi, for when we first meet the Weather-god he is already "king in heaven." Just how the rebellion is accomplished is not quite clear. Is it possible that Earth, like her Greek counterpart, conspired with her offspring (if indeed they were such) to bring about Kumarbi's downfall? Considering Earth's probable connection with the birth of Teshub and his siblings, this is quite likely; perhaps we have here a merging of Gaia and Rhea in the person of Earth.

The second Hittite myth relevant to the theme in question is entitled the "Song of Ullikummi" and contains many important parallels to the previously discussed Typhon story.[50] Kumarbi, having been dethroned, has intercourse with a rock; from this unnatural union is produced the Stone-monster[51] (also termed the Diorite after

---

46 Apparently Earth becomes pregnant thereby, although the names of the divinities she bears are unclear.

47 *MAW*, pp. 157–158.

48 *Ibid.*, p. 158.

49 Cf. also the birth of Erichthonios: Hephaistos, desiring to wed a reluctant Athena, struggles with her, and in the course of this struggle his seed falls on the ground; Gaia is thus impregnated and in due time gives birth to Erichthonios (cf. Rose, *op. cit.*, p. 110).

50 Text and translation published by Güterbock, *JCS* 5:135–161 (1951), 6:8–42 (1952).

51 There is an interesting counterpart to this in Phrygian mythology; cf. Arnobius, *Adversus Nationes* 5.55, Pausanias 7.17.10–12. Papas, the Phrygian "Zeus," inseminates a rock called Agdos and begets Agdistis, an indolent hermaphrodite monster who, initially at least, is not unlike Ullikummi in some respects. The Phrygian monster, however, is castrated by the gods and thereby

the substance of which the monster is composed), or Ullikummi. Conceived by his father in order to avenge the latter's overthrow, Ullikummi is destined to be a rebel against Teshub.[52] That Typhon was born with a similar purpose in life can be seen from a passage in the *Dionysiaca* (2.565–568) wherein Kronides (an epithet of Zeus), after wounding the monster sorely, chides him saying: "A fine ally has old Kronos found in you, Typhoeus! . . . A jolly champion of Titans!' "

The young Ullikummi is placed on a shoulder of the Atlas-like Upelluri and allowed to grow: "In one day one yard he grew, but in

transformed into the mother-goddess figure Cybele. The blood produced by the castration causes a marvelous pomegranate or almond tree to spring up, and the fruit of this tree impregnates Nana, daughter of the river god Sangarios. Nana gives birth to Attis, who later castrates himself out of love for Cybele.

Agdistis' birth and early resemblance to Ullikummi may possibly indicate a relationship between the two traditions. Save for the castration motif, however, which might conceivably be implied in Ullikummi's loss of power after being cut from Upelluri's shoulder, the rest of the story does not have any clear Hittite parallels.

52 Ullikummi is not the only rebel to oppose Teshub's power; there is also a text (Güterbock, *Kumarbi*, pp. 10–13, Text 1; *MAW*, pp. 161–164) which describes the rebellion of a god known to us only by the highly ambiguous word sign KAL (cf. Güterbock, *MAW*, p. 161, who claims that neither the reading Sumerian LAMA, Akkadian *LAMASSU*, nor the Hittite reading Inara [an Anatolian goddess; cf. the Illuyanka myth, *MAW*, p. 151] fits the context). This text presents some interesting, although not conclusive, parallels to the Greek myths concerning Prometheus and his defiance of Zeus. Unfortunately the KAL text (if indeed it is a separate text) is extremely fragmentary; the tablet is broken in such a way that we possess neither the beginning nor the final colophon that would indicate the name of the text and its exact relationship to the other two texts. Nevertheless, the events described almost certainly follow the ascension of Teshub; whether they precede or follow the Ullikummi affair is, however, much less certain.

Unlike Prometheus, KAL actually seems to have assumed the kingship for a time, for when we first meet him he is described as taking "the reins and [the whip] out of the Storm-God's [i.e., Teshub's] hands" (i.18–19). Like Prometheus, however, and unlike Typhon and/or Ullikummi, KAL eventually submits. Addressing the Weather-god as "my lord," he is subjected to some form of bodily punishment involving mutilation; cf. the fate of Prometheus bound to a rock (or mountain) and continually mutilated by an eagle (*Theogony* 521). There are other aspects of KAL's rebellion which also seem broadly similar to that of Prometheus. In the text, one of the chief objections raised against KAL is that he encourages mortals to be lax in their sacrificial duties: Ea, who apparently had appointed KAL to the kingship, later becomes dissatisfied with his protégé's conduct and claims that " 'just as he [KAL] himself is rebellious, so he has made the countries rebellious, and no one any longer gives bread or drink offerings to the gods' " (iii.18,40); Prometheus, too, is accused of encouraging humans to withhold sacrificed food from the gods (cf. *Theogony* 535). While there seems to be no connection here between KAL and either the creation of mankind or man's knowledge of fire, the Hittite rebel can be seen to occupy a role broadly similar to that of Prometheus: a champion of mortals in their dealings with the gods. Furthermore, KAL's downfall, like that of Prometheus, is apparently the result of a plot hatched by the gods and implemented by the chief god's lieutenant (i.e., Teshub's vizier Ninurta [*MAW*, p. 164]; cf. the role played in Prometheus' punishment by Hephaistos [*Theogony* 520]).

one month one furlong he grew . . . when the fifteenth day came the Stone had grown high. And in the sea on his knees like a blade he stood. Out of the water he stood, the Stone . . . , and the sea up to the place of the belt like a garment reached . . . ; he was lifted, the Stone, and up in Heaven the temples and the chamber he reached" (I.23–32). This can be compared to Nonnos' description of Typhon cited earlier, that is, feet in water and head "crushed" against the clouds.

The first of the gods to see Ullikummi is the Sun-god, who reports his terrified observations to Teshub. The latter goes to see for himself, and when he does so he weeps, for apparently he can see no way of overcoming this monster. His sister, Ishtar (Aranzah?) comforts him and tries to enchant Ullikummi by music (cf. Kadmos' charming of Typhoeus while recovering Zeus's sinews [*Dionysiaca* 1.409–534]). Here, however, we learn that the Stone is deaf and blind. So Teshub decides to fight him, but to no avail, for the monster is too powerful. The gods retreat from this battle, fought in the shadow of Mount Hazzi (i.e., Mount Kasios on the Syrian coast), and retire to Kummiya,[53] the city of Teshub. Ullikummi follows, endangering even Teshub's wife Hebat. At this point Tashmishu enters the picture. After climbing a tower to tell Hebat of her husband's defeat, he suggests to Teshub that they visit Ea,[54] the Babylonian god of wisdom and witchcraft (cf. the *Enūma-Elish,* shortly to be discussed, wherein Ea occupies a prominent position), and together they journey to the wise god's home in Apsuwa (the Babylonian Apsu).[55] Ea, willing to help, first ascertains that Upelluri has no knowledge of what is resting on his shoulder and then orders the "former gods" (i.e., those who ruled in heaven before Alalu, such as Enlil, the Sumerian storm-god) to produce the "ancient tool" (a sickle?) used at one time to separate Earth and Heaven. With this tool Ea cuts Ullikummi from Upelluri's shoulder and thus magically renders him powerless.[56] Here, too, we have a parallel to the Greek tradition, for Apollodorus, as we have seen, described the use of a cutting tool (i.e., the "adamantine sickle") by Zeus in his struggle with Typhon. The same tool, of course, was used against Ouranos by Kronos, and some authorities,

---

53 Apparently located in the mountains of southeast Anatolia; Güterbock suggests (*MAW,* p. 166) that the name Ullikummi itself simply means "Destroyer of Kummiya."

54 Güterbock, "The Hittite Version of the Hurrian Kumarbi Myths," p. 129. In col. iii.19—22 there is the suggestion that Anu wants to make Ea king instead of Teshub; cf. P. Meriggi, "I miti di Kumarpi, il Kronos Currico," *Athenaeum* 31:101–157 (1953).

55 Güterbock, *op. cit.*

56 *Ibid.*

both ancient and modern, have interpreted the castration of Ouranos as a symbolic separation of heaven and earth.[57] It is interesting that the Hittites preserve a tradition of a primeval cutting tool once used to separate heaven and earth, and which must later be used to defeat Ullikummi, although no specific tool is mentioned in the account of Anu's castration. Perhaps in the latter case the teeth of Kumarbi have been substituted for the stone "teeth" of a neolithic sickle (i.e., the "ancient cutting tool").

When word reaches the gods that Ullikummi has been rendered powerless, they join together under the leadership of Teshub and attack the monster. From here on the text is unreadable; however, we may assume with Güterbock[58] that Teshub and his fellows are ultimately victorious. For it appears that here, as in the Greek tradition, the new "king in heaven" must meet this final challenger so as to validate his position as perpetual ruler, and there is no doubt that Teshub, like Zeus, is able to accomplish this validation. It should be noted, though, that the conflict here is much more general than in the Greek tradition. Perhaps in the conflict between Teshub and Ullikummi we have a merger of the Titanomachia and the Typhon fight.

THE PHOENICIAN VERSION

In the *Phoenician History* of Herennios Philo of Byblos, known only through the works of Eusebius (*Praeparatio Evangelica*) and Porphyrius (*De Abstinentia*), is contained a version of the "Kingship in Heaven" which closely parallers the two just discussed, a version that has often been regarded as an intermediary between those of the Hittites and the Greeks. Philo's date is uncertain, although the best evidence leads me to believe that he wrote during the latter half of the first century A.D.; Clemen places his birth in the last years of the reign of the Emperor Claudius.[59] Claiming to have obtained his information from the works of a certain Sanchunjathon, a Phoenician scholar who, he asserts, "lived before the Trojan War," Philo attempts to reconstruct the "history" of his city and to trace the origins of its gods. He begins by outlining a four-generational sequence of "kings in heaven," all of whom are intimately associated with the city of Byblos and its environs.

According to Philo, the first "king in heaven" is named Eliun (or

---

57 W. Staudacher, *Die Trennung von Himmel und Erde* (Tübingen, 1942), pp. 61 f.

58 Güterbock, *op. cit.*, p. 130.

59 Clemen, *op. cit.*, p. 2.

Hypsistos "Highest") (I.14),[60] who with his wife Bruth (i.e., Beirut) comes to live in Byblos. They give birth to a son called Ouranos and a daughter named Ge or Gaia. Ge and Ouranos marry and produce four sons: El (who is also referred to as Kronos), Baitylos, Dagon, and Atlas (I.16). A quarrel ensues between Ouranos and his wife, and El (or Kronos) and his siblings side with their mother. Ouranos then tries to destroy his rebellious offspring, but El, on the advice of Hermes, whom he has taken as a counselor, forges a sickle (or spear?) and with it drives out his father. El then becomes "king in heaven" (or at least in Byblos), but turns out to be a bad ruler, casting out his brother Atlas and murdering a son and a daughter. Meanwhile, Ouranos has fled unharmed. He sends Rhea, Astarte, and Dione, his young daughters, to plead his case before El. These three El takes to wife,[61] and by each he produces a number of children. The most important of these is Baal[62] (or Baaltis), who succeeds him.

Thirty-two years later, El lures his father back to Byblos, into an ambush, and castrates him (cf. *Theog.* 175). Thus, the castration theme is present, although it does not accompany the deposition of the "Heaven figure" as it does in the Greek and Hittite-Hurrian versions. Furthermore, what appears to me to be a crucial element is lacking here: the idea that castration is a necessary step in reducing the power of the Heaven figure. In Philo it seems but an afterthought. Castration figures again in Philo's account, although this time it is self-inflicted. For some obscure reason El mutilates himself thirty-two years after so altering his father.

Finally, the fourth generation (in the person of Baal) takes over the heavenly kingship. This transfer of power is apparently made without much conflict, an occurrence unique in the distribution of the theme. Typhon is mentioned by Philo along with the children of El, but there is no mention of a fight.[63] Moreover, the role of the "Zeus figure" (Baal) is minor when compared with that played by him in the Greek and Hittite-Hurrian versions, and in the Iranian, Norse, and Babylonian versions as well.

---

60 The numbers enclosed by parentheses refer to lines in the original text of the *Phoenician History*; the translation is by Clemen.

61 There is a close parallel to this in the Iranian tradition wherein the "Kronos figure" Zohak marries two of Jamshid's sisters after deposing him. See Wikander, "Hethitiska myter hos greker och perser," p. 52.

62 Cf. the relationship between El and Hadad, the god of thunder and lightning, as delineated in the Ras Shamra texts. The association of Baal and Hadad has long been recognized in the Caananitic tradition; cf. W. F. Albright, *Archaeology and the Religion of Israel* (Baltimore, 1946), pp. 72–74; S. H. Hooke, *Middle Eastern Mythology* (Harmondsworth, 1963), pp. 86–87.

63 Clemen, *op. cit.*, p. 28.

In view of its late date and the high probability that its author was thoroughly familiar with Hesiod, many scholars have been skeptical of this Phoenician "Theogony," labeling it a poor attempt at syncretism. The discovery of some Hurrian texts at Ras Shamra, however, wherein the double name El-Kumarbi occurs,[64] has thrown a new light on the matter. As El is clearly identified by Philo with Kronos, it is reasonable to infer that there was some sort of a Kronos-El-Kumarbi syncretism present in northern Syria, at least, as early as 1400 B.C. If this is correct, then it is also quite reasonable to infer with Güterbock that the Phoenician tradition here forms a link between the Hittite-Hurrian version and the later Greek version, and that what formerly appeared as rank syncretism on Philo's part can now be seen as antedating rather than reflecting the Hesiodic version of the theme.[65]

But there still remain other possibilities. That the Phoenicians undoubtedly received elements of the Kumarbi myth from the Hittites as the latter expanded their empire after 1500 B.C. is not questioned here; indeed, the Ras Shamra evidence renders it almost certain. What is questioned, however, is the assumption that the Phoenicians were necessarily the link in a chain of diffusion from northern Syria to Greece. There is always the possibility that the theme reached Hesiod and/or his immediate sources directly from the Hittite-Hurrian region. This alternative is enhanced somewhat by L. R. Palmer's assertion[66] that the Luvians, first cousins to the Hittites, invaded the Peloponnesus and Crete at the beginning of the second millennium B.C., and that the first speakers of Greek arrived several centuries later. If Palmer is correct in this assertion, and there is good reason to believe that he is, then it is remotely possible that the "Kingship in Heaven" theme was taken over by the Greeks along with other aspects of Luvian culture.[67] Another possibility, that the theme was borrowed directly from Babylonia during Mycenaean times, is discussed presently.

THE IRANIAN VERSION

It was Stig Wikander who, in 1951,[68] first demonstrated the presence of the "Kingship in Heaven"—if indeed the term "heaven" is appli-

---

64 Güterbock, "The Hittite Version of the Hurrian Kumarbi Myths," p. 133.

65 A further argument against interpreting Philo wholly in syncretistic terms is that he preserves a "pre-Ouranos" figure, i.e., Eliun; cf. the position of Alalu in the Hurrian-Hittite version.

66 L. R. Palmer, *Mycenaeans and Minoans* (2d ed.; London, 1965).

67 Palmer (*ibid.*) suggests that the name Parnassos is derived from a Luvian form meaning 'place of the temple' (Luvian *parna-*, 'temple,' plus the suffix *-ass-* denoting appurtenance).

68 "Hethitiska myter hos greker och perser."

cable in this instance—in the Iranian tradition. Bypassing the more ancient and mythological Avestan literature, Wikander pointed out that a threefold set of royal usurpers similar to those present in the Greek, Hittite-Hurrian, and Phoenician traditions occupies a prominent position in Firdausi's *Shāhnāmeh,* which was composed about A.D. 976. Despite its relatively recent date and the high probability that its author was familiar with Greek myth, the *Shāhnāmeh* has long been recognized as a repository of popular traditions not elsewhere represented in Iranian literature. This would certainly appear to be true as far as the theme in question is concerned.

In any event, the three Iranian kings cited by Wikander as comparable with Ouranos, Kronos, Zeus, *et al.*, are Jamshid, Zohak, and Feridun, who occupy, respectively, positions four, five, and six in Firdausi's king list. Jamshid is preceded by three relatively indistinct figures, Kaiumers (equals Gayōmart in the *Avesta*), Husheng, and Tahumers. These three do not seem to be related to their successors in any important sense—Jamshid is made the son of Tahumers, but little else is said about the relationship between them. Thus it is Jamshid who occupies the Ouranos-like position, despite his lack of an autochthonous or truly divine origin.

Jamshid, whose name corresponds to that of Yima Xšaēta[69] in the *Avesta,* is said to have ruled for some seven hundred years, and the early portion of this reign is described as a sort of Golden Age, when men were at peace with one another and the land was bountiful. But this state of affairs did not last. "Then it came about that the heart of Jamshid was uplifted with pride, and he forgot whence came his weal and the source of his blessings."[70] Wikander, in discussing the position of Jamshid, notes that he "règne d'abord sur une humanité heureuse, mais il commet ensuite le premier péché, ce qui amène la perte de la Gloire Royale et sa chute."[71] Wikander also remarks that some texts show Jamshid as having been deceived by "une figure féminine qui aurait inspiré ses transgressions et causé sa chute."[72] Thus, we have some indication that here, too, there is a Gaia-like figure somewhere in the background.[73]

Jamshid is eventually overthrown by Zohak (equals Aži Dahāka in the *Avesta*), who in terms of our model occupies an ambiguous position. He is at once Typhon and Kronos. Both in his physical ap-

---

69 Literally the "first man."

70 Helen Zimmern, *The Epic of Kings* (New York, 1926), p. 4. For a more recent translation, see R. Levy, *The Epic of Kings, Shāh-nāma* (Chicago, 1967).

71 "Histoire des Ouranides," p. 13.

72 *Ibid.*

73 Wikander, "Hethitiska myter hos greker och perser," p. 41.

pearance and in his relationship with the third member of the trio, Feridun, who occupies the position of Zeus figure, Zohak strongly resembles Typhon. Yet he enters the epic occupying the position of a Kronos figure. Like Typhon, his physical appearance is characterized by the presence of snakes growing from his shoulders;[74] yet he is the one who overthrows Jamshid and who commits the inevitable act of mutilation, although in this instance it is not castration but rather a sawing in half.[75]

There are two interesting parallels here to the Phoenician version. Like El, Zohak waits a hundred years before mutilating his deposed enemy: "in the hundredth year [after his overthrow] the impious shah [Jamshid] appeared one day beside the Sea of Chin. Zohak clutched him forthwith, gave him no respite, and, sawing him asunder, freed the world from him and the fear that he inspired."[76] A second parallel can be seen in the fact that Zohak, like El, marries two sisters who stand in close kinship to him—only in this instance they are sisters of the deposed first-generation ruler (Jamshid).

Wikander emphasizes the similarity between the saw that cut Jamshid in half and the sickle that castrated Ouranos. "Azdahak ou un autre ennemi le mutile avec une 'scie' . . . cette 'scie' est évidemment identique à la 'serpe aux dents aigues' d'Hésiode."[77] He also characterizes Zohak as the "neveu" of Jamshid, although nowhere in our reading of the epic is there any clear-cut statement as to the relationship, if any, between the two figures. Zohak is characterized simply as the son of an Arabian king[78] who is invited to come to Iran and replace Jamshid.

Zohak, in his turn, is overthrown by the grandson of Jamshid, Feridun (equals Thraētaona in the *Avesta*), who, like Zeus, has a marvelous childhood. Again we see the theme of the mother hiding away the child from the wrath of the father (in this case Zohak). Zohak, it seems, while having no offspring of his own, has an insatiable desire to consume human beings. Furthermore, the serpent-king dreams that Feridun will someday overcome him (cf. Kronos' foreknowledge of Zeus's coming, and his subsequent swallowing of his offspring), and on the basis of this dream "bade the world be scoured

---

74 Cf. J. Atkinson. *The Shá Námeh of the Persian Poet Firdausi* (London, 1832), p. 34.

75 Atkinson (*ibid.*) asserts that Jamshid was laid between two planks and sawed lengthwise; see also A. Warner and E. Warner, *The Shāhnāma of Firdausi* (London, 1905), p. 140.

76 *Ibid.*

77 Wikander, "Histoire des Ouranides," p. 13.

78 Warner and Warner, *op. cit.*, p. 142; cf. Wikander, "Histoire des Ouranides," p. 7, Levy, *op. cit.*, p. xvii.

for Feridun."[79] Feridun's mother first places him in the care of a wondrous cow, Purmaieh, who suckles the infant. Then, fearing that Zohak will find this hiding place, she removes him to the care of a shepherd "on the Mount Alberz" (i.e., the Elbruz?), who raises him to manhood. Here we can compare the hiding away of Zeus on Mount Ida (or Aigaion). Finally, Feridun grows to manhood and sets out to overcome his monstrous enemy. Instead of a cutting instrument, Feridun uses a club, the head of which is shaped like a cow—in memory of Purmaieh.[80] The combat between Feridun and Zohak is strongly reminiscent of the conflict between Zeus and Typhon. Again, it is a single-combat situation, not the type of group action which dethroned Kronos.

Feridun overpowers Zohak but does not actually kill him (a fusion, perhaps, of the Typhon and Kronos motifs); rather, he chains the monster to a rock[81] on Mount Demawend(?), and Zohak eventually dies of exposure. After this deed is accomplished, Feridun reigns as king, if not actually "in heaven," then certainly as a divine king in Iran.

While it is certain that the Avestan names Yima Xšaēta, Aži Dahāka, and Thraētaona correspond, respectively, to Jamshid, Zohak, and Feridun, the only clear thematic parallels between the two sets of figures are that both Yima and Jamshid can be seen to be in one respect or another primordial (although both do actually have forebears), that both were "Golden Age" rulers who "sinned," that Aži Dahāka and his later namesake share draconic characteristics, and that both are rendered harmless, respectively, by Thraētaona and Feridun. Even in the latter instance there is an important difference. Thraētaona is characterized as the "smiter" of Aži Dahāka,[82] while Feridun, as we have seen, imprisons Zohak. Thus it can be safely asserted that the theme qua theme, despite some similarities, is not present in the *Avesta*.

Nor is it to be found in the Indic tradition. To be sure, there are some very general parallels, both thematic and philological, between the Avestan figures mentioned above and some of the dramatis personae of the Indic literature. For example, Avestan Yima parallels Vedic Yama; Aži Dahāka is equivalent to the three-headed monster

---

79 Zimmern, *op. cit.*, p. 8.

80 *Ibid.*, p. 12.

81 Or imprisons him in a cave; cf. Wikander, "Hethitiska myter hos greker och perser," p. 47.

82 Warner and Warner, *op. cit.*, p. 171; the Warners suggest (p. 174) that Feridun is actually a coalescence of two Avestan figures, Thraētaona and Thrita (cf. *Yasna* 9.21–30).

Vṛtra; Thraētaona bears a resemblance to Trita Āptya, the slayer of Vṛtra (also to Indra in this context); and the cow-headed weapon (*gurz*) used by Feridun is linguistically cognate to the thunderbolt *vajra* used in the slaying of Vṛtra. But other than these isolated correspondences, together with one other possibility to be mentioned shortly in connection with the Norse version, there is no evidence for the presence of the theme in question in the *Veda*'s, *Mahābhārata*, and so on.[83] This negative evidence, so to speak, is a most important matter when it comes to the question of possible Indo-European origins, and I return to it later on.

THE NORSE VERSION

All too often there is a tendency among students of comparative mythology to equate "Norse" with "Germanic," to assume that the materials contained in the *Edda*'s, *Heimskringla*, *Gesta Danorum*, and the like, are a true reflection of common Germanic religious beliefs and practices. To make such an equation is, of course, an error; for it is abundantly clear that there were differences in religious outlook among the several branches of the Germanic-speaking peoples. One need only compare Tacitus with Saxo Grammaticus to see examples of these differences. While there are some common figures (e.g., *Tīwaz, probable prototype of Norse Týr, Anglo-Saxon Tiw, and perhaps the figure reflected in Tacitus' Tuisto),[84] any attempt to draw general conclusions about the nature of Germanic religion from any one region or era must be made cautiously.

Yet, when it comes to cosmogonic and theogonic matters we are necessarily limited to a single region and a single era: Scandinavia (primarily Iceland) in the eleventh and twelfth centuries A.D. Moreover, our chief sources,[85] the *Elder* or *Poetic Edda*, attributed to Saemund Siggfusson, and especially the *Younger*, or *Prose Edda* of Snorri Sturluson, were composed at a time when the old religion was fast giving way to Christianity (Snorri approaches his subject from an explicitly Christian standpoint), and the extent to which

---

83 For a discussion of the possible Vedic parallels here, see Wikander, "Hethitiska myter hos greker och perser," esp. p. 46.

84 Tuisto can be interpreted as meaning 'Twin'; cf. Ymir, possibly cognate with Yama, and Tacitus' Mannus, whom he combines with Tuisto and who belongs etymologically with Manu; for a discussion of Tuisto and Mannus see H. R. Ellis Davidson, *Gods and Myths of Northern Europe* (Harmondsworth, 1964), pp. 54–61, 196–199; E. O. G. Turville-Petre, *Myth and Religion of the North* (London, 1964), esp. p. 7.

85 The translations utilized are by Lee M. Hollander, *The Poetic Edda* (Austin, 1928), and Jean Young, *The Prose Edda* (Cambridge, 1954).

non-Norse materials were interwoven with the native tradition is still not wholly clear.

That Saemund and Snorri were aware—albeit dimly—of the mythic traditions of the eastern Mediterranean is entirely possible.[86] It is also possible that whatever parallels may exist between their accounts of the creation and those previously discussed in this paper are wholly or partially the result of independent invention. In any case, all the foregoing must be kept firmly in mind as we proceed to a brief examination of the Norse theogony to see if it contains materials relevant to the "Kingship in Heaven."

In the beginning was Ginnungagap (equivalent to the Greek Chaos), which can be loosely translated as "yawning void." Out of this yawning void were created initially two regions: Muspellheim on the south (i.e., a "Land of Fire") and Niflheim on the north (i.e., a "Land of Mist"). Ice crystals combined with sparks, and out of this combination there was created the first being, called Ymir. Ymir, defined as a giant of enormous proportions, lies down and sleeps. While he sleeps two things happen: first, a second autochthonous creature appears, a cow named Audhumla. While Ymir sleeps the cow nourishes him, at the same time she licks the salty ice and slowly uncovers first the hair, then the body of a third autochthon: Buri. Thus Audhumla serves as a link between these two generationally equivalent Jöntin, or "Giants" (occasionally rendered Etin). Meanwhile, in his sleep, Ymir androgynously gives birth to several offspring (*Lay of Vafthrudnir* 33): "The ice-*etin*'s [i.e., Ymir's] strong arms, beneath there grew both girl and boy, one with the other, the wise *etin*'s shanks begat a six-headed son." The latter is named Thrudgelmir. He, in turn, gives birth to the crafty Bergelmir. Thus, we have one three-generation line of descent from Ymir. As the *Lay of Vafthrudnir* (29) has it: "Ages before the earth was made, Bergelmir came to be. Thrudgelmir was that *thur*'s(?) father. But Aurgelmir [i.e., Örgelmir, or Ymir] oldest of all."

A second three-generational line descends from Buri, who, after emerging from the ice, produces a son: Bör. Bör marries a giantess named Bestla (one of Ymir's offspring?). They, in turn, produce three sons: Odin, Vili, and Vé (cf. Zeus, Poseidon, Hades). Odin and his siblings (who, unlike their Greek equivalents, become shadowy figures very quickly) are the first of the Aesir (or "Gods" as opposed to "Giants"). Their first act is to overthrow Ymir, and with him Thrud-

---

86 For a discussion of the extent to which Snorri, to say nothing of Saxo Grammaticus, was influenced by the *Aeneid*, see my paper "A Two-Dimensional Scheme for the Classification of Narratives," *JAF* 78:21–27, esp. pp. 24–25.

gelmir. Bergelmir they banish (or he escapes) to subterranean Jöntinheim (cf. Tartaros?).[87] Ymir they cut up (the tool involved is not mentioned), forming the world: "of Ymir's flesh the earth was shaped, of his blood the briny sea, of his hair, the trees, the hills of his bones, out of his skull the sky" (*Lay of Grimnir* 40).

There is a parallel to this in *Rig-Veda* 10.90, wherein Indra and others create the world from the flesh and bones of the giant Puruṣa. Another parallel can be seen in the Babylonian *Enūma-Elish,* in the use to which Marduk puts the body of the slain Tiamat. The similarities here, however, may best be explained in terms of a common folkloristic motif which has nothing specifically to do with the theme under discussion. Yet the fact that Odin and his siblings *cut* the primeval figure is significant. It is this feature, rather than the subsequent use of his remains, that is relevant for our purposes.

In any event, it is only after the Jöntin have been defeated that Odin and his brothers create mankind.[88] This, of course, is paralleled in the Greek version (i.e., the human race is only created after the final defeat of the Titans; cf. *Bibliotheca* 1.4.1).

It is our contention that the events just described contain all the essential ingredients of the "Kingship in Heaven" theme: First, there is a three-generational line of descent (although bifurcated); second, there is the mutilation of the first-generation "king" (i.e., Odin's cutting up Ymir); third, there is the banishment of a descendant of this first-generation being by one who has usurped power from him (Bergelmir is the logical inheritor of Ymir); fourth, the final and perpetual holder of power (Odin) is, together with his siblings and offspring, defined as an altogether different sort of supernatural being (i.e., "Gods" or Aesir, as opposed to "Giants" or Jöntin; cf. the Greek distinction between "God" and "Titan"). And finally, there is a battle between these Aesir and the Giants, a battle that seems to be

---

[87] In the *Gylfaginning* Snorri describes Bergelmir's flight as occurring in the context of a universal flood created from the blood that gushed from Ymir after his demise. As this is the only clear reference to a flood in Norse myth, it seems reasonable to infer that Snorri, as a Christian, felt the need of it. This is underscored by the etymology of the word *luðr,* used by him to refer to the "boat" in which Bergelmir and his wife survive the deluge. Although Snorri clearly uses the word in the context of "boat," earlier usages of the term (cf. *Lay of Vafthrudnir* 35) would seem to indicate that it meant 'coffin' or 'bier.' See E. O. G. Turville-Petre, "Prof. Dumézil and the Literature of Iceland," *Hommages à Georges Dumézil* (Brussels, 1960), pp. 211–212; see also H. Petersson, "Aisl. *luðr* 'Trog usw,'" *IF* 24:267–269 (1909), who asserts that the basic meaning here is 'hollowed tree trunk' and proposes a derivation from Indo-European **lu-tró-* (cf. Skt. *lunā̂ti,* 'cut, clip').

[88] I.e., *askr,* 'ash,' and *embla,* 'elm,' respectively, the first man and woman.

equivalent to that between the Olympians and the Titans[89] (or Giants, too, for that matter).

That the characteristic structure of the theme, as expressed in the Greek and Hittite-Hurrian tradition, is absent, must be admitted. Contained within a broad three-generational framework, however, most of the significant components of this structure are present. To put it another way, the same broad configuration is present in Norse mythology, yet the elements within this configuration are not for the most part structured as they are in the Greek tradition. Indeed, we have seen other cases, generally held to be part of the theme in question, which also deviate from this typological structure, yet which maintain the same broad configuration. We may cite here the Iranian version, wherein Zohak, who most clearly resembles Typhon, appears in the role of a Kronos figure. We may also cite the Phoenician case, wherein Baal does not have to fight his way to power, as is characteristic of the other versions—including the Norse.

It seems fair to assert that the Norse, like the Greeks, Hittites, Hurrians, Phoenicians, Iranians, and Babylonians, knew the "Kingship in Heaven" theme. Whether its presence here can best be explained in terms of diffusion or independent invention is still a moot point, although I believe that the former possibility is the more probable in view of the extremely late periods from which the primary sources date. There is, of course, the alternate possibility that the presence of the theme can be explained in terms of a common Indo-European heritage. Once again, let me defer consideration of this possibility—seemingly quite remote—until I look at the Babylonian versions.

THE BABYLONIAN VERSIONS

Like the Norse version, the two Babylonian versions deviate in a number of important respects from that which for convenience sake I have labeled the typological version (i.e., that of the Greeks). Yet these two related accounts of how the gods came to be may well prove to be far closer to the source of the theme in question than any previously considered. Although no extant text of the *Enūma-Elish* is earlier than 1000 B.C., internal evidence alone indicates that its composition probably dates at least from the Old Babylonian period,

89 I am not the first to make such an observation. Well over a century ago Jakob Grimm, in his *Teutonic Mythology* (translated from the German by J. S. Stallybrass [London, 1883], II, 275), had occasion to observe that "As the Edda has a Buri and Börr before Odinn, so do Uranus and Kronus here come before Zeus; with Zeus and Odinn begins the race of gods proper, and Poseidon and Hades complete the fraternal trio, like Vili and Vé. The enmity of gods and titans is therefore that of ases [Aesir] and giants . . . ."

that is, the early part of the second millennium B.C., and that its content may be considerably older.[90]

The *Enūma-Elish* begins with an account of the primeval state of things: "When on high the heaven had not been named,/Firm ground below had not been called by name,/Naught but primeval Apsu,[91] their begetter,/(And) Mummu-Tiamat,[92] she who bore them all,/Their waters commingling as a single body . . ." (i.1–4).[93] We see here the by now familiar pair of autochthons, in this instance defined as fresh and salt water. From this union several generations of divinities are born, including the figures (for our purposes obscure) Lahmu and Lahamu, Anshar and Kishar, and Anu. Finally, there appears the figure who, together with another shortly to be discussed, occupies the Kronos position, the "all-wise" Ea (or Nudimmud; cf. Sumerian Enki). Although the exact parentage and birth order of Ea are obscure, by all indications he is the youngest of the lot (who can, for our purposes, be reckoned as a single generation; that is, they band together and act as a generational unit).[94] If this interpretation is correct, then there is an interesting parallel here to the ultimogeniture pattern so clearly evident in the Greek version.

Under the apparent leadership of Ea, the gods of what we may term the second generation (see above) "disturbed Tiamat as they surged back and forth" (i.22). Apsu, too, is annoyed by "their hilarity in the Abode of Heaven" (i.24) and decides to do away with them. His decision is strengthened by the advice of the vizier Mummu,[95] but is opposed by Tiamat, who counsels forgiveness. Nevertheless, the gods discover Apsu's intentions. After putting Apsu to sleep with an incantation (cf. the "deep suggestions" with which Zeus beguiles Kronos[96]), Ea slays him, yet before doing so he tears off the

[90] E. A. Speiser, "Akkadian Myths and Epics," *ANET*, p. 60. It should be noted, however, that P. Walcot (*Hesiod and the Near East* [Cardiff, 1966], p. 33), suggests that the rise of Marduk to supremacy among the gods of Mesopotamia was quite late and that the *Enūma-Elish* as we know it was most likely composed around 1100 B.C. He thus concludes that "In terms of chronology, Enuma Elish now seems to stand between the Hattusas tablets and the Theogony. . . ." Nevertheless, this would not preclude earlier Babylonian and/or Sumerian prototypes wherein some other god played the part of Marduk.

[91] Sumerian Abzu; see S. N. Kramer, "Mythology of Sumer and Akkad," *MAW*, p. 120.

[92] I.e., "Mother" Tiamat; see Speiser, *op. cit.*, p. 61.

[93] The translation of the *Enūma-Elish* utilized here is that of Speiser, *ANET*, pp. 61–72.

[94] Cf. i.52, wherein Apsu plots "against the gods, his sons"; i.56, wherein Apsu's intentions are made known "unto the gods, their first-born."

[95] Not to be confused with the epithet of Tiamat; cf. i.4 and n. 92, above.

[96] See Walcot, *op. cit.*, p. 34.

former's tiara or halo (symbolic, perhaps, of sovereignty and the masculine vigor that accompanies it) and puts it on himself (i.60–69). Admittedly, I may be guilty of overinterpretation here, but it does occur to me that the act of tearing off Apsu's tiara is comparable with an act of castration. By so doing, Ea clearly renders his forbear powerless to resist, just as Kronos, Kumarbi, *et al.* render their progenitors powerless by dismembering or "biting" them. In any event, thus passes the first generation.

After having become "king in heaven" Ea[97] takes up residence upon the dead Apsu[98] and is joined by his wife Damkina. In time Damkina gives birth to the great Babylonian divinity Marduk, who is patently the Zeus figure in this version. Many lines follow describing Marduk's brilliance and prowess, for example, "He was the loftiest of the gods, surpassing was his stature,/His members were enormous, he was exceeding tall" (i.97–100). Meanwhile, Tiamat schemes in order to seek revenge for the slaying of her husband. She causes a heretofore unmentioned god, Ea's half-brother, Kingu, to be elevated to command of the Assembly of the Gods, apparently, though the text makes no mention of it, displacing Ea. She then sets about creating a host of monsters (cf. i.126). From this point on Ea fades into obscurity, and the threat presented by Tiamat and Kingu is met by Marduk. A great fight ensues. Marduk eventually slays Tiamat in single combat and destroys her host. He then captures the rebel Kingu and consigns him to Uggae, the god of the dead (iv.119–120). Afterward, Marduk and Ea create heaven and earth from Tiamat's inflated body by splitting it in two[99] (cf. the fate of Ymir). Marduk now reigns perpetually as "king in heaven."[100] He has validated his claim to sovereignty by emerging victorious in the epic duel with Tiamat.

Taken as a whole, the *Enūma-Elish* presents some remarkable parallels to the other versions of the "Kingship in Heaven," although

---

97 M. L. West, in the "Prolegomena" to *Hesiod: Theogony* (Oxford, 1966), p. 23, asserts that Ea's elder sibling (or grandfather) Anshar assumes the kingship. Nowhere in the text is this clearly evident. The only passage that may possibly reflect such a royal status is iii.1 ff., wherein Anshar sends a message to Lahmu and Lahamu via "Gaga, his *vizir*" (italics mine). Otherwise, Anshar appears as but one of the siblings (or forebears) of Ea who plays a prominent albeit essentially supporting role in the deposition of Apsu and the subsequent conflict with Tiamat.

98 There is some confusion here. Kramer suggests (*MAW*, p. 121) that Ea actually takes up residence upon Apsu's corpse. The text itself would seem to indicate that Ea names his place of residence (i.e., the location of his "cult hut"; cf. i.77) *after* his deceased parent.

99 Cf. Kramer, *MAW*, p. 121.

100 "He took from him [i.e., Kingu] the Tablets of Fate, not rightfully his, sealed [them] with a seal and fastened [them] on his breast" (iv.121–122).

there are, of course, several important structural differences. For one thing, there is a bifurcation of the Kronos figure. Taken together, the careers of Ea *and* Kingu approximate closely that of the typical second generation "king": initially, in the person of Ea, we see him usurping the kingship through a ruse and (perhaps) performing an act of emasculation; later on, in the person of Kingu, we see him defeated by the Zeus figure and consigned to what would appear to be a Tartaros-like place. In the case of Tiamat we have not bifurcation but fusion. She is at once Gaia and Typhon (cf. Zohak, who is both Kronos and Typhon). It is in the latter role, however, that she appears most clearly, and the fight between her and Marduk is strikingly similar to that between Zeus and Typhon, Teshub and Ullikummi, and so on. The relationship between Tiamat and Kingu is, of course, the opposite of that between Kronos and Typhon or Kumarbi and Ullikummi: in the Babylonian account the "king" is a creature of the monster. Yet on balance it seems clear that the theogony contained in the *Enūma-Elish* is akin to those we have previously surveyed. And given its date, it is probably their prototype.

Until recently, the *Enūma-Elish* was the only known Babylonian creation myth that came anywhere near to approximating the idea of the divine kingship. In 1965, however, W. G. Lambert published (with A. R. Millard) and subsequently translated[101] a cuneiform text (BM 74329) which may be termed for convenience' sake the "Theogony of Dunnu."[102] In it we can see essentially the same course of events as described in the *Enūma-Elish,* although the locale and figures involved are for the most part quite distinct. The date of this new text is late. Lambert and Walcot assign it to the Late Babylonian period (i.e., between 635 and 330 B.C.), altough it is suggested that it belongs to the earlier phase of this period and that, as in the case of the *Enūma-Elish,* it may contain materials originally composed perhaps as early as the beginning of the second millennium B.C.[103]

Here the action centers on the ancient city of Dunnu, an otherwise obscure place as far as the overall Babylonian tradition is concerned.[104] The text itself is far shorter and more literary than the one

---

101 W. G. Lambert and P. Walcot, "A New Babylonian Theogony and Hesiod," *Kadmos* 4:64–72 (1965). It should be pointed out that Walcot is responsible for the appended "classical commentary" (pp. 68–72); the translation and accompanying commentary are by Lambert.

102 I should emphasize that this is my term, not that of Lambert and Walcot.

103 Lambert and Walcot, *op. cit.*, p. 64.

104 *Ibid.*, pp. 67–68.

just discussed. In this instance the two autochthons are the figures Hain (unknown outside this text)[105] and Earth. Although the first three lines are incomplete, it appears that they give birth first to Sea (cf. Tiamat) by means of a plow, and then in an apparently more normal fashion to the male figure Amakandu (once again we encounter the ultimogeniture pattern). Amakandu is seduced by his mother: "[Earth] cast her eyes on Amakandu, her son, / 'Come, let me make love to you' she said to him" (lines 8–9). After marrying his mother, Amakandu slays Hain and lays him to rest in the city of Dunnu, "which he loved" (line 12). He then assumes his father's overlordship of the city (line 13). Subsequently, Amakandu marries Sea (his sister: cf. Kronos and Rhea), who gives birth to a son called Lahar. Lahar in turn slays his father, marries his mother (i.e., Sea), and assumes the kingship. He, too, produces offspring: a daughter, River, and a son, whose first name is unreadable. The latter eventually kills both Lahar and Sea (his mother), marries River (his sister), and assumes power. At this point the text is somewhat obliterated, but the pattern seems to be carried out for at least two more generations. Sons slay their fathers and mothers, marry their sisters, and usurp the sovereignty. The female figures here whose names are readable include Ga'um and Ningeshtinna. There is no clear termination to the text, which is contained on the obverse and reverse of a single tablet, although the last readable line (40) indicates that the seat of power has been transferred to the city of Shupat [or Kupat].

In this "Theogony of Dunnu" can be seen in abbreviated and somewhat redundant form the essential outlines of the theme. The fact that there are five generations rather than three is not a crucial deterrent to putting the text into comparison with the other versions. It will be recalled that both the Hittite-Hurrian version and that of the Phoenicians, to say nothing of the version contained in the *Shāhnāmeh*, all describe one or more generations as existing prior to those upon whom attention is centered. In the present case the replication follows rather than precedes the principal sequence of events. To be sure, there is a major structural problem here in that in all other versions surveyed, including the *Enūma-Elish*, there is a denouement. One figure, be he Zeus, Teshub, Baal, Feridun, Odin, or Marduk, puts a seal on the succession. In the "Theogony of Dunnu," however, Lahar is in turn overthrown, and the series of usurpations is seemingly without end. Nor do we see here any indication of emas-

[105] Lambert and Walcot suggest that the two signs *ḫa-in* may have been miscopied from the one large sign used to write the name of the corn goddess Nisaba (*ibid.*, pp. 66–67).

culation, although Lambert and Walcot, in comparing the text with Hesiod, suggest, perhaps leaning a bit too heavily upon Freud, that mother lust is equivalent to castration.[106] On this point I suggest that the very brevity and laconic nature of the text perhaps precluded the elaboration of such details as how the sovereignty was transferred (e.g., via emasculation or the "tearing off" of a tiara).

One interesting point of comparison between the Dunnu text and Hesiod's *Theogony* relates to the order in which Sea and River appear. According to Hesiod, the two figures associated with the sea, Pontos and Okeanos, emerge in succeeding generations. Pontos is essentially an autochthon, having emerged from Gaia without benefit of sexual intercourse, while Okeanos is born of Ouranos and Gaia. There is no doubt that Pontos is the sea proper, but Okeanos is more specifically defined as the 'father of rivers," the river that circles the earth (cf. *Theogony* 695–696). This order is paralleled in the "Theogony of Dunnu"; Sea is an autochthon, whereas River belongs to the third generation.[107] Lambert and Walcot also point out that there is a parallel to Hesiod in the marital relationships that obtain. The Titans regularly contract sibling marriages (cf. Kronos and Rhea), "but it is only Ouranos and Pontos who practice incest to the extent of mating with their own mother. . . ."[108] Again, in the "Theogony of Dunnu" both Sea and Earth are involved in such marriages, and matings between siblings abound.

These, then, are the Babylonian versions. So far no Sumerian counterpart has come to light, although several important Sumerian divinities are present in the texts just discussed, for example, Enki (Ea) and Anu. I do not mean to suggest that the Greek and other non-Babylonian versions of the "Kingship in Heaven" theme are necessarily based specifically upon the *Enūma-Elish* or the "Theogony of Dunnu." Rather, in one way or another all the previously discussed theogonies[109] may be based upon the immediate sources of these two Babylonian texts, sources that themselves would appear to have been Babylonian and perhaps even Sumerian. This suggestion is strengthened in that we now have two distinct versions of the theme, each dating from the early second millennium B.C., from two distinct centers of Babylonian culture, that is, Babylon proper and Dunnu.

---

106 *Ibid.*, p. 72.

107 *Ibid.*, pp. 66, 71.

108 *Ibid.*, p. 72.

109 The Norse version may be only indirectly derived from that which took shape in Babylonia some four thousand years ago; its immediate roots probably lie in the version best known to the Greco-Roman world, i.e., that of Hesiod *et al.*

The fact that one of these was a minor center adds even more strength.

CONCLUSIONS

Most of the principal points of comparison among the several versions which have been noted are summed up in the table on the facing page. The question that remains is whether or not the "Kingship in Heaven" theme is Indo-European.

Wikander's assumption that the theme is part of the Indo-European mythological inheritance is based principally upon the concordances among the Greek, Hittite, and Iranian versions. These concordances are in fact present, and there is no doubt that the three versions are part of a single tradition. But the fact that these three Indo-European-speaking communities share a common theogonic theme does not in itself mean that such a theme is part of their common mythological inheritance. By the same token, it can be said that a fair number of Indo-European speaking communities today share a common belief in how the world was created: by a God whose principal attributes are omnipotence and an intense jealously of all other pretenders to divine status. There is, of course, no doubt whatsoever that this idea was borrowed from the Judaic tradition. We have a clear record of when and where the borrowing occurred. But suppose that we did not have such a record; suppose that a Martian scholar eons hence were to be confronted with this common tradition—present, albeit, among many non-Indo-European speakers as well. Would he not be tempted to view the relationships from a genetic standpoint? Would he not be tempted to reconstruct a common Indo-European cosmogony involving "the hand of God moving across the waters," and so on?

I suggest that those who argue for an Indo-European origin as far as the divine kingship is concerned have most likely fallen into the same trap as our hypothetical Martian. The problem here is that, unlike the spread of the Judaic cosmogony, the spread of the idea of divine kingship cannot be documented. There is no clear record of events to mark its spread from ancient Babylonia to Anatolia, Phoenicia, Iran, Greece, and ultimately, perhaps, to Scandinavia. There is nothing here comparable with the conversion of Clovis or the ministry of St. Patrick. Yet spread it did, from one religious system to another, the initial impetus being perhaps the prestige of the Babylonian tradition. By the time the theme reached Scandinavia (if indeed it did not evolve there independently), the Babylonian roots had long since become obscure, and the prestige would have been

COMPARISON OF FIGURES IN

VERSION	FIRST GENERATION FIGURE	SECOND GENERATION FIGURE
Greek	*Ouranos**: autochthon; marries Earth (Gaia); sires	*Kronos*: castrates *Ouranos* with sickle and exiles him; swallows offspring; marries sister (Rhea); sires
Hurrian-Hittite	*Anu*: son of Alalu; deposes father; sires	*Kumarbi*: castrates *Anu* by biting and deposes him; swallows offspring (?); from *Anu*'s seed and *Kumarbi's* spittle is born
Phoenician	*Ouranos**: offspring of Eliun; marries Earth (Ge, Gaia); sires	*El* (*Kronos*): drives out *Ouranos* with sickle; later castrates him; kills a son and a daughter; marries his three sisters; sires
Iranian	*Jamshid*: preceded by three earlier kings; is overthrown by	*Zohak* (monster-like "nephew" [?]): later saws *Jamshid* in half; marries *Jamshid*'s two sisters; is deposed by
Norse (two lines)	*Buri*: autochthon; sires	*Bör*: sires
	Ymir: giant autochthon; licked from ice by cow; androgynously begets	*Thrudgelmir*: sires
Babylonian *Enūma-Elish*	*Apsu**: autochthon; marries *Tiamat*; sires	*Ea*: deposes *Apsu;* is apparently supplanted by *Ea*'s half-brother, *Kingu*. *Ea* sires
"Theogony of Dunnu"	*Hain*: autochthon; marries Earth; sires	*Amakandu*: slays *Hain,* marries mother (Earth), then sister (Sea); sires

* These figures provoke filial rebellion by exiling or attempting to destroy their eventual successors.

NOTE: The italicized names are those of the principal figures involved in the "Kingship in Heaven."

"KINGSHIP IN HEAVEN" THEME

THIRD GENERATION FIGURE	MONSTER
Zeus: deposes *Kronos*; must validate his position by slaying	*Typhon*: creature or offspring of *Kronos*; is killed in single combat around Mt. Kasios and Cilicia.
Teshub: deposes *Kumarbi*; must validate his position by rendering powerless with "ancient tool" and slaying (?)	*Ullikummi*: offspring of *Kumarbi*; defeated near Mt. Hazzi (Kasios).
Baal: deposes *El*; later *El* castrates self. *Baal* reigns perpetually.	Although *Typhon* is mentioned, there is no clear monster figure.
Feridun (*Jamshid's* exiled grandson): reigns triumphantly after defeating	*Zohak*: parallels *Typhon;* after being clubbed in single combat and left enchained, dies on Mt. Demawend(?). Represents fusion of second generation and monster.
Odin: who reigns perpetually after killing and cutting up *Ymir* and banishing *Bergelmir* to Jöntinheim.	*Ymir*, from whose corpse the universe is formed, represents fusion of first-generation figure and monster.
Bergelmir.	
Marduk: deposes *Kingu* and banishes him (to Uggae); reigns perpetually after slaying	*Tiamat*, from whose corpse the universe is formed, represents fusion of first-generation figure and monster.
Lahar: slays *Amakandu*; marries Sea; deposed eventually by offspring.	No clear monster figure.

that of the Greco-Roman tradition, to which it had diffused perhaps two millennia earlier.

Two of the chief reasons for ruling out an Indo-European origin are the absence, previously noted, of the theme in the Indic tradition and its very late appearance in that of ancient Iran. Also important in this connection is its absence in the ancient Celtic tradition. Admittedly much of our knowledge of Celtic religion is confined to those elements of it that persisted in Ireland; yet even here, given the care taken by the medieval Irish monks to preserve their heritage, one would assume that if the theme had been present before the arrival of Christianity it would have carried over. But only by the most Procrustean of methods can one make a case for its presence in the traditions relating to the Túatha Dé Danann and their predecessors. It is simply not present.

Thus, that neither the *Veda*'s, the *Avesta,* nor the *Lebor Gabála* know the theme is highly significant. With the exception of the Norse, all known versions center upon Mesopotamia. Even Egypt does not seem to have known a clear version of the "Kingship in Heaven."[110] Its diffusion to Greece, usually thought to have been accomplished via Phoenicia,[111] may indeed have been much earlier than heretofore suspected. Lambert and Walcot suggest that the mythical conception of a divine kingship may have diffused directly from Mesopotamia to Greece during the Late Helladic period and cite recent archaeological evidence (e.g., the presence of Babylonian cylinder seals at Thebes) indicative of widespread Mycenaean-Mesopotamian contacts.[112] Its diffusion to the Hittites would probably have been accomplished via the Hurrians, who had come into close contact with the mainstream of Mesopotamian civilization by the middle of the second millennium B.C. Its late diffusion eastward to Iran may reflect more immediately the Hesiodic and/or Phoenician versions rather than the Babylonian versions themselves (cf. the very specific parallels between Zohak and Typhon). But whatever the course taken, its absence in at least three widely separated and important Indo-European traditions, coupled with the early dates

---

110 But Lambert and Walcot, *op. cit.*, p. 69, point out that there is an Egyptian tradition according to which Sky devoured her children, quarreled with her husband, Earth, and therefore they were separated; for the relevant text. see H. Frankfort, *The Cenotaph of Seti I at Abydos* (London, 1933), p. 83.

111 Güterbock, "The Hittite Version of the Hurrian Kumarbi Myths," pp. 133–134.

112 Lambert and Walcot, *op. cit.*, p. 72. Walcot, as we have seen (see n. 90), has since modified his views and is convinced that the theme most likely diffused to Greece only after sustained contact had been reestablished with the Near East in the eighth century, B.C. (*op. cit.*, p. 47).

of the Babylonian versions, would seem to give powerful support to my contention that it is of Babylonian[113] and perhaps even ultimately of Sumerian origin.

No discussion of Indo-European origins would be complete without reference to Professor Dumézil's theory of a common tripartite social and supernatural system, a system that is clearly evident in most of the ancient Indo-European speaking domain.[114] Dumézil himself has refrained from any attempt to apply the tripartite model to the idea of the "Kingship in Heaven," despite the fact that at first glance, at least, the three-generational sequences would seem to offer a fertile field in this regard. Even Wikander, in many ways Dumézil's most brilliant disciple, and, as we have seen, the chief proponent of the Indo-European origin theory, has refrained from attempting such an application.[115] The closest Dumézil has come to the problem is the suggestion[116] that the proto–Indo-European mythology possibly included a tradition that Heaven was the last and only surviving offspring of a great water deity (probably female), who drowned all but one of her children as soon as they were born. His suggestion is based upon a comparison between the Norse god Heimdallr and the Vedic divinity Dyauḥ. Both are connected with water. Heimdallr is said to have had nine mothers, who were conceived as "sea waves"; Dyauḥ and his seven brothers (the *Vasus*) are linked with the river goddess Gaṅgā (Ganges), who drowns seven of the eight siblings, leaving only Dyauḥ to reach maturity (cf. *Mahābhārata* 1.3843–3963).

Certainly the personifications of sea and heaven play parts in both

---

113 The historical relationships proposed here are generally congruent with those proposed by Steiner (*op. cit.*, p. 104), who sees the *Enūma-Elish* as the immediate source of two unattested versions of the theme which he labels "X" and "Y." The "Y" version, Steiner suggests, ultimately reached Greece and manifested itself in Hesiod's *Theogony*. The Hurrian-Hittite version reflects both the "X" and the "Y" versions, although the former would seem to be the most immediate source. He also suggests that the "X" version perhaps gave rise to a third unattested version, "Z," which, together with the Hesiodic version, is reflected in Philo's "history." If Steiner is correct, it might be suggested that his hypothetical "Z" version could have diffused to Iran as well as to Phoenicia (cf. the specific correspondences between Philo and Firdausi as noted in the table and elsewhere); the Hesiodic version would be the immediate source of that contained in Snorri's *Edda*.

114 The most succinct statement of Dumézil's theory can be found in his *L'idéologie tripartie des Indo-européens* (Brussels, 1958). For a brief analysis of this theory see my article "The Comparative Indo-European Mythology of Georges Dumézil," *JFI* 1:147–166 (1964); for a more extended discussion of Dumézil's ideas see my *The New Comparative Mythology: An Anthropological Assessment of the Theories of Georges Dumézil* (Berkeley and Los Angeles, 1966).

115 Cf. *ibid.*, pp. 63, 85.

116 "Remarques comparatives sur le dieu scandinave Heimdallr," *EC* 8:263–283 (1959).

the Greek and the Babylonian versions of the divine kingship (cf. Pontos, Tiamat), but in neither case do we have any clear identification of the drowning of all but one of their offspring. Moreover, Heimdallr plays no part whatsoever in the Norse version, nor do any of the other traditions surrounding the rather otiose Dyauḥ come anywhere near to approximating the sort of divine succession so crucial to the presence of the theme in question. In short, it would seem to me that, even though Dumézil may well be correct in his suggestions as to the Indo-European roots of the traditions surrounding the births of Dyauḥ and Heimdallr, it would not be germane to the problem at hand. The presence of such a common Indo-European tradition would in no way alter my convictions as to the origin of the theme.

One of the most interesting suggestions yet made from a Dumézilian standpoint is that previously mentioned by F. Vian[117] relative to the Greek Typhon myth. As Vian sees it, Zeus's battle with the monster derives from an isolated story paralleling what Dumézil[118] and others have suggested is the typical Indo-European myth of a fight between a second-function or warrior figure and a tricephalic monster (cf. Indra versus the son of Tvaṣṭar, and the like). This story later fused with a widespread non-Indo-European dragon-slaying account (which had also diffused to the Hittites; cf. the Ullikummi and Illuyanka narratives)[119] that had been introduced into Greece by the Phoenicians in the early eighth century B.C. Thus, according to Vian, by the time of Hesiod the story as it is generally known in Greek mythology had fairly well crystallized. It is interesting that in later versions of the Typhon episode (i.e., those of Apollodorus and Nonnos) the details undergo progressive elaboration and become more and more similar to those of the Hurrian-Hittite version. As noted, the Hittite description of Ullikummi before Mount Hazzi is almost identical with Nonnos' description of Typhon.

If Vian is correct, then some intriguing possibilities present themselves. Perhaps the Hittites, too, grafted the dragon-slaying myth onto an inherited Indo-European three-headed monster tale and, like their Greek cousins a thousand years later, eventually fused this with the Babylonian account of the divine kingship. Thus there would be three distinct strata in both the Greek and Hittite versions: (1) the Indo-European account of the slaying of the tricephalus,

---

117 *Op. cit.*

118 *Horace et les Curiaces.*

119 For a thorough discussion of the dragon-slaying myth, see J. Fontenrose, *Python: A Study of Delphic Myth and Its Origins* (Berkeley and Los Angeles, 1959).

(2) the dragon-slaying myth, and (3) the "Kingship in Heaven" theme proper. Of course, it is by no means clear that the monster-slaying episode is disassociated in its origins from the rest of the theme under discussion. It is just as easy to make a case for the presence of this figure in the person of Tiamat—although its presence in the "Theogony of Dunnu" is less clear.

In sum, while it presents some alternative possibilities of interpretation of certain specific episodes associated with the "Kingship in Heaven," I do not feel that Vian's arguments relative to Typhon add anything substantive to the argument favoring an Indo-European origin for the theme as a whole, and I must reiterate my conclusion that it is most probably rooted in the Babylonian tradition.

The Threefold Death: An Indo-European Trifunctional Sacrifice?

DONALD J. WARD, *University of California, Los Angeles*

In one of his investigations of Germanic heroic and mythological traditions,[1] Georges Dumézil speculates that the Norse heroic traditions treating the careers of Hadding and Hunding (and sometimes Frotho), represent euhemerizations of the careers of the Norse gods, Njördr and Freyr. According to Dumézil, the two phases in the career of Hadding represent the two phases in the career of Njördr, the first phase being the "Vanic" period, during which Njördr was firmly associated with the third function, and the second phase being the period during which the god became the protégé of Odin and, in so doing, became a divinity of the first function. Dumézil finds evidence that supports his hypothesis in an episode in Book I of Saxo Grammaticus. In this episode, the hero Hunding meets an accidental death when he falls into a vat of beer. Upon learning the news of Hunding's fate, Hadding hangs himself. Dumézil sees in this episode the survival of a sacrificial myth in which the death by drowning in a vat involves a ritual of the third function, whereas death by hanging represents a ritual of the first function.

The hypothesis of Dumézil is thus based on the assumption that, in Germanic religion, there were once separate sacrifices performed for the divinities of the first and third functions. This assumption, however, has not been tested. Therefore, I have investigated the available sources in order to establish whether there is a correlation between the classes of Germanic divinities and the sacrifices made to them,

[1] *La Saga de Hadingus* (Paris, 1953), pp. 118–159.

and, if so, whether there are corresponding practices found among other Indo-European peoples.

It has long been established that, in Germanic religion, the practice of sacral hangings was associated with the cult of Odin, who, according to Dumézil, represents the Varunaic half of the Indo-European first function. The very epithets Hangi, Hangagoð, Hangatýr, and Galgavaldr, all of which are borne by Odin, indicate such a relationship. There is, moreover, a myth in which Odin himself is envisioned as hanging in a tree for nine days (*Hávamál* 138), saying that he was "given to Odin, I myself, to myself, in the tree of which no one knows from what roots it grows". Snorri, furthermore, writes (*Ynglingasaga* 7) that Odin "sometimes roused the dead out of the earth or sat under the hanged, and therefore he was called the lord of ghosts or the king of the hanged." There is, in addition, evidence from German folklore which indicates that Wotan, the South Germanic counterpart of Odin, was similarly associated with hanging. Various folk legends tell of the one-eyed personification of the wind who leads the raging army of the souls of the hanged across the heavens. One fourteenth-century source even refers to this host of lost souls as "Wutanes her."[2]

An account of an actual sacrificial ritual, during which a human victim is offered to Odin by hanging, has been preserved in the *Víkarssaga* as well as in the Danish history of Saxo Grammaticus (6.5). In both sources there is an account of the hanging of King Víkar, whom the hero Starkadr offers to Odin. That such sacral hangings belong to an early stratum of Germanic religion is confirmed by the earliest reports of sacrificial practices among Germanic peoples. Prokopios, for example (*De bello Gotico* 2.15, 23), describes the victory celebration of the Thulites and reports that prisoners of war were hanged in trees.[3] Orosius writes of a similar ritual after the Cimbrian victory over the Romans (*Historia adversus paganos* 5.16). Similarly, Adam of Bremen wrote in the eleventh century (*Gesta* 4.27) that horses, dogs, and men were hanged in the sacred grove at Uppsala.

The second sacrificial ritual mentioned by Dumézil involves the drowning of a human victim in a vat or tub. Dumézil's contention

[2] See K. Meisen, *Die Sagen vom wütenden Heer und wilden Jäger* (Münster in Westfalen, 1935), p. 72. See also O. Höfler, *Kultische Geheimbünde der Germanen* (Frankfurt, 1934), pp. 1–83.

[3] According to Pliny the Elder (*Naturalis Historia*, 18.3), a similar hanging ritual was practiced by the Romans. There is also evidence of such a sacrifice in ancient Greece. See M. P. Nilsson, *Griechische Feste von religiöser Bedeutung mit Ausschluss der Attischen* (Leipzig, 1906), pp. 234–237.

that this kind of sacrifice represents an Indo-European third-function ritual is given support by the occurrence of this motif in various heroic and popular traditions of Indo-European speaking peoples. Elsewhere within Germanic tradition one reads that Fjölnir, son of Yngvifreyr (*Heimskringla* 1.24–25) drowns after falling into a vat of beer. In Greece, the motif is found in the story of the Thessalian Piasos[4] and in that of Glaukos, son of Minos and Pasiphae, who drowns after accidentally falling into a vat of honey (Apollodorus, *Bibliotheca* 3.3.1). Similarly, in Ireland there are several heroes who are reported to have drowned in a vat of beer during a festival.[5] The motif can also be found in Scandinavian and German variants of the folk legend "The Death of Pan," in which a dwarf is reported to have fallen into a brewing vat.[6]

The occurrence of this motif in widely separated areas, each of which is occupied by an Indo-European speaking people, points to the possibility that it was based on an Indo-European mythological theme, which was associated from the earliest times with a sacrificial ritual, and which had been adopted into various heroic and popular traditions. Further evidence of such a ritualistic drowning among Indo-European peoples will be adduced in the course of this investigation. For the present, however, I wish to focus upon the evidence of this practice in Germanic tradition.

The most convincing single piece of evidence that links ritualistic drowning with Germanic divinities of the third function is found in chapter 40 of Tacitus' *Germania*. Tacitus reports that the sacred wagon of Nerthus was sprinkled with water, after which slaves were drowned as an offering to the goddess.

It has long been established that Nerthus, a female counterpart of the Norse Njördr, is a divinity of fertility and abundance. Moreover, the practice of sprinkling water on the wagon of the goddess is obviously an example of ritualistic imitative magic of the kind found all over Europe in fertility and rain-producing rituals. Such practices have been observed in rural areas of Germany in this century.[7] It is apparent that the ritual described by Tacitus was performed with the intent of promoting fertility, and the fact that the mode of human sacrifice to the fertility divinity took the form of drowning lends con-

4 A. Yoshida, *RHR* 168:155–164 (1965).

5 See J. de Vries, *Keltische Religion* (Stuttgart, 1961), pp. 46–48.

6 See G. Hermansen, "Die Sage vom Tode des grossen Pan," *Classica et Mediaevalia* 2:239–242 (1939).

7 G. Gesemann, *Regenzauber in Deutschland*, Diss. Kiel (Brunswick, 1913), pp. 23–34.

siderable support to Dumézil's hypothesis that drowning involves a ritual of the third function.

Various observations recorded by other early historians reveal that sacrificial drowning was an important ritual in Germanic religion from early times. Orosius (*Historia* 5.16) writes that after the Cimbrian victory over the Romans, horses were drowned in a river. Adam of Bremen (schol. 134) describes a human sacrifice by drowning in a spring at the sacred grove of Uppsala. In the ninth-century *Vita Vulframmi* (chap. 8) it is reported that two youths were sacrificed to the sea by being abandoned on a sandbar, to be swept away by the rising tide. This identical method of sacrifice is evidently reflected in the episode in Snorri's *Skaldskaparmál,* in which the dwarfs, Fialarr and Galarr, are taken by the giant, Suttungr, to a sandbar at sea, where they are likewise abandoned to the rising tides.[8] This means of doing away with victims is also reported to have been used in penal execution. In the *Heimskringla* (*Ólafssaga Tryggvasonar,* 70) Eyvindr kelda and his followers are bound and likewise abandoned on a sandbar as punishment for a crime. These cases are of particular importance for this investigation. The three reports deal respectively with an actual sacrifice, a literary-mythological motif, and a criminal execution. In all three cases the identical method is used for doing away with the victim. This combination of evidence indicates that ancient religious practices can survive long after their religious function has been forgotten. The report in Snorri's *Edda* indicates that the mythological theme, based on a sacrificial ritual, can survive as a literary motif. Similarly, the report in the *Heimskringla* indicates that the method of killing used in penal executions can evolve from earlier sacrificial practices. Whether the penal execution represents an offering to the offended god or demon, as Karl von Amira and others have tried to prove,[9] remains problematic; it is unlikely that this contention can ever be established with any degree of certainty. Nevertheless, I believe that one can show that, in certain recorded criminal cases, the punishment was determined by the type of crime committed, and, furthermore, that this relationship reflects the tripartite structure of Germanic society.

Once again, the most convincing evidence is to be found in Taci-

---

[8] According to the *Additio Sapientum* XI of the Lex Frisionum, those who violated the temple of an unnamed divinity had their ears slashed, were castrated, and then drowned.

[9] *Die germanischen Todesstrafen: Untersuchungen zur Rechts- und Religionsgeschichte,* Abhandlungen der Bayerischen Akademie der Wissenschaften, Philosophisch-philologische und historische Klasse XXXI, 3. Abhandlung (Munich, 1922), pp. 1–415.

tus' *Germania.* In chapter 12, Tacitus discusses penal executions and he states specifically that the crime determines the punishment: *distinctio poenarum delicto.* He then informs us that *proditores et transfugas* ('traitors and deserters') were hanged from trees, whereas *ignavos et imbelles* ('cowards and nonwarriors') and *corpore infames* were drowned in mires and bogs. The term *ignavos et imbelles* is a traditional combination in classical Latin. Cicero, among others, made frequent use of this word pair. The expression means, in fact, more than just 'cowards and nonwarriors,' but evidently was used to refer to the effeminate, the unmanly, and the timid. Thus when Tacitus adds to this expression the term *corpore infames* it is evident that he is referring to a particularly flagrant kind of homosexuality or other unnatural sexual vice considered to be depraved enough to warrant capital punishment.[10]

Thus the pattern that has been established for human sacrifice evidently holds true for human execution as well. Crimes of treason, that is, crimes against the sovereign state (first function), are punished in the same manner in which victims are sacrificed to the sovereign divinity: by hanging. And sexual crimes (third function) are punished in the same manner in which sacrifices are made to the divinities of fertility: by drowning.[11]

Execution by drowning has a long history in Europe, and it would be almost impossible for a single investigator to assemble all the evidence for this practice.[12] There is, furthermore, the question of whether the results would warrant—at least for this study—such an undertaking. In spite of the evidence adduced above, which reveals a relationship between the sacral offering and penal execution, one cannot automatically assume that every instance of drowning as punishment—especially those of a later date—is sacral in origin.

There are, however, a few cases of execution by drowning which deserve special attention. In a remarkable investigation, in which a

---

10 See N. Beckman, "Ignavi et imbelles et corpore infames," ANF 52:78–81 (1936).

11 That sacrifices and executions were performed by drowning in bogs has been confirmed by the many archaeological finds of human corpses in the mires of Denmark and North Germany. See, for example, G. Bibby, *The Testimony of the Spade* (New York, 1956), pp. 402–406. A passage in the *Kjalnesinga saga,* moreover, tells that people who were to be sacrificed (*blótuðu*) were cast into a bog which was called *Blótkelda.* According to the *Flateyjarbók,* when the Norwegian queen Gunnhildr arrived at the court of King Haraldr, the latter sent his slaves and "guests" to greet her. They seized the queen amid great tumult and jeering and drowned her in a deep morass.

12 See Amira, *Todesstrafen,* pp. 140–143. See also F. Ström, *On the Sacral Origin of the Germanic Death Penalties,* Kungliga Vitterhets Historie och Antikvitets Akademiens Handlingar, Del 52 (Stockholm, 1942), pp. 171–188.

great amount of data was assembled, Heinz Goldschmidt was able to show that in the Low Countries of Europe—with isolated examples in London and Magdeburg—a common form of execution during the late Middle Ages was by drowning in a vat.[13] The drowning generally took place at night and was performed in secret. Goldschmidt attempts to show that this practice had its origin in heathen sacrificial practices and was only later adopted as a form of execution. Although such a contention is difficult to prove, the similarity of this practice with the motif of accidental drowning in a vat, which was discussed above, is too striking to be dismissed as mere coincidence.

One case cited by Goldschmidt warrants special attention. On February 18, 1478, George Duke of Clarence was secretly executed in the Tower of London by order of his brother, King Edward IV. Although the manner in which the execution was conducted was kept a secret, it was generally assumed that the Duke was drowned in a butt of malmsey wine. One such report is found in Robert Fayan's *New Chronicles of England and France,* published in 1516: "This yere, that is to meane ye XVIII daye of February the duke of Clarence . . . brother te the kynge, thanne beyng prysoner in ye Tower, was secretly put to deth and drowned in a barell of malmsye within the sayd Tower."[14]

Since the murder was performed in secret, one will probably never know with certainty whether the drowning in the vat of wine was the actual means by which the victim was killed. But since Goldschmidt has been able to show that this practice represented a traditional means of execution in the Low Countries during the late Middle Ages, such a situation must be considered a possibility. Until such time as new evidence can be adduced, however, this question will have to remain open.

Yet, one point is clear. Since the populace of London associated the murder of the Duke with the motif of drowning in a vat of wine, it is evident that this motif was, at that time, a part of the popular tradition. It has already been shown that this motif occurs in the heroic traditions of Greece, Ireland, and Denmark. We are thus once again

[13] "Das Ertränken im Fass: Eine alte Todesstrafe in den Niederlanden," *Zeitschrift für vergleichende Rechtswissenschaft* 41:423–470 (1925); 42:248–288 (1927).

[14] Ed. H. Ellis (London, 1811), p. 666. M. Murray (*The Divine King in England* [London, 1954], p. 117) argues that the slaying of Clarence was actually the ritualistic sacrifice of the King's representative as part of a rite in which, originally, the king himself was the divine victim. This is an attractive hypothesis which, if tenable, could contribute much to this investigation. Unfortunately, the entire structure of Murray's theories rests on a foundation of conjecture.

confronted with a familiar pattern, namely, a literary motif and a penal execution, both of which show the identical method of killing the victim. But one important element is lacking to make the pattern complete. Although evidence has already been adduced which shows that sacrificial drowning was an important ritual in early Germanic religion, there are no written records indicating that a vat or a tub was used in which to drown the victims. There is, however, archaeological evidence that confirms the existence of such a sacrifice. On the kettle of Gundestrup there is depicted a scene in which a large man in a robe—evidently a priest—is pushing a human victim head-first into a large tub.[15] It is evident that this scene depicts a sacrificial ritual during which a human victim was drowned in a tub.

This evidence fills the gap in the pattern. The identical method of killing occurs as (1) an actual sacrificial practice, (2) a literary motif, and (3) a penal execution. This evidence, viewed in its totality, confirms the contention of Dumézil that the motif of Hunding's death by drowning in a vat of beer, as recorded in Saxo's history, represents the euhemerization of a mythological theme, which originally was associated with a third-function sacrifice. Furthermore, since this motif occurs in Greece, Denmark, England, and Ireland, it is probable that the sacrificial myth in question dates back to the period of Indo-European unity. This myth was borne by the various migrating peoples to their respective new homelands where, in each instance, it later became euhemerized and was adopted into the respective heroic and/or popular narrative tradition.

Before concluding the discussion of Germanic third-function sacrifices, I should like to adduce some relatively late evidence that shows that such sacrifices survived in Europe with remarkable tenacity. In several areas of Europe there are documents in which are recorded incidents of humans having been buried alive for the purpose of warding off the black plague. One such document is a letter, dated August 7, 1604, from King Christian of Denmark to the sheriff of Lundenaes in which the king directs that a woman, who buried her child alive, be executed. The crime had taken place in the year 1603, the same year the plague was raging in Denmark.[16]

Several folk legends recorded in Scandinavia preserve evidence of the same practice. Children were reported to have been buried alive

---

15 S. Müller, *Nordische Altertumskunde* (Strasbourg, 1897–1898), II, 164–165.

16 See H. Knudsen, "En hest levende begravet," *Samlinger til Jydsk Historie og Topografi*, 4. Raekke (1922), IV, 299–303. As late as the eighteenth century, there is a report of live burial having been performed to ward off disease. According to a court record from Sunnerbo in Småland, a woman was forcibly nailed in a coffin during the epidemic that raged there in 1712. See Ström, *op. cit.*, p. 205.

in the hope of warding off the dreaded plague.[17] Remnants of this practice have, moreover, survived to relatively modern times, for there is evidence from several European areas that, as late as the latter half of the nineteenth century, farm animals were buried alive to avert hoof-and-mouth disease among cattle.[18]

From Ireland, there are similar reports that human sacrifice was practiced as a means of warding off disease. One such report is found in the *Rennes Dindšenchas*:

> During the Trena of Taillte, at sunrise
> I twice invoked Mac Erca
> The three plagues to remove
> From Erin, though it be a woman's command.
> Their hostages were brought out;
> The drowning of the bonds of the violated treaties
> Immolating the son of Aedh Slane
> To Mac Erc—it was not a cause for shame.[19]

From these lines one learns that human victims, in this case a group of hostages, and a captive prince, were sacrificed by drowning for the purpose of warding off the plagues. At this point it should be mentioned that, according to the tripartite theory of Dumézil, one of the important functions of the divinities of the third estate is to insure general well-being and to combat disease. Thus the above passage is additional evidence supporting the contention that sacrifice by drowning was associated with the divinities of the third function.

In the cases adduced from Germanic-speaking areas, as seen above, the method used to sacrifice the victims was not by drowning but by burial alive. It can, I believe, be assumed that, in relatively arid regions, in which there were no swamps or bogs, the practice of live burial could easily have supplanted that of drowning in a mire. Or, stated in other terms, burial alive as a sacrificial practice can be viewed as being in complementary distribution with sacrifice by drowning.

---

17 Variants of the legend have been collected in Dalsland (M. Hofberg, *Svenska folksägner* [Stockholm, 1882], p. 122), in Halland (J. Kalén, *Halländska folkminnen, lokalsägner och övertro från Fagered* [Stockholm, 1927], p. 207), and in Blekinge (E. Wigström, *Folkdiktning, visor, sägner, sagor, gåtor, ordspråk, ringdansar, lekar och barnvisor* [Copenhagen and Göteborg, 1880–1881], I, 285). For further examples, see Ström, *op. cit.*, p. 206.

18 See P. Heurgren, *Husdjuren i norsk folktro* (Örebro, 1925), p. 249. See also Knudsen, *op. cit.*, p. 299.

19 See W. Stokes, "The Bodleian Dinnshenchas," *Folk-Lore: A Quarterly Review of Myth, Tradition and Custom* 3:467–516 (1892). The *Dindšenchas* are pieces of verse and prose of the fourteenth and fifteenth centuries which treat noteworthy locations in Ireland.

Additional evidence supporting the contention that burial alive can be associated with Dumézil's third function can be found in medieval legal documents. During the Middle Ages, one means of performing capital punishment in cities in Germany was by live burial. The records show that there was a relationship between this type of punishment and the nature of the crime committed. According to Jacob Grimm,[20] this type of execution was preferred for cases of theft, bestiality, sex crimes, and for the murder of illegitimate children. These crimes constitute specific violations of property, wealth, and sex, all of which belong to the domain of the third function. This evidence reveals a rather astonishing continuity in the correlation between the type of crime committed and the manner of punishment from the time of Tacitus to relatively modern times.

Since the evidence adduced thus far seems to confirm a correlation between the sacrifice and the ideological structure in the case of the first and third functions among Germanic peoples, one might expect a similar correlation in the case of the second function. There is, however, only a small corpus of evidence regarding special sacrifices to a Germanic god of war. Jordanes (*Getica* 5.41) stresses that the Goths worshiped Mars, who may represent Thor, the Germanic war god, with the spilling of much human blood (*humani sanguinis effusione placandum*). The report has a parallel in a much later document, namely in the *Norman History* of Dudo of St. Quintin,[21] who informs us that the Vikings, prior to embarking on a warring raid, sacrificed human life and smeared their bodies with the blood of their victims. Presumably if warriors performed such a blood sacrifice as described by Jordanes and Dudo, the sacrificial instrument would be a weapon of war.[22]

A pattern thus begins to emerge from the evidence thus far assembled. Among Germanic peoples, there were essentially three methods of offering a human victim to the divinities: noose, water, and weapon. These three means of execution, moreover, correspond to the three social classes, and to the three classes of divinities. Admittedly, the evidence for the second function sacrifice is meager.

---

20 *Deutsche Rechtsaltertümer*, 4. vermehrte Ausgabe, eds. A. Heusler and R. Hübner (Leipzig, 1899), II, 275–277.

21 *De Moribus* I.2. There is confirmation of a blood sacrifice to Thor in the Icelandic *Eyrbyggja saga* 10, in which a sacrificial temple is described in which there was a large flat rock called "Thor's stone". The saga tells how the victim's back was broken across the stone which had become red with the blood of many victims.

22 See Amira, *op. cit.*, pp. 166–208, for evidence of execution and sacrifice with a weapon among various Indo-European peoples.

The relative lack of evidence of this type of sacrifice among Germanic peoples can, I believe, be attributed to the fact that much of the sacrificial activity associated with warfare was frequently devoted to the cult of Odin, the "God of the Dead,"[23] and not to Thor, the war deity.

There are, however, other reasons for the relative lack of evidence of this kind of sacrifice. In contrast with the Mediterranean peoples, warfare for the Germans involved not warriors alone, but the entire community. Tacitus, for example (*Germania* 8), stresses the fact that women were present during battle, baring their breasts as a gesture to remind the men of that to which their wives would be exposed if the battle were lost. Tacitus also mentions (*Germania* 7) that women were on hand during battle to tend the wounds of their men. It is evident that, in Germanic society, all three social classes would have a profound interest in the outcome of battle and even share in the victory celebration. A passage in Saxo confirms this contention. In writing about the division of spoils after victory, Saxo (5.152) states that each of the social classes acquired its share of the booty. The chiefs were given the gold and silver, the warriors were given weapons, and the common people were given the ships. It can thus be seen that the society was divided into three classes, and this division corresponds precisely to the tripartite structure as posited by Dumézil.

One can imagine that it became a tradition among Germanic peoples to celebrate a victory with an elaborate festival during which not only a division was made of the booty, but offerings were made to the appropriate divinities of each of the three social classes. Evidence of such a celebration has been recorded by Orosius who writes that after the Cimbrian victory over the Romans (*Historia adversus paganos* 5.16), the victorious barbarians hanged prisoners in trees, cast silver and gold into the water, and drowned horses in the river. These three kinds of offerings correspond strikingly to the three social classes and to their respective kinds of sacrifices. The hangings clearly represent an offering to Odin, the drowning of the horses is apparently a third-function sacrifice, and the offerings of gold and silver conceivably could represent a second-function ritual.[24]

---

23 See E. Mogk, *Die Menschenopfer bei den Germanen*, Abhandlungen der Königlichen Sächsischen Gesellschaft der Wissenschaften, Phil.-Hist. Klasse XXVII, 17:603–643 (Leipzig, 1909). Mogk, who wrote long before Dumézil, and thus was not trying to defend a tripartite hypothesis, likewise concluded that the victory offerings made to Odin did not take the form of sacrifices made to a divinity of war, but were apparently made in honor of the "God of the Dead."

24 A similar tripartite celebration may be alluded to by Tacitus (*Annales* 1.61)

Additional evidence of a tripartite sacrifice after battle can be observed in an illustration from the seventeenth century by J. van Ossenbeeck entitled "Kriegsgreuel." In this illustration a victory celebration is depicted during which prisoners of war are sacrificed. One prisoner is shown hanging in a tree. Another is being decapitated by sword. And off to one side a large vat is shown, in which another prisoner has apparently been drowned.[25] This painting seems to confirm the pattern of noose, weapon, and water as means of carrying out human sacrifice.

One might, of course, raise the valid objection that a painting of the seventeenth century is scarcely the place where one would expect to find evidence of ancient Germanic sacrificial practices. Nevertheless, the trifunctional victory celebration, with the traditional sacrifices, is depicted in surprising detail. I suggest three possible explanations: (1) The artist had access to sources that described earlier victory celebrations; (2) the victory celebrations, with the three kinds of sacrifices, survived in form long after their original religious significance had been forgotten and, as such, were still practiced in the Thirty Years' War; (3) the artist created a scene of horror from his imagination alone, and made no attempt to depict a traditional celebration.

It is probably impossible to determine which, if any, of the three explanations represents the correct one, at least until such time as new evidence can be adduced. For the present, I am inclined to look upon the second explanation as the one that best explains the scene depicted by the artist.

In short, the evidence thus far points toward the following tentative conclusions: Germanic peoples not only performed separate sacrifices to their respective classes of divinities, but also performed a trifunctional rite after victory in battle. During these celebrations offerings were made simultaneously to the three classes of deities. Admittedly, this conclusion has been reached on the basis of a rela-

---

when he writes that the site at which Germanic tribes celebrated their victory over the Romans in the battle of the Teutoburg forest was marked by skulls hanging on trees, broken weapons, and the bones of horses scattered about. Of course, the weapons and the bones of the horses could be merely battle remnants. The drowning of horses as a sacrifice is documented in ancient Greece. For example, Homer writes (*Iliad* 21.130–132) that horses were drowned in honor of the river god, Skamandros. Moreover, there is evidence that horses and bulls were drowned in honor of Poseidon. See L. Farnell, "Sacrifice (Greece)," in *Encyclopaedia of Religion and Ethics*, ed. J. Hastings (New York, 1958), XI, 12–18.

25 G. Hirth, *Kulturgeschichtliches Bilderbuch aus drei Jahrhunderten* (Leipzig and Munich, 1883), V, 1616, pl. 2396. Ossenbeeck was born in Rotterdam in 1627 and died in Regensburg in 1678.

tively small corpus of material, and additional data would be needed before one could accept the findings as fact. Such supporting evidence can be found in other Indo-European religious traditions.

Of all Indo-European religions, the Celtic can provide the best comparative data. Among the most important sources for Celtic religion is the first-century Latin poem *Pharsalia* by Lucan and the commentaries written by the scholiasts between the fourth and ninth centuries. Just as Adam of Bremen mentions three distinct divinities for Germanic peoples, so does Lucan mention a triad of deities for the Celts, namely, Esus, Taranis, and Teutates. Similar to Germanic religion, there were separate kinds of human sacrifice performed in honor of each of the gods.

Just as in Germanic religion hanging was associated with the cult of Odin, the *Commenta* to Lucan mention that the victims offered to Esus were hanged and left suspended until their limbs wasted away.[26]

It would be convenient to conclude that the figure of Esus represents a first function, that is, an Odinic-Varunaic, divinity. But this conclusion involves some difficulty. First, the *Commenta* to Lucan provide precious little information regarding the functions of the divinities. Second, in Celtic religion Lug is apparently the true counterpart of Odin-Varuṇa, and thus hanging ought to be linked with Lug rather than with Esus. Yet Esus is generally hard to pin down—the *Commenta* equate him both with Mercury and with Mars—and since Lug is not mentioned by Lucan, it can be assumed that Esus has moved into the Odinic-Varunaic slot.[27]

The *Commenta* to Lucan report that the human victims offered to Taranis were sacrificed in quite a different manner. The victims were placed in a large basket-like structure which was then ignited, cremating those inside.[28] This kind of sacrifice has also been recorded by Strabo, who writes that a large structure was made of wood and straw into which all kinds of animals and humans were cast. The structure was then ignited, creating a bloody holocaust.[29]

---

26 *M. Annaei Lucani Commenta Bernensia*, ed. H. Usener (Leipzig, 1869), I, 445: "Hesus Mars sic placatur: homo in arbore suspenditur usque donec per cruorem membra digesserit." Elsewhere in this same paragraph Esus is equated, not with Mars, but with Mercury. Hereafter cited as *Commenta*.

27 For further discussion of this problem, see de Vries, *Keltische Religion*, pp. 97–100, who likewise concludes that Esus represents an Odinic divinity.

28 *Commenta*, I, 445: "Taranis Ditis pater hoc modo aput eos placatur: in alueo ligneo aliquod homines cremantur."

29 De Vries (*op. cit.*, p. 222) adduces numerous parallel episodes from Celtic heroic tradition in which a hero is killed by cremation. De Vries argues convincingly that such episodes represent survivals of sacrificial myths.

The third divinity mentioned by Lucan, Teutates, was honored by still another means of human sacrifice. According to the *Commenta*, a man was thrust headfirst into a vat, and was held in that position until he drowned.[30] In this passage, Teutates is equated with Mercury, a fact that might lead one to believe that we are again confronted with a first-function divinity. Since Esus, however, who is also equated with Mercury, most likely represents the Celtic first-function sovereign divinity, and since Teutates is associated with the rite of drowning victims in a vat, which has been shown to be a third-function sacrifice, it is highly probable that Teutates represents the Celtic third function. This contention is supported by the etymology of the name: **teutā́*, 'people,' indicating that he was a divinity of all the people, and, as such, his role would be parallel to the roles of other third-function deities of Indo-European tradition.

The material that has been adduced for Celtic religion reveals a striking agreement with the situation found in Germanic religion. In each case, there is a triad of divinities representing the three social classes, and each of the gods is honored by a separate kind of human sacrifice. Moreover, the pattern for Celtic tradition is remarkably similar to that found in Germanic tradition. In the latter, the three means of doing away with the victim were by noose, weapon, and water, whereas in Celtic religion, the three methods are noose, fire, and water. And as in the Germanic sources, the noose was associated with the first-function sacrifice, and water with the third-function sacrifice. Only in the case of the second function does one find an apparent inconsistency. In Germanic religion the weapon was used, whereas in Celtic religion fire was preferred. The two methods of sacrificing a victim are apparently in complementary distribution. That is, killing by weapon and by fire represent variants of a single class of sacrificial practice.

There are, moreover, further parallels with Germanic religious practices. For example, it has been shown that Germanic peoples celebrated their victories with simultaneous sacrifices to the three classes of divinities. Similarly, in Celtic tradition, there is evidence of such "trifunctional" rituals. This evidence is found chiefly in the ancient heroic literature of Ireland and specifically in the complex of motifs known as the "Threefold Death."

The earliest record of the theme is found in Adhamnán's seventh-century account of the life of St. Columba.[31] The Irish saint propheti-

[30] *Commenta*, I, 445: "Teutates Mercurius sic apud Gallos placatur: in plenum semicupium homo in caput demittitur ut ibi suffocetur."

[31] Adhanmhnán's *Life of St. Columba*, ed. W. Reeves (Edinburgh, 1874), I, 36.

cally informs Aedh the Black that he will die three different deaths. He will be wounded in the neck with a spear, fall from a tree into the water, and he will drown. One can speculate that the fall from the tree represents a variant of hanging. Indeed, evidence adduced below shows that such is precisely the case. The conclusion to this episode seems to be somewhat garbled: Aedh is wounded, falls from a boat, and drowns.

This episode corresponds in striking detail to two Latin poems written by Bishop Hildebert of Le Mans in the early twelfth century.[32] In each of the poems a boy asks the gods how he will die. Venus replies that he will die in a noose, Mars says by a weapon, and Neptune says by water. The youth climbs a tree above a river, falls in such a way that his sword pierces his breast, and his head is submerged. Once again, the three methods of death correspond to the tripartite sacrificial practices: noose, weapon, and water. The fact that the noose is the predicted form of death, and the actual death occurs by a fall from a tree, confirms the above assumption that the prediction of death by a fall from a tree actually represents death by hanging.

A variant of this tale occurs in the poems ascribed to Saint Moling as they appear in the *Anecdota* of Michael O'Clery, and which are associated with the Irish legend of Suibhne Geilt.[33] Although the *Anecdota* date from the seventeenth century, the material is obviously very much older. There are brief references to the poems as early as the ninth and tenth centuries.[34] Grag, who has killed Suibhne, is told by St. Moling that he will die by a weapon, by being burned, and by drowning. Grag is relieved to hear this prophecy, for he knows that, since man can die but once, the prophecy must be wrong. Nevertheless, fate is inevitable, for when Grag is climbing an oak tree, he is wounded by his spear, falls from the tree into a fire, and then into the water in which he drowns. Once again, we find the identical pattern: noose (represented by a fall from the oak tree), weapon, and water. There is, however, a new element, namely, fire. It has already been shown that, in Celtic religion, fire apparently replaced the weapon as a means of killing in the second-function sacrifice. Curiously, in this source, both a weapon and fire are mentioned.

The same episode occurs in the Irish life of St. Moling,[35] with an important addition. In this account, the punishment of the villain is

---

32 *Patrologia Latina*, ed. J. Migne. See K. Jackson, "The Motive of the Threefold Death in the Story of Suibhne Geilt," in *Essays and Studies presented to Eoin MacNeil* (Dublin, 1940), pp. 535–550.

33 MS Brussels 5100–5104, quoted from Jackson, *op. cit.*, p. 539.

34 J. G. O'Keeffe, *Buile suibne, Being the Adventures of Suibhne Geilt*, Irish Texts Society XII (London, 1913). See Jackson, *op. cit.*, p. 540.

35 See W. Stokes, "The Birth and Life of St. Moling," *RC* 27:285–287 (1906).

evidently associated with the crime that was committed. For Grag is not only guilty of killing Suibhne, but also of having stolen cattle. The theft of cattle apparently represents a violation of the third estate, whereas the killing of Suibhne could represent a second-function violation. A third crime is not mentioned, and one can only speculate that the threefold death was once associated with a crime against each of the three functions.

A variant of the episode is also to be found in the account of the exploits of King Diarmaid, who lived in the sixth century. The account is recorded in the eleventh-century *Silva Gadelica*.[36] It is predicted that King Diarmaid will meet death by three different means, by a weapon, by burning, and by drowning. During a festival, the king is wounded with a spear, the house is burned over him, he creeps into a vat of beer to avoid the flames, and drowns. The fact that the death of the king is reported to have taken place during the celebration of a festival is of special importance. I suggest that this account represents the euhemerization of a sacrificial myth which was associated with a periodic festival during which a human victim, most likely a king, was sacrificed simultaneously to the three classes of divinities.

The same story is told of Aidhedh Muirchertaig mac Erca in a fourteenth-century manuscript[37] in incomplete fashion, for only two of the deaths are reported. During a festival, Mac Erca's house is burned, and, to avoid the flames, the hero climbs into a vat of beer and half burns and half drowns. That this version is incomplete is confirmed by allusions to the hero's death in other manuscripts, one dating from the twelfth century, the other from the thirteenth.[38] In both cases, it is mentioned that Mac Erca died by three different means, by a weapon, by burning, and by drowning. Once again, one is confronted with what appears to be the survival of a sacrificial myth, in which it is told how a victim is sacrificed simultaneously to the three classes of divinities.

This theme of the threefold death later became a part of popular oral tradition and was told as a kind of a "fate tale" in which the hero's fate was determined from birth. As the story becomes further removed from its religious background, the manner in which the hero suffers death undergoes changes. This development is not surprising. When the ritualistic significance is forgotten, the only im-

---

36 *Silva Gadelica*, ed. S. O'Grady (London, 1892), I, 86–88; II, 80–84.

37 W. Stokes, "The Death of Muirchertach Mac Erca," *RC* 23:395–437 (1902).

38 E. J. Gwynn, *The Metrical Dindsenchas*, Royal Irish Academy, Todd Lecture Series VIII–XII (Dublin, 1903–1935), XI, 200. See also *Codex Palatio Vaticanus*, Todd Lecture Series III (Dublin, 1892), p. 397.

portant aspect is that the hero dies three deaths, and the manner in which he dies becomes of ever-decreasing importance.

The theme occurs in legends recorded in the British Isles, and is associated with the careers of Myrddin, Merlin, and Lailoken.[39] In the *Vita Merlini* by Geoffrey of Monmouth,[40] Merlin predicts that a youth will die in a tree, by a fall from a rock, and drown. The youth later suffers all three deaths simultaneously. In the account treating the figure of Lailoken, the three deaths are by stoning, beating, piercing with a stake, and by drowning.[41] In a Welsh fate tale, it is predicted that a youth will die by snakebite, by a fall from a tree, and by drowning.[42] The boy later climbs a tree, is bitten by a snake, falls and breaks his neck—a variant of the hanging motif—and drowns in a river below.

The modern folktale treatment of the threefold death has a wide distribution, having been recorded in variants from Ireland to Iran. A relatively complete comparison of these tales can be found in a recent monograph by R. Brednich,[43] and therefore they need not be treated here in detail. Instead, in referring to these tales, I limit my remarks to the place where the tale was collected, and to the manner in which the hero suffers the threefold death.

Estonia:	Hunger, fire, and water.[44]
	Fall from tree, snakebite, ax wound.[45]
Low German:	Hanging on willow branch, drowning.[46]
Slovene:	Snakebite, fall from tree, drowning.[47]
Bulgaria:	Snakebite, fall from tree.[48]
Greece:	Snakebite, fall from cliff, burning.[49]
Iran:	Fall from tree, snakebite, drowning.[50]

---

39 Jackson, *op. cit.*, pp. 543–546.

40 The *Vita Merlini*, ed. J. Parry, University of Illinois Studies in Language and Literature X, no. 3 (Urbana, Ill., 1925), pp. 44–54, lines 245–415.

41 Jackson, *op. cit.*, p. 546.

42 T. Williams, *Iolo Manuscripts: A Selection of Ancient Welsh Manuscripts in Prose and Verse from the Collection of the Late E. Williams* (Llandovery, 1848), p. 202.

43 R. Brednich, *Volkserzählungen und Volksglaube von den Schicksalsfrauen*, FFC 193 (Helsinki, 1964), pp. 138–145.

44 A. Aarne, *Estnische Märchen und Sagenvarianten*, FFC 25 (Helsinki, 1918), p. 136.

45 O. Loorits, *Estnische Volkserzählungen*, Fabula, Supplement, Series A.1, no. 197 (Berlin, 1959), p. 204.

46 G. Henssen, *Bergische Märchen und Sagen*, Märchen aus deutschen Landschaften 1, no. 67 (Münster in Westfalen, 1961), pp. 115–116. O. Schell, *Bergische Sagen*, 2. Aufl., no. 101 (Elberfeld, 1922), p. 37.

47 Brednich, *op. cit.*, p. 142.

48 *Ibid.*, p. 143.

49 B. Schmidt, *Griechische Märchen, Sagen und Volkslieder* (Leipzig, 1877), p. 68.

50 D. Lorimer and E. Lorimer, *Persian Tales* (London, 1919), pp. 233–234.

The motif of the snakebite, which is especially well represented in East Europe and Asia, evidently represents a secondary intrusion. It occurs only in the tales that have been collected at a relatively recent date, and is totally lacking in the older written sources. Hanging—and its variant, fall from a tree—burning, wounding with a weapon, and drowning are all motifs that occur in the earliest sources and evidently have belonged to the tradition from the earliest times.

A study of the distribution of the modern folktale, and consideration of the oldest written sources, apparently leaves only one tenable conclusion regarding the origin and dissemination of the tale. The tale had its origin in ancient Ireland and then spread by diffusion to the various European and Asian locations. But there is an alternative explanation. One can assume that the theme was a part of the mythology of the Indo-Europeans and was borne by the migrating Indo-European peoples to their respective new homelands, and then, in each new area, the tale became a part of the local narrative tradition. Or, stated in other terms, one can explain the distribution of the tale either by the "diffusion" theory or by the "Indo-European" theory. Although I favor the diffusion theory in explaining most of the variants and their distribution, I believe that, in at least one instance, the Indo-European theory represents a more plausible explanation. Such an instance is represented by a variant of the tale as it was recorded in a Low German dialect by Gottfried Henssen in the town of Untersiebeneick in the year 1927.[51]

In this tale a prophet tells a mother in labor that her child should not be born during that hour, for "wenn dat Kenk en de Stond te Welt köm, dan köm et to en doadonglöcklichen Doad: entweder et höng seck op oder et verdrönk."[52] The child, alas, is born during the fateful hour. As it becomes old enough to walk, every effort is made to avert the prophesied death. The child is never allowed to play alone. Later the child, under close supervision, is playing near the water when it becomes entangled in a willow twig (*Wiedenstruck*), falls into the water, and is simultaneously strangled and drowned.

Of particular importance in this tale is the occurrence of the motif of strangulation by a willow twig, a motif that does not occur in any of the other variants of the tale. There is a curious parallel to this motif in a narrative recorded many centuries earlier in the same general North Germanic area. It is to be found in the accounts of the death of the Danish king Víkar. The story exists in two prose versions.

---

51 Henssen, *op. cit.*, p. 204.

52 "If the child should come into the world during that hour then it would suffer a wretched death: it will either hang itself or drown."

One account is in the Danish history of Saxo Grammaticus (5.5), the other in the *Víkarssaga*, which had been intercalated in the Icelandic *Gautrekssaga*. Fragments of the episode also occur in verse form in the *Víkarsbálkr*.

In the version preserved in the *Gautrekssaga*, we learn that King Víkar sails to Hörðaland with his army, but is held up by a headwind at some holms. Sacrificial chips (*blótspán*) are dropped to ascertain the will of the gods, and it is determined that Odin desires a man for hanging. The victim is to be selected by drawing lots. The lot falls to King Víkar himself, and it is decided to hold a conference the next day. During the night Odin appears and commissions Starkadr to send King Víkar to him, giving him for the purpose a spear that looks like a reed. The following morning the king's counselors decide, on Starkadr's advice, to arrange a sham sacrifice. Just near the scene is a small pine tree, at the foot of which is a stump. A narrow twig stretches above the stump. Starkadr has the entrails taken from a newly slaughtered calf. He steps onto the stump and makes a noose out of the soft entrails and ties it to the narrow, supple twig. Starkadr thereupon says to the king: "Now is a gallows ready for thee, O king! and it looks not very dangerous. Come hither, then, that I may lay the noose about thy neck." The king replies: "If this arrangement is not more dangerous for me than it appears, I do not expect it to harm me; but if it is otherwise, may destiny take its course." He then stepped onto the stump, Starkadr laid the noose about his neck and stepped down from the stump. Starkadr now touched the king with the reed and said: "I now give thee to Odin." Thereupon Starkadr released the pine twig. At this point, three curious events occur: The reed turned into a spear and pierced the king, the stump fell from under his feet, and the soft entrails of the calf became a strong willow twig (*viðju*), and the branch flew up and lifted the king into the branches where he was strangled.

In the account that appears in Saxo's history, there are only a few, but nevertheless important, differences. According to Saxo, Odin wishes the death of Víkar, and to achieve this end he grants to the hero, Starcatherus, superhuman strength and the life-span of three human lives. The hero makes the noose, not out of a calf's entrails, but out of willow twigs (*ex viminibus*). In both cases, however, the actual strangulation occurs by means of willow twigs, the same manner by which the child in the Low German folktale was strangled.

A close examination of the death of Víkar reveals that the king loses his life by the simultaneous occurrence of three events. The reed becomes a spear and wounds the victim, the stump falls over, the pine twig flies up, and the king is strangled by the entrails that have become a strong willow branch. It is thus probable that one is here confronted with a variant of the theme of the threefold death. This contention is supported by the account in Saxo's history. Saxo states specifically that Odin is using Starkadr as a tool to acquire the life of Víkar, and he grants to the hero the life-span of three human lives. The payment of the threefold death is thus a threefold life, and with this payment a kind of divine balance of life and death is maintained.

It is, moreover, probable that in this Germanic version of the threefold death, the means of execution was originally by noose, water, and weapon. One can imagine that it became increasingly difficult to make plausible an accident in which the victim is hanged and drowned simultaneously. In Celtic tradition this problem had been solved in an obvious manner; the hanging motif had been weakened to merely that of falling from a tree. Here in Germanic tradition a similar solution was reached; the motif of drowning had been weakened by merely indicating that the victim fell from a stump.

This contention is supported by the occurrence of the drowning motif in the Low German variant of the tale of the threefold death which was already discussed. In the German tale the child suffers a simultaneous twofold death by drowning and by strangulation when it becomes entangled in a willow twig (*Wiedenstruck*) and falls in the water. The occurrence of the willow twig strongly suggests that this tale is related—not directly to the Celtic tradition, as are many of the variants of the tale—but to the Germanic accounts of the sacrifice of Víkar. In view of this evidence, it can now be assumed that the drowning motif was part of the Germanic treatment of the threefold death, and it is thus probable that this motif was originally associated with the accounts of the sacrifice of King Víkar.

An important element shared by the Irish heroic legends, the popular folktale, and the Germanic treatment of this theme is the establishment in advance of the mode of death, either by dream, by prophets, or—in the case of the *Víkarssaga*—by the drawing of lots and the appearance of Odin in person. In each of the traditions an attempt is made to avert the threefold death. But fate cannot be cheated, nor can the gods be deprived of their victim. Death is the one incontrovertible fact of life. There is no escape, thus the three prophesied manners of death inevitably work simultaneously to deprive the victim of his life.

The evidence adduced thus far indicates that both Germanic and Celtic religion knew the three separate kinds of human sacrifice, corresponding to the three classes of divinities and to the three classes of society. Moreover, each tradition knew the legend of the threefold death in which all three modes of human sacrifice functioned simultaneously. One question, however, remains unanswered: What is the nature of the relationship of the theme as it occurs in the Celtic and Germanic traditions? One could assume that the Germanic version of the legend represents an intrusion from Celtic tradition. There is certainly enough evidence of prolonged and intensive contact between the two peoples to justify such an assumption. On the other hand, the relationship of the Germanic treatment of the legend with the Celtic treatment seems to be a distant one indeed. The Germanic legend, with the use of the willow twig, the reed, and with the dedication of the victim to Odin, seems to represent a distinct tradition, deeply imbedded in Germanic religion. Moreover, the motif of death by fire, an important element in many of the Celtic variants, is totally missing from the Germanic treatments of the theme. In view of this evidence, one must look for another explanation of the relationship of the two traditions.

If the relationship cannot be explained by diffusion, then the only tenable explanation that remains is the assumption of a common ancestor to both traditions. Since it has been established that the narrative tradition is based on sacrificial practices, and since it has been shown that these practices reflect the Indo-European tripartite ideology as posited by Georges Dumézil, I suggest that this common ancestor lies in the religion of the Indo-Europeans.

The Threefold Death in Finnish Lore

JEANNINE E. TALLEY, *University of California, Los Angeles*

Outside the Indo-European sphere there is an interesting and peculiar appearance of the trifunctional sacrifice in the Finnish ballad "Mataleena."[1] In the following passage Christ exposes the sins of Magdalen with these words:

Kussas kolme poikalastas?—	Where are your three sons?—
Yhden tuiskasit tulehen,	The first you burned in fire,
toisen vetkaisit vetehen,	The second you drowned in water,
kolmannen kaivoit karkeesehen.	The third you buried in the earth.
Sen kuin tuiskasit tulehen,	The one you burned in fire
siit' ois Ruotsissa ritari;	Could have been a knight in Sweden;
sen kuin vetkaisit vetehen,	The one you drowned in water
siit' ois herra tällä maalla;	Could have been a burgher in this country;
sen kuin kaivoit karkeesehen,	The one you buried in the earth
siit' ois pappi paras tullut.	Could have been a good priest.

In this passage the three social classes of priest, knight, and burgher are represented, and correspondingly three distinct means of killing: burial, burning, and drowning respectively. Burial, in this instance, seems to have supplanted hanging.

How did this motif find its way into the popular tradition of a non-Indo-European people? As D. J. Ward indicated above, the folktale version of the "threefold death" spread by diffusion and is attested in Estonia, yet not in this type of ballad. The southern European variants of the ballad do not have this motif, but rather closely

[1] For the entire Finnish text see Elsa Haavio, *Ritvalan Helkajuhla* (Helsinki, 1953), pp. 180–181.

follow the narrative as it is preserved in a thirteenth-century Latin manuscript of Jacobus a Voragine. Julius Krohn[2] believed that the ballad spread from southern Europe northward into Germany and Scandinavia. "Magdalen," as Krohn also points out, has not survived in Germany; yet, there is a fragmentary text from Lausitz which he quotes.[3] Below is a free translation of the text:

> A beautiful maiden, Aria, goes on Sunday to fetch water. An old man comes who requests a drink from her. "The water is not clean; there is dust and dirt in it." "The water is certainly clean, but you are impure." "Prove it." "Go to church with a wreath on your head." Before her departure it withers. In the churchyard nine headless boys surround her. "Mother, why do you still go with the wreath on your head?" "Please forgive my crime!" "We surely could, but not God." She goes to church to receive holy water, gets down on her knees before the altar and makes the sign of the cross, but at that instant sinks into the earth.

The death of the children and their illegitimacy are merely alluded to respectively by the mention of the nine headless children and the withering of the wreath, which indicates that Aria is no longer a virgin. The significance of this text is that it combines two different ballads, "Magdalen" and "The Cruel Mother," and suggests that the inclusion of the motif from "The Cruel Mother" first occurred in Germanic tradition before spreading to the Scandinavian countries and the British Isles. In Germany there are many variations of "The Cruel Mother" and many titles for the narrative which differ in finer details but which conform in the overall narrative pattern. Among the more popular names by which the ballad is known are: "Höllisches Recht,"[4] "Die Rabenmutter,"[5] and "Die Kindsmörderinn."[6] A passage quoted from *Des Knaben Wunderhorn* suffices to illustrate the handling of the motif in the German ballad.

> Trägst du ein Kränzlein rosenroth,
> Du hast ja schon drei Kinder todt.
> Das erste hast in Wasser getragen,
> Das ander hast in Mist vergraben,
> Das dritt in hohlen Baum gesteckt
> Und mit Eichenen Ruthlein zugedeckt.

---

2 Julius Krohn, *Kantelettaren tutkimuksia*, I (Helsinki, 1900), 32–33.

3 For the original text see Leopold Haupt and Johann Ernst Schmaler, *Volkslieder der Wenden* (Grimma, 1841–1843), I, no. 290; II, no. 197.

4 See Achim von Arnim and Clemens Brentano, *Des Knaben Wunderhorn* (Berlin, 1846), II, 205.

5 A. Wilhelm von Zuccalmaglio, *Deutsche Volkslieder mit ihren Original-Weisen* (2d ed.; Berlin, 1840), p. 203.

6 Joseph Georg Meinert, *Alte teutsche Volkslieder in der Mundart des Kuhländchens* (Hamburg, 1817), p. 164.

Almost unanimously Finnish folklore scholars have concluded that the Finns borrowed "Magdalen" from Sweden; in the Swedish variants, however, the children are thrown into a lake, a river, or the sea, thus representing only the sacrificial ritual of the third estate. In addition to this aspect, the Swedish ballads do not mention the member places of the sons in the social structure. Because these two items are lacking in Swedish ballads, it is possible that the Finns borrowed directly from the Germans. Conceivably this borrowing could have occurred sometime between the twelfth and sixteenth centuries, since the Hanseatic League brought Germans into direct contact with the Finns. In Gotland, at Visby, the League founded a center of commerce. Many vessels sailed from Visby to Turku in quest of fish and furs, the merchants often spending their winters in Finland waiting for the spring market.[7]

Lines similar to those in the Finnish "Magdalen" also occur in the Finnish lyrical song, "Leino Leski" ("The Pitiable Widow"). In this song a widow has been told to leave her castle because of an ensuing battle. The widow, however, defies the advice proudly announcing that she is not to be pitied and that she is not without means since she has three sons to protect her:

> One is a bishop in Turku,
> The second a knight in Sweden,
> The third a burgher in this country.
>
> It happened that death heard this,
> Standing below the wall
> Already the bishop from Turku was killed,
> The knight from Sweden was killed,
> And the burgher from this country.[8]

Both the ballad and the song are isolated examples of the triadic social class structure in Finnish tradition. The ballad has been preserved in western Finland only in Ritvala in the province of Häme where it was traditionally sung in the Helka (Whitsuntide) festival until the nineteenth century. "Leino Leski" was sung mainly in Ingria and the Karelian Isthmus but has never been collected in western Finland.

There is, for the time being, no reason for asserting that the Indo-European social structure was wholly or even partially paralleled by the early Finns. Further investigations may uncover more examples

---

7 Matti Kuusi, "Keskiajan kalevalainen runous," *Suomen kirjallisuus*, I (Helsinki, 1963), 273–397.

8 For the complete Finnish text see Kaarle Krohn, *Suomen muinaisrunoja* (Helsinki, 1930), pp. 137–138.

in support of such an assumption. For the present, however, one may only suggest that, after the ballad was transmitted to Finland, the Finns conserved the motif combining the Indo-European triadic social structure with the tradition of the trifunctional human sacrifice. Social patterns introduced by Swedish rule may well have afforded secondary reinforcement of its practical relevance.

Indo-European Elements in Baltic and Slavic Chronicles

ROBERT L. FISHER, JR., *University of California, Los Angeles*

The search for Indo-European elements in ancient Slavic and Baltic paganism presents the investigator with a formidable challenge. On the one hand, the data are meager and of comparatively recent date, while on the other hand, what data we do possess are contained for the most part in Christian documents, and are thus distorted by the hostile attitudes of the authors toward the very paganism that they were trying to suppress. Furthermore, since no myths have survived qua myth, we are destined to be limited to euhemerization of older Indo-European beliefs. Aside from individual items of an Indo-European character which poke through the surface of the sea of Christianization like partly submerged mountain peaks, there are few legends that, as systems, present a consistent tripartite *Weltanschauung*. Thus, the investigator

> quaesitisque diu terris, ubi sistere possit,
> in mare lassatis volucris vaga decidit alis.[1]

Recently Georges Dumézil recorded his own findings and incorporated those of A. Yoshida and others who have been working with euhemerized myth in the Slavic area. They have usually dealt with the *byliny*, some of which are quite late ("la plus ancienne peut-être du XIVe siècle").[2] These workers have primarily bypassed the older

---

1 Ovid, *Metamorphoses* 1.307–308.

2 Dumézil, *Mythe et épopée: L'idéologie des trois fonctions dans les épopées des peuples indo-européens* (Paris, 1968), p. 625. See also Roman Jakobson

sources (eleventh and twelfth centuries), such as *The Russian Primary Chronicle*. Recently V. N. Toporov investigated the gods as they are enumerated in this chronicle, in the *Igor' Tale*, and various other works. He has concerned himself directly with the ancient Slavic pantheon, and not with euhemerization. Toporov has postulated the following order:[3]

First function: Stribogŭ = Varuṇa-Mitra
Second function: Perunŭ = Indra
Third function: Volosŭ = Nāsatya

Although Perunŭ and Volosŭ are well placed in their respective functions, Stribogŭ is relegated to the first function primarily on the strength of a doubtful etymology: *Stri-bogŭ* < **pətri-bhagos*. Then Stribogŭ would be parallel to *pitā́ dyauḥ*, Ζεῦ πάτερ, Jupiter, IE **pətēr diēus*. The main objection here is that regardless of whether or not the etymology is correct, little is really known of Stribogŭ, except his name. There are no myths or legends that explain his function in the system.

The Slavic pantheon is further complicated by the addition of Iranian elements: the god Xŭrsŭ, and possibly Simarĭglŭ which may be a copyist's error for "Sim, a household spirit, and Rigl, a spirit of the harvest."[4] It is even plausible that the Slavic pantheon is an artificial organization of gods drawn from native Slavic sources and scholarly borrowing from Persia. Vladimir may have had a strong reaction to the encroachment of Christianity, and therefore tried to establish a standardized state religion. At any rate, so little is known about the ancient Slavic gods that the researcher must rely heavily upon euhemerization.

There is, however, one piece of *terra firma* which does directly concern the gods themselves, and this is a surprisingly clear example of tripartite ordering. In Grunau's *Preussische Chronik* of the sixteenth century, there is a description of a tapestry (*bannir*) that portrays three heads, two on the top and one on the bottom, looking up at the

---

and Marc Szeftel, "The Vseslav Epos," in *Russian Epic Studies*, Memoirs of the American Folklore Society 42 (1947), where they discuss the intrusion of the folktale of Volx Vseslav'evič into *The Russian Primary Chronicle*. This legend appears as the biography of Prince Vseslav of Polock (1044–1101). The hero has been analyzed from an Indo-European tripartite point of view by Dumézil and Yoshida (see Dumézil, *op. cit.*, pp. 625–628). For the south Slavic version of this tale see Gojko Ružičić and Roman Jakobson, "The Serbian Zmaj Ognjeni Vuk and the Russian Vseslav Epos," *AIPhO* 10:343–355 (Brussels, 1950).

[3] V. N. Toporov, "Fragment slavjanskoj mifologii," *Akademija Nauk SSSR, Institut slavjanovedenija, Kratkie soobščenija* 30:26 (1961).

[4] S. H. Cross and O. P. Sherbowitz-Wetzor, *The Russian Primary Chronicle: Laurentian Text*, Medieval Academy of America Publication 60 (1953), p. 222 n. 55.

others. Patollo (Pickols, Pickollos, and so on) is depicted as an old man with a pale, deathly color; he wore a white cloth over his forehead like a "morbant."[5] He is the one on the bottom. Lucas David (*ibid.*, p. 91) reports that "Patollo or Pickollos" is the most important Prussian deity; he is "the god of death" who has "the power to kill." "Pocols atque Pocols" is glossed "Pluto, Furiae," and "Pocclum inferni ac tenebrarum deum" as well as "Pocollom aereorum spirituum deum," and "Pocullus deus spirituum volantium sive cacodaemonarum." Pickollos seems to be derived from the same root as Lithuanian *pykstù*, "be angry," a sense that resembles that of Odin (*Wō-ðanaz). Both Varuṇa and Odin are described as pale, old men—gods of the underworld and death. White is also the color associated with the first function.

The other two figures are: Perkunas, depicted with an angry mien, and Potrimpo, portrayed as a young, beardless man with ears of corn around his head and a happy expression. Perkunas is a well-known counterpart of Thor and Perun. Potrimpo can be none other than the third-function god on a par with Freyr. His name is far less transparent. Since he is the god of water, rivers, and streams, attempts have been made to divide his name into *po*, "under," and **trimpus*, "water" (the closest word actually attested in Old Prussian is *trumpa*, "fluvius").[6]

A search into Nestor's *Russian Primary Chronicle* for euhemerized Indo-European myth is rewarding. Nestor sets forth the legendary history of the Kievan state: its earliest beginnings, the reigns and personalities of its first rulers. The question of the historicity of the early kings of Kiev is far from settled. The earliest king, Rurik, is the most hazy, and this haze lifts as the chronicler approaches the time of St. Vladimir. Much of the early history contains a great deal of popular legend, and the chronology of succession is riddled with numerous impossibilities. For example, it is unlikely that Igor' could be Rurik's son because Igor' is said to have married Olga in 903, although his own son, Svjatoslav, was not born until 942. More important, the second attack of Oleg on Constantinople is another report that is completely unsubstantiated by Byzantine documents. The chronicle hopelessly confuses the dates of Olga's journey to Byzantium as well as the date of her baptism. At any rate, even if all those rulers are historical, real figures, very little is known of them, and it is obvious that much oral tradition has been draped around

---

5 N. K. Chadwick, *The Beginnings of Russian History: An Enquiry into Sources* (Cambridge, 1946), p. 25.

6 Theodore R. von Grienberger, "Die Baltica des Libellus Łasicki: Untersuchung zur litauischen Mythologie," *Archiv für slavische Philologie* 18:80 (1896).

these early personages. The exact characterizations of their personalities with exemplifying stories, and their order of succession, are manipulated in such a way as to suggest a euhemerization of some underlying myth. It may also represent an unconscious ordering of fact and tradition "en accord avec le système triparti." Finally, considering the long discourses on folk beliefs, portents, apocrypha, and hagiographic miracle lore—all presented as indisputable fact—it should not be surprising to discover such discrepancies.

The legend of the establishment of the Kievan state begins essentially with an entry under the years 860–862 in the Nestor Chronicle. It was at this time that the disunited Slavic tribes, suffering from internecine conflicts, requested the overlordship of the Varangians in a last-ditch effort to achieve stability: "Our land is rich, but there is no order in it; come and rule and have dominion over us."[7]

The important part of the entry for these years is the designation of Rurik as a ruler of Novgorod and the succession of Oleg upon the other's death. It is not entirely farfetched to assume that Rurik and Oleg were corulers of Novgorod, as seems to have been a widespread custom among the Scandinavians of that time (cf. Chadwick, *op. cit.*, p. 25). If this were the case, then plausibly Rurik and Oleg could be candidates for the same position occupied by Romulus and Remus when they were the early cosovereigns of Rome.

There are other similarities in the two histories. First, Romulus violently wrests control from Remus;[8] such violence is not surprising considering the former's Varunaic nature. Although Rurik dies peacefully, Oleg, the Varuṇa figure, does assume sole rulership. Second, Romulus becomes a syncretized personality since the Ramnes (< Remus), a tribe devoted to religious and administrative authority, is said to have been founded by the victorious twin. Parallel to this is the syncretism of many Mitraic traits in the personality of Oleg.

By way of contrast, nowhere does the chronicler suggest any change in the basic nature of these two rulers; they were always sovereigns. Whereas, both in Roman tradition and in the Hadingus story, there is a metamorphosis from third- to first-function characteristics of these rulers. So little is known about Rurik, however, that assumptions about his personality are extremely difficult.

---

[7] Cross and Sherbowitz-Wetzor, *op. cit.*, p. 59. Incidentally, this "calling of the princes" has been rejected by most modern scholars on the basis of archaeology and Greek and Oriental records. Apparently the Scandinavians had entrenched themselves in northern Russia before the ninth century, and then proceeded south as traders and warriors. For full argument, see pp. 35–50 and 233–234 n. 20.

[8] Livy, *Early History of Rome*, I–IV of *The History of Rome from its Foundation*, trans. Aubrey de Sélincourt (Harmondsworth: Penguin Books, 1967), p. 24.

Nevertheless, what can be reasonably assumed is that Oleg and Rurik were cosovereigns of Novgorod, and that the Varuṇa figure became the sole ruler upon the death of his partner.

There are a number of aspects to the legends concerning Oleg that suggest a Varunaic character. First, there is his singular method of winning battles. Under the years 880–882, Nestor reports that Oleg traveled to Kiev, which at that time was held by Askold and Dir, two Norsemen who were not of Rurik's clan but had captured the city. Oleg was of Rurik's clan and was the regent for Igor', Rurik's son. Because of his kinship to Rurik, Oleg considered himself to be the rightful ruler. Nestor goes on to relate (Cross and Sherbowitz-Wetzor, *op. cit.*, p. 61):

> He [Oleg] then came to the hills of Kiev, and saw how Askold and Dir reigned there. He hid his warriors in the boats, left some others behind, and went forward himself bearing the child Igor' . . .he sent messengers to Askold and Dir, representing himself as a stranger on his way to Greece on an errand for Oleg and for Igor', the prince's son, and requesting that they should come forth to greet them as members of their race. Askold and Dir straightway came forth. Then all the soldiery jumped out of the boats, and Oleg said to Askold and Dir, "You are neither princes nor even of princely birth." "Igor" was then brought forward, and Oleg announced he was the son of Rurik. They killed Askold and Dir.

In this story there is no long siege, no attempt at integrity, and little bloodshed. But there is a trick and a lie. Also, Oleg emphasizes his own princeliness, his sovereignty, his "race." Oleg calls himself "a stranger," and there is that irony of his lie because he says he is on a mission for "Oleg and Igor'." All these elements point clearly to similar features of Varuṇa and Odin. Just as Odin manipulates warriors, but never enters the actual killing himself, here Oleg merely asserts his authority over Kiev, brushing aside its rulers who seem to stand dumbfounded and paralyzed before his authority. Oleg merely asserts his authority, and without further complications or resistance the city is his. The trick, the lie (especially with ironic overtones) are reminiscent of Odin's treachery. As does Oleg, Odin frequently appears in the guise of a stranger, and "stranger" is one of his epithets. Finally, the very name Oleg is derived from the Old Norse Helgi, "holy," borne by the Odin-related hero Helgi Hundingsbani.

There are other similar accounts of his nonparticipant manner of fighting and his emphasis on extension of authority rather than warfare. In 885 (*ibid.*, p. 61), "Oleg commanded his warriors to make wheels which they attached to the ships, and when the wind was favorable, they spread the sails and bore down upon the city from the open country. When the Greeks beheld this, they were afraid, and sending messengers to Oleg, they implored him not to destroy the city and offered to submit to such tribute as he should desire." Again the actual victory is won more by fear and by ingenuity than by brute force (as the device of the wheeled ships points out). Unlike other rulers of Kiev described later in the chronicle, there is no mention of Oleg as an actual warrior. Instead, he seems to be more of a director than a participant. Another factor brought out by this story is the blind fury of Oleg and his men which was unleashed on the Greek captives. This trait again recalls Odin (whose name means "fury" and is glossed by Saxo as "furor"). In this same passage, the victorious Oleg, upon his return to Kiev, is called "the Sage" by the people, "for they were but pagans and therefore ignorant." The word used for "sage" is *věščij*, from the same root as *vědě*, Indo-European **woyd-*, "to know," but in a supernatural sense. This same adjective is used to describe the magician Boian in the *Igor' Tale*. The best translation is "seer," "wizard."[9]

The final episode that further demonstrates Oleg's magical nature is the story of his death. He consulted magicians in order to find out how he would die. They foretold that death would come from his horse. He prudently ordered his horse to be taken care of, but never to be brought into his presence. Word came to him years later that his horse had died. He then scoffed at the magicians' prophecy and went to inspect the dead horse's bones. "He laughed and remarked, 'so I was supposed to receive my death from this skull?' [a peculiar thing to say, since the skull was never mentioned in the original prophecy], and he stamped upon the skull with his foot. But a serpent crawled forth from it and bit him on the foot, so that he sickened, and died" (Cross and Sherbowitz-Wetzor, *op. cit.*, p. 69).

His death involves a healthy respect for magic and befits a magical sovereign quite well, just as Romulus suffered a magical death or (better) disappearance (Livy, *op. cit.*, p. 35).

As mentioned above, Oleg shows Mitraic characteristics, which may represent his syncretism with Rurik (if the latter ever had such traits), in much the same way as Romulus and the Ramnes represent a syncretism of the magical and legal aspects of the first function. After his alleged attack and victory over Byzantium, Oleg concluded a peace treaty that is quite striking in its content when contrasted with the treaties drawn up by his successors. While their treaties tend to be mere nonaggression pacts (completely temporary, until more

---

[9] Tatjana Čiževska, *Glossary of the Igor' Tale* (The Hague, 1966), p. 113.

troops can be mustered, as is frequently the case with Igor'), the treaty of Oleg is much broader in scope and much more detailed. It runs on for several pages in the Nestor chronicle (pp. 64–68) and covers minutely such items as trade agreements, extradition of criminals, reparation, mutual assistance, salvage laws for lost ships, inheritance, fine for assault, and the like. The language is legalistic and sophisticated. Furthermore, much emphasis is placed on the sacredness of the oath, which is another Varunaic element. Such phrases as "an inviolable pledge binding equally on you Greeks and upon us Russes" are frequent, as are the ideas of "convention," "covenant," and "peace."

In summation, Oleg can be seen as a Varunaic sovereign of magical type based on the fact that he was a coruler of Novgorod with Rurik, that he is a nonparticipant in his wars, that he is called *věščij*, "wizard," that in many particulars he is close to Odin, and finally, because of his magical death. Oleg also has Mitraic elements as evidenced by his legalistic treaty which is unique among the early Kievan princes.

The next prince of Kiev was the grown-up Igor'. His reign is characterized by a particularly brutish and monstrous type of warfare which is in sharp contrast to the career of his successor, Svjatoslav, the embodiment of warrior ideals par excellence. Because of this distinction, it is best to interpret Igor' as a Bhīma-Vāyu type and Svjatoslav more as an Arjuna-Indra type.

Igor' ascended the throne in 913, and by 914 he had already subjected the rebellious Derevlians and had imposed a higher tribute than his predecessor, Oleg. Every entry concerning him mentions war in the same breath. Unlike Oleg, he neither enjoyed nor desired peace.

Under 935–941 Nestor recounts Igor's Greek campaign (Cross and Sherbowitz-Wetzor, *op. cit.*, p. 72): "The Russes . . . began to ravage Bithynia. They . . . laid waste the entire region of Nikomedia, burning everything along the gulf. Of the people they captured, some they butchered, others they set up as targets and shot at, some they seized upon, and after binding their hands behind their backs, they drove iron nails through their heads. Many sacred churches they gave to flames, while they burned many monasteries and villages. . . ." After his narrow escape, Igor', "upon his return . . . began to collect a great army, and sent many messengers after the Varangian beyond the sea, inviting them to attack the Greeks, for he desired to make war upon them." In 944 he finally collected this great army and "advanced upon the Greeks . . . thirsting for revenge." But the Byzantine Emperor managed to buy off the Russian invader and his allies, and Igor' "bade the Pechenegs to ravage Bulgaria" (*ibid.*, p. 73).

His treaty with the Greeks is a simple document which ends (*ibid.*, p. 76): "May they [the transgressors of the treaty] not be protected by their own shields, but may they be slain by their own swords, laid low by their own arrows or by any of their own weapons, and may they be in bondage forever." These threats and curses stand out against the more sophisticated Greek stipulations which echo many points of Oleg's treaty.

After concluding this agreement, Igor' lived in peace until "autumn came, [when] he thought of the Derevlians, and wished to collect from them a still larger tribute" (*ibid.*, p. 78).

In 945 he sought that extra tribute and "collected it by violence. . . ." He returned home loaded with booty, but halfway he had second thoughts; "being desirous of still greater booty, he returned on his tracks with a few of his followers."

Prince Mal of the Derevlians heard of his return for more tribute. They described Igor' as a "wolf come among sheep" who "will take away the whole flock one by one, unless he is killed." They slew Igor' since he had but a small retinue with him.

At this point, Nestor inserts the legend of Olga, Igor's wife, and her threefold revenge for his murder. This is discussed below, but now it is important only to note that an additional tale whose motif is revenge follows the biography of a prince devoted to savage warfare, torture, ravaging for its own sake, revenge, and the exacting of tribute. On account of these characteristics of the Igor' legend, it is best to see him as a Bhīma-Vāyu personality.

The tone of the reports changes radically with the years 956–964, when Svjatoslav became prince of Kiev. Although his career is extremely warlike, Svjatoslav is described as having a "valiant army," and, "stepping as light as a leopard, he undertook many campaigns." Typical of Nestor's new vocabulary is (year 965): "He sallied forth against the Khazars." His nature is clear; he is a brave warrior—so much so that his sovereignty as prince is almost totally eclipsed. He eats and lives just like one of his infantrymen (*ibid.*, p. 84): "Upon his expeditions he carried neither wagons nor kettles, and boiled no meat, but cut off small strips of horseflesh, game, or beef, and ate it after roasting it on the coals. Nor did he have a tent, but he spread out a horse-blanket under him, and set his saddle upon his head: and all his retinue did likewise." He does not employ the sneak attack, but sends messengers, announcing his intention to fight. His bravery is well attested (971, after a Bulgarian victory): "But Svjatoslav cried to soldiery, 'Here is where we fall! Let us fight bravely, brothers and companions!' " (*ibid.*, p. 87). And once when outnumbered by Greeks (*ibid.*, p. 88): "Now we have no place whither we may flee. Whether we will or no, we must give battle. Let us not disgrace Rus', but rather sacrifice our lives, lest we be dishonored. For if we flee, we shall be disgraced. We must not take to flight, but we will resist boldly, and I will march before you. If my head falls, then look to yourselves."

One episode from the same year incontrovertibly demonstrates Svjatoslav's second-function character. The Emperor took council how he might halt Svjatoslav's onslaught. First, they tempted him with gifts and gold, but he took no notice and gave the riches to his servants. On the second try, they brought him arms, which he duly admired and praised. The envoys told the Emperor: "This man must be fierce, since he pays no heed to riches, but accepts arms."

Svjatoslav, fearing a counterattack after his Greek victories, decided to make a peace treaty. It is recorded in a small declaration that does not have the legal bent of Oleg's, or the fierce curses and threats of Igor's. It simply states his promise not to attack Greek lands. Curiously though, he mentions that if anyone breaks the oath, "may we become as yellow as gold" (*ibid.*, p. 90). This may be a reference to the infliction of jaundice by the Slavic equivalent of Varuṇa for oath-breaking.

Svjatoslav died by the sword in a campaign against the Pechenegs. With consistency, the death is appropriate to the life he led as a warrior. Svjatoslav must be considered a second-function figure because of his love of war, his valor, his preference for arms over riches—all of which sets him apart from the vicious Igor'.

In 973 the reign of Jaropolk began. His rule was brief, and he was treacherously assassinated (but the chronology of this part of the chronicle is particularly confused). Jaropolk was a victim in many ways of his aggressive brother Vladimir (later Saint). Jaropolk fled his brother and was besieged for a winter in the city of Rodnya. The chronicle adds: "There was a great famine there, and we have to this day a proverb which speaks of famine as in Rodnya" (*ibid.*, p. 92). Vladimir also stole his brother's wife who had been brought from Greece and married to Jaropolk "on account of the beauty of her countenance." Both the famine, the mention of his wife's beauty, and her abduction have to do with the third function, and in this sense Jaropolk can be seen as its representative. This is scant evidence. One might suggest, however, that the third function would not be presented as sovereign. In Roman tradition, the only candidates for a representative of the third function are Ancus Martius and Servius Tullius. The latter seems to be more of a Bhaga-Aryaman sovereign, and the former is concerned with establishing legal boundaries, administration, and other practicalities, although Rome is said to have prospered during his reign. In Slavic tradition there is no other candidate, since the next king is the historically attested Vladimir who is legendarily very complex. Perhaps the legends of Jaropolk were overshadowed by those of Vladimir. In the chronicle, Jaropolk seems to be a stepping-stone for Vladimir's rise to power. At any rate, the case for Jaropolk as a third-function figure is inconclusive.[10]

In conclusion, the legends of the Nestor Chronicle surrounding the first four kings in the founding of the Kievan state were viewed as a continuation of Indo-European tripartite myth (such as is found in the legends of the early Roman kings), or a tripartite ordering of ancient Slavic lore. The shadowy Rurik had a coruler, Oleg, who displays mostly Varunaic features combined with Mitraic, legalistic

[10] The *jarŭ* in Jaropolk's name would seem to indicate 'frenzy,' but with sexual overtones: German 'Brunst' (cf. ζωρός, 'strong, fiery, lively,' most often used with reference to wine, but sometimes also to drugs; Old Russian *jarŭ*, 'streng, herb,' Serbo-Croatian *jȁra*, 'Hitze vom Ofen'). This reference to virility strengthens the case for his third-function character. Thus Jaropolk parallels Oleg in so far as he bears a name characteristic of his function: Olĭgŭ is from Old Norse Helgi, 'holy,' pointing to his connection with magic.

Both second-function figures have less transparent names. Igor' is < Old Norse Yngvarr < **InguhariR*. Yngvi is quoted by J. de Vries as a poetical word for 'prince, warrior' (*Altnordisches etymologisches Wörterbuch* [Leiden, 1961], s.v.). Rudolf Much (*Die Germania des Tacitus* [2d ed.; Heidelberg 1954], p. 53) suggests that Ing(ui) is another name for Freyr on the basis of the name Ingaevones, a maritime tribe among whom Nerthus (Freyr) was especially worshiped. He would segment the word Ing-aevones (< **aiwa-*, *aiwō-*, *aiwī*, Old English *ā(w)*, Old Saxon *ēo*, Old High German *ēwa* 'law, right'), meaning 'those who follow the law of Ing, the people of the cult of Ing.' On the other hand, Ing- may be a cognate of Greek ἔγχος, 'spear,' since both occur in such compound names as Ingimarr (<**InguimāriR*) and ἐγχεσί-μωρος, 'great with the spear, fighting with the spear' (cf. Gaulish Seg-mārus, Old Church Slavic Vladi-měrŭ, and so on). Although Igor's personality and warrior function are clear, unfortunately the same cannot be said of the origin and meaning of his name.

Svjatoslavŭ < *svjatŭ-*, Old Church Slavic *svętŭ*, 'holy' (cf. Avestan *spənta-*, Lithuanian *šventas*). *Spənta-* would perhaps be best translated as 'strong, supernaturally powerful.' (For a detailed summary of the arguments and for a complete list of Baltic, Slavic, and Iranian cognates, see H. W. Bailey, "Iranian Studies III," *BSOS* 7:275–298 [1934]). Since this word is used most often for divine beings who are good and beneficial to mankind, the Slavic meaning 'holy' is a natural development from an earlier epithet meaning 'strong, supernaturally powerful.' Perhaps this connotation of 'strong' (of good beings) has found its way to the Arjuna figure here, because he represents the "chivalrous," "socially acceptable" warrior as opposed to Igor', the sheer embodiment of uncontrolled destruction.

I would be inclined to think that the fact of the different linguistic sources of these names (Old Norse and Slavic) does not vitiate the proposal of their semantic unity within a mythological system. Just as the third-function figures may be called the Aśvins in one area and the Διόσκουροι in another, so even within a mixed language area the semantic slots may be filled with words from different linguistic traditions.

features. Igor' appears as a Bhīma-Vāyu figure, and Svjatoslav as an obvious Arjuna-Indra figure. Jaropolk has some third-function characteristics, but the evidence is insufficient for any definite conclusion.

There is yet another episode in the Nestor Chronicle in which further Indo-European elements can be seen. This is the story of Olga's triple revenge on the Derevlians for the murder of her husband, Igor'. As was seen above, Igor' was slain by the Derevlians. His widow was then approached by the Derevlian Prince Mal who asked for her hand in marriage, since he wished "to obtain possession of Svjatoslav, and work [his] will upon him." Mal sent his "best men, twenty in number" as envoys (*ibid.*, p. 78). Olga welcomed them, stated her willingness to marry Prince Mal, but added that she wished to honor the envoys the next day before her people. She bade them to refuse to go by horse or on foot, but to insist on being drawn through the city in their boat. That night she had a deep trench dug near the castle. After the envoys had been drawn to the castle and were "puffed up with pride," their boat was thrown into the ditch and they were buried alive. This completed the first phase of her revenge.

Next she sent a message to the Derevlians, saying that "if they really required her presence, they should send their distinguished men, so that she might go to their prince with due honor, for otherwise her people in Kiev would not let her go." The Derevlians accordingly "gathered together the best men who governed the land of Dereva, and sent them to her." Upon their arrival, Olga had a bath prepared for them; they were locked in the bathhouse, which was then set afire, "so that the Derevlians were all burned to death."

For her final act of revenge, she told the Derevlians that she was on her way and to "prepare great quanities of mead in the city . . . that . . . I may hold a funeral feast for him [Igor']. . . . When the Derevlians were drunk, she bade her followers fall upon them. . . . So they cut down 5,000 of them. . . ." Although Olga went on to further revenge by besieging their city the following year (946), this is another story, which is to be kept separate from the legend of her three-leveled scheme to go among the Derevlians under the pretense of a marriage proposal.

This legend shows that Olga brought revenge upon all three social classes: warriors, rulers, common people, in that order. "Best men" seems to refer to warriors in the first phase of her revenge because, first, they were not used to being treated as rulers, since they were "puffed up with pride" when shown honor. Second, they are specified as twenty handpicked men, not the distinguished men "who governed the land of Dereva." Her last victims are the people at large, the five thousand participants in their own funeral feast.[11]

This tripartite social scheme is rather straightforward, but the methods of killing the representative members of each social group present problems from an Indo-European point of view. Live burial is usually taken as appropriate to the third function, while death by fire and by the sword belong to the second function. The live burial is exceptional in that it involves the ship. Since there is a strong Scandinavian influence on the ruling house of Kiev, perhaps here there is a reference to "ship burials in stone barrows on the edge of the sea described in Norse sagas. In such stories it is sometimes said that a man builds for himself a barrow during his lifetime, and that he enters it while he is still alive with his ship's crew. Frequently in these sagas, we read of the Norse heroes breaking into such barrows, and finding a ship fully manned with a crew richly dressed and laden with treasure, seated, like the Derevlians, on the cross benches" (Chadwick, *op. cit.*, p. 29.). Thus, more likely, this episode is connected with the Scandinavian theme of ship burial, and not with an appropriate form of execution with respect to Indo-European ideology.

The second execution is by burning, a death that befits the second function, not the first function as here. One can only suggest that since the first function seems to have taken over second-function characteristics in the Slavic world (stress on warrior activity, lack of firmly entrenched priestly class), perhaps it has also taken on the form of second-function execution. Considering the general discontinuity, however, it seems better not to view the executions as consistent with an Indo-European outlook.

The last massacre involves the common people. From the fact that it occurs at a feast and involves their drunkenness, a good third-function method of killing would be expected. The story states explicitly, however, that the means of death was the sword.

In conclusion, Olga's revenge is truly tripartite since she extends her killings to all three social classes. But the same cannot be said of her methods of execution for each class.

---

[11] Another tripartite death may appear in *The Chronicle of Henry of Livonia* (Leonid Arbusow and Albert Bauer, *Heinrici Chronicon Livoniae* [Hannover, 1955]). Bishop Berthold, while consecrating the cemetery at Holm, is the object of a planned murder by the pagans: (p. 9) "alii in ecclesia concremare, alii occidere, alii submergere concertabant. . . ." There are, however, difficulties. Although the third-function death (by drowning) and the second-function death (by fire and sword) are represented, there is no first-function death. Here, since a priest is the potential victim, one would especially anticipate mention of hanging or falling. Nevertheless, it is suspicious that his Livonian parishioners thought of killing him in three ways—two of which, drowning and burning, seem to entail extra effort, since it would have been an easy matter to "cut him down" (*occidere*).

Aspects of Equine Functionality

JAAN PUHVEL, *University of California, Los Angeles*

From early Europe, the Near East, and Western Asia we possess an immense amount of archaeological, antiquarian, ethnographic, mythological, and folkloristic material concerning the horse. In the face of this welter of data, Indo-Europeanists concerned with mythic and religious matter must apply severe methodical selectivity in order to winnow structurally significant information from the mass of raw material. It is hence my purpose in this paper to pursue the role of the horse as an integral component of such Indo-European mythic and religious structures as are congruent with a tripartite concept of social and religious organization, and to eschew the pitfalls of universal or diffusional accordances.

Not much has been accomplished so far on the specific subject that interests us. Collections of antiquarian lore,[1] ethnographic treatises,[2] and paleological investigations[3] are not primarily concerned with Indo-European protocivilization in its mythic and religious aspects. The only viable starting point in past research is a kind of triptych depicting Indo-European horse sacrifice, the centerpiece of which is the well-documented and much-studied Ancient Indic *aśvamedha* ritual. One side panel is composed of the Roman *October Equus* as interpreted by Georges Dumézil, the other by Celtic analogues first adduced by Franz Rolf Schröder. A critical study of these compositions is needed as a basis for further forays. All other stray informa-

1 Such as J. von Negelein, *Das Pferd in arischen Altertum* (Königsberg, 1903).

2 On the lines of W. Koppers, "Pferdeopfer und Pferdekult der Indogermanen," *Wiener Beiträge zur Kulturgeschichte und Linguistik* 4:279–409 (1936).

3 Of the type of F. Hančar, *Das Pferd in prähistorischer und früher historischer Zeit, ibid.*, 11 (1955).

tion concerning horse sacrifice among Indo-Europeans must take a back seat until this is accomplished.

The *aśvamedha* is exceedingly well endowed with descriptive and exegetic matter. Apart from such Rig-Vedic hymns as 1.162 and 1.163, Paul-Emile Dumont treated the relevant White Yajur-Vedic (*Vājasaneyi Saṃhitā, Śatapatha Brāhmaṇa, Kātyāyana Śrautasūtra*) texts in his book *L'Aśvamedha* (Paris, 1927), adding material from three Black Yajur-Vedic *Śrautasūtra*'s (*Āpastamba, Baudhāyana, Vādhūla*) and from *Mahābhārata*, Book 14 (*Āśvamedhikaparvan*), and later performed the same service for the Black Yajur-Vedic variants of the *Taittirīya Brāhmaṇa*.[4] Further editorial work was done by Shrikrishna Bhawe.[5] Any number of more general works[6] afford a summary description.

The *aśvamedha* is a ritualistic production with a cast of thousands, incorporating many adjutory rites and representing in a sense the sum of Ancient Indic sacrificial pageantry. Trying to strip away excrescences, the central proceedings may be summarized as follows:

The start of the rite was made in the spring, with the king as patron and the four main priests (*adhvaryu, hotar, udgātar,* and *brahman*) as officiators. During the preliminary celebrations the king had to spend the night chastely with his favorite wife by the *gārhapatya* or domestic fire. A prize stallion was selected as the prospective victim and subjected to a number of ceremonies, including sprinkling in a pool, at which time a dog was killed and thrown under it. The stallion was then set free to roam, accompanied by a hundred gelded or aged horses and four hundred young men of different castes who were to guide it toward the northeast and keep it from contact with mares and from further immersion in water. This roaming took a whole year, and in the meantime a number of preparatory rituals took place at home. Toward the end of the year a huge fire-altar was erected, and the king underwent a seven- or twelve-day initiation (*dīkṣā*) involving fasting and other observances. During this time the entire stage was prepared, including a new hearth for the *gārhapatya* fire and the procurement and installation of the *soma*-supply. The main ritual took three days. On the principal, second day of sacrifice the king drove in a war chariot drawn by the sacrificial stallion and three other horses. The victim was anointed

4 *Proceedings of the American Philosophical Society* 92:447–503 (1948).

5 *Die Yajus des Aśvamedha* (Stuttgart, 1939).

6 Recently, for example, J. Gonda, *Die Religionen Indiens,* I (Stuttgart, 1960), 168–173; J. Campbell, *The Masks of God: Oriental Mythology* (New York, 1962), pp. 190–197.

by the three foremost wives of the king, and its mane and tail were fitted with 101 pearls. The sacrifice took place at twenty-one stakes, the three principal victims being the stallion, a hornless ram, and a he-goat. Altogether 366 or 609 victims were prescribed (according to *Taittirīya* and *Vājasaneyi* sources, respectively), but the wild beasts among them were released rather than killed. The stallion was smothered to death, whereupon the *mahiṣī* or chief queen symbolically cohabited with it under covers, while the entourage engaged in obscene banter. Then followed the cutting up of the victim, disposal of the parts, further blood sacrifices, ablutions, and disbursement of priestly honoraria.

In the *Śatapatha Brāhmaṇa* and in several *Śrautasūtra*'s the *aśvamedha* description is accompanied by what in most respects amounts to a summary replication of its ritual in the form of human sacrifice. This *puruṣamedha* involved the procuring of a *brāhmaṇa* or *kṣatriya* victim by purchase from his family for a thousand cows and a hundred horses. After initial rites he was set free for a year and humored in everything except sexual indulgence. The ritual itself took five days, versus three for the *aśvamedha*. The victim was adorned and throttled on the second day much like the horse, together with a hornless ram and a he-goat. The liturgy was taken mostly from the *Puruṣasūkta* and the funeral hymns of the tenth mandala of the *Rig-Veda*. The queen had intercourse with the dying or dead victim. Rather than a menagerie of animals, an accompanying human massacre was prescribed, which in some sources reached 184 persons of all social strata.

What was the relationship of these two rituals? Oldenberg and others saw in the *puruṣamedha* a figmental replication of the *aśvamedha*, thus disclaiming its historical reality. It is evident that to the Brāhmanic and Sūtric compilers the *puruṣamedha* was a somewhat unreal appendage to the horse sacrifice, almost a theoretical afterthought. In epic and classical literature there is no instance of its performance, except for the preposterous statement in *Mahābhārata* 1.3773 that Ayutanāyin performed ten thousand *puruṣamedha*'s. The Pāli Canon repeatedly rejects both *aśvamedha* and *puruṣamedha*, but this occurs in a blanket condemnation of all bloody sacrifices.

The historical *puruṣamedha* was thus at best obsolete, at worst unreal. Willibald Kirfel, in his article in the Walther Schubring dedication volume,[7] has made a case for the historicity of the *puruṣamedha* as a one-time practical means of actually begetting a royal

[7] *Beiträge zur indischen Philologie und Altertumskunde* (Hamburg, 1951), pp. 39–50.

heir when for some reason the king was unable to do so. Kirfel brings medical evidence for reflex-conditioned tumescence and emission in victims of hanging and decapitation and assumes a similar set of circumstances in the cohabitation of the *mahiṣī* and the *puruṣa*. Thus the *aśvamedha* would appear to be rather a substitute sacrifice for the *puruṣamedha*, with the symbolic element prevailing. Yet matters are not so simple, nor does Kirfel assume them to be. In the classical *aśvamedha* the king is triumphantly in charge, as dedicant to Prajāpati, the Lord of Creation, and the whole performance is guaranteed to make him victorious, sinless, happy, and glorious, as in Yudhiṣṭhira's great ritual in *Mahābhārata* 14. The cohabitation part, with the queen in the star role, is somehow extraneous to the central concept, although occasionally childlessness propels the sacrifice, as with King Daśaratha in *Rāmāyaṇa* 1. Kirfel assumes that the horse ritual of the invading Indo-Aryans fused on Indic soil with an agricultural fertility rite involving human sacrifice. The horse supplanted the human victim in the resulting conflation, yet the traits of the Pre-Aryan rites came to dominate the end product. Koppers distinguished what he called "Southern" elements in the *aśvamedha* from Indo-European-based inner-Asian imports, and it is those that would mainly correspond to the indigenous *puruṣamedha* features assumed by Kirfel. We may grant Kirfel that the total *aśvamedha* is a specifically Indic product. That it contains Pre-Aryan matter is well possible, but I find less convincing the specific assumption that Indo-European horse sacrifice and Pre-Aryan human sacrifice were conflated in such a way that the result was predominantly horse oriented in form but wholly Pre-Aryan in sacrificial and sexual substance. In short, I admit that there were transformations in the Indic horse sacrifice away from an Indo-European prototype, but not that the latter necessarily excluded connections with human sacrifice or sexual practice.

Let us turn now to one of the side panels of the previously mentioned triptych. That the Roman *October Equus* is a reflection of an Indo-European ritual of horse sacrifice has long been assumed, but Dumézil has made the comparison with India more plausible and precise.[8] As pieced together from Polybius, Plutarch, Festus, and Paulus Diaconus, the Roman ritual may be summarized as follows: After a horserace on the Campus Martius on the Ides of October, the right-side horse of the victorious chariot was immolated to Mars with a spear. The people of Suburra and of the Sacra Via fought over the

---

[8] Most recently and comprehensively in *La religion romaine archaïque* (Paris, 1966), pp. 217–229.

head of the horse; if the former caught it, they fixed it on the wall of the Turris Mamilia; if the latter, on that of the Regia. The tail was carried speedily to the Regia, and drops of blood from the tail were sprinkled on its hearth.

There are important differences from the *aśvamedha,* notably the manner of killing and the absence of the erotic element. But there are also broad similarities, for example, the dedication to Mars in Rome and the clear anteriority of Indra to Prajāpati as the one-time recipient of the *aśvamedha* (see e.g., Koppers, *op. cit.*, p. 337), and further the patronage of the *kṣatriya-rājā* in India and the role of the Regia in Rome. There are further specific accordances of the curious type that tends to exclude chance, such as the designation of the *equus bigarum victricum dexterior* in Rome and the *Śatapatha Brāhmaṇa* injunction (13.4.2.1) that the *aśvamedha* victim must "excel on the right part of the yoke," or the role of the horse's tail in both rituals.[9]

A similar singularity has been pointed out by Dumézil in "Quaestiuncula Indo-Italica 17."[10] Dio Cassius (43.24.2–4) describes how, as a result of a mutiny of troops in Rome in 46 B.C., Caesar had one ringleader summarily executed, whereupon two others were ritually killed on the Campus Martius by the pontiffs and the Flamen Martialis, and their heads deposited in the Regia. In these proceedings it seems that Caesar, in preparation for assuming royal power, was reviving an obsolescent ritual of human sacrifice which was a replication of the *October Equus.* It places the relationship of *aśvamedha* and *puruṣamedha* in a truer light, to the extent of indicating that in an Indo-European warrior-class horse sacrifice the substitution of a human victim for the horse was possible. Thus the horse sacrifice was not a toning down of the human sacrifice; rather the human victim represented an upgrading of the rite, a *Potenzirung,* as Albrecht Weber long ago described the *puruṣamedha* in his article "Über Menschenopfer bei den Indern der vedischen Zeit."[11]

Now for the other side panel. It is best subsumed in the words of the outraged Geraldus Cambrensis in his *Topographia Hibernica* (*ca.* A.D. 1185), which Schröder first collocated with the *aśvamedha*:[12]

> There is in a northern and remote part of Ulster, among the Kenelcunil, a certain tribe which is wont to install a king over itself by an excessively savage and abominable ritual. In the presence of all the people of this

[9] Dumézil, "Quaestiuncula Indo-Italica 3," *REL* 36:130–131 (1959).
[10] *REL* 41:87–89 (1963).
[11] *ZDMG* 18:269 (1864).
[12] *Zeitschrift für Celtische Philologie* 16:310–312 (1927).

land in one place, a white mare is brought into their midst. Thereupon he who is to be elevated, not to a prince but to a beast, not to a king but to an outlaw, steps forward in beastly fashion and exhibits his bestiality. Right thereafter the mare is killed and boiled piecemeal in water, and in the same water a bath is prepared for him. He gets into the bath and eats of the flesh that is brought to him, with his people standing around and sharing it with him. He also imbibes the broth in which he is bathed, not from any vessel, nor with his hand, but only with his mouth. When this is done right according to such unrighteous ritual, his rule and sovereignty are consecrated.

Here is something that was consummated in the full Middle Ages in the Celtic hinterlands on a far fringe of the Indo-European world. Its principal ties to the *aśvamedha* have often been affirmed since 1927, and I would reiterate what I wrote back in 1955,[13] that the Gaulish Arvernian royal name Epomeduos is synonymous with the royal name Aśvamedha in the *Rig-Veda* (5.27.4–6) and is the same type of exocentric compound (the Indic *bahuvrīhi* Aśvamedha being anterior to the descriptive *tatpuruṣa* name of the ritual). I am interested to find that V. V. Ivanov and V. N. Toporov[14] present this collocation as unchallenged and unreferenced fact. The ritual sacrifice of a horse may well have been a pan-Celtic Indo-European inheritance, a royal rite that was part of a consecration ceremony. In this respect it should belong with the Indic *rājasūya* rather than the *aśvamedha* proper, and there are other differences as well. The coitional element is there, but among the Celts it involves the king and a mare, versus the queen and a stallion in India. In the flush of collocation this discrepancy has been overlooked or de-emphasized, and I read with surprise: "Mit Recht bemerkt Schröder, dass es ohne Belang ist, wenn im irischen Ritus im Vergleich zum indischen die Rollen vertauscht sind: hier Königin und Hengst, dort König und Stute."[15] I think that this difference is far from inconsequential and in fact provides us with a wedge for penetrating from the ritualistic to the mythological level in dealing with Indo-European equine tradition.

There is ample reason to suspect a hierogamous mating as the mythical underpinnings of the horse sacrifice.[16] The nature of this mating is clearly discernible in Celtic traditions and involves a representative of the second or warrior function with the transfunctional

---

13 *Language* 31:353–354.

14 *Sanskrit* (Moscow, 1960), p. 18.

15 Jan de Vries, *Keltische Religion* (Stuttgart, 1961), p. 244.

16 See, for example, H. Ringgren and Å.V. Ström, *Die Religionen der Völker* (Stuttgart, 1959), pp. 148, 210–211, 358, 389–390, 409–410.

goddess figure. This figure has paled in Indic tradition, apart from its epicized survival in Draupadī as the consort of the Pāṇḍavas, but is eminently present in the Iranian Anāhitā, to whom various heroes in her Yašt (*Yašt* 5) sacrifice "a hundred stallions, a thousand cattle, ten thousand sheep." Their recipient is the trifunctional Arədvī Sūrā Anāhitā ("Moist, Heroic, Immaculate"), whose set of epithets probably hides the Iranian counterpart of the Vedic goddess Sarasvatī, that is, *Harahvatī, 'rich in waters,' which survives in the name of the province of Arachosia.[17] It seems likely that horses represented a warrior-function offering to Sūrā, cattle (not specifically bulls) a third-estate tribute to Arədvī, and sheep were an appropriate first-function sacrifice to Anāhitā. Similarly in the Roman *suovetaurilia* the bull was sacrificed to Mars, the pig to Tellus (Earth), and the sheep to Jupiter, although the whole rite is oriented toward Mars. The bull, ram, and boar figure in the Greek *trittyes* (offered to Poseidon, Apollo, Asklepios, the Dioscuri, and others), while the Indic *sautrāmanī* (dedicated to Indra Sutrāman) was made up of bull, ram, and he-goat, sacrificed to Indra, Sarasvatī, and the Aśvins, respectively. Thus, as long as the horse figures on the triple list for the second function, the third level exhibits either cattle (as with Anāhitā) or goat (in the *aśvamedha*), with the sheep or hornless ram in the first-function position. The bull is in complementary distribution with the horse, for when it appears in the second-function spot, it is to the exclusion of the horse, whereas the third level shows goat or pig.

The same goddess can be traced in the East Slavic Mokoš ('Moist,' cf. Russ. *mokryj*) and in Mati Syra Zemlja 'Mother Moist Earth.' In the Celtic area the presence of such a figure is preeminent, and in several varieties. The Gaulish Terra Mater and the three Matres or Matrae or Matronae, in whom I suspect a trifunctional triad, are matched in insular tradition by the divine ancestress Irish Danu, Welsh Dôn, and especially by the goddess Ériu, with whom every king of Tara was symbolically wedded in a conferral of sovereignty. In most manifestations this goddess figure exhibits manifold equine elements. The Gaulish Epona (Regina) of mostly iconographic fame as a riding or horse-surrounded goddess, and her legendary Mabinogi counterpart Rhiannon < *Rīgantona, 'Queen,' are subject to suspicions of original hippomorphism.[18]

The Irish goddess Macha of Ulster, or rather the three so-named figures, are a textbook case of a trifunctional female deity in some-

---

17 See H. Lommel, *Asiatica: Festschrift Friedrich Weller* (Leipzig, 1954), pp. 405–413.

18 See, for example, J. Gricourt, *Ogam* 6:28 (1954).

what euhemerized triple transmission. Their tales are preserved chiefly in the story of the sickness of the Ulstermen and in the *Rennes Dindšenchas,* and are conveniently summarized in several recent treatments.[19] The first Macha was a prophetess and wife of Nemed mac Agnomain, a druidic figure connected with the word for "shrine." The second Macha was the daughter of Aed Ruad ("The Red"), herself called Mongruad, 'Red-maned.' Her father had contracted with two other kings, Dithorba and Cimbaeth, that each should reign supreme for seven years in the framework of a triumvirate. On Aed's death Macha claimed for herself his due term of sovereignty, made her claim stick by force of arms, and ruled for seven years. She was finally killed by Rechtaid Rigderg, whose name also reeks of the red color symbolism of the warrior class.

The third Macha, wife of Crunniuc mac Agnomain, was forced by King Conchobar of Ulster to a race against horses, while in the last stages of pregnancy. She won, then immediately gave birth to twins, and died uttering a curse on the Ulstermen which led to their annual so-called childbed sickness.

This splitting of the one Macha into three distinct personalities is symptomatic of tensions within the trifunctional system. I cannot subscribe to Dumézil's claim that the second Macha represents the conflict of warriors with the first function; it is rather that the warriors' relationship with the trifunctional goddess has gone sour, from mating to hostility, as it is apt to do in Irish lore. But the cruelty of Conchobar to the third Macha, like the indignities suffered by Rhiannon, is directly relatable to the Western Indo-European mythical tensions embodied in the Norse Aesir-Vanir conflict, the Fomorian troubles in Ireland, and the Sabine War. For it is undeniable that the transfunctional goddess exerts a particular hegemony over the third function and is thus caught in the middle of any conflict opposing the third to the others. As Macha shows, this goddess is the mother of twins, and we might recall that the third-function horsemen twins of India, the Aśvins, also had some trouble with Indra before their admission to the upper-class *soma*-sacrifice.

The activities that led to split personalities in the case of Macha are visible elsewhere among the Celtic avatars of the transfunctional goddess. The names of Cuchulainn's three divine instructresses, Scathach ('Modest'), her daughter Uathach ('Terrible'), and Aife ('Handsome'), sound suspiciously trifunctional. That they are aspects of one and the same goddess it made clear by Uathach's advice that

---

[19] E.g., Gricourt, *ibid.*, pp. 25–30; Dumézil, *RHR* 146:5–17 (1954); de Vries, *op. cit.*, p. 128.

Cuchulainn should at swordpoint wring from Scathach a triple set of boons: instruction in warfare, Uathach's hand in wedlock, and a foretelling of his future, for Scathach was also a prophetess.[20] For what it is worth, I add this straw to Dumézil's trifunctional stack.

The figure of Medb is, if I may say so, the euhemerized Celtic super-Matrona, a sovereignty-conferring warrior-harridan and fountain of sexuality alike, whose nearest undebased parallels are the warrior goddesses Morrigu and Badb. Her relation to the former is evident from the fact that Medb and Morrigu both figure as interchangeably active in various versions of the prelude to the *Táin*, and diverse bird symbolisms tie her closely to the ornithomorphic Badb.[21] Her taurine fixation on the Donn of Cooley does not obliterate her horse symbolism. Thus her lover Fergus was known as Ro-ech, 'Big Horse,' and the third of her four husbands (besides Conchobar of Ulster, Tinne of Connacht, and Ailill of Leinster) was named Eochaid, a name also borne by the two husbands of Tailtiu, the divine nurse of the god Lug who closely resembles Ériu herself. The name Eochaid may be connectible with Old Irish *ech*, 'horse,' and with the epithetal string Eochu Ollathir Ruadrofessa 'Horse, All-father, Red Great Sage' that characterizes the god Dagda. I doubt that Medb's name means simply 'intoxication' or the like, and would rather interpret it as a Celtic *Meduā, uncompounded feminine parallel to the Arvernian Epomeduos, much as Badb corresponds to the Gaulish Cathubodua. The linguistic history would be the following: While the Indic name *Aśva-medha-* contains either an IE **mad-dho-* or **mey-dho-* (cf. *mádati*, 'be drunk,' or *máyas-*, 'strength'), a Proto-Celtic **Ekwo-medu-* would contain IE **médhu*, 'mead,' 'ritual beverage,' hence 'ritual involving drunkenness,' and the *-o-* or *-ā-* of *Epomeduos* or the abstracted **Meduā* is a *samāsānta* suffix characterizing the compound as a whole. It is therefore methodically incorrect to compare *Medb* directly with Welsh *meddw* as a thematic Celtic adjective **medwo-* derived from **medu*. I therefore submit that in Celtic tradition there exist traces not only of the royal sacrifice of and mating with a mare performed by kings who sometimes bore the name *Ekwomeduos, but also of a ritual myth of the mating of the transfunctional goddess, sometimes called *(Ekwo-)meduā, with a probably hippomorphous second-function representative. The offspring of such mating was a set of divine twins, typically of third-estate character.

---

20 See T. P. Cross and C. H. Slover, *Ancient Irish Tales* (New York, 1936), p. 165.

21 See, e.g., J. Dunn, *The Ancient Irish Epic Tale Táin Bó Cúalnge* (London, 1914), pp. 88, 274.

I am, of course, taking a calculated risk in awarding so much primacy to the Celtic material. The voice of caution would remind me that very little is known about a transfunctional goddess in the Roman, Germanic, and Indic pantheons, that the whole Aegean and Near Eastern area swarmed with goddess types that could influence the Iranian cults, and that some autochthonous survival might account for the proliferation of the Celtic Matronae. Yet I think that the very strong tripartite structuring of the Iranian and Celtic data argues for their primacy. The absence of the sexual element in Roman horse sacrifice is no surprise, for early Roman ritual is exceedingly nonerotic, in probable overreaction to Etruscan overindulgence. The transfunctional goddess, however, exists in Roman religion as Juno Seispes, Mater, Regina at Lanuvium, as Dumézil has pointed out.[22] In the Germanic pantheon, the complications caused by the sharp Aesir : Vanir dichotomy and the sexual ambivalence of the Vanir have wrought transfunctional havoc. Traces of the goddess no doubt survive in the Tacitean Nerthus and the masculinized Norse Njördr, whose career combines both Vanir and Aesir periods and is euhemerized in Saxo's figure of Hadingus.[23] In India the epic survival of the goddess in Draupadī is proof enough, and her disappearance from the pantheon is part and parcel of the trend that reduces goddesses to vague echoes of their consorts, onomastically and otherwise. She is doubtless present in Sarasvatī, and the latter's receipt of the ram offering in the *sautrāmanī* shows that her transfunctionality once reached all the way to the first function, like that of Anāhitā.

Let us return now to the *aśvamedha*. We can at this point better appreciate why the ritual does not check out well, mythically speaking. The reason is that it has been cut adrift from the cult myth that once explained its meaning. In compulsive ancient Rome this was no serious matter, for ritual petrifacts were readily perpetuated there in a vacuum. But the *aśvamedha* must have floundered, ever since at some point its prototype ceased to depict the ritual union of king and goddess, owing probably to a downgrading of the goddess. The king's role as the patron of a great horse festival persisted, the detail was elaborated and absorbed Pre-Aryan matter, not of a *puruṣamedha* type, but rather the typical Near Eastern ritual union of queen or goddess and beast. The usual bull of those rituals has, however, not supplanted the horse, or there would be no *aśvamedha*. The Indo-European pattern of theriomorphic hierogamy was clearly King and Mare, the Near Eastern and Aegean one Queen and Bull (e.g., Eu-

[22] *Eranos* 52:105–119 (1954).
[23] See Dumézil, *La Saga de Hadingus* (Paris, 1953).

ropa, Pasiphae in Cretan saga, wife of Archon Basileus in Greek religion, and so on). The Indic *aśvamedha* is thus a halfway house of transformation.

This ritualistic enactment of the hierogamic myth, even in the transmuted *aśvamedha* form, redounded to the weal of the canonically constituted total society, as subsumed in the whisperings of the *adhvaryu* into the ear of the victim during the preparatory ceremonies: blessings were to accrue successively to priesthood (*brahman*), royalty (*rāṣṭra*), cow, ox, horse, woman, chariot fighter, and youth; male offspring, rain, plentiful ripe fruit, and peaceful enjoyment were to result. Dumézil[24] has not only elucidated the detail of this tripartite listing but has compared it with Italic formulae like the Umbrian *nerf arsmo ueiro pequo castruo frif*, 'heroes, priesthood, men and beasts, fields and fruits' (cf. the corresponding lexical petrifacts of the type Avestan *pasu-vīra*, Vedic *vira-pś-á-*) and with Varro's division of human activity on analogous lines.[25] It is highly likely that such pandemic lists played an ancient part in Italic lore and belonged to the ritual that we still imperfectly glimpse in the *October Equus*.

Traces of the Indic cult myth probably survive in the traditions concerning Saraṇyū and her offspring. The basic texts from the *Rig-Veda* (10.17.1), Yāska (*Nirukta* 12.10), and Śaunaka (*Bṛhaddevatā* 6.162-7.7) were discussed by Maurice Bloomfield,[26] to which A. Blau added the corresponding Purāṇic *itihāsa*'s.[27] More recently H. Lommel has reexamined the material.[28] In brief summary, Tvaṣṭar had twin children, Saraṇyū and Triśiras. The latter was the three-headed monster that came to grief at Trita Āptya's hands but does not figure further in this myth. Saraṇyū married Vivasvat and bore twins, Yama and Yamī. She then created a double of herself, Savarṇā, left the children in her care, and fled in the form of a mare. Vivasvat mistook Savarṇā for his wife and begot Manu. When Vivasvat later realized that the real Saraṇyū had left as a mare, he changed himself into a stallion, found her, and begot on her the twin Aśvins.

The novelistic Purāṇic elaborations need not concern us here; what matters is that a rather primal goddess, a daughter of the demiurge Tvaṣṭar, or her double, is the mother of three sets of deities: Yama and Yamī, Manu, and the Aśvins. Yamī beside Yama, known only from their *saṃvādana* (*Rig-Veda* 10.10), like the Iranian *Yamīk* be-

---

24 "Quaestiuncula Indo-Italica 9," *Latomus* 20:257–262 (1961).
25 L. Gerschel, *Latomus* 17:65–72 (1958).
26 *JAOS* 15:172–188 (1893).
27 *ZDMG* 62:337–357 (1908).
28 *ZDMG* 99:243–257 (1950).

side *Yam*, may be merely a folkloristic foil to her brother.[29] Yama himself, like the Iranian Yima Xšaēta, the son of Vīvahvant, does mean 'Twin' and can be reconstructed beyond Proto-Indo-Iranian, in view of the Tacitean Germanic anthropogonic deities Tuisto, 'Twin' and Mannus. Tuisto is "terrae editus," Mannus his son. A primal relationship is thus not excluded, and possibly in the proto-myth Yama-Manu and Tuisto-Mannus were the twins born of a primal goddess. This goddess may well have been a Germanic equivalent of the Celtic earth mother Tailtiu, and the horse form was thus one of her manifestations. It is not impossible that a fission and duplication of a uniform prototype involving a mating of god and polyvalent goddess in horse form, and the production of hippomorphic issue of the third estate, should be postulated. Twins tend to multiply, and thus the grouping that we see in the Saraṇyū myth finds its cumulative explanation. Whether the Germanic Alcis-twins of Tacitean attestation should also be adduced I cannot say. In any event let us remember that the Aśvins have alternative parents (Nāsatya, the Aśvin proper, has Sumakha, and Dasra is the son of Dyauḥ [Divó nápāt]). Thus it is not so much the detail of the offspring that matters as the whole hippomorphous situation. It is noteworthy that the goddess is the one who primarily appears in horse form, in conformity with the postulated Indo-European pattern.

Much as one may in the Greek Dioscuric traditions vaguely glimpse a great deal that reminds one of the Indo-European Divine Twins, even so there is a vast amount of roughly relevant horse mythology particularly associated with Poseidon. Yet, since this presentation has as its theme functionality on an Indo-European level, and since the Greek pantheon is not so readily analyzable, detailed structuring would be gratuitous. With regard to the Saraṇyū myth let us merely be mindful of its curious similarities with the Arcadian tale of Demeter Erinys and her mating as a mare with Poseidon Hippios, producing a daughter Despoina and the horse Areion.[30] Other variants exist, also involving Poseidon and a Boeotian Erinys bearing the horse Areion whom Herakles used against Kyknos, and Poseidon and Medusa producing Pegasos whom Bellerophontes rode against the Chimaira.[31] On the rebound from Adalbert Kuhn's etymological identification of Saraṇyū- with Ἐρῑνύ́ς,[32] one should be very careful about V. Pisani's fresh attempt to connect Βελλεροφόντης with Vṛtra-

[29] Thus Lommel, *op. cit.*, pp. 253–255.
[30] See Pausanias 8.25.4–10; Apollodorus 3.6.8.
[31] See, e.g., J. Fontenrose, *Python* (Berkeley and Los Angeles, 1959), pp. 367–371.
[32] *Zeitschrift für vergleichende Sprachforschung* 1:439–470 (1852).

hán.[33] It is also easy to think of Ixion's union with the Hera double Nephele ('Cloud') in connection with the Savarṇā (Purāṇic Chāyā, 'Shadow'), and of the birth of Kentauros who mated with mares to produce the race of Centaurs. All this is singularly inconclusive, as is the slender Greek evidence for horse sacrifice.[34] The Dioscuri have their own hippomorphism and attendant traditions which are equally difficult to evaluate. In short, Greece disappoints the comparativist.

No other branch of Indo-European affords significant answers that I know of. In the context of this study, little of structural significance can be garnered from the stray attestations of horse sacrifice or other sacral equine lore among the Iranians (including Scythians), Thracians (such as Spartacus' killing of his war-horse *in extremis*),[35] Illyrians, Balts, Slavs, and Germanic peoples (e.g., the well-known manipulation of a horse phallus in the Old Norse Völsi-rite). Catalogues of such data have often been assembled (e.g., by Negelein, Koppers, and Capozza, *opera cit.*) but remain repositories of ethnological curiosities rather than mythical matter.

Sometimes, however, there are tantalizing questions. For example, why does the Hittite Law Code expressly exempt from punishment bestiality with horses or mules, after sternly penalizing such practice with cattle, sheep, and pigs? The horse is not an attested sacrificial animal in Hittite religion, except perhaps at burials. Such discrimination is strange when confronted with the sweeping injunction of *Leviticus* 20.15: "And if a man lie with a beast, he shall surely be put to death, and ye shall slay the beast." What is the relation of this Hittite attitude to the horse deity Pirwa? It is of uncertain gender and etymology but definitely related in name to Hittite *pirwa-*, *peru(na)-*, 'rock,' whether of Hattic origin (*pir-*, 'stone') or of Indo-European provenance (Sanskrit *párva(n)-*, *párvata-*, and so on). Nothing functionally viable can be extracted from these data.

The only one who has attempted some sort of functional summary of the horse in Indo-European religion is Dumézil.[36] He finds the horse heavily connected with the Varuṇa half of sovereignty but absent from the Mitra half. Yet "Mars" (i.e., Tiw) in Germany did receive horse sacrifices (Koppers, *op. cit.*, p. 286), and "Mars Thincsus" was certainly the Germanic juridical sovereign of the Mitra type. At the warrior level Dumézil finds the horse reigning

---

33 *Annali, Istituto Orientale di Napoli, Sezione linguistica* 7:48–51 (1966).

34 See, e.g., Koppers, *op. cit.*, pp. 291–292, and F. Schachermeyr, *Poseidon und die Entstehung des griechischen Götterglaubens* (Munich, 1950), *passim.*

35 According to Plutarch, *Crassus* 11.8–9, discussed by M. Capozza in *Critica Storica* 2:251–293 (1963).

36 In the last chapter of *Rituels indo-européens à Rome* (Paris, 1954).

supreme, with some competition from the bull, whereas the ass seems to replace the horse at the third-estate level.

I have a feeling that Dumézil has stayed too much on symbolistic ground and in this instance abstained from mythological analysis. It would be easy enough to go on collecting materials on such lines, for example, trying to distinguish functionally oracular horse, war-horse, and workhorse (or death mount, at the third-function level), and to speculate on possible color symbolism in white coursers, bay steeds, and black horses, respectively. I have chosen a divergent tack and hope that it will prove to be a horse of a different color: in brief, the basic Indo-European equine myth involves the mating of a kingship-class representative with the hippomorphous transfunctional goddess, and the creation of twin offspring belonging to the level of the third estate.

The Divine Victim: Aspects of Human Sacrifice in Viking Scandinavia and Vedic India

JAMES L. SAUVÉ, *University of California, Los Angeles*

1.

The study of Ancient Indic and Scandinavian mythology requires a special comparativistic approach. This approach involves a typology that seeks to resolve the comparativistic problems stemming from the wide temporal and spatial separation of the historical periods and places under examination. The relative chronology of Vedic India and Viking Scandinavia permits taxonomic juxtaposition, even though the two temporal loci are separated by an absolute time gulf of about two millennia. The terms "relative" and "absolute," as employed above in their sense proper to typology, express the chronological credibility of confronting Vedic India (*ca.* 1000 B.C.) and Viking Scandinavia (*ca.* A.D. 1000) almost as though their historical situations were the same. In an absolute chronology the two periods are, strictly speaking, beyond comparison, but relatively they are yet comparable because they represent mutually analogous developmental phases. For the purposes of typologically describing and naming mythohistorical phenomena, it is permissible to regard the two ages as artificially synchronic. This synchronization is justifiable by its heuristic possibilities. Among the latter is the eventuality that features may be disclosed in a relevancy that may otherwise escape attention, and that genetically related or relatable factors can be rendered accessible to scientific scrutiny.

Information on pagan Scandinavian human sacrifice survives mainly in historical accounts by foreigners, Eddic allusions to mythological details, the saga literature, and the *Gesta Danorum* of Saxo Grammaticus. Eyewitness accounts recall the physical reality of the sacrifices and recount aspects of their execution. There exist also the poetic reflections of what are probably real emanations of a religious outlook that embraced human sacrifice. Finally, there is the more or less legendary information contained in Saxo's quasi-history. Because Germanic paganism was not merely superseded but was extirpated by Christianity, we know nothing firsthand of the pagan ritual or cult. The barbaric ritual knowledge was doubtless suppressed immediately by the missionaries and proselytes of the invading religion. Ritual "science" is the effective support of the total religion in all cases known to me, and this ritual arsenal must be disarmed as soon as possible by the overthrowers in the course of a religious conversion. The ancient religious converters strove to destroy heathen cultic paraphernalia and idols. It is not surprising, therefore, that all authentic pagan Norse ritual knowledge was obliviated.

Vedic religion was never suppressed, and throughout the Indic evolutions very ancient and archaic elements were transformed, reoriented, and variously perpetuated. Some elements were perpetuated virtually unmodified in their primitive form, although their orientation within the religious consciousness may have become displaced. These more or less archaic survivals provide valuable testimony of early practices. The authentic ritual literature, which lacks an exact counterpart in the Norse tradition, is our principal source for the comparativistic data used in this study. This early ritual literature contains actual prescriptive information for application in the priestly performance of the *puruṣamedha* or human sacrifice. We are fortunate that the *puruṣamedha* is ritually documented, because this important rite can offer abundant clues to possible interpretations of laconic accounts of human sacrifice in non-Indic traditions. The *puruṣamedha* was an even more powerful and efficacious rite than the already tremendously powerful (and expensive) *aśvamedha* or horse sacrifice. The only loftier sacrifice ever named is the *sarvamedha,* the all-sacrifice, which was doubtless largely or entirely *livresque* and was probably conceived as a hyperbolic epitome of the *aśvamedha* and *puruṣamedha.* Extensive evidence indicates that the latter two sacrifices were historically real and performable. The epics and mythological sources provide sufficient evidence pointing to the one-time existence of human sacrifice among the Vedic Aryans.

The disposition of the Indic data is significantly different from that of the Scandinavian records. In ancient Scandinavia the actual practice of religious human sacrifice is historically attested beyond doubt, but no genuine Norse ritual texts survive. On the other hand, the extant Indic ritual texts detailing the *puruṣamedha* contain internal evidence showing that the practice of human sacrifice was already obsolete or obsolescent at the time of their composition. The Indic and Scandinavian records contrast meaningfully for the typologist.

The problem of the historical significance of human and animal sacrifice in ancient India has provoked various reactions among scholars. Whether any ground has been gained toward its resolution remains to be evaluated and demands comparativistic attention. In 1897 J. Eggeling wrote:[1]

> With regard to the earliest phase of Vedic religion, there is no direct evidence to show that the horse-sacrifice was already at that time a recognized institution. . . . Seeing, however, that animal sacrifices generally are not alluded to in the Riksaṁhita, whilst there is every reason to believe that they were commonly practised from remote antiquity, this absence of earlier positive evidence regarding the horse-sacrifice cannot be taken as proving the later origin of that institution . . . there are sufficient indications to show that even human sacrifices were at one time practised among the Aryans of India, as they were among their European kinsmen.

Today we can affirm that a horse sacrifice was indeed current in Indo-European times, and we can also be quite certain that the silence of the *Rig-Veda* is by no means authoritative or constraintive. Eggeling's statements represent a sober and reasoned standpoint which we can now afford to amplify.

The individual dispositions of the early Indic and Scandinavian records seem incongruent. Nevertheless, symbolic coherencies exist in comparable patterns, and it is these symbolic elements that I am investigating.

I have purposely left out of account the comparison of *Rig-Veda* 10.90, the *Puruṣasūkta,* with the cosmogonic slaughter of the giant Ymir as told in Norse mythology, simply because it is necessary to define what was meant by the immolation of a man, and to discover the efficacy of human sacrifice for the archaic consciousness, before attempting an interpretation of those myths. Still, I am convinced that those myths can be understood only within the framework of

---

1 *Sacred Books of the East,* vol. 44, p. xvii. I have taken the liberty of modernizing the transcription of Old Indic words when they occur in the quotations.

studies on Indo-European human sacrifice. Reference to the *Puruṣasūkta* cannot be avoided, but a true comparativistic analysis must remain in abeyance.

2.

In Book 4 of Adam of Bremen's *History of the Archbishops of Hamburg-Bremen,* written in the eleventh century, there is a description of the pagan temple and some religious proceedings at Uppsala, the last stronghold of heathendom in the North. Section 27 reads as follows in its entirety (with the exception of one medieval annotation):[2]

> For all their gods there are appointed priests to offer sacrifices for the people. If plague and famine threaten, a libation is poured to the idol Thor; if war, to Wotan; if marriages are to be celebrated, to Frikko. It is customary also to solemnize in Uppsala, at nine-year intervals, a general feast of all the provinces of Sweden. From attendance at this festival no one is exempted (*a,* [omitted scholion]). Kings and people all and singly send their gifts to Uppsala and, what is more distressing than any kind of punishment, those who have already adopted Christianity redeem themselves through these ceremonies. The sacrifice is of this nature: of every living thing that is male, they offer nine heads (*b,* scholion 141 [137]: Feasts and sacrifices of this kind are solemnized for nine days. On each day they offer a man along with other living beings in such a number that in the course of the nine days they will have made offerings of seventy-two creatures. This sacrifice takes place about the time of the vernal equinox), with the blood of which it is customary to placate gods of this sort. The bodies they hang in the sacred grove that adjoins the temple. Now this grove is so sacred in the eyes of the heathen that each and every tree in it is believed divine because of the death and putrefaction of the victims. Even dogs and horses hang there with men. A Christian seventy-two years old told me that he had seen their bodies suspended promiscuously. Furthermore, the incantations customarily chanted in the ritual of a sacrifice of this kind are manifold and unseemly; therefore it is better to keep silence about them.

Adam's account is laconic, but in consideration of his last statement we must be thankful to learn anything at all of the barbaric Norse practices. The "manifold and unseemly" incantations are precisely the variety of ritual knowledge we would be most fortunate to possess for linguistic and religious historical purposes, but which we would least expect to find preserved in a land overwhelmed by Christianity. Still, Adam's book does contain remarkably valuable and useful information. A scholion to the section preceding the one I quoted above

[2] This translation is borrowed from F. J. Tschan, *Adam of Bremen: History of the Archbishops of Hamburg-Bremen* (New York, 1959).

makes the additional remarkable observations:[3] "Near this temple stands a very large tree with wide-spreading branches, always green winter and summer. What kind it is nobody knows. There is also a spring at which pagans are accustomed to make their sacrifices, and into it to plunge a live man. And if he is not found, the people's wish will be granted."[4] It would thus appear that drowning was also a sacrificial technique at Uppsala. Notably, this scholion reveals the existence of a huge tree and its evident cultic eminence. This tree is beyond doubt the terrestrial, cultic counterpart of the world-ash Yggdrasill that figures prominently in Norse mythological literature. The cultic tree probably presided over those others in the grisly grove where Adam's Christian informant saw human bodies hanging. Perhaps we may suppose that distinguished victims were suspended from the great tree.

3.

The cult of the god Odin is known to have especially involved human sacrifice during the Viking age. The literary reflections of Odin's mythology display a broad symbolic perspective in which human sacrifice has found expression. Two literary motifs furnish minimally the essential comparative materials. The first is the episode of King Víkar in the *Gautrekssaga*,[5] and the second is the enigmatic *Rúnatals þáttr* contained in the *Hávamál* (138–145). A superficial survey of these two sources suffices to disclose the salient symbols of human sacrifice relevant to the Odin cult. An analysis of the symbolism reveals the religious contextuality of Odinic human sacrifice. Here we approach the comparativistic object of the present study—the role of god as divine victim in ancient Scandinavia and India.

The tale of the death of King Víkar at Odin's behest is recounted in the *Gautrekssaga* and by Saxo in the *Gesta Danorum*.[6] For the purposes of this article the differences in the two versions are of no consequence. The story recalls that King Víkar was to be made the mock victim of a sacrifice to Odin and was to be hanged by means of a fake noose. The god, however, insisted on the real victim, and, evidently with his powerful magic, at the last moment turned the sham noose into an all too real hangman's line, while Starkadr, ad-

---

3 *Ibid.*, p. 207 n. *Scholion* 138 (134).

4 A. Weber, "Über Menschenopfer bei den Indern der vedischen Zeit," *ZDMG* 18:268 (1864), refers to a probable Indic drowning sacrifice.

5 E. O. G. Turville-Petre, *Myth and Religion of the North* (New York, 1964), p. 44 and elsewhere.

6 *Ibid.*, p. 205.

ministering the coup de grâce, pierced Víkar's body with a spear. The death imagery of the *Gautrekssaga* portrays Víkar hanged from a tree, stabbed by Odin's spear in Starkadr's hand.

A common form (perhaps the predominant form) of human sacrifice for Odin was by hanging from a tree or gibbet, accompanied frequently by stabbing with a spear (Odin's weapon) for good measure. Many cases of hanging associated with Odin exist in the literature. Saxo relates that the Odin-hero Hadingus ended his life by hanging himself in public.[7] Hanged men and men killed with a spear belonged to Odin, who was actually a death god, or god of the dead, although not a god of the netherworld. Truly, Odin's *Einherjar* was an army of dead men.

Stanzas 138–145 of the *Hávamál* are uncannily difficult to interpret with certainty in every respect and probably reflect Christian/pagan syncretism in the poetic structure of their imagery; yet their content does not plausibly derive from sources other than the pagan Odinic tradition. The similarity of the hanging Odin with the crucified Christ is obvious and well noted, but, as at least Van Hamel[8] and Turville-Petre[9] have convincingly shown, every detail is thoroughly consistent with pagan religiosity and the worship of Odin. The Crucifixion can, of course, be studied in its Mediterranean setting as a typological parallel to the divine sacrifices under scrutiny here, but an analysis of the biblical event itself cannot further a comparative study of Indic and Norse mythology in a way that might facilitate the identification of maximally archaic and perhaps genetically related features in the Indo-European mythological traditions. Internal analysis of the Germanic records has already proved sufficiently that *Hávamál* 138–145 is essentially pagan.

Considered within the framework of the sacrificial religious tradition from which they spring, the relevant verses of the *Hávamál* constitute part of the answer to the question of the meaning of human sacrifice to the pagan Norse mentality. In a wider scholarly context, the immolation of the god Odin is a problem that must be stated and clarified before late Norse paganism can be fully understood. This essay seeks to prepare a statement of the problem and to indicate the avenue toward its resolution. While risking the evils of an obscure procedure, I allow the statement of the problem and its resolution to appear in an implicit fashion. For this study, *Hávamál* 138 is the crucial locus for which India will supply the exegetic key. Stanzas

---

7 *Ibid.*, p. 216.

8 A. Van Hamel, "Odin Hanging on the Tree," *APhS* 7:260 (1932).

9 Turville-Petre, *op. cit.*, p. 43.

139 ff. record how Odin seized the runes and prospered. The god himself narrates 138:

Veit ek at ek hekk vindga meiði á naetr alla níu geiri undaðr ok gefinn Óðni sjálfr sjálfum mér á þeim meiði er mangi veit, hvers hann af rótum renn.	I know that I hung on the windy tree for nine full nights, wounded with a spear and given to Odin, myself to myself; on that tree of which none know from what roots it rises.[10]

Van Hamel offers a very persuasive interpretation of this Eddic passage, without considering the problem of the more pervasive meaning of Odin's act to a pagan religious sensibility. Van Hamel does not investigate the poetic mythological manifestation as part of a consciousness which countenanced human sacrifice, nor does he evaluate the god's action with respect to the manner in which human victims were consigned to him. Furthermore, he tried to demonstrate that Odin's deed in the *Hávamál* amounted to an act of martyrdom rather than sacrifice. I contest the distinction between martyrdom and sacrifice as applied to a source like the *Hávamál,* but I do admit that many of Van Hamel's criteria and explanations are interesting for their own sake: for example, that martyrdom construes blind powers, whereas sacrifice intends to win over the free will of a god. The application of Van Hamel's criteria to Odin and the *Hávamál* is deceptive, however, and fails to discover the most important content of the episode in the poem.

Van Hamel has also discussed the semantic realm within which we should consider *gefinn* as it occurs in the *Hávamál.* Rather than 'geopfert,' it means 'geweiht' and was used in this sense when children were dedicated to a god as *living* pledges. This is also the verb used in the story of Víkar where a human victim (King Víkar) is consigned to Odin: Starkadr: *nu gef ek þik Óđni,* 'now I give you to Odin.' Still, the question remains as to what meaning there is in the notion of a god being consecrated to *himself,* as Odin is in *Hávamál* 138. Van Hamel thinks that there is meaning in such a statement as *gefin sjálfr sjálfum mér* only if it is conceived as exemplary of what he considers a pretheistic variety of Norse thinking, that of those Norsemen who believed in their own strength only (*á matt sinn ok megin*). Supposedly these men would not be representative in their world view of an

---

[10] Translation after *ibid.,* p. 42.

atheistic perspective following the decline of the pagan religion, or of any theistic viewpoint, but of the cultural stage prior to the development of the pagan religion! As Van Hamel puts it (*op. cit.*, p. 265), "this mentality points to a social state anterior to that where gods are worshipped." How many contemporary historians of religion would take that remark seriously? To me, Van Hamel's primitivistic explanation seems incredible in every respect. Van Hamel goes on to say that Odin's ecstatic act generates his *ásmegin* ('divine power') to its acme. Somehow the god creates a force that cows the runes and coerces them into his control. By means of a magical state of sublimation, wherein he gives himself up to his own magical essences, Odin conquers and captures the runes. In his comprehension of the Odinic *method*, Van Hamel comes very close to an adequate realization of the content of the *Rúnatals þáttr*.

While Van Hamel correctly understood Odin's overt method, he is, unfortunately, incorrect in believing that a secular, shamanistic explanation of the hanging Odin will suffice, and that Odin's actions exemplify the orientation of men who belong to a pretheistic cultural level. As we shall see, Odin's behavior is eminently theistic in the utmost degree and typologically resembles that of the Indic Prajāpati (lord of progeny), the prototype par excellence of the divine victim, who suffers self-immolation within a reflexively creative and productive ritual syndrome. The assertion that Odin is martyred, not sacrificed, pays no attention to the obvious and hardly inconsequential fact that he suffers precisely the same ritual death as might befall one of his human sacrificial victims. Odin does indeed die a ritual death by means of which he appropriates the power of death, symbolized in the runic magic that raises the dead to momentary eloquence. Van Hamel's criterion for sacrifice, cited above, could never apply to Odin's act or to Prajāpati's self-transformation and self-immolation as exposited by the Indic *Uttaramīmāṃsā* literature which is discussed below. Odin is truly sacrificed to himself and not merely martyred. Odin hung for nine nights on the world tree, which recalls the nine-day festival at Uppsala referred to in Adam of Bremen's *History*. Odin was stabbed with a spear and hanged like his victim, the unfortunate Víkar (for instance), so that it seems obvious that the god and the sacrificial victim were intentionally confounded in the *Hávamál*. This realization induces us to seek the meaning of the Norse hanging sacrifice in connection with a ritual repetition of the self-willed immolation of the god. Especially considering that Odin sought Víkar's death, we should regard King Víkar henceforth as an Odin surrogate and the prototype of the *human* sacrificial offering who fulfills the role of the supreme god in the capital sacrifice. The parallels between Odin's techniques in the *Hávamál* and the arts of ancient and aboriginal sorcerers and magicians merely supply another avenue of research and do not compromise the study of the hanging Odin as a self-immolated divine victim.

4.

Van Hamel and others have correctly observed that the tree with unknown roots upon which Odin hangs can be none other than the world tree, the holy ash Yggdrasill. This tree is the sustainer of the worlds and represents an organic *axis mundi*. Yggdrasill is the Norse representative of the abundantly attested and remotely archaic "tree of life" symbol. This symbol was taken seriously by many of the ancients and was frequently an innermost constituent of ancient and primitive religions. The primitive pancultural Eurasian cosmology is unthinkable without the *axis mundi*, the tree of life, and the cosmic center, all of which freely combine in the ancient conceptions. Indo-European mythology is a pancultural Eurasian phenomenon, and those studies that overlook the "tree of life," or dismiss it as marginal or incidental in importance, must fail to evaluate properly, or even approximately, many aspects of some Indo-European religions and mythologies. The importance of the *axis mundi* in Germania is well known and not easily overlooked; witness the Saxon *Irminsūl* and its historic role in the conversion of the most die-hard continental Germanic pagans. The cosmic column could be conceived variously by the Germanic people as a tree or a simple stave, without evident sense of contradiction. The manifestation of a universal center shaft is prolific in all its forms in India as well. It was natural and probably necessary, in terms of the religion of ancient Scandinavia, that the poet of the *Hávamál* should portray Odin as immolated on the world tree. Yggdrasill, of course, is the sacred tree of the Aesir and, symmetrically, we have already observed in Adam of Bremen's account how the great temple of Uppsala had a terrestrial replica of Yggdrasill. The practice of offering human victims on trees, as at Uppsala, must have entailed the will to sacrifice at the symbolic universal center in the presence of the cosmic sustainer. The close association of human sacrifice and the *axis mundi* greatly facilitates a comparativistic study. The symbolism of the world tree or *axis mundi* usefully serves typology because it is so widespread among variant traditions and so esoterically meaningful within the individual religions.

5.

Indic data relating to conceptions of the cosmic column and its sacrificial and mythological symbolism are abundant. But there are difficulties of taxonomy and interpretation caused by the mode of expression given to the world-tree symbol. In Vedic India we encounter a language of symbolic forms of the highest sophistication, surpassed nowhere in world literature. Kuiper (*IIJ* 8:117 [1964]) correctly emphasizes that the Vedic passages that allude to the world tree or axis refer to an esoteric mystery. For that reason, naturalistic interpretations of the imagery of those passages misapprehend the symbol. Recent attempts have succeeded in taxonomically securing the identity of the tree and column symbol and have established the world tree as paramount among Indic symbols.[11]

The great tree flourishes in various forms throughout Vedic and later Indic literature; especially as the *aśvattha* (*Ficus religiosa*) or *pippala* tree. The *aśvattha* tree is a noteworthy feature of the Vedic texts and, as Linnaeus' *nomen* indicates, it is religiously significant. Its Old Indic name might mean 'horse stead' or 'horse abode.' The *aśvattha* was honored in later times as the *bodhi* tree of Gautama Buddha. Another related though distinct tree often confused with the *aśvattha* is the *nyagrodha* or banyan tree (unmentioned by the *Rig-Veda*). The *nyagrodha* (Sanskrit *nyagrodha, vaṭa, bhāṇḍīra,* or *parkaṭī,* i.e., *Ficus bengalensis* or *Ficus indica*) is the *bodhi* tree of Kāśyapa. The *pippala* (*aśvattha*) and the *nyagrodha* are among the largest Indian trees and are often known as *vanaspati* (usually translated 'lord of the forest'), a name that is also applied to the fire-god Agni.[12]

The tree of life is encountered in Indic literature and religion in various guises and is symbolically identifiable and partly cofunctional with the universal column, even when the latter is not conceived as an organic tree, or when the tree has been transformed into a colossal stave as in the case of the *skambha* of *Atharva-Veda* 10.7 and 10.8 (and elsewhere).[13] The *skambha* ('supporter'),[14] which is the sustainer of the universe, is portrayed by the author of *Atharva-Veda* 10.7.20–

[11] F. D. K. Bosch, *The Golden Germ* (The Hague, 1960).

[12] *Ibid., passim.*

[13] Cf. M. Lindenau, "Die Skambha-Hymnen des Atharvaveda," *Zeitschrift für Indologie und Iranistik* 3:235–279 (1925).

[14] *Ibid.,* p. 247: "Es liegt hier wohl eine etymologische Anspielung auf Skambha vor, die wir zur Wurzel *skab, skabh* (idg. Dublette), lat. *scabo* 'schabe' stellen; *skambha* scheint ursprünglich etwa soviel wie 'behauener Baumstamm' bedeutet zu haben, woraus sich der Begriff 'Pfeiler, Stütze' entwickelte."

21 as fashioned from the trunk of a tree in a way comparable with the formation of the *Irminsūl* of the Saxons. But the same hymn also characterizes the *skambha* as still possessing branches, so that we must accept the sustainer as symbolically heteromorphic.

6.

The symbolism of the world axis as the sacrificial center provides a comparativistic point of orientation. In Indic sacrificial texts the *yūpa* or stake, to which the creature to be immolated is bound, can be a specially selected tree still in the forest, which is prepared for use in the ritual. The cosmic axis that, as explained above, can be visualized as a leafy, growing tree or as a simple shaft, is symbolized in the *yūpa*. In the *Rig-Veda*, the Āpri hymns, which are ritually connected with animal sacrifices, refer to or address the *yūpa* as *vanaspati*. It is quite clear that the *Rig-Veda* comprehends the *yūpa* as *vanaspati*.[15] The *vanaspati*,[16] as explained above in section 5, is itself the *aśvattha*, or terrestrial avatar of the cosmic tree. The *yūpa*, as the symbol of the cosmic axis, is the necessary locus of the human and animal sacrifice and is simultaneously an alternative form of the tree of life.

The comparison of the employment of the *yūpa* in the Indic sacrifices with the similar function of the tree or gibbet in Ancient Scandinavia discloses concordances between the Indic and Norse practices. In India, the *paśu* or sacrificial animal (*paśu* was also applied to the human victim) was tied to the *yūpa* by a cord or rope and strangled to death if the blood sacrifice was actually performed fully. The strangulation death in India and the hanging death of the Odin victim resemble each other. Variant means of sacrificial killing were also in use.[17]

---

[15] H. Oldenberg, *Sacred Books of the East*, vol. 46, p. 12. Oldenberg is not alone in his perception of the *yūpa* as *vanaspati*.

[16] The name *vanaspati* is applied both to the *aśvattha* and to Agni, who is also otherwise associated with the *aśvattha*.

[17] Unfortunately, I must leave out of this paper the pressing discussion of Varuṇa and his noose as related to human sacrifice. In a religious-historical study in depth, as opposed to typological groundwork, Varuṇa versus Odin would become important immediately. Eggeling, too, emphasized the importance of Varuṇa (*Sacred Books of the East*, vol. 44, p. xx): "Of any connection of the sacrificial horse with Prajāpati, on the other hand, as of the Prajāpati theory of the sacrifice generally, clearly shadowed forth in the Puruṣa-sūkta, and so decidedly dominant during the Brāhmaṇa period, no trace is to be found in the earlier hymns. Indeed, if we have any right to assume that the horse-sacrifice was known and practised in the earlier times, it can scarcely be doubted that King Varuṇa must have been the deity to whom this victim was chiefly consecrated."

7.

I offer here a brief overview of the *puruṣamedha* literature in ancient India and a review of some of the most noteworthy aspects of the rite. The ritual of the human sacrifice is briefly described in the thirteenth *kāṇḍa* of the *Śatapatha Brāhmaṇa* (*White Yajur-Veda*), and a list of the special victims is supplied by *Vājasaneyi Saṃhitā* 30.5–22 (*White Yajur-Veda*). The sacrifice is not mentioned in the *Taittirīya Saṃhitā* (nor evidently in the *Maitrāyaṇī* or *Kāṭhaka Saṃhitā*'s), but a slightly differing list of victims is given in the *Taittirīya Brāhmaṇa*. The ritual of the *puruṣamedha* is detailed as well in five of the *Śrautasūtra*'s, viz. those of *Śāṅkhāyana* (to the *Rig-Veda*), *Āpastamba* and *Hiraṇyakeśin* (both to the *Taittirīya Saṃhitā*), *Kātyāyana* (to the *White Yajur-Veda*), and *Vaitāna* (to the *Atharva-Veda*). Of these, however, only the *Śāṅkhāyana* and *Vaitāna Śrautasūtra*'s actually prescribe the real killing of the human *paśu*. The others have the human victim released at the last moment, or have an animal put to death in his place, under the ritual pretense that the animal is a man.

The *puruṣamedha* is a *pañcarātra* ('five-night') sacrifice which according to *Kātyāyana* (21.1.2) is to be initiated only by a member of the *brāhmaṇa* or *rājanya* castes. According to *Śāṅkhāyana* (who prescribes real killing) it achieves everything that is not yet attained by the potent *aśvamedha*. In many particulars the *puruṣamedha* rite duplicates the ritual of the horse sacrifice. Whereas in the latter a horse, *gomṛga*, and *aja tūpara* form the nucleus of the assemblage of victims consecrated en masse to Prajāpati, in the human sacrifice a man occupies the place of the horse. *Śāṅkhāyana* says that the *puruṣapaśu* is supposed to be a brahmin or kshatriya who has been purchased for the price of a hundred horses and a thousand cows. Like the horse in the *aśvamedha*, the human victim is permitted to go unfettered for a year preceding his sacrificial death, under the provision that he remain sexually chaste during that year of freedom. Prajāpati himself is sometimes called the year, and the *Bṛhadāraṇyakopaniṣad* (1.2.4) states that when Prajāpati became the sacrificial horse who was to prepare for his voluntary immolation, he contained his semen for a length of time equivalent to a year. Upon its release, the semen *became* the year (*saṃvatsaram*), which, we are told, had not yet existed.

The number of victims offered at a single performance of the *puruṣamedha* could be large (according to *Śatapatha Brāhmaṇa*, 166 persons on eleven *yūpas*). The lists of potential and ritually desirable victims given by the *Śatapatha Brāhmaṇa*, the *Taittirīya Brāhmaṇa*, and the *Vājasaneyi Saṃhitā* are interesting because of the bizarre and peculiarly detailed personal and physiognomic requirements to which each of the victims must individually conform.

The performance of the *puruṣamedha* entailed recitation of the "Puruṣa-Nārāyaṇa" hymn, *Rig-Veda* 10.90. This cosmogonic *sūkta* narrates the primordial, prototypical sacrifice of a special man (*puruṣa*) conceived as a divine being. The *Brahma Purāṇa* (*adhyāya* 161)[18] gives a commentary to the *Puruṣasūkta*. The passage provides an inkling of how the *Puruṣasūkta* was understood in antiquity and so might contribute to a realization of the meaning of the immolation of the divine victim. A notable feature of the Purāṇic story is the identification of the *yūpa* with *kāla* ('time'). The world tree itself can be found associated with temporal symbolism. The passage also exploits an ambiguity in the meaning of the word *guṇa*, employing it in a context that recalls the primary meaning of 'bond' or 'cord' simultaneously with the derived meaning 'quality.' The contextual implication is that the three *guṇa*'s bind the *puruṣa* to the sacrificial post (*yūpa*) of time (*kāla*). The passage says that Brahman had prepared for a cosmogonic sacrifice in which *kāla* would be the *yūpa*, and the three *guṇa*'s would be the bonds for tying the victim, but no *paśu* was available (161.39: . . . *naiva tatrābhavat paśuḥ*). Brahman says forlornly (161.40): *Vinaiva paśunā nāyam yajñaḥ parisamāpyate*, 'without a victim this sacrifice cannot be instituted.' There follows a dialogue between Brahman and the bodiless goddess of speech (*ākāśavāg aśarīriṇī*) within (*nityā*) Brahman, which results in a *puruṣa* sacrifice.[19]

8.

The *puruṣamedha*, like the *aśvamedha*, bears a singular relationship to Prajāpati, the lord of progeny, frequently called "father" by the *Śatapatha Brāhmaṇa*. The *Uttaramīmāṃsā* texts declare that it is Prajāpati himself who is sacrificed in the form of a horse, as an entity undergoing immolation and himself immolating. Thus, the opening sections of the *Madhukāṇḍam*, at the very beginning of the *Bṛhadāraṇyakopaniṣad*, unroll the fantastic and awesome symbolism of the *aśvamedha* and define how the symbols extoll Prajāpati's cosmogonic self-slaughter. The god and the victim are unequivocally identified.

---

18 Ānandāśrama Sanskrit Series 28 (Poona, 1895), p. 378.

19 *Ibid.*, *adhyāya* 161.40–44: "tato mām avadad devī saiva nityā 'śarīriṇī // ākāśavāg uvāca --- paurusenātha sūktena stuhi tam puruṣam param // brahmovāca --- tathetyuktvā stūyamāne devadeve janārdane / mama cotpādake bhaktyā sūktena puruṣasya hi // sā ca mām abravīd devī brahman mām tvam paśum kuru / tadā viśāya puruṣam janakam mama cāvyayam // kālayūpasya pāśve tam guṇapāśair niveśitam / barhisthitam aham praukṣam puruṣam jātam agrataḥ //."

The limitless labyrinths of the *Brāhmaṇa*'s enfold yet another transition of role and identity beyond the synthesis of god and victim. The role and power of Prajāpati are bequeathed to the patron of the sacrifice whenever he initiates it. So, as L. Renou writes:[20] "The human sacrifice is the most efficacious of all: it makes the sacrificer equal to Prajāpati, the great victim." The *Śatapatha Brāhmaṇa* clearly supports this portrayal of the patron's relation to the process of the sacrifice. Eggeling, in the introduction to his translation, has made some definitive paraphrases which, by virtue of their insight and clarity, are worth quoting at length:[21]

> Prajāpati, who here takes the place of the puruṣa, the world-man, or all-embracing personality, is offered up anew in every sacrifice: and inasmuch as the very dismemberment of the Lord of Creatures, which took place at that archetypal sacrifice, was in itself the creation of the universe, so every sacrifice is also a repetition of that first creative act. . . . The theologians of the *Brāhmaṇas* go, however, an important step further by identifying the performer, or patron, of the sacrifice—the Sacrificer, with Prajāpati—. . . . As regards the symbolic connection of the Sacrificer himself with the sacrifice, there can at any rate be no doubt that it was an essential and an intimate one from the very beginning of the sacrificial practice.

In other words, such a connection is essential to Vedic religion, since this religion was fundamentally sacrificial. This comprehension of the role of the sacrificer has the utmost importance for an adequate understanding of archaic Indic religion and of those religions that are comparable with it. The point of view Eggeling represents is abundantly supported in the testimony of the *Pūrvamīmāṃsā* and *Uttaramīmāṃsā* texts themselves. This viewpoint and the perspectives disclosed by its implementation in an analysis of human sacrifice can provide the clue to the real and pervasive meaning of the utterance of the self-immolated Norse magical deity: *gefinn Óðni, sjálfr sjálfum mér*, 'given to Odin, myself to myself.'

9.

Typologically, the Indic *yūpa* (*i.e.*, *vanaspati*, *aśvattha*, and so on) is categorially equivalent to the sacrificial trees at pagan Uppsala, and,

20 *Vedic India* (Calcutta, 1957), p. 96.

21 Eggeling, *Sacred Books of the East*, vol. 43, pp. xv–xvi. H. Oldenberg ("Der geopferte Gott und das Agnicayana," *Nachrichten von der Kgl. Gesellschaft der Wissenschaften zu Göttingen, Phil.-hist. Kl.* 1917 [1918], pp. 6–8) disagreed with Eggeling's conception of Prajāpati (*puruṣa*) as victim, but Oldenberg's objection is not well made because he denied Prajāpati's victimhood principally on the grounds that it did not fit into the Frazerian symptomatic paradigm of the dying god. His text-critical objection adduced in a footnote is unconvincing.

seen through the mythopoetic prism of the *Hávamál*, to Yggdrasill in its role as the hanging Odin's gibbet. The word used in *Hávamál* 138 which is usually rendered as 'tree' is Old Icelandic *meiðr*. F. Ström[22] argues that the word *meiðr* means 'pole, gallows,' rather than 'tree,' although he evidently accepts the translation as 'tree' in the *Hávamál*. Apparently the term was often used in poetry with the meaning 'tree.' The semantic parallelism of *yūpa* and *meiðr* is quite close. The symbolic perception of both *Hávamál* 138 and the Vedic Āpri hymns which contain the word *vanaspati* deepens and expands prismatically when we consider that the *vanaspati*, in the capacity of a *yūpa* in the blood sacrifices of the Vedic *Ārya*, resembles the role of trees in the Uppsala cult.

As mentioned in the foregoing sections, the horse sacrifice and the human sacrifice are interrelated. Adam of Bremen's Christian informant asserted that at Uppsala horses and dogs could be seen hanging on trees next to men. The relationship of the horse to the world tree is itself an important subject, especially in the religions and mythologies of the Indo-European area. Again, in connection with the practice and mythology of human sacrifice and the divine victim, the horse and its association with the world tree is curious. As we saw above, one of the Indic names for the celestial tree, *aśvattha*, is probably equine in content. The *aśvattha*, however, is also involved with the hieratic fire god Agni[23] and, as mentioned before, shares with him and the *nyagrodha* tree the name *vanaspati*, which is also the Rig-Vedic appellation for the personified *yūpa*. The intimate rapport between Agni and the tree is episodically expressed by the *Śatapatha Brāhmaṇa* in the myth of Purūravas and Urvaśī, but the *Taittirīya Brāhmaṇa* (1.1.3.9, quoted by Sāyaṇa in his commentary on *Rig-Veda* 1.65, which tells of Agni's flight into the waters) astonishingly enunciates the heteromorphic and congruent characters of Agni, the horse, and the *aśvattha* tree combined: *agnir devebhyo nilāyata aśvo rūpam kr̥tvā so 'śvatthe saṃvatsaram atiṣṭhat*, 'Agni hid from the gods. Having made [himself into] the form of a horse, he abode in the *aśvattha* [tree] for a year *(saṃvatsaram)*!' This is an amazing confluence of identities and events, but *Rig-Veda* 10.27.14*a* almost surpasses the *Taittirīya Brāhmaṇa* with the bewildering image of a large, shadowless, leafless horse: *br̥hánn acchāyó apalāśó árvā tasthaú mātá víṣito atti gárbhaḥ*, which Geldner renders, 'ein hoher, schattenloser, unbelaubter [Baum], ein Renner [ist er]—die Mutter steht still, ent-

---

22 *On the Sacral Origin of the Germanic Death Penalties* (Stockholm, 1942), pp. 119–120.

23 Bosch, *op. cit., passim.*

bunden frisst das Kind. . . .' Murray Fowler[24] has done the service of calling attention to this startling Vedic image, while trying, by comparativistic means, to reclaim some of the scorched earth left by pioneers like Ludwig, who translated the opening line: 'hoch, schattenlos, laublos, beweglich ist der himmel.' This scholar tried to make his bland translation palatable by adding the acrimonious comment: "unrichtig muss *arvā* sein, da ein vernunftiger mensch doch wohl von einem laublosem ross nicht sprechen kann." I, for one, find Ludwig's leafless sky *unrichtig* and his point of view absurd.

Fowler correctly identifies the image in the first line of *Rig-Veda* 10.27.14 as a hippodendron and believes like Grassman that its ultimate referent is Agni of the *aśvattha.* Agni's heteromorphology associates him with the *aśvattha,* but for reasons that differ substantially from the one adduced by Fowler, who evidently believed in the sufficiency of the naturalistic explanation that fire (Agni) is felt to be inert and latent in wood (*aśvattha* tree).

The comparison of the *aśvattha* with Yggdrasill is natural and elementary. Yggdrasill, too, is a hippodendron. As has been well known since Sophus Bugge, *drasill* is an Old Icelandic poetic word for horse, while *Yggr* ('the terrible') is a name of Odin, as evidenced by *Grímnismál* 54:

Óðinn ek nú heiti
Yggr ek áðan hét.

Odin am I now called,
Yggr was I called before.

Most scholars have wanted to construe Yggdrasill as meaning 'Ygg's [Odin's] horse,' with the meaning extended to 'Odin's gallows' and into the Norse semantic realm wherein 'horse' equals 'gallows' and doubles as a potent death symbol. Two facts oppose the unqualified acceptability of this definition. First, the tree is alternatively called *Yggdrasills askr* ('Yggdrasill's ash-tree'), as though *Yggdrasill* itself were another name for the god Odin. Second, everyone[25] notices that for the meaning 'Ygg's horse' we should expect the form of the word to be **Yggsdrasill,* which has not been found. There is a theoretically possible solution if, as I suggest, we interpret the compound as endocentric in meaning and signifying 'Ygg, the horse.' Seen in this way, however, not only is Yggdrasill (that is, *Yggdrasills askr*) a hippodendron, but Odin himself is unmasked in a hippomorphic *Gestalt* like

---

24 *JAOS* 67:273 (1947).

25 E.g., Jan de Vries, *Altnordisches etymologisches Wörterbuch* (Leiden, 1942), pp. 676–677.

the one assumed by both Prajāpati and Agni, and, heteromorphically, Odin assumes the form of a hippodendron as well! His case would be analogous to that of Agni according to *Taittirīya Brāhmaṇa* 1.1.3.9. In my opinion, these considerations and possibilities seem theoretically quite likely and plausible. The heteromorphic propensities of the Indo-European gods are already well recognized.

10.

The time has come to survey the more general implications of this study and to define the common motivation that seems to underly those portions of the Indic and ancient Scandinavian sacrificial traditions that involved and employed human sacrifice after a divine example.

Prajāpati is not the only Indic divine victim, but at least in his hippomorphic manifestation in the *aśvamedha* he offers the best prototypical example for a typology. His identification with the *puruṣa* is at hand but is less explicit, probably because of the flagging metaphysical support for human sacrifice within the ancient Indic religious orthodoxy. Seeking the motivation for the kind of human sacrifice studied here, we need not search endlessly through the labyrinthine brahmanical texts, even if we could not already intuit or deduce the driving will to appropriate divine, cosmic power by means of a ritual, karmic quasi-science. The *Śatapatha Brāhmaṇa* and the *Bṛhadāraṇyakopaniṣad* (originally a part of the total text of the former) fulfill their ancient function of exegesis, explaining clearly enough the import of the sacrifice. At the beginning of the *puruṣamedha* ritual the *Śatapatha Brāhmaṇa* declares (13.6.1, after Eggeling): "Puruṣa Nārāyaṇa desired, 'Would that I overpassed all beings! would that I alone were everything here [this universe]!' He beheld this five-days sacrificial performance, the Puruṣamedha, and took it, and performed offering therewith; and having performed offering therewith, he overpassed all beings, and became everything here. And, verily, he who, knowing this, performs the Puruṣamedha, or who even knows this, overpasses all beings, and becomes everything here." For an Indic text, the above could not be more straightforward. In our terms, an ontological issue is at stake. If the *yajamāna*, the sacrificial patron, cannot *be* god, then at least by means of the brahmanical magical "science" he can appropriate divine power and surmount existential heights rivaling the stations of the gods whenever he performs the sacrifice modeled after the ultimate godly act, the self-sacrifice that unleashes total power. The concept of appropriation at the sacrifice obviously motivates the *yūpārohaṇa*, the mounting of the sacrificial post erected at the symbolic center of all existence, whereby the *yajamāna* thirsts to acquire the being and energy of the absolute center, the symbolic cosmic axis. The extent of the sacrificial victory in ontological terms is most spectacularly expressed by *Bṛhadāraṇyakopaniṣad* 1.2.7:[26] He[27] desired:

> "Would that this [body] of mine were fit for sacrifice! Would that by it I had a self (*ātmanvin*)!" Thereupon it became a horse (*aśva*), because it swelled (*aśvat*). "It has become fit for sacrifice (*medhya*)!" thought he. Therefore the horse sacrifice is called Aśva-medha. He, verily, knows the Aśva-medha, who knows it thus.
>
> He kept him [i.e., the horse] in mind without confining him. After a year he sacrificed him for himself. [Other] animals he delivered over to the divinities. Therefore men sacrifice the victim which is consecrated to Prajāpati as though offered unto all the gods.
>
> Verily, that [sun] which gives forth heat is the Aśva-medha. The year is its embodiment (*ātman*).
>
> This [earthly] fire is the *arka*. The worlds are its embodiments. These are two, the *arka* sacrificial fire and the Aśva-medha sacrifice. Yet again they are one divinity, even Death. He [who knows this] wards off repeated death (*punarmṛtyu*), death obtains him not, death becomes his body (*ātman*), he becomes one of these deities.

The Upanishadic identity of the horse sacrifice with death parallels the Norse perception of the horse as death symbol.

Human sacrifice conforming to the example of the lugubrious Odin envisages the attainment of a goal similar to that of the Brahmanic practice. Odin achieved a mighty victory over death when he dangled from the world tree for nine nights, and secured possession of the powerful runes, effective over the dead, thus attaining a dual ontological supremacy over the realms of the living and the dead. As in the case of Prajāpati, immortality as it applies to Odin can be properly understood only as a litotes formula for the expression of superabundant life that encompasses and assimilates even death and can never be compatible with the Platonic terms of Judeo-Christian theology. Odin's ontological mastery of two realms was, however, a momentary and designed transcendence of an immutable and basic dualism in the Norse religious tradition. At the *Ragnarök* Odin's magical cosmic grip would loosen and the inimical forces would dislodge him.

Whatever the contrast between the Vedic and Viking traditions, in the goals of human sacrifice they appear to maintain consonance. The

---

[26] Translation after R. E. Hume, *The Thirteen Principal Upanishads* (2d ed., London, 1934), pp. 75–76.

[27] Prajāpati.

ultimate divine act of self-sacrifice was perceived as the eschatological mystery wherein the last possible cosmic potentiality was actualized in the person of the sacrificer. The religious institution of human sacrifice pursued the model of the godly archetype as the supreme sacrificial mystery which mobilized the maximum possible magical propensities of the offering.

The Separate Functions of the Indo-European Divine Twins

DONALD J. WARD, *University of California, Los Angeles*

Although the new comparative Indo-European mythology owes its existence almost exclusively to Georges Dumézil, some of the most brilliant studies to emerge from the new discipline have come not from Dumézil but from the Swedish scholar Stig Wikander. In 1947 Wikander made a highly significant contribution when he was able to show conclusively that much of the great Indian epic, the *Mahābhārata*, represented euhemerized Indo-Iranian mythology.[1] With this one article, the entire study of Indo-European mythology and the theories of Georges Dumézil acquired new stature, for Wikander, working within the framework of Dumézil's system, was able to produce startling and convincing results. In a more recent investigation[2] Wikander was able to uncover the first totally convincing evidence of Indo-European mythology among Germanic-speaking peoples, and the implications of this study are just making themselves felt among historians, mythologists, and philologists.[3] But of all of Wikander's studies, none is more remarkable than the one in which he again turned to the euhemerized mythology of the *Mahābhārata* and investigated the twin heroes, Nakula and Sahadeva,[4] the twin

1 "Pāṇḍavasagan och Mahābhāratas mytiska förutsättningar," *RoB* 6:27–39 (1947).

2 "Från Bråvalla till Kurukshetra," *ANF* 75:183–193 (1960). See also "Germanische und indo-iranische Eschatologie," *Kairos* 2:83–88 (1960).

3 See, for example, J. de Vries, *Heldenlied und Heldensage* (Bern and Munich, 1961), pp. 147–149.

4 "Nakula et Sahadeva," *OS* 6:66–96 (1957).

sons of the Vedic divinities, the Aśvins. Wikander was able to show that each member of the heroic pair had a quite distinct personality, and that each played a distinct role in the epic. Nakula, the heroic, handsome warrior, is a breaker and trainer of horses. He is also reported to have "eyes of fire" and "the shoulders of a lion." Sahadeva, on the other hand, is of a sweet, peaceful temperament and is associated with domestic duties and with the care of cattle. He is considered to be especially virtuous, modest, patient, intelligent, and just.

Wikander points out that the one twin, in his role as warrior, represents Dumézil's second function, while his brother, interested in domestic duties and animal husbandry, represents the third function.[5] This association of each twin with a separate function was, according to Wikander, already well defined during the period of Indo-European unity. This hypothesis, however, encounters difficulty, for in the *Rig-Veda* the Aśvins are characterized and invoked as equals. Wikander has carefully analyzed the Vedic hymns and has discovered a number of subtle differences between the brothers which are all variants of a sharp, fundamental distinction. For example, the identical traits and functions (fertility and warfare) associated with the heroes Nakula and Sahadeva are also characteristic of the Aśvins and are furthermore reflected in their epithets. These epithets, although generally applied to both divinities, invariably occur in pairs, and in nearly always the same order. This recurring order, which is parallel to the order of epithets used individually for Nakula and Sahadeva, is a strong indication that originally one set of epithets belonged to the one Aśvin, and the other set belonged to the second Aśvin. Moreover, the post-Vedic texts call the one twin Nāsatya and the other Dasra, both forms being in the singular.[6] Wikander supports his conclusions with evidence found in the Iran-

[5] The Indo-European tripartite structure, which, according to Dumézil, is reflected not only in the mythology, but in society as a whole, makes a clear distinction between the functions of the divinities. The first function is essentially the religio-political function involving the priests and the kings (Mitra-Varuṇa). The second function is that of warfare, involving warriors (Indra). The third function is essentially economic, involving fertility, wealth, and general well-being (Aśvins).

[6] Although in the *Rig-Veda* both names generally occur in the dual, there is one hymn (4.3.6) which speaks of one Nāsatya. Other scholars have also concluded that these were originally the individual names of the Aśvins. See P. S. Sastri, "The Semantic History of the Words Nāsatyāu and Dasrāu," *Journal of Oriental Research* (Madras) 17:232 (1946). Similarly P. Collinet ("Vedic Chips," *Babylonian and Oriental Record* 3:196 [1888–1889]) contends that Nāsatyā was originally a singular that became a dual and was then applied to both twins much like the Roman "Castores."

ian *Avesta,* in which there is only the figure of a demon named Naŋhaithya (*Vidēvdāt* 10.9, 19.43). This name corresponds to the Vedic Nāsatya, a favorite epithet of the Aśvins. The *Avesta* treats this figure as malevolent, thereby revealing an instance of Zoroastrian damning of an Aryan divinity. As Wikander has shown,[7] all divinities associated with warfare and with the horse were rejected by the Zoroastrian religion. Consequently the one Aśvin, who exhibited the more warlike nature, and who was associated with the horse, was demoted to the role of a demon in the new religion. The second twin, the peaceful youth, who was concerned with more domestic chores and with the cow, should have found ready acceptance in the Zoroastrian pantheon. Wikander believes to have found him in the figure of Atar, son of Ahura Mazdāh. Although this final point is not as convincing as the remainder of the brilliant study, Wikander has nonetheless shown conclusively that the Vedic Aśvins originally had distinct characteristics and functions, and that from the beginning the one twin was associated with the second function and the other twin with the third function.[8]

The implication of Wikander's study is, of course, that this distinction of the Indo-Iranian twin gods dates back to the period of Indo-European unity and was evident in the original stratum of Indo-European mythology. Such a conclusion, however, should not be reached too hastily. The concept of twin divinities having totally distinct characteristics and functions is by no means limited to Indo-European mythology but is worldwide in distribution. This universal concept has arisen logically from the widespread notion that a multiple birth is the result of multiple conception.[9] As the result of this belief, one frequently encounters the notion that a pair of twins cannot possibly be sired by a single father. The attitudes recorded in some of the legends collected by the Brothers Grimm attest that this

---

7 "Nakula et Sahadeva," p. 81.

8 *Ibid.*, pp. 82–83. Various scholars have sensed the essential difference between the Aśvins, even though the evidence indicating such distinction is subtle. For example, C. Renel (*L'évolution d'un mythe: Açvins et Dioscures* [Paris, 1896], p. 63) sees the one twin embodying the fire element of the sacrifice, whereas the second embodies the liquid element. F. Cornelius (*Indogermanische Religionsgeschichte* [Munich, 1942], p. 65) contends that the one twin was the coachman and the second the warrior in the celestial chariot, G. L. Chandavarkar ("Aśvins as Historical Figures," *Journal of the University of Bombay* 3:81 [1935]), contends that the Aśvins owe their existence to a single mortal who became deified and thus led a twofold existence, human and divine. Thus the concept of two Aśvins, one divine and one mortal, is supposed to have developed.

9 For examples from various ethnographic sources, see L. Sternberg, "Der antike Zwillingskult im Lichte der Ethnologie," *ZEthn* 61:167–69 (1929). See also A. H. Krappe, *Mythologie universelle* (Paris, 1930), p. 65.

belief was still current in Europe in relatively modern times. For example, legend number 521: "Es ist unmöglich, daß dieses Weib drei Kinder von einem Mann haben könne ohne Ehebruch."[10] Similarly, legend number 584: "Es ist unmöglich, daß ein Weib zwei Kinder auf einmal von einem Vater habe."[11]

Notions of the dual paternity of human twins have played a role in the formation of mythological traditions involving divine twins as they occur throughout the world. A typical example is provided by the mythology of the Apapocuva Indians of south Brazil. The pantheon of this tribe includes a pair of divine twins, one of whom is the son of a high deity, "Our Great Father," while the second twin is considered the son of a lesser divinity, "Our Father Knower of All Things."[12]

Since twin deities are frequently considered to have been begotten by different fathers, the twins often are very different in nature. For example, in the Old Testament Esau is the bold, vigorous huntsman, while his brother Jacob is a docile shepherd. Among the Brazilian Apapocuva, the elder of the twin deities is a powerful god who resides in heaven; the younger brother, on the other hand, is of minor importance and resides in the east with his mother. Generally throughout the Americas the elder of twin deities is clever and capable, while the younger is a foolish, lazy blockhead.[13]

Among the mythological traditions of Indo-European peoples, various pairs of Greek divine twins were reported to have been begotten by separate fathers. According to Pindar (*Nemean Odes*, 10.150), Polydeukes was begotten by Zeus, while Kastor was fathered by Tyndareos.[14] Similarly, the twin Amphion (musician) was fathered by Zeus, whereas Zethos (huntsman) was fathered by the mortal Epopeus. Moreover, Zeus begot Herakles, whereas the mortal Amphitryon begot his twin brother, Iphikles.

A parallel to the Greek tradition is encountered in Vedic religion. The twin Aśvins, like the Dioscuri, are both called Divó nápātā, 'Sons of God'[15] (*Rig-Veda* 1.117.12), yet they are likewise reported to

---

[10] Brüder Grimm, *Deutsche Sagen* (Berlin, 1956), p. 493.

[11] *Ibid.*, p. 584. The identical notion is found in lines 38–42 of the twelfth-century poem of Marie de France, *Le Frene.*

[12] See A. E. Jensen, *Mythos und Kult bei Naturvölkern* (Wiesbaden, 1951), p. 341.

[13] A. Métraux, "Twin Heroes in South American Mythology," *JAF* 59:114 (1946).

[14] See also Pausanias 4.31.7, 3.26.2; Apollodorus 3.10.5.

[15] The identical name is preserved in Baltic mythology where the twins are called Dieva dēli in Latvian, and Dievo suneliai in Lithuanian, both of which mean 'Sons of God.' Moreover, the Greek Διὸς κοῦροι has the identical meaning. All three forms are not only related in meaning but etymologically as well.

have had different fathers. One of the twins is the "blessed offspring of the sky," while the other is the son of the mortal Sumakha (*Rig-Veda* 1.181.4).

In view of this evidence, the distinction in the function and character of the Vedic twins as worked out by Wikander is in no way surprising. If, as in the case of Dioscuric traditions the world over, the twins were considered the products of two different fathers, the distinction in their behavior and in their religious function is only to be expected. Since this phenomenon is universal, one could justifiably question the contention that the divergences between the Aśvins represent an exclusively Indo-European trait.[16] In the case of the Indo-Iranian tradition, however, we do not merely have a distinction between the twin deities, we have a highly specialized difference, that is, one twin is associated with warfare, horses, and strength, and the other is associated with domestic duties, cattle, fertility, and is a gentle being. We thus have a uniquely Indo-European manifestation of a universal Dioscuric trait.[17] For, although distinctions between twin divinities are encountered everywhere, the specific one found in the Indo-Iranian tradition is by no means worldwide in its distribution.

Wikander's contention that this distinction between the Indo-Iranian divinities belongs to the original stratum of Indo-European mythology, as well as the entire tripartite theory of Dumézil, would gain in strength if one could find evidence of such a differentiation among the other Indo-European Dioscuric pairs. I believe that it can indeed be detected, although, as in the case of the *Rig-Veda*, it is not always immediately discernible. Before discussing the details, however, I should like to adduce evidence that shows that various Indo-European Dioscuric pairs were, in general, associated with the "second and third functions."

That the Vedic twins were associated with both the warrior and fertility function is well known. Regarding the second function they help Viśpalā in contest (*Rig-Veda* 1.112.10), they protect mortals in combat (10.143.4), they grant victory in war (8.35.12). Similarly, the Greek Dioscuri are renowned for their role as warriors. They bat-

---

16 Similarly, the evidence of a distinction between other Indo-European Dioscuric pairs, e.g., Kastor was mortal, Polydeukes divine, Kastor was the "breaker of horses," Polydeukes a boxer (*Iliad* 3.326; *Odyssey* 11.298), cannot in itself be considered as belonging exclusively to the Indo-European tradition.

17 For a discussion of uniquely Indo-European traits of "Dioscurism" occurring within the framework of a universal "Dioscurism," see R. Goossens, "Notes de mythologie comparée indo-européenne," *NClio* 1/2:13–14 (1949–1950). See also D. Ward, *The Divine Twins: An Indo-European Myth in Germanic Tradition*, Folklore Studies, 19 (Berkeley and Los Angeles, 1968), pp. 8–29.

tle with Idas and Lynkeus over cattle. They lead the storming of the fortress at Aphidnae to liberate their sister.[18] Even the Latvian Sons of God were reported to have been equipped with a sword.[19]

The third function is also associated with the various twin divinities. Many Vedic hymns invoking the Aśvins praise their ability to promote fertility. They are praised for placing the germ in all female creatures (1.157.5), and for giving fertility to the bride (10.184.2). They give a child to the wife of the eunuch (1.117.24) and milk to the barren cow (1.112.3). Evidence of the Dioscuri functioning as divinities of fertility is relatively scant. They were frequently honored at important festivals and banquets where offerings of food were made to them,[20] indicating that they may have been divinities of the harvest. There are, moreover, countless reliefs and coins that depict the twins with a horn of plenty, sheaves of grain, and other agricultural products.[21] Furthermore, the eggshell hats (piloi) of the twins were evidently fertility symbols. Moreover, the Roman Castor was associated with the goddess of fountains, Juturna, indicating that he was worshiped as a fertility deity.[22] Similarly, in the mythology of the Baltic region, the twin Sons of God were envisioned working with agricultural implements, helping to till the soil and sow the seeds, thus indicating that they functioned as divinities of the harvest and of fertility. One Latvian song, for example, reports that the twin gods had plows of gold and seeds of silver.[23] Moreover, they bring the yeast and add it to the beer,[24] and they are associated with the "golden dew" that covers the green meadows.[25]

The evidence above makes it clear that in the various Indo-European traditions, the Divine Twins were associated with both the second and third functions. The evidence that each twin was originally associated with only one of these functions is more difficult to uncover.

In Greek mythology this contrast is stressed when Pindar (*Pythian*

---

18 For a more complete listing of the episodes in which the Dioscuri provide divine aid in battle, see A. Furtwängler, "Die Dioskuren," *Ausführliches Lexikon der griechischen und römischen Mythologie* (Leipzig, 1884), I, 1, cols. 1156–1157.

19 M. Jonval, *Les chansons mythologiques lettonnes* (Paris, 1929), song no. 34019, with French translation.

20 Furtwängler, *op. cit.*, cols. 1167–1168.

21 F. Chapouthier, *Les Dioscures au service d'une déesse: Étude d'iconographie religieuse* (Paris, 1935).

22 See R. Schilling, "Les Castores romains à la lumière des traditions indo-européennes," in *Hommages à Georges Dumézil* (Brussels, 1960), pp. 177–192.

23 Jonval, *op. cit.*, song no. 33904.

24 *Ibid.*, p. 40.

25 *Ibid.*, song no. 33954.

Odes 5.9) uses the epithet χρυσάρματος, 'in a golden chariot,' to refer to Kastor alone. Moreover, Kastor was honored as the founder of the horse race, while Polydeukes was honored for having invented the hound races. The dog is clearly an animal associated with house and farm, whereas the horse, especially in ancient Greek civilization, is an animal of warfare. An even more remarkable contrast is made in *Homeric Hymn* 33.3, which calls Kastor ἱππόδαμος, 'breaker of horses,' and mentions ἀμώμητον Πολυδεύκεα, 'the faultless [virtuous] Polydeukes.' It is in the Roman sources, however, that this fundamental distinction is most clearly expressed. In a recent study, R. Schilling has demonstrated that the Roman knights, whose cavalry charge at Lake Regillus in 499 B.C. saved the Roman infantry from a rout, had already worshiped Castor as a patron of their class.[26] The reason that one brother alone was worshiped, instead of both Dioscuri, is evidently that Kastor alone was the warlike youth, associated with the horse. His docile, virtuous brother would have been poorly suited for the needs of an elite knighthood. Further evidence of this contrast occurs in Dio Cassius (57.14.9), who reports that the younger Drusus was "so prone to anger that he even inflicted blows upon a distinguished knight and received on this account the nickname Castor."[27] This report indicates that the Romans evidently carried the contrast between the Dioscuri to an extreme. Not only was Castor considered warlike and aggressive, but rash and hot-tempered as well. Pollux, who was unquestionably a more passive figure, and who was more involved with domestic functions, gradually faded into the background.

Although there is evidence of Germanic peoples having worshiped the Divine Twins,[28] the source material is generally too scant to enable the scholar to discern a difference between the Germanic divinities.[29] A possible exception is furnished by Hengist and Horsa, who were reported to have led the Anglo-Saxon invasions of the British Isles.[30] The names of the brothers mean 'stallion' and 'horse,'

---

26 *Op. cit.*

27 K. Scott, "Drusus, Nicknamed 'Castor,'" *CPh* 25:155 (1930).

28 See Ward, *op. cit.*, also "Kudrun: An Indo-European Mythological Theme?" *Indo-European and Indo-Europeans* (Philadelphia, 1970).

29 If one accepts Dumézil's hypothesis that the gods Freyr and Njördr represent the Germanic twins (*La Saga de Hadingus* [Paris, 1953], pp. 118–159), one could build a strong case for each of these divinities representing a separate function. Dumézil, however, does not offer enough evidence to prove his contention.

30 During the migrations various Germanic peoples were reported to have been under the leadership of such pairs, for example the leaders of the Vandals were

respectively, indicating that the same theriomorphic concept associated with other divine pairs of the Indo-European tradition was known also among Germanic peoples.

Of particular interest regarding these sources is that the one brother, Horsa, gradually disappears from the scene, leaving Hengist as the sole leader of the invaders. We are already familiar with the gradual disappearance of one member of a Dioscuric pair, namely in the Roman sources in which the passive, docile Pollux is overshadowed by his more aggressive, warlike brother. One can speculate that a similar distinction was responsible for the demise of Horsa during the heroic age. As an aggressive heroic warrior Hengist was doubtless praised in lay and legend. His more docile brother, as a representative of the third function who may have been a patron of herdsmen and farmers, was excluded from the heroic songs, and thus his name is often missing from those records that tell of the exploits of Anglo-Saxon heroes.

One can further speculate that in Germanic religion there developed a dual aspect of the sacred horse. The one aspect may have represented the horse as an animal of warfare, and the other as an animal of the farm and of fertility. Similar to the Indo-European tradition in which the one twin divinity was associated with the horse and the other with the cow, the one Germanic twin, Hengist, may have been associated with the war-horse, while his brother, Horsa, may have been linked with the farm animal. This hypothesis is, admittedly, based on speculation. Nevertheless, the curious distinction in the names of the pair, viz. Hengist/Horsa, may well point to such a dual aspect of the horse.

Other than the fact that Horsa gradually fades into oblivion, the records of the exploits of the heroes offer no evidence of separate functions. A folk legend recorded in modern Germany however, offers a remarkable example of a pair of brothers with distinct functions. The legend reports that an aged count, when near death, decided to bestow upon his two sons the implements that would determine their respective careers. To the one son he gave a sword and the instructions to use his strength to defend the castle. To the other son he gave a plow, and he instructed him to work the fields of the valley "peacefully."[31]

Ambr and Assi, the leaders of the Langobards were Ibor and Aio, and the leaders of the Asdingi were Raus and Raptus. The evidence points clearly to a euhemerization of Dioscuric divinities in each of these cases. See N. Wagner, "Dioskuren, Jungmannschaften und Doppelkönigtum," *ZDPh* 79:1–17, 225–247 (1960). See also Ward, *The Divine Twins*, pp. 50–56.

[31] H. Stötzel, *Die Sagen des Ahrtals* (2d ed.; Bonn, 1953), p. 44.

Although it may seem fantastic to assume that this modern legend represents the survival of an ancient mythological tradition, the similarity with the Indo-European theme is so striking that this legend cannot be ignored. Not only are the brothers given distinct roles to play, the distinction is precisely of the kind that is typical of other Indo-European pairs. The one brother, who bears the sword, represents the second function, while his brother, who works with the plow, represents the third function. I suggest that a euhemerized myth of the Germanic divine pair survived in oral tradition and came to be recorded in the form of a folk legend.

An even more striking treatment of this theme occurs in Spanish heroic tradition. Samuel Armistead has worked with the legends that treat the illegitimate birth of the Spanish hero, the Cid.[32] Armistead is able to demonstrate that at one time there were two contemporary epic traditions involving the hero's birth. According to the one tradition, the Cid was a twin who was begotten when a knight forced himself upon a peasant woman. The woman later lay with her husband, at which time the twin brother was conceived. The most complete evidence of this theme has been uncovered in a passage of the second redaction (*ca.* 1504) of the *Compendio historical,* originally written by Diego Rodríguez de Almela *circa* 1479. The passage in question attempts to discredit the report of the Cid's illegitimate birth.[33]

> Note also inasmuch as some say that the Cid was a bastard they are mistaken about it. And the way in which those who have not read his history and chronicle say this is as follows: That is, that Don Diego Laínez, father of the Cid, before marrying Dona Teresa Nunez, mother of the Cid, on Saint James day in Vivar forced a peasant woman, a miller's beautiful wife, at her house, and she conceived a son at that time. And the peasant, her husband, when he came home from the mill, seized her that same day, and she conceived another son at that time. And when they were to be born, the knight's son was born first. And he looked like his father, very lively and full of grace; and the peasant's [son looked] like his [father], very coarse. And when both brothers were five or six years old, the knight's son made hobby-horses out of wood and lances and swords and other things pertaining to arms. And he called the young boys "knights" and ran about from place to place, and all his activities had to do with weapons and knighthood. And the peasant's son made little oxen out of clay and plows of wood. And with these things and other sticks,

[32] This information will eventually be published by Armistead in an article entitled "Two Rival Traditions Concerning the Parentage of the Cid." I am grateful to Professor Armistead for providing me with this information and for the translation of the manuscript material.

[33] "Compendio historial," 2d redaction, Biblioteca Nacional Madrid, MS 1525, formerly F–115, fol. 248*r*, known as MS F.

> which he had in his hand, he would plow along the floor, saying 'Gee up here!' and 'Gee up there!' and those who saw them marvelled at it. Don Diego Laínez then took his son, who was called Fernán Díaz. And when he was of age to bear arms he was a good knight and brave.

The relationship with the universal Dioscuric pattern, whereby the one twin is begotten by a divinity and the other by a mortal, can be clearly discerned in this passage, even though the material has been euhemerized. The theme of the dual paternity of the twins remains, and with it the distinction in the character of each of the twins. Moreover, the distinction is of the specialized type that has been encountered in the Indo-European tradition. Namely, the one twin represents the second function, is consequently of heroic, warlike character, and is associated with the horse, while the other twin represents the third function, is of a docile, gentle nature, and is more interested in cattle, plows, and farming than in warfare. I suggest that this contrast between the Spanish hero and his twin brother not only represents the same contrast as one encounters in Indo-European mythology, but that this episode in the career of the Cid represents a heroic euhemerization of an Indo-European Dioscuric myth. The question of just how this theme found its way into the Spanish heroic tradition is left open at this time. This aspect of the problem, however, certainly warrants further investigation.

These various bits of information regarding the character and function of the Indo-European twins when viewed singly may not appear too significant, but viewed altogether they add up to an impressive sum of evidence, showing clearly that the distinction in the function of the twins, as posited by Wikander for the Indo-Iranian tradition, is true for other Indo-European traditions as well. Moreover, this distinction bears a clear imprint of the tripartite ideology of the Indo-Europeans.

Reflections on "yaoždā," with a Digression on "xvaētvadaθa"

JACQUES DUCHESNE-GUILLEMIN, *University of Liège*

Georges Dumézil published an article some twenty years ago entitled "A propos de latin *ius*."[1] After recalling that the term has only a profane value, namely 'area of maximal action or pretension,' but must previously have had a half-juridical, half-religious one, still reflected in *iurare* and *ius iurandum*, he asked the question: "What religious value?"

The answer seemed to lie in a comparison between Avestan *yaoždā*, which in the *Vidēvdāt* means chiefly 'to purify from the contagion of dead matter,' and Latin *iusta facere* ('to perform certain religious ceremonies called *denicales feriae*'). On the day of cremation, a bone was severed from the corpse; this *os resectum* (usually a finger bone) was then buried at the *denicales feriae*. If, however, the person had perished at sea (*in navi necatus*), no *denicales feriae* were to take place, since the family was then said to be *pure*: *decrevit P. Mucius*, Cicero writes in *De Legibus* 2.22, *familiam puram, quod os supra terram non extaret*. This seems to prove, Dumézil writes, that *iusta facere* means not only granting the dead what they have a right to receive, but also purifying the family. The same would be expressed in Varro (*De lingua latina* 3.4) as *familiam purgandam*. Hence an intimate connection between *iusta facere* and *yaoždā* can be deduced, with the common meaning 'to purify from defilement by death.'

In sending me the offprint of this article ten years after it appeared (I did not yet know him when it was published, and it was only in

[1] *RHR* 134:95–112 (1948). [A considerably revised version of this article may be found in *Idées romaines* (Paris, 1969), pp. 31–45.]

1958 that I asked for it), Dumézil wrote one of those pregnant dedicatory lines of which he has a wonderful mastery, and which typify the constant revision to which a lifetime of work is being submitted by one of the most active, everlastingly young minds of our time: "Après dix ans, bien des choses sont à changer." He did not say which; but now, in his excellent *La religion romaine archaïque* (Paris, 1966), although the phrase *iusta facere* is mentioned, no reference at all is made to *yaoždā*. Why? This is the question I tackle below.[2]

Is the reason for Dumézil's change of mind to be found in an article published in 1955 by J. de Bie in *Le Muséon*?[3] The author tries to reconstruct the semantic evolution of *yaoždā*, drawing his evidence exclusively from Avestan texts. He distinguishes three stages, after first sketching the evolution of the Mazdean religion as he sees it. The first is a purely ethical stage, then (in his own words) "dans la fixation progressive du culte mazdéen, toute purification se lie de plus en plus fermement à des rites magiques bien définis," with reference to J. Darmesteter and A. Carnoy. From this far too simple background three successive semantic values of *yaoždā* seem to emerge:

1) 'to put in a state of moral purity, exempt from evil.' *Yasna* 44.9 speaks of *yaoždā*'ing the *daēnā*, an act performed, according to *Vidēvdāt* 10.19, through good thoughts, good words, and good deeds. *Yašt* 8 speaks in the same way of *yaoždā*'ing the *urvan*, the *daēnā*, the *aŋhvā*;

2) the second stage is reflected in numerous passages of the *Vidēvdāt* in which *yaoždā* means 'purifying from the contagion of dead matter,' representing a shift from ethics to magic;

3) in the third stage even water is supposed to have been defiled by dead matter and must be purified; such is the case also of other inanimate objects, cult implements, and the like.

De Bie summarizes his view as follows: originally the word designated the internal, moral attitude of "sinless, well disposed toward the Good and Ahura," both in the passive sense of 'agreeable' and in the active one 'devoted.'

This linear evolution is allegedly that of the Mazdean religion itself. But such an assumption is obviously wrong. We recognize in the *Avesta* many elements older than the Gathic reform with which

[2] Dumézil also wrote an article on *mos*, "Ordre, fantaisie, changement dans les pensées archaïques de l'Inde et de Rome" (*REL* 32:139–160 [1954], comparing the term with Sanskrit *māyā́*. This collocation also has been quietly dropped in *La religion romaine archaïque*.

[3] "Yaoždā, étude d'un terme religieux avestique," *Le Muséon* 68:145–161.

they must later have been merged; defilement by contact with dead matter could have been one of them. Linguistically de Bie takes practically no account of the semantic correspondences found in *yaoš*, 'exemption from dead matter,' and Sanskrit *yoṣ*, 'welfare, health, happiness.'

We conclude that de Bie's article cannot have impressed Dumézil very much. What then can have made him find fault with his own?

Perhaps de Bie, a beginner in Avestan, who has since gone over to the study of Greek grammar by means of computers, was misled by the chronological order that Bartholomae followed in his dictionary: beginning with Gathic passages, followed by the later Avestan ones. It is useful, in this case, to examine first the passages in which the meanings are similar to the Vedic ones. Such a procedure will be more in line with what Dumézil has done.

The first examples demonstrate a connection, in both Sanskrit and Avestan, between the term under study and life:

Rig-Veda 1.189.2 and elsewhere: *tokā́ya tánayāya śáṃ yóḥ*, 'sei für den leiblichen Samen zu Wohl und Heil.' Such a prayer is addressed to the waters in *Rig-Veda* 6.50.7 and 5.53.14, as pointed out by Dumézil in "A propos de latin *ius*."[4] A parallel is present in the Avestan hymn to the goddess of waters, Anāhitā: *yā vīspanąm aršnąm xšudrå yaoždaδāiti . . . hāirišinąm ząθāi garəwąn yaoždaδāiti . . . hāirišīš huzāmitō daδāiti . . . vīspąm hāirišinąm dāitīm raθwīm paēma ava.baraiti (Yašt* 5.2), 'Who *yaoždā*'s the semen of all the males, the embryos of the females for birth; gives the females an easy childbirth; provides them with milk at the right moment.' To which may be compared further on in *Yašt* 5.5: *hā mē āpō yaoždaδāiti hā aršnąm xšudrå hā xšaθrinąm garəwąn hā xšaθinąm paēma*, 'she *yaoždā*'s me the waters, the semen of the males, the embryos of the women, the milk of the women."

The next example in *Yasna* 48.5 is subject to a new interpretation, as distinct from Humbach's translation: . . . *vanhuyå čistōiš šyaoθanāiš ārmaitē yaoždå mašyā(i) aipī ząθəm vahištā gavōi vərəzyātąm*, '. . . mit den Werken der guten Erkenntnis, o Gemässheit, . . . die mit dem Menschen auch seine Nachkommenschaft gesund macht, soll der Kuh gegenüber angewandt werden.' Humbach makes *čisti-* the implied subject of *vərəzyātąm*, but if we take *ārmaiti-* instead we obtain a rather remarkable agreement with the passage from *Yašt* 5.2 quoted above, since Armaiti is the Gathic substitute for Anāhitā: 'Armaiti, who also *yaoždā*'s man and his progeny.'

The second group consists of passages dealing with purification

---

[4] *Op. cit.*, p. 100.

from defilement by death. In *Vidēvdāt* 6 and elsewhere, the verbs *pairi.yaoždā* and *us.snā, frasnā* are employed as near equivalents. One instance of *yaoždā* (*Vidēvdāt* 8.100) suffices: 'Here I am, one who has touched the corpse of a man, and who is powerless in mind, in tongue, in hand. Do *yaoždā* me!'

In the third group *yaoždā* is extended to the soul, *urvan, daēnā,* or *aŋhvā,* as in *Yasna* 44.9: *yąm yaoš daēnąm (yaož)dąnē,* 'die Gesinnung, die ich mir heilwirkend machen will,' and this is accomplished by means of good thoughts, good words, and good deeds.

In the fourth group, fire has to be purified, for instance *Zaraθuštrəm ātrəm pairi.yaoždaθəntəm* (*Yasna* 9.1).

In the fifth group, the act has to do with ritual cleanliness of implements.

It seems, then, from the main objects undergoing *yaoždā,* namely, the semen, living beings, the soul, and fire, that we would be entitled to deduce an intrinsic affinity between *yaoš* and life, and perhaps a new etymology: **yewes* <**yew,* 'young,' compare Sanskrit *yoṣā,* 'woman,' and Sogdian *ynč* <**yavanikā.*[5]

To test this hypothesis, we may examine the means by which the act is performed. We read in the descriptions of the *barəšnūm* ceremony that purification is made with water, sand, and *gōmēz.* Why is *gōmēz,* 'bull's urine,' used? Is it assumed to have life-giving properties because it is near the semen and perhaps mingled with it, thus a plausible antidote to anything connected with death?

According to *Vidēvdāt* 8.13, however, corpse-bearers may be purified not only with the urine of cattle, but also with the mingled urine of a man and a woman who have performed the *xvaētvadaθa.*

A DIGRESSION ON *XVAĒTVADAΘA*

History repeats itself. In 1888 the Parsi Darab Peshotan Sanjana published a book, *The Alleged Practices of Next of Kin Marriage in Old Iran* (London, 1888). The following year H. Hübschmann showed that although the Avestan evidence for the practice alluded to in the title is not decisive, inasmuch as no definition of *xvaētvadaθa* is given, the material in Greek and other foreign authors is overwhelming.[6] This did not deter another Parsi, Jamshid Cawasji, from writing another book, *Marriage in Ancient Iran* (Bombay, 1965), in which he tries to revive Sanjana's theory that *xvaētvadaθa* had nothing to do with next-of-kin marriage. This may be pardon-

[5] See J. Duchesne-Guillemin, "Autres miettes," *Acta Orientalia* 30:73–74 (1966).
[6] "*Ueber die persische Verwandtenheirath,*" *ZDMG* 43:308–312 (1889).

able on the part of zealous people who tend to represent their religion as it should be, rather than as it is; what seems less pardonable is for a European scholar such as Otakar Klima in his rejoinder "Zur Problematik der Ehe-Institution im alten Iran"[7] to have made a rather heavy refutation of the Parsi thesis without reference to his predecessor Hübschmann or to L. H. Gray's "Marriage, Iranian, Next-of-Kin."[8] He seems at least to have known Hübschmann's article, since he refers in a footnote to the very volume of *ZDMG* in which it appeared. Why then not cite him?

It is certainly a pity that Klima completely ignored Gray or Otto Schrader, whose hints as to the origin of this Mazdean usage he might otherwise have followed. I allude to Schrader's *Reallexikon der indogermanischen Altertumskunde* (Strasbourg, 1901), revised by Alfons Nehring more than thirty years ago, a work that needs yet another edition.

Anyhow, this is what may be said *en attendant*. Three hypotheses are possible as to the origin of this usage: (1) It may be a survival from a state of savagery, in which free intercourse between the sexes prevailed; (2) or it may be an exaggeration of a particular rule of marriage; (3) or it may have been borrowed from some indigenous population of western Asia.

The third hypothesis may be rejected for lack of evidence, despite what Ghirshman writes: "Many figurines of a naked goddess have been found on prehistoric Iranian sites. This goddess probably [I do not see what makes this probable!] had as a consort a god who was at once and the same time both her son and her husband. Undoubtedly [this seems just a manner of speaking!] it is in this primitive religion that we should seek the origin of marriage between brothers and sisters—a custom common in Western Asia, which the Persians and later the Nabateans inherited from the indigenous population—or of the marriage, less often recorded, between mother and son."[9]

The other two hypotheses are less fragile. The first one is based on Celtic facts. Among the ancient Britons, according to Caesar (*Bellum Gallicum* 5.14) and Dio Cassius (*Historiarum Romanarum* 76.12; 62.6), women were the common property of their husbands. In Ireland, if we are to believe Strabo (*Geographica* 4.4) and Jerome (11.7), intercourse with wives of other men, with mothers and sisters was frequent, and kinship ties were not an obstacle to marriage: Lugaid,

---

7 *AO* 34:554–569 (1966).

8 *Encyclopaedia of Religion and Ethics*, ed. J. Hastings (New York, 1925), VIII, 456–459.

9 R. Ghirshman, *Iran* (London, 1961), p. 44.

king of Ireland, married his mother; a king of Leinster had his two sisters as wives.

The second hypothesis is illustrated among the ancient Balts. It is true that Christoph Hartknoch's statement in *Alt- und neues Preussen* seems at first sight rather to bear out the first one:

> . . . das die alten Preussen in ihrem Heyrathen gantz und gar auff keine Blut-Freunschaft oder Schwägerschaft gesehen, sondern haben auch Bluts-Verwandten einander geheyrathet und ist damit niemand ausgeschlossen gewesen als eine rechte Mutter. Denn dasz sie auch ihre Stiefmütter haben heyrathen können . . . auch bey den Littauen hat es vor Zeiten in dem Heydenthum frey gestanden die Stiefmütter zu Weibern zu nehmen.[10]

But the explanation furnished by Jacobus, "ein Päbstischer Gesandter," proves that the passage alludes not to unruliness but to a perfectly justified rule: "Cum enim pater aliquam uxorem de pecunia communi sibi et filio emerat, hactenus servaverunt, ut mortuo patre, uxor eius ad filium devolveretur, sicut alia hereditas de bonis communibus comparata."[11]

The early Indo-European woman thus seems to have been regarded as either a toy or a chattel. But neither theory can account for the position accorded to women amongst the ancient Germans. The famous passages in Tacitus (*Germania* 7–8) that follow seem to support the view that they were human counterparts of sorts of the trivalent goddess of the Indo-Iranians: *ad matres, ad coniuges uulnera ferunt; nec illae numerare et exigere plagas pauent, cibosque . . .*, 'the men take their wounds to their mothers and wives, and the latter are not afraid of counting and examining the blows, and bring food . . .' (all this representing the third function); *et hortamina pugnantibus gestant,* 'and encouragement to the fighting men' (second function); *inesse quin etiam sanctum aliquid et prouidum putant, nec aut consilia earum aspernantur aut responsa neglegunt,* 'more than this, they believe that there resides in women an element of holiness and prophecy, and so they do not scorn to ask their advice or lightly disregard their replies' (first function).

But if we are confronted with the three Dumézilian functions, why do they appear in the reverse order, unless perhaps it be because woman belongs first of all to the third function? We further miss what Scott Littleton refers to as the "corner-stone," namely the character-

---

10 See "Von den Hochzeiten der Alten Preussen," in *Alt und neues Preussen* (Frankfurt and Leipzig, 1684), chap. xi.

11 *Ibid.*

istic division of the first function into two halves. This makes the proof of trifunctionality uncertain.

Be that as it may, this enhanced position of woman would seem to take us back to the very ancient system of matriarchy, and it is perhaps in this context that we must interpret the indications of the *xvaētvadaθa* (for lack of a better explanation), since obviously in a matriarchal system the only way for a boy to inherit the family's possessions is to marry his sister.

Presumably next-of-kin marriage is motivated by the desire to preserve the family from outside interference, a desire for some kind of purity. Consequently the urine of a couple united in *x^{v}ētōdas* is a valid substitute for *gōmēz* because it is particularly immune from outside factors, with their possibly noxious influence. Such urine, and by extension *gōmēz* in general, thus appears to have been valued mainly for its cathartic powers rather than its lifegiving properties. With this may be compared the Pahlavi usage: the word, when not merely transcribed *yoždas*, is translated by *pāk kartan*, or *hac vinās pāk dāštan*. And in the *Bundahišn*, when the semen of the Primeval Bull (or of Gayomart) is "purified" by the light of the moon or sun, the verb used is *pālūt*, 'to cleanse.'

If we now follow the same line backward in trying to determine the original meaning of *yaoždā*, we deduce that the connection of this term with life and death is only secondary and extrinsic, and that it means essentially 'to render pure.' We must now go back one step further and take Latin *ius* into account. This will be my third and final approach.

An evolution parallel to that of *ius, iustus* is found, historically attested, in Latin *proprius* and its Romance representatives. In Latin the word means 'belonging to someone particularly.' In the Romance languages it came to signify 'fitting' and was borrowed into English with that meaning. The *Oxford English Dictionary* tells us that from 1225 on, *properly* is attested in the sense of 'fittingly, suitably, appropriately, as it ought to be or as one ought to do; rightly, correctly, duly, well; in accordance with social ethics or good manners'; *proper* also has the meaning 'answering fully to the description; thorough, complete, perfect, out-and-out, now only slang and colloquial.'

The last stage in the evolution was reached in French, in the sixteenth century, when *propre*, which hitherto had meant 'appropriate, fit,' came to signify 'clean.'

Given the parallel, the semantic evolution of Latin *ius, iustus* can be reconstructed as follows: starting from 'exact sphere or domain' it went through the notion of 'how it should be' to that of 'untouched by violence; healthy.' This last stage is indirectly attested in *iniuria,* defined as follows in *Rhetorica ad Herennium* 4.25.35: "Iniuriae sunt quae aut pulsatione corpus, aut conuitio aures, aut aliqua turpitudine vitam cuiuspiam uiolant." Hence English *injury, injure* (this meaning does not appear in French except in the phrase *les injures du temps,* a Latinism attested only from the seventeeth century onward). The connection between bodily integrity and "justice" is still illustrated in the phrase used when someone stumbles and falls: "Are you all right?"

We have therefore no difficulty in accepting the usual etymology of Latin *ius* as **yewes,* from **yew,* 'to join, to fit'; hence**yewes,* 'what fits, is fitting' (cf. French *justesse-justice*), or 'what is exact, unmixed, pure.' The connection of this notion with life is then accidental: life is considered as pure from death, unhampered, unsullied by it. If this meaning is frequently attested it is only because life and death are so particularly important in the religion.

The notion is easily further extended to the soul, which will be considered good because not diminished, not weakened by evil; and finally it will extend also to inanimate objects.

The application to life and death certainly dates back at least to Indo-Iranian times. We have noted a precise identity between Vedic *tokā́ya yóṣ* and the Avestan passages, both Gathic and later, in which Anāhitā or her substitute Armaiti favors the purification of the semen. The question is, last but not least, did not this extension date back still further and is it not reflected in Latin? This boils down to interpreting *iusta facere*: we are brought back to our beginning, without perhaps being any the wiser for all our roamings. To be precise, how can we interpret the passages in Cicero and Varro quoted above? What does *familiam puram* mean in the Ciceronian passage where it denotes the family of a person killed at sea? In the absence of a good Latin dictionary, the answer is difficult (the *Thesaurus* has not yet reached the letter *P*!). Does the phrase mean, as Dumézil first suggested: 'not subject to the necessity of being purified from a connection with a dead body'; or does it after all mean simply 'not subject to the obligation of performing certain just actions, *iusta*'? Similarly, does *ad familiam purgandam* in Varro simply mean 'to relieve the family from a moral obligation'? Is it this second possibility that caused Dumézil to hesitate and then, in *La religion romaine archaïque,* drop all reference to *yaoždā* in dealing with *ius*?

The Three Functions of Indo-European Tradition in the "Eumenides" of Aeschylus

UDO STRUTYNSKI, *University of California, Los Angeles*

It was some thirty years ago that Georges Dumézil added the dimension of comparative mythology to the field of Indo-European studies, transforming the beneficiaries of a common linguistic heritage into the bearers of a socially oriented mythological tradition, unique and distinct from that of the other peoples of the ancient world. Central to Dumézil's thought is the notion of Indo-European tripartition: the "three functions" of Indo-European ideology comprising the characteristics of sovereignty, physical prowess, and fertility, wealth, and nourishment, which are represented on the level of social classes by a hierarchy of priests, warriors, and herdsmen-cultivators. This trifunctional pattern of thinking pervades all significant aspects of social life, amounts to a definition by the people of themselves, and finds reflection in the structure of their pantheon. Thus there are first-function gods related to the class of priests and characterized by sovereignty; second-function gods, patrons of the warrior class, who display military prowess; and third-function gods in whose charge has been placed the health, sustenance, and wealth of the entire people.[1]

While the pivotal areas where Indo-European traditions have been found, the Indo-Iranian, Roman, and Germanic, have provided ample comparative evidence in support of Dumézil's thesis, ancient

---

1 Cf. C. Scott Littleton, *The New Comparative Mythology: An Anthropological Assessment of the Theories of Georges Dumézil* (Berkeley and Los Angeles, 1966), pp. 4–6.

Greek myth reflects but few Indo-European traits.[2] These few have already been noted by Dumézil and his followers.[3] Still, continuing research makes it possible from time to time to add to their number. In a tradition such as that of Greece, however, which has been fragmented and hidden under continuing change, any traces of an Indo-European heritage which might be uncovered are not often easily recognizable.[4]

Certainly this is the case with the plays of Aeschylus. Although Aeschylus is for all intents and purposes the earliest of the Greek tragedians,[5] he is first and foremost a man of letters whose thought is his own. Aeschylus' dependence upon Hesiod is not slavish, writes Friedrich Solmsen,[6] and from this it can hardly be argued that his thinking was influenced by an even more distant Indo-European tradition. Nevertheless, elements of Indo-European thought have already been found in one of his plays. Dumézil[7] has noted that in the *Persians*, the lines of the dialogue between the ghost of Darius and Atossa (714–715) parallel the words of Dārayavahu in the Old Persian inscriptions.

---

[2] Cf. G. Dumézil, *L'idéologie tripartie des Indo-Européens* (Brussels, 1958), p. 91: "La Grèce—par rançon sans doute du 'miracle grec', et aussi parce que les plus anciennes civilisations de la Mer Égée ont trop fortement marqué les invahisseurs venus du Nord—contribue peu à l'étude comparative: mêmes les traits les plus considérables de l'héritage y ont été profondement modifiés." See also Littleton, *op. cit.*, p. 54 n.

[3] G. Dumézil: *Jupiter Mars Quirinus IV* (Paris, 1948), p. 176, and note (quote from an important unpublished work by L. Gerschel); *La Saga de Hadingus* (Paris, 1953), p. 152 n. 1; *Hommage à Lucien Febvre* (Paris, 1953), II, 27–31; *Latomus* 14:183–184 (1955); *Aspects de la fonction guerrière chez les Indo-Européens* (Paris, 1953), p. 152 n. 1; *Hommage à Lucien Febvre* (Paris, 1953), II, 25–32; *Latomages à G. Dumézil* (Brussels, 1960), pp. 215–224; *Les origines de Thèbes* (Paris, 1963), pp. 229–244; J.-P. Vernant: *RHR* 157:21–54 (1960); *Les origines de la pensée grecque* (Paris, 1962), pp. 34–35; A. Yoshida: *RBPh* 42:5–15 (1964); *RHR* 166:21–38 (1964); *RBPh* 44:5–11 (1966); L. R. Palmer, *Achaeans and Indo-Europeans* (Oxford, 1955); M. Lejeune, *Hommages à G. Dumézil* (Brussels, 1960), pp. 129–139; E. Benveniste, *RHR* 130:5–12 (1945).

[4] Cf. G. Dumézil, "Les 'trois fonctions' dans le ṚgVeda et les dieux indiens de Mitani," *BARB* 47:265–298 (1961), esp. pp. 280–281, where the criteria for recognizing trifunctional structures are given: 'Deux règles de bon sens s'imposent: 1° Pour qu'on soit en droit de reconnaître une intention de classement trifonctionnel, il faut que les trois termes, dans la syntaxe et plus encore dans la pensée, soient homogènes (trois dons ou qualités d'un dieu, trois prières des hommes, etc.) . . . . 2° Il faut écarter toute éxegèse qui, pour une, à plus forte raison pour deux des fonctions, se fonderait sur l'interprétation solicitée de termes équivoques ou imprécis."

[5] Cf. Gilbert Murray, *Aeschylus: The Creator of Tragedy* (Oxford, 1940).

[6] *Hesiod and Aeschylus* (Ithaca, 1949), pp. 178–224.

[7] Dumézil, *op. cit.*, pp. 294–298; also *Mythe et épopée* (Paris, 1968), pp. 617–621.

Darius asks:

τίνι τρόπῳ; λοιμοῦ τις ἦλθε σκηπτὸς ἢ στάσις πόλει;

In what manner [was the power of Persia destroyed]? Did some onslaught of plague or sedition come upon the state?

Atossa responds:

Οὐδαμῶς· ἀλλ' ἀμφ' Ἀθήνας πᾶς κατέφθαρται στρατός.

Not at all, but near Athens our whole army has been destroyed.

Each of the three means of destruction mentioned represents an attack on one of the three functions. Plague destroys the physical well-being of a people and refers to the third function; sedition indicates a crisis of sovereignty, thus referring to the first function; and the annihilation of Persia's military power represents a defeat for the second-function warrior class. Significant is the fact that it is the destruction of all of Persia, of the society as a whole, which is at issue. For this reason,[8] all three functions must be mentioned, despite the fact that the actual fall was a second-function matter.

What must be kept in mind about this example, however, is the fact that while it is unquestionably Indo-European, it does not belong to the tradition of Greece but to that of Iran. As Dumézil points out, "La publicité que le Grand Roi (Darius I) avait donnée à ses succès, à ses expériences, à ses pensées, avait pu par bien des intermédiaires, depuis les Ioniens de l'empire jusqu'aux prisonniers de Salamine, de Platées, d'Eion, atteindre les Athéniens ses vainqueurs et vainqueurs de son fils."[9]

Unlike the *Persians*, the *Eumenides* is a play that concerns itself with traditions that are distinctly and exclusively Greek. But before examining these traditions for whatever traces of Indo-European thought they might contain, it is necessary to isolate them from what might be properly called the literature of the play.

This task has been immeasurably simplified by the work of Jean Defradas,[10] who has examined the legend of Orestes upon which Aeschylus drew, in the light of its development from the earliest versions, through the transformations it experienced at the hands of the priests of Apollo at Delphi, until it gained currency in Athens at the end of the fifth century B.C. At that time the legend recounted how Orestes, son of Agamemnon, on the orders of Delphic Apollo avenged his father who had been murdered on his return from

---

[8] Cf. Dumézil, "Les 'trois fonctions' dans le Ṛg Veda . . . ," p. 285. The three functions occur when the issue is "tout ce qui compte dans le monde. . . ."

[9] *Ibid.*, p. 294.

[10] *Les thèmes de la propagande delphique* (Paris, 1954), esp. pp. 160–207.

Troy by Aegisthus and Clytemnestra. After Orestes has killed his mother he is pursued by her Erinyes, but Apollo, who had ordered the crime, wards off the Erinyes, and taking the guilt upon himself, sees to it that Orestes is acquitted by a human tribunal.[11]

This version is radically different from what is found in Homer's *Odyssey* (1.30 ff., 3.93 ff., 3.247–275, 3.301–312, 4.514 ff.). There the punishment of one's father's murderer is a question of honor. In the later classical conception of the problem, personal honor is replaced by a moral debt to the person killed. This development, however, gives rise to the question whether it is not a greater crime to fulfill one's duty when avenging the murder of one's father demands the killing of one's mother. Thus, as soon as the act of revenge ceases to be automatic and a moral conflict arises, the intervention of a god becomes necessary.[12] The vengeance that Orestes takes upon his mother is not a natural duty and for this reason must be considered a crime. Only a god can order Orestes to commit this crime and then assume the responsibility for it. The purification of Orestes is then part and parcel of a new concept of the problem. The Homeric avenger becomes a murderer who is soiled by his act and has need of a religious purification of it. Apollo is the proper purifier because he purified himself from Python's blood and drew Orestes to himself as he had drawn Herakles, soiled by the blood of his children.[13] For this reason Defradas can write,[14] "Oreste tient, dans la mythologie delphique, une place à part: il est étroitement lié au dieu de Pythô, au point que l'on a cru pouvoir l'identifier avec lui."

A comparison of Homer and Aeschylus reveals that the latter introduced a number of new themes: the curse of the House of Atreus; the problem of Orestes; Agamemnon's own guilt as compared with that of Clytemnestra; and finally the shifting of the role of the principal murderer from Aegisthus to Clytemnestra. Certainly the theme of the son who murders his mother is not unique in

---

[11] Defradas, *op. cit.*, p. 160: "Telle est la version de la légende qu'Eschyle a mise au point et que les tragiques ont à peu près adoptée après lui. Tous ont imputé à Apollon le parricide d'Oreste, soit pour justifier le héros, soit pour accabler le dieu." Cf. Aeschylus, *Choephori* 269 ff.; Sophocles, *Electra* 32 ff., 1264, 1376 ff.; Euripides, *Electra* 399 ff., 971 ff., 1190 ff., 1244 ff., 1296.

[12] *Ibid.*, p. 164. Cf. also C. Robert, *Die Griechische Heldensage* III.2 (Berlin, 1926), p. 1318. On the obligation of vengeance, cf. G. Glotz, *La solidarité de la famille dans le droit criminel en Grèce* (Paris, 1904), pp. 48 ff.

[13] Defradas, *op. cit.*, p. 165: "Nous n'hésiterions donc pas, même s'il n'existait pas des raisons de fait plus convaincantes, à affirmer *a priori* que l'Orestie n'a pu naître qu'à Delphes, en vertu de son contenu."

[14] *Ibid.*, p. 160.

Delphic literature. There is the legend of Alcmaeon,[15] son of Amphiaraus, who is ordered by the Delphic oracle to kill his mother in revenge for her designs upon his father's life. His deed brings the Erinyes of his mother down upon him until his subsequent purification at Delphi. There are also the versions of the Oresteia of Pindar and Stesichorus which attest the Delphic influence.[16] Both these authors share with Aeschylus this trait that Clytemnestra is the principal murderer of Agamemnon. Pindar shares one other trait with the author of the *Eumenides*: he presents Orestes as forced to punish his mother by virtue of the patriarchal law whose Dorian character is a significant aspect of the Delphic tradition. One need only compare this story of Orestes with that of Periander, tyrant of Corinth, who killed his wayward wife with impunity. Not only was vengeance by her relatives out of the question, but Periander himself was later counted among the seven sages.[17]

This patriarchal law plays a role in the *Eumenides* when Apollo introduces it as part of the defense argument during the trial of Orestes (658 ff., 736 ff.). Apollo's position is that the father is superior to the mother because his seed is the true source of life. The murder of a father is then a greater crime against the "élan vital" of nature than is the murder of a mother. When Athena joins her voice with Apollo's, the argument carries the day against the Erinyes. Defradas' following comment can be applied to this:

> Ce système patriarcal devait appartenir en propre à une idéologie dorienne. La société dorienne, indo-européenne dans son essence, s'est opposée semble-t-il, à la société égéenne, où dominait le matriarcat. Dans la mesure où un système religieux est l'expression d'un système social, nous constatons que les religions préhelléniques, où dominent les divinités féminines, divinités de fécondité, ont été remplacées par des religions à prédominance masculine: Zeus, maître de l'Olympe, domine Héra; Zeus Olympien devient à Olympie le maître de l'Altis, où régnait avant lui une divinité féminine, dont le cult était célébré à l'endroit où s'élévera l'Heraeon.[18]

He concludes by saying: "Nous trouvons chez Eschyle un écho de ce mépris des guerriers pour les femmes, une sorte d'appel à la

---

15 Diodorus Siculus 4.66; Pausanias 8.24.8.

16 Defradas, *op. cit.*, pp. 173–181.

17 Cf. Herodotus 3.50–53; Diogenes Laertius 1.94; Glotz, *op. cit.*, pp. 235 ff.; Defradas, *op. cit.*, p. 187: "celui-ci, à la suite de Kypsélos régna en tyran sur la ville de l'Isthme au début du VIe siècle, à l'époque où nous avons signalé les premières manifestations d'une pensée delphique."

18 Defradas, *op. cit.*, p. 187. Cf. also Charles Picard, *Les religions préhelléniques: Crète et Mycènes,* Collection Mana (Paris, 1948), pp. 81 ff.; cf. J. Jolly, *Recht und Sitte* (Strasbourg, 1896), p. 49, for Indic parallel.

solidarité des combattants contre la femme qui a tué un soldat, quand Apollon oppose à la mort de Clytemnestre celle d'Agamemnon."[19]

The Delphic aspects of the Orestes legend can be summed up as the following: Apollo orders the murder of Clytemnestra;[20] Apollo announces the purification of Orestes at Delphi;[21] and Apollo defends Orestes by an argument that clearly favors the notion of patriarchy over that of matriarchy. It is the presence of Apollo and his close ties to Orestes which form the core of the Delphic legend. With this core Aeschylus has fused the Attic traditions of the founding of the Areopagus at Athens and the establishment of the cult of the Eumenides, just as in the Prologue to the play he presented an Athenian version of the installation of Apollo at Delphi.[22]

There are, however, two Athenian institutions in the domain of criminal law which also attest contact between Delphi and Athens: the Delphinion and the Exegetes. Both apply to the case of Orestes. In addition to the Areopagus and the Palladion, there was a third tribunal at Athens which was the "most sacred" (ἁγιώτατον), that of the Delphinion, where it was decided whether or not a crime was permissible (ὅσιον) in accord with the religious laws.[23] The tradition of the Delphinion was brought to both Delphi and Athens by Cretan navigators in the eighth century. Therefore one must speak of an assimilation of a Cretan god and Apollo at Delphi, and then of Apollo at Delphi, and Apollo, god of the Delphinion, at Athens. In assigning to Apollo the role of defense counsel in his play, Aeschylus was giving a Delphic and even more ancient—and thus more venerable—origin to an Athenian legal fact.[24]

---

19 Defradas, *op. cit.*, p. 188. The comment about the warrior's contempt for women refers to the Spartans, of whom Agamemnon was king. Cf. Pierre Roussel, *Sparte* (Paris, 1939), pp. 51 ff. Cf. also *Eumenides* 625–627.

20 Aeschylus, *Choephori* 269 ff.; *Eumenides* 64–84, 465 ff., 590 ff.

21 *Eumenides* 238–240. Orestes is purified by the sacrifice of a pig, cf. *Eumenides* 280–283. See also P. Amandry, "Eschyle et Eleusis," *AIPhO* 9:32–35 (1949), who doubts the Delphic nature of the pork-blood purification. Cf. Defradas, *op. cit.*, p. 189.

22 *Ibid.*, p. 190. But A. Yoshida ("Le fronton occidental du temple d'Apollon à Delphes et les trois fonctions," *RBPh* 44:6–9 [1966]) finds a Delphic trifunctional structure: Zeus, Athena, Dionysos, which might have a parallel in the prologue to the *Eumenides* wherein we find in this order Zeus, (Apollo) Loxias, Athena (Pronaia), the nymphs, and Bromios (Dionysos). Considered as a trifunctional ordering, this but reinforces the argument of this article.

23 Defradas, *op. cit.*, p. 191; cf. also the Law of Dracon in *Inscriptiones Graecae* 1.115; Demosthenes, *Contra Aristocrates* 66, 74; Aristotle, *Constitution of Athens* 57.3; Pausanias 1.28.10.

24 Defradas, *op. cit.*, p. 192. There is banishment from Attica for the murderer

An Athenian legal tradition even more relevant to the case of Orestes is that of the Exegetes.[25] These were interpreters of ancestral religious laws and were associated with the purification of the criminal in matters concerning the family. The function of the Exegete was to determine if there were any extenuating circumstances when a crime was committed. Apollo was associated with these exegetes at Athens in decrees appearing about the middle of the fifth century.[26] Since these texts apply to the πάτρια, the laws of the ancestors, Apollo can be connected with them, not directly as the Pythian god, but as Apollo πατρῷος, the ancestor of the Ionians, father of Ion, who was in the fourth century assimilated to the god of Delphi.[27]

Direct reference to the tradition of the Exegetes can be found in the texts of Aeschylus. In the *Choephori,* Electra, interrogating the Chorus how she should best honor the memory of her father, employs precisely the word that designates the act of the exegete: (118) Τί φῶ; διδάσκ' ἄπειρον ἐξηγουμένη. Later Orestes is asked by the Chorus, as an exegete might be asked, in what manner Agamemnon's death was to be revenged on his wife and her lover (552 ff.): ἐξηγοῦ φίλοις. In the *Eumenides* Apollo himself appears as an exegete. The Chorus of the Erinyes asks Orestes (595): ὁ μάντις ἐξηγεῖτό σοι μητροκτονεῖν; And Orestes, turning to Apollo, asks the god as one would ask an exegete, to bear witness on his behalf (609 ff.): Ἤδη σὺ μαρτύρησον· ἐξηγοῦ δέ μοι, Ἄπολλον, εἴ σφε σὺν δίκῃ κατέκτανον.

This additional link which the traditions of the Delphinion and the Exegetes provide between Orestes and his purifier Apollo causes Defradas to observe,[28] "Tous les Apollons convergent dans l'Apollon pythien . . . Apollon devient le prototype de meurtrier légitime qui se soumet à la purification après la mort de Python."

---

until a reconciliation between him and the parents of his victim is achieved; cf. Glotz, *op. cit.*, pp. 309 ff. This theme is picked up in the *Eumenides* where Orestes tells of wandering in exile before reaching Athens (443 ff.).

25 Texts concerning the existence of Exegetes in Athens are listed in Defradas, *op. cit.*, p. 205.

26 *Ibid.*, p. 198; cf. also a decree in 431 to accord a sacrifice to Apollo in *Inscriptiones Graecae* 1.78: τοῖ ['Απόλλονι θῦσαι ἐπ]ειδὲ ἀνεῖλεν ἑαυτόν ἐχσεγετὲ[ν γενόμενον 'Αθεναίοι]ς, and an analog in *Inscriptiones Graecae* 1.77.9 ff.: [κατὰ τὲν μαντέιαν hέ]ν ho 'Απόλλον ἀνhεῖλ[εν] ἐχ[σ]εγόμε[νος τὰ πάτρια]. Cf. also Plato, *Republic* 4.427c.

27 Defradas, *op. cit.*, pp. 198–199. Judging from what Defradas says, one might consider that a gradual assimilation of the two Apollos began earlier than the fourth century and that the *Oresteia* of Aeschylus represents a step in this process.

28 *Ibid.*, 204.

Defradas[29] has already alluded to the Indo-European character of Apollo's argument in favor of patriarchy, which links the god of Delphi to the Spartan warrior class. A. Yoshida[30] has indicated that the traditions found at Delphi are in some instances marked by Indo-European traits. What now remains to be done is to show how Apollo, the dragon-slayer, relates to Indo-European tradition.

Aeschylus lets Apollo allude to his feat of slaying the Python in the lines with which he wards off the Furies from Orestes by threatening them with physical violence (179–183):

> Out of this temple! I command you, go at once!
> Quit my prophetic sanctuary, lest you feel
> The gleaming snake that darts winged from my golden bow,
> And painfully spew forth the black foam that you suck
> From the sour flesh of murderers.[31]

The presence of the bow and the metaphor "snake" for "arrow" refer to the weapons with which Apollo killed the Python. While the Homeric hymn mentions only one arrow that kills a dragoness, in the legend of Simonides the dragon is male and is called Python. Apollo vanquishes him with a hundred arrows.[32] A version that appears to have been the most popular after 300 B.C. has Apollo killing the dragon at Delphi with many arrows and then leaving for Tempe or Crete to be purified of blood pollution. Another Delphic account, this time in euhemerized form, tells how the son of a certain Krios, who ruled in Euboea, plundered Apollo's shrine at Delphi. Apollo promises to send his arrows upon this bandit and then have himself cleansed of blood pollution by the Cretans.[33] Finally, a Sicyonian legend mentions how Apollo and Artemis came to Aigialeia seeking purification for the killing of Python.[34]

The guilt that the death of the dragon brings upon the slayer is best paralleled in the Indic tradition of the warrior god, Indra, whose slaying of the tricephalic dragon Viśvarūpa is a sin.[35] The

---

29 *Ibid.*, 188.

30 *Op. cit.*, pp. 5–11.

31 All English quotations from the *Eumenides* are from P. Vellacott's translation: *The Oresteian Trilogy* (London, 1956). Cf. C. Kerényi, "Apollo Epiphanies," in J. Campbell, ed., *Papers from the Eranos Yearbooks I: Spirit and Nature* (New York, 1954), pp. 49–74.

32 Joseph Fontenrose, *Python: A Study of Delphic Myth and Its Origins* (Berkeley and Los Angeles, 1959), p. 15.

33 *Ibid.*, pp. 19–20.

34 *Ibid.*, pp. 57, 199. Cf. also Pausanias 2.7.7 ff.

35 Cf. Vian, *Les origines de Thèbes*, p. 103, for numerous other instances of dragon slayings by warrior figures (as well as third-function figures) in Indo-

nature of this sin, which is recounted in the fifth chapter of the *Mārkaṇḍeya Purāṇa,* has been explained by Dumézil:[36] "Indra tue d'abord le monstre Tricéphale, meurtre nécessaire, car le Tricéphale est un fléau menaçant pour le monde, et cependant meurtre *sacrilège,* car le Tricéphale a rang de brahmane et il n'y a pas de crime plus grave que le brahmanicide."

Fontenrose[37] recognizes another parallel between Apollo and Indra, this time in the legend of Indra's killing of the dragon Vṛtra: "As early as Rig Veda 1.32 Indra fled after Vritra's death. In later sources his flight and death are combined with his need for purification after blood guilt. In this the Indra-Vritra myth offers a remarkable parallel to the Apollo-Python myth in both Delphian and Sicyonian versions."

It might be added that the legend of Indra's killing of the three-headed son of Tvaṣṭar has been compared by Dumézil with the Roman legend of the battle between the three Horatii and the three Alban Curiatii, found in the first book of Livy. The third of the Horatii can be related to Trita Āptya, Indra's helper in the dragon slaying. Trita Āptya incurs guilt by killing a relative and a Brahman; the third of the Horatii, upon returning to Rome, slew his sister because she mourned the death of the Alban to whom she was betrothed. Both Trita Āptya and the Roman champion then had to undergo ritual purification.[38]

In the *Eumenides,* the story of Orestes offers some striking parallels to that of Trita Āptya and the third Horatius. In each case the crime is defined as the murder of a relative. In each case the murderer must be cleansed of his guilt. Orestes kills his mother upon the command of Apollo. Trita Āptya kills the three-headed dragon as the helper and ally of Indra. Both Apollo and Indra themselves undergo or have undergone ritual purification.

From these parallels, and bearing in mind that the legend that provides the core for the play of Aeschylus is itself Delphic and therefore exposed to the influence of Indo-European thought, it is tempting to assume that the Apollo who appears in the *Eumenides,* by virtue of his patriarchal bent, his near identification with Orestes, both as criminal and as purifier, and the parallels that his own

---

European tradition. For another Greek example of dragon slaying as a sin, cf. *ibid.*, p. 117 and *passim;* see also Fontenrose, *op. cit.*, pp. 306–320; both discuss the legend of Kadmos who killed the dragon-son of Ares.

36 Dumézil, *L'idéologie tripartie,* p. 30.

37 *Op. cit.*, p. 199.

38 Dumézil, *Aspects de la fonction guerrière,* p. 40.

Python-slaying has in the Indo-European tradition of the warrior class, is a god of the second function.[39]

Turning our attention to Athena, we find a goddess who has done as much as has Apollo in aiding the cause of Orestes, if not more. Yet there is a difference in their characters and in the means they employ to achieve their common end. While Apollo succeeds only in antagonizing the Erinyes, Athena opposes them with moderation and reason. Apollo threatens the Furies with shafts from his bow; he acts as defense counsel for Orestes. Athena promises the Erinyes a new kind of justice and establishes the court of the Areopagus over which she presides as impartial judge.

Yet she is not impartial. When the votes of the jurors are evenly divided between conviction and acquittal, Athena casts hers in favor of Orestes in a speech in which she reveals herself to be a member of the patriarchal party whose argument Apollo had put forward earlier (735 ff.):

> No mother gave me birth. Therefore the father's claim
> And male supremacy in all things, save to give
> Myself in marriage, wins my whole heart's loyalty.
> Therefore a woman's death, who killed her husband, is,
> I judge, outweighed in grievousness by his.

When the Erinyes protest the verdict and threaten to inflict sorrow and pestilence upon Athens in revenge, Athena soothes them with kind words, telling them that they have suffered neither dishonor nor defeat. When this course seems ineffectual, her tone changes (825 ff.):

> I alone among the gods
> Know the sealed chamber's keys where Zeus's thunderbolt
> Is stored. But force is needless.

Athena then offers the Erinyes an honored place in the society. In so doing, she describes her own social role in the following way (914 ff.):

> I will conduct their valiant arms to victory,
> And make the name of Athens honored through the world.

These last lines are the only clear indication in the play of what Athena's function is.[40] Yet in their light the other lines that have been quoted fall into place. Athena is at the side of Apollo, the second-

---

39 Another treatment of Apollo as a second-function figure, this time, however, of Apollo the physician who is related through Asklepios to Rudra, is found in H. Grégoire, R. Goossens, and M. Mathieu, *Asklèpios, Apollon Smintheus et Rudra*, MARB 45.1 (Brussels, 1949).

40 Orestes, it is true, referred to Athena as a warrior when he first approached her shrine at Athens; cf. *Eumenides* 295 ff.

function god, and cooperates with him in the defense and purification of Orestes. It was she who gave him sanctuary at Athens from the wrath of the Furies, just as Apollo had done at Delphi. And it was to her that Apollo had sent Orestes, that she might free him from his pursuers once and for all.

Yet Athena takes on dimensions larger than Apollo, not only in her founding of the court of the Areopagus which brings legal jurisdiction to the warrior function, but in her concern for the defense of the city from the fury of the Erinyes. Apollo represents the ruder aspects of the warrior function (cf. Rudra and the Maruts, n. 39 above), while Athena is entirely civilized (cf. Indra). She is anxious to avoid civil strife in Athens (854 ff.). Her acts of conciliation are motivated by this concern, but it is Athena's great power, her knowledge of how to wield the thunderbolt of Zeus, which allows her to be generous with a defeated enemy. Athena is more important than Apollo because she is responsible for the military protection and regulation of the entire Athenian society.[41] Her second-function role in the play thus does not depend entirely on her relationship to Orestes. Rather, it is outlined in unequivocal terms by the poet when he contrasts the function of the goddess with that of the newly established Eumenides. Athena is par excellence the warrior goddess of Athens.

What is found in the play is found also in the tradition. Athena is a second-function figure not only at Athens[42] but, as Yoshida[43] has noticed, also at Delphi, where as Athena Pronaia she is depicted as fighting under the command of Zeus against the giants. Like Indo-European goddesses in general, however, and specifically the Indic Sarasvatī and the Iranian Arədvī Sūrā Anāhitā, Athena also appears as a transfunctional figure. In the feast of Panathenaia held at Athens she is described as Hygieia, Polias, and Nike (*Inscriptiones Graecae* 2^1.163), which Vian[44] has noted as representing the third, first, and second functions, in that order.

---

41 Orestes is a second-function figure by virtue of his identification with Apollo. Athena as his judge exercises authority over a second-function figure. Yet the founding of the Areopagus is of the first function (Mitra), and the general guardianship of Athens makes Athena seem more like a sovereign Aryaman figure (in Dumézil's opinion).

42 For treatments of the warrior-function of Athena cf. M. P. Nilsson, *Die Anfänge der Göttin Athene* (Copenhagen, 1921); *Geschichte der griechischen Religion*, I (2d ed.; Munich, 1955), 433–437; W. F. Otto, *Die Götter Griechenlands* (Bonn, 1929), pp. 44–61; M. W. M. Pope, *AJPh* 81.113–135 (1960); Vian, *Les origines de Thèbes*, pp. 139–140.

43 *Op. cit.*, p. 7.

44 *La guerre des géants*, p. 257. Cf. also L. Deubner, *Attische Feste* (Berlin, 1956), pp. 26–27.

The term "function," as Dumézil uses it, refers in this broadest sense to a sphere of power and responsibility. Yet it is not a sphere that exists in isolation. Each function is, as Littleton points out, "in a mathematical sense, a function of the others." Apollo's power rests in his being lord of Delphi, and his responsibility is the protection and purification of Orestes. Athena is also the protectress of Orestes, but she is guardian of Athens as well. Apollo's weapon is the traditional bow with which he killed Python. Athena, however, alludes to wielding the thunderbolt of Zeus, which is an indication that the authority she exercises in the play of Aeschylus is not her own, but has been delegated to her by the lord of Olympus. This reference to Zeus is but one of many in the text which reveal that Zeus, although he never appears on stage or speaks a line, is very much at the center of the action.

In the Prologue the priestess of Delphi, recounting the history of the oracle, gives Zeus the prominent position. Not only is he the god who established his son Apollo as present ruler and *προφήτης Διός* (*Eumenides* 19, 616 ff.), the interpreter to mankind of his father's word and will; he is also the supreme Fulfiller who guarantees that what has been prophesied will come to pass. The Delphic oracle, in effect, begins and ends with Zeus.

The subservient roles that Athena and Apollo play with respect to Zeus are recognized by the Erinyes. They address god and goddess as daughter and son of Zeus (415, 150). The Erinyes themselves agree to let Orestes be tried because they trust Athena's wisdom and her father's name (435–440). The arguments and evidence put forward during the first trial are full of references to Zeus. Apollo tells the Erinyes that Clytemnestra's crime cannot go unpunished because the marriage of Zeus and Hera serves as a model for the sanctity of all marriage bonds (154 ff.). His patriarchal argument, that a wife's murder of her husband is a worse crime than a son's murder of his guilty mother, is based on this model. And Athena, in freeing Orestes, echoes these sentiments by announcing that for her the father's word was law because she herself had no mother (735 ff.). The issue of the trial is decided by one consideration only: the will of Zeus. Apollo presents the deciding argument when he announces that Zeus himself commanded the killing of Clytemnestra (610 ff.). Next to this fact all arguments pale. Orestes slew by the will of Zeus as interpreted by Apollo (616 ff.); Zeus acquits him through the mouth of Athena (797 ff., 763, 663 ff.).[45] And so Athena can say to the Erinyes (824 ff.):

---

[45] Murray, *op. cit.*, pp. 196–204.

> You call on Justice: I rely on Zeus. What need
> To reason further?

A link between Zeus and Orestes is found in the concept of the suppliant. Orestes is told by Apollo to go to Athena as a suppliant (78 ff.). Athena protects Orestes the suppliant because Zeus is the protector of suppliants who purified Ixion (440). Apollo has no fears that his shrine will be polluted as a result of his purification of Orestes because Zeus, who had set the precedent with Ixion, did not suffer any pollution as the result of his act (715 ff.). In an earlier play of Aeschylus, *The Suppliant Maidens,* Zeus himself is characterized as a suppliant (1):[46] Ζεὺς μὲν ἀφίκτωρ. This adds a new dimension to the conflict. Apollo has already been identified with Orestes and shown to be the mouthpiece of Zeus. Now Orestes is linked to Zeus as a suppliant. The guilt for the murder of Clytemnestra is passed on from Orestes to Apollo and from Apollo to Zeus, and each must answer for it. The purification of Orestes occurs at the hands of Apollo, but also at the hands of Zeus. Not only do Orestes and Apollo plead before the court: Zeus, in the final lines of the play, is described as "Zeus the Pleader" who "crowned persuasion with success" (972–974). In justifying the act of Orestes, Zeus has justified himself.

It is a success in which Apollo does not directly share. Orestes gains his life and regains his innocence. There his story ends. But Athena gains freedom from civil strife in Athens (854 ff.), the recognition and acceptance of her Areopagus, and a reconciliation with the Erinyes who become the patron goddesses of wealth, fertility, and nourishment. This is the second part of the story, the main part, for which the trial and acquittal of Orestes serve only as a test case. This is the success that Zeus gains through his role as Pleader, that human justice tempers the justice of nature with reason and intelligence.[47] But he gains it in the same way as he pleads, indirectly and from a distance.

Littleton[48] points out that Dumézil has been loath to regard Zeus as a first-function figure. His weapon, the thunderbolt, is found in Indo-European tradition, as Yoshida[49] has remarked, "dans les

---

46 *Ibid.*, 201.

47 Cf. Vian in his paper "Le conflit entre Zeus et la Destinée," *REG* 55:198 (1942); Murray, *op. cit.*, 84–85; Solmsen, *op. cit.*, p. 163: "It is justice and moderation which save him and ensure the eternal duration of his kingdom. Just as the Areopagus, the incorruptible organ of Justice, will be forever a bulwark of Athens, so the spirit of Justice will be a stabilizing factor for the world government of Zeus."

48 *Op. cit.*, pp. 196–197.

49 *Op. cit.*, p. 9.

mains des dieux de la deuxième fonction." But Zeus does not make use of his weapon. Nor does Athena, who refers to it. It looms only as a distant threat, as distant as Zeus himself. Yet distance does not hinder his efficacy. Zeus is in command of the action through his agents, and the final victory goes to him. The power and responsibility that Athena and Apollo have as second-function figures derive from Zeus. By virtue of his sovereignty he cannot be considered as belonging to any other than the first function. Yoshida himself admits that the thunderbolt in the hands of Zeus at Delphi, "semble avoir eu . . . plutôt la valeur d'un moyen d'action royal qui permettait au dieu souverain de diriger l'action de loin sans s'y engager véritablement." This, too, is the thunderbolt-wielding Zeus who appears in the eighth book of the *Iliad*.[50]

The alliance between the first and the second functions, as manifested by Zeus, Athena, and Apollo, is a theme common to Indo-European tradition. The two superior functions unite to conquer the third and thus bring the latter into the social system. Dumézil[51] has isolated three instances of this theme. In India the third-function Aśvins were not incorporated into the society of the gods until after a violent conflict with the "two forces" (*ubhe vīrye*), which was followed by a reconciliation and a pact. In Germanic tradition there is the war between the Aesir, the dominant group of gods to which Odin, Týr, and Thor belong, and the lower group of Vanir, comprising Freyr, Njördr, and Freyja. After their defeat, the Vanir are brought into the community. In the Roman tradition of the Sabine war it is not gods but men who fight, but as Dumézil has repeatedly pointed out, early Roman "history" is euhemerized Indo-European myth. The first book of Livy describes how the Romans under their early kingship were a militarily strong people but lacked women to bear their next generation. Sabine women were noted for their voluptuousness, to say nothing of their fertility. But their king, Titus Tatius, would not agree to let the Romans marry them. The women were then tricked into entering Rome, where the Romans took possession of them. In the battle for their release Titus Tatius was defeated by the Romans. The incorporation of the Sabines into Roman society is revealed by the list of the three original

[50] Cf. *Iliad* 8.69–77, 133–138, 170–171, 402–406, 416–420, 455–456, and see Nilsson, *Geschichte der griechischen Religion*, I (2d ed.), 368–369.

[51] *L'idéologie tripartie*, pp. 56–57. For some ideas on binary structural oppositions in Germanic myth cf. Einar Haugen, "The Mythical Structure of the Ancient Scandinavians: Some Thoughts on Reading Dumézil," *To Honor Roman Jakobson: Essays on the Occasion of his Seventieth Birthday* (The Hague, 1967), pp. 855–868.

Roman "tribes," the third of which is called *Titienses* after Titus Tatius, and is charged with the maintenance of physical well-being.

At the end of the *Eumenides,* Athena asks the Erinyes to stay at Athens and accept a new role, now that the power of Zeus has robbed their old function of all significance. They ask her (892 ff.):

> What prerogatives are mine?

She answers:

> Such that no house can thrive without your favour sought.

Then they ask (901 ff.):

> What blessings would you have me call upon this land?

And she replies:

> Such as bring victory untroubled with regret;
> Blessing from earth and sea and sky; blessing that breathes
> In wind and sunlight through the land; that beast and field
> Enrich my people with unwearied fruitfulness,
> And armies of brave sons be born to guard their peace.[52]

In Celtic tradition there is a fragment from the mythological cycle which recounts the second battle of Moytura (Mag Tured), wherein the Túatha Dé Danann defeat the Fomorians. One of the vanquished is Bress, once king of both peoples, but deposed because of avarice and forced to serve as guarantor of nourishment and prosperity for seven years without compensation. The account of how he saves his life from his conquerors provides an interesting parallel to the final scene between Athena and the Erinyes. The dialogue takes place between Bress, the first-function god Lug, and the judge Maeltne:[53]

> BRESS: It is better to give me quarter than to slay me.
> LUG: What then, will follow from that?
> BRESS: If I be spared, the kine of Erin will always be in milk.
> LUG: *That* does not save thee: thou hast no power over their age or their offspring (?) though thou canst milk them.

Bress tries a second time:

> BRESS: Tell your brehon that for sparing me the men of Ireland shall reap a harvest in every quarter of the year.

---

[52] For other instances in Greek tradition where Athena is seen awarding third-function responsibilities, cf. Colin Austin, "De nouveaux fragments de *l'Erecthée* d'Euripide," *Recherches de Papyrologie IV* (Extrait): *Travaux de l'Institut de Papyrologie de Paris* (Fascicule 5), Publications de la Faculté des Lettres et Sciences Humaines de Paris-Sorbonne, Série "Recherches" 36 (Paris, 1967), pp. 19, 33, 57.

[53] W. Stokes, trans., "The Second Battle of Moytura," *RC* 12:52–130 [esp. pp. 104–107] (1891). See also H. D'Arbois de Jubainville, *L'épopée celtique en Irlande* (Paris, 1892), pp. 405, 415, 442–444.

LUG TO MAELTNE: Shall Bres be spared for (giving) the men of Ireland a harvest of corn every quarter?

MAELTNE: This has suited us: the spring for ploughing and sowing, and the beginning of summer for the end of the strength of corn, and the beginning of autumn for the end of the ripeness of corn and for reaping it. Winter for consuming it.

The third time Lug proposes Bress' task:

LUG: How shall the men of Ireland plough? How shall they sow? How shall they reap? After making known these three things thou wilt be spared.

BRESS: Tell them that their ploughing be on a Tuesday, their casting seed into the field be on a Tuesday, their reaping on a Tuesday.

This fragment from Celtic tradition, the Aesir-Vanir conflict, and the Sabine war, as well as the battle of the Aśvins in India, all speak of a reconciliation between figures of the first two superior functions and figures who perform third-function activities already before they are incorporated into the system and defined as the third function. In Aeschylus the Erinyes are not third-function figures before their transformation. True, they are earth goddesses, chthonic figures whose mother is Night[54] (860 ff.), but their province is the revenge of blood crimes, wherein they resemble other Indo-European figures such as the Roman Parcae and the Germanic Norns;[55] it is not the nourishment and general well-being of a people.

The Aeschylean conception of the Erinyes would seem to be based on Hesiod.[56] Although he does not call them daughters of Night as Aeschylus does, Hesiod does mention them as having sprung from the blood of Ouranos when he was overthrown and emasculated by Kronos. What Aeschylus has done is to identify them with the Hesiodic Keres who are born of Night and who relentlessly pursue the sinner until he is punished (*Theogony* 220–222). Among the other children of Night, Hesiod lists the Moirai, which gives Aeschylus the opportunity to call the Erinyes their sisters "by the same mother." This new structure allows the Erinyes to be reconciled with Zeus after the acquittal of Orestes, since Zeus' insistence upon this acquittal was the basis for his reconciliation with the Moirai, a fact that the final chorus celebrates (1045–1046):[57] Ζεὺς Παντόπτας οὕτω Μοῖρά τε συγκατέβα.

---

[54] Clémence Ramnoux, *La nuit et les enfants de la nuit dans la tradition grecque* (Paris, 1959).

[55] A. Yoshida's opinion. With similar figures in two other independent Indo-European traditions, the Erinyes are clearly Indo-European.

[56] Cf. Solmsen, *op. cit.*, pp. 178–224.

[57] Murray, *op. cit.*, p. 204.

The probable source of the concept "Eumenides" or "well-disposed ones" is the Attic feast of the Semnai. As Solmsen (*op. cit.*, p. 201) writes, "In effecting the transformation, Aeschylus made use of a well-established Athenian cult, that of the *Semnai* or *Eumenides*, who were worshipped in a cave on the slopes of the Areopagus and to whom—perhaps even at Aeschylus' time—those acquitted by the jury of the Areopagus used to offer sacrifice (cf. Pausanias 1.28.4 and 2.11.4)." Deubner[58] points out that they remain subterranean creatures (thus chthonic like the Erinyes) but then goes on to say, "Von dem Opferfest war . . . das Geschlecht der Eupatriden wegen seiner genealogischen Beziehungen zum Muttermörder Orest ausgeschlossen. . . ."

What occurs at the end of the play is simply a shifting of emphasis from the conflict between Orestes and the Erinyes to Zeus and the Moirai.[59] The tradition of Orestes itself provides a common ground where the Erinyes and the Eumenides meet. But after the acquittal Orestes and Apollo depart from the scene, and Zeus through the person of Athena confronts the Furies whose justice he has replaced with his own. At this point they are still Erinyes and represent no more than that aspect of the third function which engages in conflict with the two superior functions. It is only by accepting their new role that they become Eumenides; they assume the proper responsibilities of the third function which, working in cooperation with the other two, provides a basis for the life of the entire society. One has the impression from reading Aeschylus that a social charter is being drawn up and that a new society is just now coming into its own (916–926):

> I will consent to share Athene's home,
> To bless this fortress of the immortal powers
> Which mighty Zeus and Ares
> Chose for their habitation,
> The pride and glory of the gods of Greece,
> This prayer I pray for Athens,
> And guardian of their altars.
> Pronounce this prophecy with kind intent:

---

58 *Op. cit.*, p. 214.

59 Cf. F. Vian, *REG* 55:204 (1942): "L'oeuvre principale des Moires est l' 'antique partage' qui a assigné à chacun sa place et son rôle dans le 'cosmos'. C'est ce partage qui a donné aux Erinyes le Tartare pour séjour et pour fonction le châtiment des crimes et des affaires de sang." But on page 205 he makes the point that Zeus's function is to execute the laws. The function of the Erinyes has been transferred to Zeus; it is a first-function activity that they have lost. Thus they retain and make the most of what remains: their chthonian third-function character.

Fortune shall grace her land with healthful gifts
From her the rich earth engendered
By the sun's burning brightness.

In these lines are found a recapitulation and a reinforcement of the trifunctional structure found throughout the play: (1) Zeus, (2) Apollo and Athena, (3) Eumenides. Here this society is headed by the first-function god Zeus; and he is followed by Ares, in Greek tradition the unequivocal god of war. To these the Eumenides will add their name and their powers. This triad takes its place among other instances of Athenian trifunctionality: the four Ionian tribes: first-function Dias, second-function Athenaïs and Posidonias, third-function Hephaistias;[60] in Aristotle's *Constitution of Athens*[61] the third-function Archon in charge of goods and possessions, the first-function Basileus whose realm is the celebration of mysteries and the direction of all sacrifices, and the second-function Polemarchos whose role was to keep an eye on strangers in and out of Athens. The social charter of Aeschylus is headed and embraced by Athena, representing her country and her people, who under the transfunctional aspect of Panathenaia[62] stands as the supreme symbol for the unity of Athens.

---

[60] H. Jeanmaire, *Couroi et Courètes* (Lille, 1939), p. 125. Cf. Dumézil, "Les trois fonctions dans quelques traditions grecques," in *Hommage à Lucien Febvre* (Paris, 1954), II, 25–32, esp. p. 26, for the Ionian tribes and the trifunctional structure of Plato's ideal city; see also J.-P. Vernant, *Les origines de la pensée grecque* (Paris, 1962), p. 35.

[61] Chaps. 56, 57, 58; cf. Vian, *Les origines de Thèbes*, p. 240.

[62] Cf. L. Gerschel, "Coriolan," in *Hommage à Lucien Febvre* (Paris, 1954), II, 37. Here Athena could well be herself a rising third-function figure, as was Arədvī Sūrā Anāhitā and the Commagene of Antiochus I, whose "third function" was the entirety "Commagene my Country."

Some Possible Indo-European Themes in the "Iliad"

C. SCOTT LITTLETON, *Occidental College*

It is fair to say that, of all relevant ancient Indo-European traditions, that of the Greeks presents by far the greatest number of difficulties to contemporary students of Indo-European myth and epic. For the common, tripartite ideological inheritance, so clearly demonstrated by Georges Dumézil and his colleagues in the myths and epics of the Indic-, Iranian-, Italic-, and Germanic-speaking communities,[1] is all but absent in the Greek tradition—despite the fact that this tradition is certainly the most voluminous and best preserved of the ancient Indo-European traditions. As Dumézil puts it, "La Grèce—par rançon sans doute du «miracle grec», et aussi parce que les plus anciennes civilisations de la Mer Égée ont trop fortement marqué les envahisseurs venus du Nord—contribue peu à l'étude comparative: même les traits les plus considérables de l'héritage y ont été profondement modifiés."[2]

Yet here and there, tucked away in a variety of contexts, a few bits and pieces of the common Indo-European ideology have come to light,[3] proving that the Greeks were not altogether ignorant of the

---

1 Perhaps the most succinct statement of Dumézil's thesis can be found in his *L'idéologie tripartie des Indo-européens* (Brussels, 1958), p. 31. For a comprehensive discussion of Dumézil's work, together with that of his disciples and critics, see my *The New Comparative Mythology: An Anthropological Assessment of the Theories of Georges Dumézil* (Berkeley and Los Angeles, 1966).

2 Dumézil, *op. cit.*, p. 91.

3 See Dumézil, *Jupiter, Mars, Quirinus* (Paris, 1941), pp. 257–260, wherein the tripartite character of Plato's *Republic* is discussed; "Les trois fonctions dans quelques traditions grecques," *Hommage à Lucien Febvre* (Paris, 1953), II, 25–32;

ideology to which, as Indo-European speakers, they were heirs. One of the more recent (1964) and significant additions to this meager store of evidence concerning the persistence of the Indo-European ideology in the Greek tradition is A. Yoshida's[4] suggestion that it is expressed in the embellishments on the shield of Achilles, as described by Homer in Book 18 of the *Iliad.* The purpose of this paper[5] is to build upon this foundation and comment upon the extent to which the *Iliad* as a whole may perhaps reflect the common Indo-European ideology. This is, of course, a matter that cannot possibly be dealt with adequately in a paper of this scope. Yet given the high probability that Yoshida is correct in his interpretation of the shield of Achilles (I had come to similar conclusions before encountering Yoshida's article), a few observations relative to the epic's chief figures and events are in order, if only to point the way for further investigation.

First, however, let us hear what Yoshida has to say about the shield.

Pointing out that Homer begins his description of the embellishments with images of the earth, the sky, and the constellations (center of the shield), and ends it with an image of the sea (outermost rim)–images that, he suggests, reflect a conventional cosmogonic scheme–Yoshida goes on to assert that

> Entre ces deux ensembles, c'est au contraire une série de scènes décrivant la vie des hommes qu'a ciselées l'artiste. Or cette description est faite de trois parties, nettement distinctes, respectivement consacrées aux activités rélévant d'une des trois fonctions de l'idéologie indo-européenne.
>
> Dane la figuration d'une ville en paix (490–508), sont représentés un mariage (490–496), puis un procès (497–508), deux des grandes manifestations du domaine juridique, c'est-à-dire de la première fonction.
>
> La figuration d'une ville en guerre, qui vient ensuite (490–540), com-

---

Aspects de la fonction guerrière chez les Indo-Européens (Paris, 1956), pp. 93 ff., wherein the career of Herakles is discussed from an Indo-European standpoint. Others who have applied Dumézil's theory to Greek data include F. Vian, "La triade des rois d'Orchomène: Étéocles, Phlégyas, Minyas," *Hommages à Georges Dumézil* (Brussels, 1960), pp. 215–224, and A. Yoshida, "La structure de l'illustration du bouclier d'Achille," *RBPh* 42:5–15 (1964); "Survivances de la tripartition fonctionnelle en Grèce," *RHR* 166:21–38 (1964); "Sur quelques coupes de la fable grecque," *REA* 67:31–36 (1965); "Piasos noyé, Cléité pendue et le moulin de Cyzique: Essai de mythologie comparée," *RHR* 168:155–164 (1965); "Le fronton occidental du Temple d'Apollon à Delphes et les trois fonctions," *RBPh* 44:5–11 (1966).

[4] "La structure de l'illustration du bouclier d'Achille."

[5] I should like to thank Professors Jaan Puhvel and Donald Ward for their most helpful comments and suggestions relative to this paper. Special thanks are due Professor Atsuhiko Yoshida who, although not a participant in the symposium in which this paper was initially read, has nevertheless contributed a great deal to its final form through his invaluable criticisms and suggestions.

prend essentiellement des combats, c'est-à-dire l'expression la plus typique de la deuxième fonction.

Ces tableaux antithétiques de la vie citadine sont complétés par ceux de la vie rurale, d'abord les travaux de l'agriculture, puis ceux de l'élevage (541–589), c'est-à-dire les deux parties principales de l'activité nourricière qui est un des principaux aspects de la troisième fonction; de plus, dans la scène du χορός qui suit (590–606), des jeunes gens et des jeunes filles, beaux et richement habillés, exécutent une danse joyeuse en se tenant par la main et font l'admiration de la foule immense qui entoure: jeunesse, beauté, richesse, joie populaire, tous ces éléments appartiennent aussi à la complexe troisième fonction. . . .[6]

The third-function character of the final scene, Yoshida suggests, is strengthened by its mention of Ariadne: "grande déesse minoenne de la végétation." To this I might add that there is also a great deal of evidence for the association of dancing with a host of third-function figures, especially the divine twins, in other Indo-European traditions.[7]

It should be emphasized that this interpretation of the shield of Achilles is phrased in thematic, contextual terms, and does not pretend to be predicated upon any set of philological premises, other than the fact that the author of the tradition was an Indo-European speaker. Nevertheless, as mentioned earlier, it does seem to me that Yoshida is correct in his assumption that the tripartite Indo-European ideological principles are expressed here and that their expression unfolds in the canonical order so frequently found in Indic, Iranian, Roman, and Norse materials. The uniqueness of *this* expression is itself an interesting phenomenon, for if we examine that other famous Greek shield, the shield of Herakles as described by Hesiod, no clear parallels emerge. Although Hesiod's description of the Theban hero's shield is perhaps modeled after the Homeric passage in question, and despite certain very specific points of similarity, notably the wedding sequence on the shield of Herakles, wherein people "were bringing the bride to the groom, and the loud bride-song was arising" (line 274), the general character and order of the scenes depicted are distinct from those on the shield of Achilles.

Why Hesiod failed to organize his description in terms of the Indo-European ideology is a moot question, especially in view of the strong probability that he was a younger contemporary of Homer (or at least of the author of the *Odyssey*).[8] Lattimore suspects that

---

6 Yoshida, "La structure de l'illustration du bouclier d'Achille," pp. 7–9.

7 For a discussion of this point, see Donald Ward, *The Divine Twins: An Indo-European Myth in Germanic Tradition* (Berkeley and Los Angeles, 1968), pp. 50–51.

8 Cf. Richmond Lattimore, *Hesiod* (Ann Arbor, Mich., 1959), p. 13.

the bulk of the description of the shield of Herakles (from line 57 on) may well be the work of a late interpolator.[9] If this view is correct, then perhaps by the time these later lines were composed the hold of the Indo-European ideology had largely given way, although there is nothing in the first fifty-six lines that would clearly indicate its presence. The problem is further complicated by the fact that in most other contexts Herakles is, as Dumézil has shown,[10] one of the most "Indo-European" of Greek figures.

Withal, despite Hesiod's failure to express the common Indo-European ideology in a closely analogous context, its presence in at least one important Homeric passage raises the question of whether or not the *Iliad* as a whole reflects this ideology.

Although it is certainly correct to assert that the *Iliad* is concerned primarily with the behavior of Achilles, his withdrawal and subsequent return to the fray, and only secondarily with the siege of Troy, it must never be forgotten that it is against this latter backdrop that the events relative to Achilles' "wrath" take place. Indeed, it is against this backdrop of internecine military conflict that *all* the events described by Homer take place. Therefore, it seems fitting to begin by asking whether there are any other Indo-European mythic (or quasi-mythic) counterparts to such internecine strife.[11] The answer is, of course, yes: to name but a few samples, the conflict between the Pāṇḍavas and the Kauravas, as described in the *Mahābhārata*; the conflict between Aesir and Vanir, which forms an important element in the Norse tradition; the conflict between the Romans and the Sabines, as described by Livy, *et al.*[12] In all such cases one segment of the society comes into conflict with another segment, even though these segments may be formally distinguished, as in the case of the Romans versus the Sabines.

Now among the more interesting of Dumézil's suggestions as to the character of the proto-Indo-European mythology is that it contained a myth concerning a conflict or "war" between representatives of the first two functions and those of the third.[13] The clearest

---

9 *Ibid.*, p. 9.

10 Dumézil, *Aspects de la fonction guerrière*, pp. 93 ff.

11 That the Achaean-Trojan confrontation was internecine seems certain; see for example Helen Thomas and F. H. Stubbings, "Lands and Peoples in Homer," in A. J. B. Wace and F. H. Stubbings, eds., *A Companion to Homer* (London. 1963), pp. 283–310, esp. 285–288.

12 For a discussion of the Indo-European character of the conflict between the Romans and the Sabines, see Dumézil, *La religion romaine archaïque* (Paris, 1966), pp. 79–84.

13 *Ibid.*; see also Littleton, *op. cit.*, pp. 11–13.

reflexes of this assumed protomyth are to be found in the Norse and Italic conflicts just mentioned. In the Norse case it is certain that the Aesir, the dominant group of gods, to which Odin, Týr, and Thor belong, are representatives of the first two functions, and that the Vanir, the losers in the struggle, to which Freyr, Njördr, and Freyja belong, are third-function figures. In the Italic case, the Romans, under the leadership of the warlike Tullus Hostilius (second function), and after the successive reigns of Romulus and Numa (first function), engage in a conflict with their neighbors, the Sabines, who, as devotees of luxury, "la tranquillité," and "la volupté," are manifestly representatives of the third function.[14] In both cases, the representatives of the third function—Vanir and Sabines—are defeated and eventually integrated into the social and/or supernatural system, rendering it complete. (Elsewhere, I have suggested that this theme of a "war between the functions" might well serve to explain, or sanction, perhaps, the lowly position of the cultivator in Indo-European society; he was the last to be admitted to it).[15]

Assuming Dumézil is correct in his interpretation of these two mythical (in the Roman case quasi-mythical) conflicts, is it possible to view the conflict between the Achaeans and the Trojans in the same light? The answer depends upon the extent to which it is possible to assert that Homer, or at least the tradition upon which he drew, conceived of the Trojans in third-function terms.

To begin with, there is the famous Judgment of Paris, which, according to Dumézil, contains perhaps the clearest single Greek expression of the tripartite ideology.[16] At the behest of Zeus, Paris agrees to award the golden "apple of discord" to the fairest of the goddesses. The choice is between the regal Hera, the warlike Athena, and the voluptuous Aphrodite. So as to influence him in his choice, each goddess, seen by Dumézil as representative of one of the three functions, offers Paris a gift: Hera offers world sovereignty (first function); Athena promises military prowess (second function); and Aphrodite tenders the gift of earthly pleasure (third function). Paris chooses Aphrodite, and thus, by alienating Hera and Athena (i.e., the first two functions), he sets the stage for what is to come. It is quite clear that, in making this choice, he has aligned himself and his people with a third-function divinity. Indeed, throughout the epic, the *only* divine being firmly committed to the Trojan cause is Aphrodite; the other two former contestants in that prototypical

[14] Dumézil, *ibid.*
[15] Littleton, *op. cit.*, p. 13.
[16] Dumézil, "Les trois fonctions dans quelques traditions grecques."

beauty contest never waver in their commitment to the Achaean cause.

Further evidence of the extent to which the Trojans, both individually and collectively, manifest third-function characteristics can be seen in Homer's descriptions of the city and its inhabitants. The city itself is consistently depicted as a center of wealth and a rich prize waiting to be sacked (cf. 2.133, 9.278, 22.116–118, and elsewhere); indeed, one of the reasons why Achilles withdraws from the fight is his expectation that he will be shortchanged when the spoils are distributed (1.164–171). Evidence of third-function characteristics can also be seen in the emphasis among the Trojans upon family life and the relationships therein. Perhaps the best example of this can be found in Book 6, wherein Andromache, her infant son in her arms, implores Hector to withdraw from the war (390 ff.). With the bitterness of one who prefers peace to war, Hector tells his wife that he must continue to fight; yet before taking leave of his family he finds the time to kiss and fondle his offspring (465–481). Moreover, throughout the conversation between Hector and Andromache there is the implication that the cause is lost and that she and all the rest of the Trojan women will be carried off by the victorious Achaeans. Here, of course, we can compare the fate of the Sabine women.

In this connection it may be recalled that Dumézil has suggested that third-function figures, although primarily concerned with the maintenance of tranquillity and physical well-being, are often depicted as armed in a protective capacity. Typically, they do not instigate conflicts, but they are not exempt from them should they arise or should the domestic peace be threatened. The Roman figure Quirinus is often referred to as Mars *qui praeest paci*, and there are *arma Quirini*. The Norse Freyr is armed with a sword, and the Indian epic heroes Nakula and Sahadeva (projections of the Aśvins) carry weapons and engage in battle.[17] Although the chief Trojan figures, especially Hector, are depicted as doughty warriors, their prowess is displayed solely in defense of their homes and families; they are never portrayed as aggressors.

Turning to a consideration of the principal Trojan figures themselves, it is possible that Hector and Paris are projections of the twin third-function figures so frequently encountered in the pantheons of the ancient Indo-European-speaking communities (e.g., the Vedic Aśvins, the Greek Dioscuri). In order to support this contention, it is necessary to consider two of the chief figures in that other Indo-

[17] G. Dumézil, "Remarques sur les armes des dieux de 'troisième fonction' chez divers peuples indo-européens," *SMSR* 28:1–10 (1957).

European epic, the *Mahābhārata*. Some years ago (1947) Stig Wikander was able to demonstrate that the principal protagonists of the Indian epic were transpositions of the major Vedic divinities, and as such reflected the three Indo-European ideological functions.[18] Yudhiṣṭhira was seen to be a projection of Mitra and thereby a representative of the first function; Arjuna and Bhīma, respectively, were projections of the warrior divinities Indra and Vāyu; while Nakula and Sahadeva were projections of the twin Aśvins. In 1957, Wikander focused his attention upon the latter two figures and sought to differentiate them in terms of their respective roles in the narrative.[19] Nakula, for example, is handsome, fearless, and a breaker of horses; Sahadeva is defined as peace-loving, an indifferent warrior, and a keeper of cattle. Furthermore, although together they clearly serve as representatives of the third function, the differences between them would align Nakula more closely with the second function, while his brother is more firmly a representative of the third. In the *Rig-Veda*, common epithets reflecting the third function are used to refer to the Aśvins, although these epithets invariably occur in pairs, and almost always in the same order. This order parallels the epithets used individually in the *Mahābhārata* for Nakula and Sahadeva. Moreover, many post-Vedic texts refer to one of the twins as Nāsatya and the other as Dasra. Wikander concludes that this distinction goes back to Proto-Indo-European times (or at least to the period of Indo-Iranian unity).[20]

If we examine the epithets and characters of Hector and Paris, some interesting parallels emerge. The most common epithet of Hector is ἱππόδαμος, 'breaker of horses.' Paris, however, is never so characterized; indeed, in his youth he was associated with the care of sheep, having been weaned by a band of shepherds.[21] Hec-

---

18 Stig Wikander, "Pāṇḍava-sagan och Mahābhāratas mytiska förutsättningar," *RoB* 6:27–39 (1947).

19 S. Wikander, "Nakula et Sahadeva," *OS* 6:66–96 (1957).

20 *Ibid.* Further evidence can be found in the *Avesta*, wherein there is only a single demon, Naŋhaithya, whose name corresponds to Nāsatya. The more benevolent twin seems to have survived demonization and persists, Wikander believes, in the person of Atar, son of Ahura Mazdāh; see also Ward, "The Separate Functions of the Indo-European Divine Twins," above, pp. 194–195.

21 Cf. Apollodorus 3.148. Paris' childhood conforms to the general heroic pattern, as delineated by O. Rank, Lord Raglan, and J. Campbell: although born of Priam and Hekabe, he was exposed at birth on Mount Ida as a result of prophecy that he would bring about Troy's ruin. Like Oedipus, however, he was reared by shepherds, and it was only after reaching manhood that he was able to claim his birthright. The etymology of his name is obscure. H. Frisk (*Griechisches etymologisches Wörterbuch*, II [Heidelberg, 1965], p. 275) suggests that it is perhaps Illyrian in origin.

tor's character is that of a valorous and chivalrous warrior; Paris, despite his chief epithet, Alexandros ("Warrior, Champion), is characterized as an indifferent fighter (e.g., his duel with Menelaus, wherein he survives only with the aid of Aphrodite), and as a man devoted to the maintenance of physical well-being (or at least to his own sensual enjoyment). In short, the distinction between the two Trojan princes is broadly reminiscent of that between Nakula and Sahadeva.

Yet if Hector's principal epithet and character resemble those of Nakula, his name would seem to be derived from the same Indo-European source as Skt. *sáha-* (cf. Avestan *hazah-*, Gothic *sigis*; from Proto-Indo-European **seĝh-*, 'to withstand, to uphold').[22] One possible explanation of this metathesis, so to speak, is that at some point before Homer crystallized the tradition, the name of the Nakula figure had disappeared, and his epithets and personality came to be assumed by the surviving Sahadeva figure, that is, Hector. At the same time, it would appear that the *theme* of a functional distinction between the two did manage to persist, and that many aspects of the Sahadeva figure—though by no means all—were transferred to a new figure whose name has no connection with the Indian version, that is, Paris. One aspect that did not shift was the association with cattle-keeping. It is remotely possible that the epithet "Alexandros," together with the curious equine simile that occurs in connection with Paris near the end of Book 6 (506–512), wherein his movements are likened to "some stalled horse who has been corn-fed at the manger . . . ," may be dim survivals of an earlier identification with the Nakula figure. By the same token, despite his epithet and military prowess, certain aspects of Hector's character would seem to reflect Sahadeva; he is, as we have seen, a man who prefers peace to war, a man who would much prefer to live in harmony with his neighbors. Like Sahadeva, Hector is also a would-be peacemaker, and this, too, may be a survival of his former identification.

Whatever the reasons for this transposition, it seems to me that the very existence of a philological connection between Hector and Sahadeva, coupled with the thematic parallels that can be demonstrated between the two sets of heroic siblings, are sufficient to make a strong case for the assumption that Hector and Paris are reflexes of the common Indo-European twin figures. The absence of any lineal connection between the Trojan pair and their divine counterparts (Kastor and Polydeukes), a connection that, as I have said, can

[22] Cf. J. Pokorny, *Indogermanisches etymologisches Wörterbuch* (Bern, 1959), p. 888.

be demonstrated in the Indian tradition, does not appear to be an insurmountable obstacle here.

Indeed, the Dioscuri can be brought into the picture, for as the daughter of Leda, Helen is their sister.[23] Thus, while Kastor and Polydeukes are not seen as lineal kinsmen of the Trojan princes, the implication of an affinal relationship seems quite clear. Elsewhere among the ancient Indo-European traditions associated with the twins there is usually a close female relative present, oftentimes a sister, less frequently a spouse; compare, for example, Sarasvatī, Freyja, and, as Donald Ward has recently suggested, Kudrun and Sītā.[24] That Helen, sister of the Dioscuri, and wife to Paris, fits this pattern is a distinct possibility.

In sum, the Trojans, individually and collectively, seem to represent the third function. If this is correct, then the next task is to consider some possible Achaean candidates for the honor of representing the first two functions.

By all odds, the most logical candidate for the second-function honors is the wielder of the shield discussed previously, Achilles—or, more properly, Akhilleus. He is far and away the most warlike figure in the epic. But what is more, his recalcitrant behavior, as described by Homer, generally conforms to what appears to be a common Indo-European pattern when it comes to warrior figures. Like Indra, Starcatherus, and Herakles, he is culpable. In his *Aspects de la fonction guerrière*,[25] Dumézil suggested that the Indo-European warrior typically commits three characteristic "sins," each of which is a violation of one of the three ideological principles. Indra, for example, is an accomplice in the murder of a Brahman (the three-headed son of Tvaṣṭar, chaplain of the gods), displays cowardice in the slaying of Namuci (with whom he had sworn a treaty), and commits adultery with Ahalyā, wife of Gautama. Starcatherus (Starkadr), as described by Saxo Grammaticus in Books 6–8 of the *Gesta Danorum*, commits a similar set of "sins": he strangles a king (Wicarus of Norway), displays cowardice in battle, thereby causing a war to be lost, and, for a price, agrees to kill the Danish king Olo while the latter is in the act of bathing and thus unable to defend himself.[26] In the case of

---

23 They do, of course, have separate fathers: Kastor is generally viewed as the son of Tyndareos; Polydeukes and Helen are fathered by Zeus.

24 D. J. Ward, "Kudrun: An Indo-European Mythological Theme?" *Indo-European and Indo-Europeans* (Philadelphia, 1970).

25 *Op. cit.*; also in *Heur et malheur du guerrier* (Paris, 1969).

26 This action, although it lacks the sexual component, does involve both money and bathing, and the act of bathing is conducive to a sense of physical relaxation and well-being. To kill a bather is to kill one who, for the moment at least, is

Herakles, "le seul héros panhellénique," as Dumézil calls him, the sin against the first function involves the murder of his children in defiance of the command that he perform the twelve labors, a command issued by his sovereign, Eurystheus, and confirmed by the Delphic Oracle. His sin against the second function involves the cowardly slaying of Iphitos, who had come to claim his broodmares. His sin against the third function involves his abduction of Astydamia and, subsequently, of Iole. Like Indra, whose powers wane with each "sin," Herakles becomes impotent and eventually succumbs as a result of his misdeeds.

Although the parallels are admittedly imperfect, Achilles, too, commits a set of sins against the established order of things. To begin with, he defies the authority of his commander-in-chief, Agamemnon, and withdraws from the war. Moreover, the immediate cause of his defiance is the command that he give up a slave girl (Briseis). Thus, in this one brief but crucial sequence (1.130 f.) can be seen all the elements in the culpability of the Indo-European warrior. Achilles defies authority (first function); he withdraws from the conflict (second function); and he falls victim to his sexual desires (third function). The Achaean hero's defiance of authority and refusal to fight, to say nothing of his concern with his own sensual enjoyment, are themes that occur over and over as the epic unfolds. In the case of the latter theme, it is clear that during his withdrawal he lives in a manner far more suited to a third-function figure than to a representative of the second function. He has become concerned with his own physical well-being to the exclusion of any concern with the proper performance of his warrior role. A good example of this can be seen in the famous interchange between Achilles and Odysseus, wherein Odysseus, acting as Agamemnon's emissary, offers vast riches, women, and so on, if only he will return to the war (9.252 f.). It would appear that in this context, at least, Achilles is treated *as if* he were a third-function figure.

Another aspect of Achilles' career which bespeaks the third function is his transvestitism at the court of Lykomedes of Skyros. The story, not contained within the framework of the *Iliad* proper (cf., for example, Apollodorus 3.174), is that Thetis had dressed her son as a girl and had hidden him among Lycomedes' women, her purpose being to spare him from certain death in the then imminent war. Achilles' location does not long remain a secret, however, and,

---

neither a sovereign nor possessed of effective physical prowess, and would seem to relate to the third function (cf. Littleton, *The New Comparative Mythology*, p. 124).

in what would appear to be an adumbration of their later embassy, Odysseus and Diomedes trick the transvestite into joining the expedition by leaving his armor in the women's quarters. His excessive interest in these warlike appurtenances betrays his true sex, and he eventually joins the fleet at Aulis.[27]

Unlike the other culpable heroes previously discussed, Achilles does manage to redeem himself. He returns to the war bearing the trifunctionally illustrated shield, overcomes Hector, and materially advances the Achaean cause—which, as I have suggested, in essence appears to be the cause of the first two functions. Yet Achilles, too, is doomed; his invulnerability does not last indefinitely. Although his death does not occur within the framework of the *Iliad* proper, it is clear that it is imminent. In Book 18, for example, when Achilles announces his decision to avenge Patroklos' death, Thetis "spoke to him letting the tears fall: / 'Then I must loose you soon, my child, by what you are saying, / for since it is decreed your death must come soon after Hector's' " (18.94–96).[28] Later on we learn from Xanthos, Achilles' chariot horse (whom Hera had given the power of speech), that this "decree" had come from " 'a great god and powerful Destiny' " (19.410), or, in other words, from the divine representatives of the first function.

That Achilles, like Herakles *et al.*, does eventually pay the supreme price for his defiance of sovereign authority is congruent with what appears to be a major aspect of the common Indo-European ideology: the ambivalent position of the warrior, especially vis-à-vis representatives of the first function. For he is at once vitally necessary and a threat to the maintenance of the social order. Malinowski once suggested that myths are fundamentally created to serve as pragmatic "charters" for behavior.[29] If this dictum be correct, then in the case of the Indo-European warrior the charter would appear to read: be valorous in battle, but never forget that you are ultimately subject to the authority of your sovereign, for if you do, you are doomed. That such a charter is implied in the account of the "wrath" of Achilles seems quite probable.

---

27 This episode has a number of counterparts elsewhere among the Indo-European traditions relating to second-function figures; cf., for example, the episode in the *Mahābhārata*, Book 4 (the *Virāṭaparvan*), wherein Arjuna, posing as a eunuch, becomes a dancing master in the harem of King Virāṭa. See Dumézil, *Mythe et épopée* (Paris, 1968), pp. 71–72.

28 This and other English translations of Homer are taken from Richmond Lattimore, *The Iliad of Homer* (Chicago, 1951).

29 B. Malinowski, "Myth in Primitive Psychology," in *Magic, Science, and Religion* (New York, 1955), p. 101.

The ambivalent character of the Indo-European warrior is also expressed in a general tendency to separate mythical and epical warriors into two distinct categories: the chivalrous and the bestial.[30] Perhaps the best attested examples of this dichotomy can be seen in the Vedic differentiation between Indra and Vāyu, and the subsequent epic distinctions between Arjuna and Bhīma. Arjuna, more directly a transposition of Indra, exemplifies all that is noble and chivalrous; Bhīma, more immediately linked to Vāyu, is boorish and ill-tempered, and exhibits a savage bloodlust.

If we examine the several major figures of the *Iliad*, especially the Achaean warriors, it is possible to see a number of examples of this sort of differentiation, although none of them are as clear-cut as the dichotomy between Arjuna and Bhīma. The most obvious candidate for the Bhīma position, it seems to me, is the lesser (or Locrian) Aias (Latin Ajax). Rose points out that this Aias is the one hero for whom Homer shows personal dislike.[31] And with good reason, for unlike Achilles or his more chivalrous, if slow-witted, namesake (Aias of Salamis), Aias of Locris is insolent, given to sudden outbursts of violence, ill-mannered, and in general not a very pleasant figure. Perhaps his character is best summed up in Idomeneus' words: " 'Aias, surpassing in abuse, yet stupid, in all else you are the worst of the Argives with that stubborn mind of yours' " (23.483–484). Furthermore, Aias of Locris, like Vāyu, is consistently described as extremely swift of foot; this is a characteristic that seems to go with warrior figures of the Vāyu type, one that perhaps ultimately reflects the idea of the "ill wind" that can cause sudden and violent destruction. Aias of Salamis presents a different picture; although slow-witted, he is nevertheless possessed of many Arjuna-like character traits, among them loyalty, steadfastness, and a generally good humor. Indeed, the distinction between the two Aiases does in many respects parallel the Arjuna-Bhīma distinction, although admittedly the greater Aias' lack of sagacity does not conform to the Arjuna model. Nevertheless, from this perspective, it is curious that two warriors exhibiting in many respects opposite personality traits would bear the same name. Perhaps we have here a dim reflection of a common Indo-European warrior figure, possessed of a "Jekyll-and-Hyde" personality structure, who in the Indian tradition underwent onomastic as well as characterological bifurcation.

In addition to the greater Aias, there are several other major candidates for the Arjuna position. One, of course, is Achilles him-

30 Dumézil, *Aspects de la fonction guerrière.*

31 H. J. Rose, *A Handbook of Greek Mythology* (New York, 1959), p. 236.

self, despite his culpability—Indra, too, it must be remembered, was culpable. It is Achilles who, after rejoining the army, bears the trifunctional shield in the climactic struggle with Hector. Moreover, even at his most recalcitrant, Achilles is ever concerned with his honor, and with assumed assaults upon that honor by Agamemnon and others. Yet an equally good case can be made for Achilles as a representative of the Vāyu figure. In the first place, he is described as the swiftest of all the Achaeans (see above); second, his behavior is wrathful and capricious and in many respects resembles that of Bhīma. In short, Achilles' character reflects *both* aspects of the Indo-European warrior figure, and it is impossible to assign him definitely to one or another category.

Another figure that should be mentioned in this connection is Diomedes, who, with the possible exception of Hector, is perhaps the most consistently honorable and chivalrous of Homer's heroes. Unlike Achilles, he is never given to fits of temper, never defies his commander-in-chief, and in general can be counted upon for steadfast and valiant service. Unlike the greater Aias, he is noted for his good advice and quickwittedness. His loyalty to Agamemnon, who on one occasion refers to him as " 'you who delight my heart' " (10.234), is never in question. Perhaps these traits can best be seen in Book 10, wherein Diomedes volunteers to lead a commando-like expedition against the enemy. In short, in terms of personal character traits, he is by far the closest Homeric approximation of Arjuna.

Yet Diomedes' role in the *Iliad* hardly compares to that of Arjuna in the *Mahābhārata*, or to that of Indra in the *Rig-Veda*, and for this reason alone I would hesitate to rank him as *the* Homeric Arjuna figure. That a great many inherited Arjuna-like traits went into the construction of his character cannot be doubted. Once again, we may be confronted with a case of bifurcation, in this instance between two facets of the Indo-European noble warrior: prominence in the narrative (Achilles) and consistent chivalrous behavior (Diomedes).

Finally, there is Patroklos, intimate of Achilles, a figure generally described as honorable and chivalrous in his behavior. That he, too, reflects some Arjuna-like traits seems probable; indeed, his close association with Achilles—homosexuality is not uncommon among second-function figures—may reflect the complimentary relationship between the two aspects of the warrior. Yet Patroklos' role in the epic is even less prominent than that of Diomedes, a fact that certainly must be kept in mind when considering candidates for the honor of representing the noble Indo-European warrior.

In sum, there is no *single* candidate for this position. With the exception, perhaps, of the lesser Aias, all of the figures just discussed present some Arjuna-like characteristics. The same thing, though to a lesser degree, can be said for the Bhīma figure. That the theme of the bifurcation of the warrior is present seems undeniable; its manifestation, however, is apparently collective and not centered in a single pair of figures equivalent to Arjuna and Bhīma or Indra and Vāyu.

When it comes to candidates for first-function honors, the most obvious is Agamemnon, King of Argos, and commander-in-chief of the Achaean forces. The Argive king's overall sovereign position is continually underscored by such epithets as "wide-ruling" (1.102), "lord of men" (2.612), and "shepherd of the people" (19.35). Although he engages in battle, his prowess as a warrior is rarely emphasized; rather, emphasis is continually placed upon his overlordship. In all this Agamemnon resembles Yudhiṣṭhira, eldest and leader of the Pāṇḍavas, whom Wikander has identified as a first-function figure.

Yet problems arise when we attempt to make a more precise identification, when we attempt to classify the Argive king as Varunaic or Mitraic. For it will be remembered that one of the cornerstones of Dumézil's thesis is the idea of the joint or dual sovereignty, the idea that the Indo-European conception of sovereignty was divided into two complementary aspects: the cosmic and the juridical, personified in the *Veda*'s, respectively, by Varuna and Mitra.[32] In the *Iliad* the evidence is by no means clear as to *which* aspect of sovereignty Agamemnon represents. Like Varuṇa, he is the ultimate sovereign; yet like Mitra, he is very much concerned with the affairs of men and serves (or attempts to serve) as an arbiter of disputes. On balance, however, I would suggest that he is more Varunaic than Mitraic. One reason for this suggestion is the curious impotence exhibited by Agamemnon, especially in times of crisis. Although never abdicating his position as commander in chief, he is by no means decisive and must continually rely upon others to rally his spirits and to prop him up. That impotence—admittedly more physical than mental—is a Varunaic characteristic was long ago pointed out by Dumézil.[33] More recently, in following up Wikander's analysis of the first function in the *Mahābhārata*, Dumézil has suggested that Pāṇḍu himself, "pale and impotent," yet exercising ultimate sovereignty over his offspring, can be equated with Varuṇa, and that Yudhiṣṭhira, as an incarnation

---

[32] Dumézil, *Mitra-Varuna: Essai sur deux représentations indo-européennes de la souveraineté* (Paris, 1940; 2d ed., 1948; 3d ed., forthcoming).

[33] *Ibid.*

of the principle of *Dharma,* is more clearly linked to Mitra.[34]

If Agamemnon is Varunaic, who then might be suggested as the Mitraic representative of the first function? The most promising set of candidates are those figures who most frequently serve as the Argive king's props and counselors: Diomedes, Odysseus, Kalkhas, and Nestor. Diomedes can be ruled out by virtue of his previously discussed second-function characteristics. Odysseus, though manifestly a shrewd and sagacious counsellor, is too clearly a trickster figure; he presents too many parallels to Loki, Syrdon,[35] *et al.,* to be taken seriously as an incarnation of the juridical principle. When it comes to Kalkhas and Nestor, however, the matter becomes more complex. Both figures serve as counselors; both are renowned for their wisdom rather than for their fighting abilities. Yet the contrast between them would seem to reflect that typically found between representatives of the two halves of the function in question. Kalkhas is characterized principally as a seer, as a prophet whose counsel is rooted in a supernatural ability to divine; it is he, for example, who predicts the war's duration and the role that Herakles' arrows will play in its successful conclusion. This concern with prophetic insight, with things supernatural, would seem more Varunaic than Mitraic. In contrast, Nestor is the arbiter par excellence, the adjudicator (or would-be adjudicator) of disputes among mortals; one of his principal epithets is "fair spoken." Rarely if ever does he have recourse to the kind of supernatural modus operandi employed by Kalkhas. On balance, he would appear to be much more concerned with the immediate affairs of the community than Kalkhas, and this, of course, is one of the distinguishing characteristics of the Mitra figure. Indeed, Kalkhas' relationship to Agamemnon presents some broad parallels to the relationship, as expressed in the *Rig-Veda* (cf. *Rig-Veda* 10.72.3–5), between Varuṇa and Dakṣa (or perhaps Aṃśa; cf. *Rig-Veda* 10.31.3), wherein the latter is primarily concerned with ritual relationships and (in the case of Aṃśa) with the distribution of divine fate.

In short, although Kalkhas and Nestor present a great many generalized first-function characteristics, I suggest that Nestor comes closest to meeting the requirements of a representative of the juridical half of this function.[36]

34 Dumézil, *Aspects de la fonction guerrière,* p. 75.

35 An Ossetic trickster figure; cf. Dumézil, *Loki* (Paris, 1948).

36 Professor Yoshida suggests (personal communication, April, 1969) that Nestor's character may also contain some elements reflecting what Dumézil has termed "les dieux premiers": figures who are trifunctional in definition and who serve to

These, then, are some possible Indo-European themes in the *Iliad*. If there be any validity to them, the trifunctional character of the illustrations upon the shield of Achilles, so convincingly demonstrated by Yoshida, is by no means an isolated survival of the common Indo-European ideology in Greek epic. Rather, the presence of these themes would seem to indicate that the overall tradition relative to the siege of Troy—or at least those aspects of it upon which Homer drew—was thoroughly infused with this ideology. To those who object to this conclusion on the grounds that the traditions surrounding the siege of Troy may well reflect an actual historical event, one may counter that it would not be the first time such an event has been subject to ideological reinterpretation. Gerschel, for example, has ably demonstrated that the Roman interpretations of the fall of Carthage, an undoubtedly historical event, were typically phrased in terms of the common Indo-European ideology[37]—to which the Carthaginians, as Semitic speakers, were most likely not a party.

If in fact the Trojan War did take place, it seems certain that those who took part in it were themselves the products of a tripartite social system. The Pylos tablets have yielded a picture of a society composed of three hierarchically ordered, functionally differentiated social strata: "On pourrait alors affirmer dès à present que les Mycéniens concevaient leur société comme composée essentiellement d'une classe sacerdotale (dont on ne connaît pas encore le nom collectif), d'une classe guerrière le λᾱϝός et d'une classe productrice le δᾶμος et que cette structure trifonctionnelle se retrouvait à l'échelon le plus haut de la hiérarchie dans une espèce de triumvirat constitué

introduce (or to complete) canonical lists of the representatives of the three functions; e.g., Dyauḥ, Janus, Heimdallr (cf. Dumézil, *Tarpeia* [Paris, 1947], pp. 97–100; see also "La tripartition indo-européenne," *Psyche* 2:1348–1356 [1947], where Dumézil terms the divinities in question "l'épine du système"). Like Heimdallr *et al.*, Nestor belongs to an earlier generation; he is far and away the oldest of the major Achaean figures. Moreover, he is curiously removed from the sphere of action, serving typically as a mediator and counselor rather than as an active co-sovereign. Despite his advanced age he survives the war and continues to play an important part in subsequent events; even his name may be significant here, as it can be translated "The Returner, He Who Returns." A case, too, can be made for a trifunctional character in that he is at once a counselor of the sovereign, is typically characterized as a horseman, and is described as the ruler of one of the wealthiest and most prosperous of the Achaean cities. Nevertheless, even if, as I suspect, Yoshida is correct in identifying these traits as appropriate to a "dieu premier," this would not rule out a double identification as far as Nestor is concerned, for, as we have seen, a good case can also be made for assigning him to the role of juridical counterpart of Agamemnon.

[37] L. Gerschel, "Structures augurales et tripartition fonctionnelle dans la pensée de l'ancienne Rome," *JPsych* 45:57–78 (1952).

par le ϝάναξ, le λāϝāγέτāς et le δāμοκόλος, dont chacun était attaché à l'un des trois ordres sociaux."[38] In the light of the evidence for the persistence of the Indo-European ideology in the structure of Mycenaean society, it is not unreasonable to assume that this ideology persisted in other areas of Mycenaean culture, and that, as in the much later Roman case just noted, it could have been brought to bear on the characterization of an event such as the defeat of a major commercial rival, that is, Troy.

By Homer's time the tripartite character of Greek social organization, so clearly evidenced in the Pylos texts, had largely disappeared. This disappearance seems to have owed in large measure to the disruptive effects of the Dorian invasions, the subsequent growth of Phoenician and other Near Eastern influences, and perhaps, as Dumézil phrases it (see above), the beginnings of "le miracle grec." Yet the apparent absence of social tripartition does not in itself mean that the common ideology had wholly given way. It does not mean that this ideology had necessarily disappeared in the oral traditions relative to the exploits of Achilles, Hector, *et al.*, upon which Homer must have drawn in the composition of the epic. Indeed, given the generally conservative nature of oral traditions (the *Rig-Veda* and the Irish *Lebor Gabála* are excellent examples of such conservatism within the Indo-European domain), it is entirely possible that these traditions had managed to preserve more than a modicum of their original tripartite character. Thus, though not himself the product of a tripartite society, Homer may very well have fallen heir to a body of tradition that took initial shape centuries earlier in a far more "Indo-European" social and intellectual context, that is, Mycenaean society, as revealed by the Mycenaean tablets.

There are, of course, some purely philological and stylistic grounds for assuming a connection between the *Iliad* and other Indo-European epic narratives, and these should be noted, if only in passing. For example, in Jaan Puhvel's opinion there are very sound philological reasons for deriving the Homeric hexameter from Indo-European metrical sources.[39] An interesting stylistic correspondence can be seen in the extent to which the typical Homeric enumeration, which characteristically applies an epithet to the last item

---

[38] Yoshida, "Survivances de la tripartition fonctionnelle en Grèce," *op. cit.*, p. 35. See also M. Lejeune, "Prêtres et prêtresses dans les documents mycéniens," *Hommages à Georges Dumézil* (Brussels, 1960), pp. 129–139. For earlier interpretations see L. R. Palmer, *Achaeans and Indo-Europeans: An Inaugural Lecture* (Oxford, 1954), pp. 1–22; M. Ventris and J. Chadwick, *Documents in Mycenaean Greek* (London, 1956), pp. 119–125.

[39] Personal communications, January, 1967.

or person enumerated, parallels Indic epical enumerations: for example, "These were the dwellers in Kynos and Opoeis and Kalliaros, and in Bessa, and Skarphe, and *lovely* Augeiai" (*Iliad* 2.531–532; italics mine), and "Drona, Karna, Bhūriśravas, Śakuni, the son of Sabala, and Bāhlika the *great car-warrior* (*Udyogaparvan* 5.149.1–5; italics mine).[40] The etymological tie between Ἕκτωρ and Sanskrit *sáha-* has already been noted.

In sum, although it is, as I have previously pointed out, impossible to deal adequately with a subject of this magnitude in a brief paper such as this, I do think that a strong case can be made for the Indo-European character of the *Iliad* and its principal characters and events. At the very least, the interpretations suggested here, coupled with those of Yoshida relative to the shield, would certainly seem to warrant a great deal more attention to possible Indo-European ideological themes in Greek epic than has heretofore been given.

---

[40] This translation is taken from C. V. Narasimhan, *The Mahābhārata* (New York, 1955), p. 113.

Bibliography*

ARNOLD, PAUL
1946 "Magie guerrière dans la Rome antique," *CS* 25:449–459.
1950 "Le mythe de Mars," *CS* 31:93–108.
1951 "Civilisation indo-européenne (avant-propos)," *CS* 34:216–220.
1952 "La notion de souveraineté chez les Indo-Européens: En marge de l'oeuvre de Georges Dumézil," *CS* 36:3–8.
1957*a* "Les sacrifices humains et la *devotio* à Rome," *Ogam* 9:27–36.
1957*b* "Augures & Flamines," *Ogam* 9:139–145.

BALKESTEIN, J.
1963 *Onderzoek naar de oorspronkelijke zin en betekenis van de romeinse god Mars.* Assen.

BARR, K.
1952 "Irans profet som τέλειος ἄνθρωπος," *Festskrift til L. L. Hammerich* (Copenhagen), pp. 26–36.
1954 *Avesta.* Copenhagen.

BASANOFF, V.
1942 *Les dieux des Romains.* Paris.
Review: G. Dumézil, *RHR* 127:159–161 (1944).
1943 *Regifugium, La fuite du roi: Histoire et mythe.* Paris.
1947 "Note sur la triade 'indo-européenne' à Rome," *RHR* 132:110–114. Rejoinder by Dumézil, 1947*b*.

*This bibliography lists works that either advance the study of modern-day Indo-European comparative mythology, or employ methods directly relatable to such advances, or discuss and criticize relevant theories and materials. The choice is necessarily subjective and aims for comprehensiveness rather than fully exhaustive coverage. It is nevertheless to be hoped that the list will prove usable and useful to fellow workers, now that the efforts thus codified have passed their tentative pioneer stages and must stand on their own amidst the scholarly panorama of our century.

BATANY, JEAN

1963 "Des 'Trois Fonctions' aux 'Trois États'?" *AESC* 18:933–938.

BAYET, JEAN

1947 "Nouveaux aspects de la recherche sur les siècles légendaires de Rome," *REL* 25:54–55.

1957 *Histoire politique et psychologique de la religion romaine*. Bibliothèque historique. Paris.

BENVENISTE, EMILE

1932 "Les classes sociales dans la tradition avestique," *JA* 221:117–134.

1938 "Traditions indo-iraniennes sur les classes sociales," *JA* 230:529–549.

1945*a* "La doctrine médicale des Indo-Européens," *RHR* 130:5–12.

1945*b* "Symbolisme social dans les cultes gréco-italiques," *RHR* 129:5–16.

BENVENISTE, EMILE, and LOUIS RENOU

1934 *Vr̥tra et Vr̥θragna: Étude de mythologie indo-iranienne*. Cahiers de la Société Asiatique 3. Paris.
Review: J. Przyluski, *RHR* 115:224–239 (1937).

BETZ, WERNER

1962 "Die altgermanische Religion." In W. Stammler, ed., *Deutsche Philologie im Aufriss* (2d ed.; Berlin), III, 1547–1646. Cf. 1st ed. (Berlin, 1957), III, 2467–2556.
Review: E. A. Philippson, *JEGP* 62:826–827 (1963).

BINCHY, D. A.

1970 "Celtic Suretyship, a Fossilized Indo-European Institution." In *Indo-European and Indo-Europeans* (Philadelphia).

BLOCH, RAYMOND

1946 *Les origines de Rome*. Paris.

1965 *Tite-Live et les premiers siècles de Rome*. Collection d'études anciennes. Paris.

BOYANCÉ, P.

1955 "Les origines de la religion romaine: Théories et recherches récentes," *IL* 7:100–107.

BROUGH, JOHN

1959 "The Tripartite Ideology of the Indo-Europeans: An Experiment in Method," *BSOAS* 22:69–86. Rejoinder by Dumézil, 1959*e*.

BUHOCIU, OCTAVIAN

1958 "Le mythe indo-européen d'initiation à la guerre: Le motif daco-roumain," *Ogam* 10:40–55.

CLOSS, ALOIS

1961 "Die Heiligkeit des Herrschers," *Anthropos* 56:469–480.
Review: M. Vereno, *Kairos* 4:60–61 (1962).

DAVID, MARCEL
1959 "Les 'laboratores' jusqu'au renouveau économique des XI-XIIe siècles," *Études d'histoire du droit privé offertes à Pierre Petot* (Paris), pp. 107–119.

DAVIDSON, H. R. ELLIS
1964 *Gods and Myths of Northern Europe.* Penguin Books, Baltimore.

DE MENASCE, P. J.
1947 "Une légende indo-iranienne dans l'angélologie judéo-musulmane: À propos de Hārūt et Mārūt," *AsS* 1:10–18.
Review: H. Puech, *RHR* 133:221–225 (1948).

DEROLEZ, R. L. M.
1962 *Les dieux et la religion des Germains.* Bibliothèque historique. Paris.

DEVOTO, GIACOMO
1962 *Origini indeuropee.* Florence.

DE VRIES, JAN
1942 "Rood-wit-zwart," *Volkskunde* 43:53–62 = *Kleine Schriften* (Berlin, 1965), pp. 351–359.
1951 "Der heutige Stand der germanischen Religionsforschung," *GRM* 33:1–11.
1952 "La valeur religieuse du mot germanique *irmin*,"*CS* 36:18–27.
1953 "A propos du dieu Esus," *Ogam* 5:16–21.
1954 "Über das Wort 'Jarl' und seine Verwandten," *NClio* 4:461–469.
1956–57 *Altgermanische Religionsgeschichte.* I–II. Grundriss der germanischen Philologie 12/I–II. 2d ed. Berlin.
Review: E. A. Philippson, *JEGP* 56:309–316.
1958 "L'aspect magique de la religion celtique," *Ogam* 10:273–284.
1959 "Note sur la valeur religieuse du nombre trois," *Ogam* 11:305–306.
1960*a* "Die Druiden," *Kairos* 2:67–82.
1960*b* "Die Interpretatio Romana der gallischen Götter," *Indogermanica: Festschrift für Wolfgang Krause* (Heidelberg), pp. 204–213.
1960*c* *Kelten und Germanen.* Bibliotheca Germanica 9. Bern.
1960*d* "Quelques réflexions sur la nature des Dieux Gaulois," *Ogam* 12:321–334.
1960*e* "Sur certains glissements fonctionnels de divinités dans la religion germanique," *Hommages à Georges Dumézil* (Brussels), pp. 83–95 = *Kleine Schriften* (Berlin, 1965), pp. 151–161.
1961*a* *Keltische Religion.* Die Religionen der Menschheit 18. Stuttgart.
1961*b* *Forschungsgeschichte der Mythologie.* Orbis Academicus 1.7. Freiburg and Munich.
1963 *La religion des Celtes.* Bibliothèque historique. Paris. French trans. of 1961*a* above.
1967 *The Study of Religion: A Historical Approach.* Translated with an introduction by Kees W. Bolle. New York.

DILLON, MYLES
1947 "The Archaism of Irish Tradition," *PBA* 33:245–264.
1963 "Celt and Hindu," *VIJ* 1:203–223.

DRESDEN, M. J.
1961 "Mythology of Ancient Iran." In *Mythologies of the Ancient World,* S. N. Kramer, ed. (New York), pp. 331–366.

DUCHESNE-GUILLEMIN, JACQUES
1948 *Zoroastre: Étude critique avec une traduction commentée des Gâthâ.* Paris.
1952 *The Hymns of Zarathustra: Being a Translation of the Gāthās together with Introduction and Commentary.* London. Reprinted, with a preface by Richard N. Frye (Boston, 1963).
1953 *Ormazd et Ahriman: L'aventure dualiste dans l'antiquité.* Mythes et religions 31. Paris.
1958 *The Western Response to Zoroaster.* Oxford.
1960 "De la dicéphalie dans l'iconographie mazdéenne," *Paideuma* 7:210–215 = *Festgabe für Hermann Lommel* (Wiesbaden, 1960), pp. 32–37.
1961 *Symbolik des Parsismus.* Symbolik der Religionen 8. Stuttgart. Eng. version in *Symbols and Values in Zoroastrianism.* Religious Perspectives 15 (New York, 1966).
1962 *La religion de l'Iran ancien.* Mana 1.3. Paris.
1967 "L'expansion de Baga," *Festschrift für Wilhelm Eilers* (Wiesbaden), pp. 157–158.

DUMÉZIL, GEORGES
1924 *Le festin d'immortalité: Étude de mythologie comparée indo-européenne.* Annales du Musée Guimet, Bibliothèque d'études 34. Paris.
Reviews: A. Meillet, *BSL* 25:42 (1925).
Ph. de Félice, *RHPhR* 8:576 (1928).
1925 "Les bylines de Michajlo Potyk et les légendes indo-européennes de l'ambroisie," *RESl* 5:205–237.
1926 "Les fleurs Haurot-Maurot et les anges Haurvatât-Amərətât," *REArm* 6:43–69.
1929 *Le problème des Centaures: Étude de mythologie comparée indo-européenne.* Annales du Musée Guimet, Bibliothéque d'études 41. Paris.
1930*a* *Légendes sur les Nartes, suivies de cinq notes mythologiques.* Paris.
1930*b* "La préhistoire indo-iranienne des castes," *JA* 216:109–130.
1934 *Ouranós-Váruṇa: Étude de mythologie comparée indo-européenne.* Paris.

1935 *Flamen-Brahman*. Annales du Musée Guimet, Bibliothèque de vulgarisation 51. Paris.

1938*a* "Jeunesse, éternité, aube: Linguistique comparée et mythologie comparée indo-européennes," *AHES* 10:289–301.

1938*b* "La préhistoire des flamines majeurs," *RHR* 118:188–200.

1939*a* *Mythes et dieux des Germains: Essai d'interprétation comparative*. Mythes et religions 1. Paris.

Reviews: R. Bloch, *RH* 188:274–276 (1940).
E. Dhorme, *RHR* 122:174–175 (1940).
A. Ernout, *RPh* 15:201 (1941).
A. Grenier, *REA* 41:378–379 (1939).
S. Gutenbrunner, *DLZ* 61:943–945 (1940).
A. Heiermeier, *IF* 59:115 (1944).
R. Lantier, *RA* 17:309–310 (1941).
M.-L. Sjoestedt, *EC* 4:143–146 (1948).

1939*b* "Deux traits du monstre tricéphale indo-iranien," *RHR* 120:5–20.

1940*a* *Mitra-Varuna: Essai sur deux représentations indo-européennes de la souveraineté*. Bibliothèque de l'École des Hautes Études, Section des Sciences Religieuses 56. Paris. See 1948*b*, below.

1940*b* "La tradition druidique et l'écriture: Le Vivant et Le Mort," *RHR* 122:125–133.

1941*a* *Jupiter Mars Quirinus: Essai sur la conception indo-européenne de la société et sur les origines de Rome*. Paris.

Reviews: J. Bayet, *REL* 20:182–185 (1942).
———, *RHR* 126:159–161 (1943).
Y. Bequignon, *RU* 52:199–200 (1943).
P. Boyancé, *REA* 44:143–144 (1942).
S. G. F. Brandon, *JThS* n.v.:123–126 (1944).
A. Cotard, *Hum (RES)* 16:132 (1943).
A. Grenier, *RH* 194:72–76 (1944).
R. Pettazzoni, *SMSR* 19–20:217–220 (1943–1946).
D. M. Pippidi, *RHSE* 23:278–282 (1946).
H. J. Rose, *JRS* 37:183–186 (1947).
B. Rosenkranz, *IF* 59:333–334 (1949).

1941*b* "L'étude comparée des religions indo-européennes," *NRF* 29:385–399.

1941*c* "Le nom des 'Arya'," *RHR* 124:36–59.

1942 *Horace et les Curiaces*. Les Mythes Romains I. Paris.

Reviews: J. Bayet, *REL* 20:182–185 (1942).
———, *RHR* 126:161–163 (1943).
E. Bickerman, *CPh* 41:121–123 (1946).
A. Grenier, *RH* 194:357–358 (1944).
R. Pettazzoni, *SMSR* 19–20:217–220 (1943–1946).
D. M. Pippidi, *RHSE* 23:282–283 (1946).
H. J. Rose, *JRS* 37:183–186 (1947).

1943*a* *Servius et la Fortune: Essai sur la fonction sociale de louange et de blâme et sur les éléments indo-européens du* cens *romain.* Les Mythes Romains II. Paris.
Reviews: J. Bayet, *REL* 21–22:298–301 (1943–1944).
———, *RHR* 126:163–166 (1943).
P. Boyancé, *REA* 45:325–326 (1943).
A. Grenier, *RH* 196:475–477 (1946).
R. Pettazzoni, *SMSR* 19–20:217–220 (1943–1946).
H. J. Rose, *JRS* 37:183–186 (1947).

1943*b* "Les débuts de la religion romaine." In *Mémorial des études latines* (Paris), pp. 316–329.

1943*c* "Légendes sur les Nartes," *RHR* 125:97–128.

1943*d* "O fortunatos nimium . . . ," *NRF* 31:270–286.

1944 *Naissance de Rome.* Jupiter Mars Quirinus II. Paris.
Reviews: J. Bayet, *REL* 24:362–364 (1946); rejoinder, 1948*c* (below), p. 183.
———, *RHR* 133:192–194 (1947–1948); rejoinder, 1948*c* (below), pp. 187–188.
P. Boyancé, *REA* 46:358–360 (1944).
R. Lantier, *RA* 35:229–230 (1950).
R. Pettazzoni, *SMSR* 19–20:217–220 (1946).
H. J. Rose, *JRS* 37:183–186 (1947).

1945 *Naissance d'archanges.* Jupiter Mars Quirinus III. Paris.
Reviews: J. Bayet, *REL* 24:364–366 (1946); rejoinder, 1948*c* (below), pp. 183–184.
P. Boyancé, *REA* 51:163–164 (1949).
J. Duchesne-Guillemin, *RHR* 132:175–178 (1947).
R. Pettazzoni, *SMSR* 19–20:217–220 (1943–1946).
L. Robin, *RPhilos* 137:224 (1947).

1946*a* " 'Tripertita' fonctionnels chez divers peuples indo-européens," *RHR* 131:53–72.

1946*b* "Les 'énarées' scythiques et la grossesse du Narte Hamyc," *Latomus* 5:249–255.

1947*a* *Tarpeia: Essais de philologie comparative indo-européenne.* Les Mythes Romains III. Paris.
Reviews and discussions:
J. Bayet, *REL* 25:420–422 (1947); rejoinder, 1948*c* (below), pp. 184–187.
J. Beaujeu, *REL* 37:393 (1959); rejoinder, 1960*a* (below), pp. 98–99 n. 2.
P. Boyancé, *REA* 51:164–166 (1949).
A. Brelich, *SMSR* 23:172–175 (1951–1952).
M. Leroy, *AC* 18:188–189 (1949).
V. Pisani, *Paideia* 5:55–58 (1950).

1947*b* "La triade 'Jupiter Mars Janus'?" *RHR* 132:115–123. Rejoinder to Basanoff, 1947.

1947*c* "La tripartition indo-européenne," *Psyché* 2:1348–1356.
1947*d* "Mitra-Varuna, Indra, les Nāsatya, comme patrons des trois fonctions cosmiques et sociales," *SL* 1:121–129.
1948*a* "A propos de latin 'jūs,'" *RHR* 134:95–112.
1948*b* *Mitra-Varuna: Essai sur deux représentations indo-européennes de la souveraineté.* 2d ed. Paris. See 1940*a*, above.
Reviews (1940 edition):
J. Bayet, *RHR* 124:191–196 (1941).
P. Boyancé, *REA* 43:85–87 (1941).
A. Grenier, *RH* 194:72–76 (1944).
R. Pettazzoni, *SMSR* 19–20:217–220 (1943–1946).
J. Przyluski, *RPhilos* 131:458–460 (1941).
H. J. Rose, *JRS* 37:183–186 (1947); rejoinders, *RHR* 133:241–243 (1948) and 1948*d*, pp. 12–16.
J. C. Tavadia, *IF* 59:231–232 (1948).
Review (1948 edition):
J. Gonda, *BO* 6:123–124 (1949).
1948*c* *Jupiter Mars Quirinus IV: Explication de textes indiens et latins.* Bibliothèque de l'École des Hautes Études, Sciences Religieuses 52. Paris.
Reviews: P. Boyancé, *REA* 51:166–168 (1949).
M. Leroy, *Latomus* 10:253–254 (1951).
1948*d* *Loki.* Les dieux et les hommes I. Paris.
Reviews and discussions:
J. Bayet, *REL* 27:370–371 (1949).
J. de Vries, *RHR* 146:231–235 (1954).
U. Drobins, *Temenos* 3:25–27 (1968).
A. B. Rooth, *Loki in Scandinavian Mythology.* Kungl. Humanistiska Vetenskapssamfundet i Lund, Skrifter 61 (1961). Pp. 8–9.
F. Ström, *Loki: Ein mythologisches Problem.* GUÅ 62:8 (1956). Pp. 6–9.
1948*e* "Religion et mythologie préhistoriques des Indo-européens." In *Histoire générale des religions* (Paris), I, 443–453. Cf. 1960*d*, below.
1949*a* *L'héritage indo-européen à Rome: Introduction aux séries "Jupiter Mars Quirinus" et "Les Mythes Romains."* Paris.
Reviews: J. Bayet, *REL* 27:373–374 (1949).
G. Bernard, *ECl* 18:137 (1950).
A. Brelich, *SMSR* 23:172–175 (1951–1952).
P. Chalus, *RSyn* 66:159–160 (1952).
A. Treux, *IH* 14:156 (1952).
1949*b* *Le troisième souverain: Essai sur le dieu indo-iranien Aryaman et sur la formation de l'histoire mythique de l'Irlande.* Les dieux et les hommes III. Paris.
Reviews: J. Bayet, *REL* 27:371–373 (1949).
H. Lommel, *Oriens* 7:381–385 (1954).

1949c "A propos de Vərəθraγna," *AIPhO* 9:223–226.

1950a "Les Archanges de Zoroastre et les rois romains de Cicéron," *JPsych* 43:449–463.

1950b "Dieux cassites et dieux védiques, à propos d'un bronze du Louristan," *RHA* 11:18–37.

1950c Review: A. Brelich, *Die geheime Schutzgottheit von Rom* (Zürich, 1950) and *Vesta* (Zürich, 1950), *RHR* 138:226–229.

1950d Review: Hendrik Wagenvoort, *Roman Dynamism* (Oxford, 1947), *RHR* 138:224–226.

1951a "Civilisation indo-européenne," *CS* 34:221–239. Also published as *Collège de France, Chaire de civilisation indo-européenne, Leçon inaugurale faite le jeudi, 1er décembre 1949* (Paris, 1950).

1951b "À propos du problème brahmán-flamen," *RHR* 138:255–258; 139:122–126.

1951c "L'inscription archaïque du Forum et Cicéron, *De Divinatione*, II, 36," *RecSR* 39:17–29.

1951d " 'Jupiter, Mars, Quirinus' et Janus," *RHR* 139:208–215.

1951e " 'Jupiter Mars Quirinus' et les trois fonctions chez les poètes latins du Ier siècle av J.-C.," *REL* 29:318–330.

1951f "Mythes romains," *RevP* 58 (Dec.):105–115.

1951g "Propertiana," *Latomus* 10:289–302.

1952a *Les dieux des Indo-européens.* Mythes et religions 29. Paris.
Reviews: J. Bayet, *REL* 32:454–455 (1954).
L. Gernet, *ASoc*, ser. 3, n.v.:434–436 (1952).
J. Goetz, *RecSR* 42:109–110 (1954).
M. Leroy, *AC* 22:351 (1953).
I. Meyerson, JPsych 52:403–405 (1955).
F. Mossé, *EG* 9:66–67 (1954)
E. Polomé, *Latomus* 13:285–286 (1954).
A. Vincent, *RSR* 28:91–92 (1954).

1952b "La bataille de Sentinum," *AESC* 7:145–154.

1952c *La civilisation iranienne (Perse, Afghanistan, Iran extérieur)*, ed. R. Grousset. Paris. Pp. 37–41, 61–65, 330–334.

1952d "Deux petits dieux scandinaves: Byggvir et Beyla," *NClio* 4:1–31.

1952e "La *Gestatio* de Frotho III et le folklore du Frodebjerg," *EG* 7:156–160.

1952f "Maiestas et Grauitas: De quelques différences entre les Romains et les Austronésiens," *RPh* 26:7–28.

1952g "Sur quelques expressions symboliques de la structure religieuse tripartie à Rome," *JPsych* 45:43–46.

1953a "Le *iuges auspicium* et les incongruités du taureau attelé de Mudgala," *NClio* 5:249–266.

1953b *La Saga de Hadingus (Saxo Grammaticus I, v–viii): Du mythe au roman.* Bibliothèque de l'École des Hautes Études, Sciences Religieuses 66. Paris.

Reviews and discussions:
J. Bayet, *REL* 32:457–458 (1954).
J. de Vries, *GRM* 34:186–187 (1953).
———, *RHR* 146:233–235 (1954).
L. Gerschel, *RHR* 153:254–255 (1958).
F. Mossé, *EG* 9:66–67 (1954).
I. Meyerson, *JPsych* 52:420–422 (1955).
E. Polomé, *Latomus* 14:498–499 (1955).

1953*c* "Les trois fonctions dans quelques traditions grecques," *Hommage à Lucien Febvre* (Paris), II, 25–32.

1953*d* "*Ner-* et *Viro-* dans les langues italiques," *REL* 31:175–189.

1953*e* Rejoinder to Carl Koch, "Bemerkungen zum römischen Quirinuskult," *ZRGG* 5:1–25 (1953), *REL* 31:189–190.

1953*f* "Viṣṇu et les Marut à travers la réforme zoroastrienne," *JA* 241:1–25.

1954*a* "*Meretrices* et *virgines* dans quelques légendes de Rome et des peuples celtiques," *Ogam* 6:3–8.

1954*b* "Karṇa et les Pāṇḍava," *OS* 3:60–66.

1954*c* "Iuno S.M.R.," *Eranos* 52:105–119.

1954*d* "Les cultes de la *regia*, les trois fonctions et la triade Jupiter, Mars, Quirinus," *Latomus* 13:129–139.

1954*e* "Ordre, fantaisie, changement dans les pensées archaïques de l'Inde et de Rome," *REL* 32:139–160.

1954*f* "Le trio des Macha," *RHR* 146:5–17.

1954*g* *Rituels indo-européens à Rome*. Études et Commentaires 19. Paris.
Reviews and discussions:
F. R. Adrados, *Emerita* 24:446–447 (1956).
A. Balil, *Zephyrus* 5:259–260 (1954).
J. Bayet, *REL* 32:455–457 (1954); rejoinder, 1956*a* (below), pp. 4–5.
P. Boyancé, *REA* 58:136–138 (1956); rejoinder, *REL* 34:108–111 (1956).
J. de Vries, *RHR* 147:109–110 (1955).
A. Ernout, *RPh* 31:141–142 (1957).
L. Gernet, *ASoc*, ser. 3, n.v.:332–335 (1953–1954).
M. Leroy, *RBPh* 34:300–301 (1956).
F. Le Roux, *Ogam* 7:291–296 (1955).
I. Meyerson, *JPsych* 52:405–407 (1955).
G. Oberammer, *AAHG* 10:169–170 (1957).
V. Pisani, *Paideia* 9:332 (1954).
E. Polomé, *Latomus* 13:287–290 (1954); rejoinder, *REL* 32:160–162 (1954).
H. J. Rose, *CR* 69:307–308; rejoinder, 1956*b* (below), pp. 118–123.
J. Untermann, *ZDMG* 106:409–410 (1956).

M. van den Bruwaene, *AC* 23:554–555 (1954); rejoinder, "Méthode comparative et religion romaine," *ibid.* 24:426–430 (1955).

H. Wagenvoort, *Museum: Tijdschrift voor Filologie en Geschiedenis* 61:23–25 (1956).

1954*h* "Remarques sur les dieux *Grabovio-* d'Iguvium," *RPh* 28:225–234.

1955*a* "Njǫrðr, Nerthus et le folklore scandinave des génies de la mer," *RHR* 147:210–226.

1955*b* "Notes sur le début du rituel d'Iguvium (E. Vetter, *Handbuch der italischen Dialekte* I, 171–179 [1953])," *RHR* 147:265–267.

1955*c* "Triades de calamités et triades de délits à valeur trifonctionnelle chez divers peuples indo-européens," *Latomus* 14:173–185.

1955*d* "À propos de Quirinus," *REL* 33:105–108.

1955*e* "Les 'enfants des soeurs' à la fête de Mater Matuta," *REL* 33:140–151.

1955*f* *Jupiter, Mars, Quirinus,* Trans. Franco Lucentini. Collezione di studi religiosi, etnologici e psicologici 26. Turin.

1956*a* *Aspects de la fonction guerrière chez les Indo-européens.* Bibliothèque de l'École des Hautes Études, Sciences Religieuses 68. Paris.

Reviews: P. Boyancé, *REL* 34:398–399 (1956).
A. Brelich, *SMSR* 27:146–148 (1956).
M. Eliade, *NNRF* 4:336–338 (1956).
A. Ernout, *RPh* 31:142 (1957).
I. Meyerson, *JPsych* 53:244–245 (1956).
E. Polomé, *Latomus* 16:186–188 (1957).
G. Redard, *Kratylos* 1:135–144 (1956).
R. Schilling, *RHR* 159:243 (1961).
M. van den Bruwaene, *AC* 25:531–534 (1956).

1956*b* *Déesses latines et mythes védiques.* Collection Latomus 24. Brussels.

Reviews: F. R. Adrados, *Emerita* 25:222–223 (1957).
G. Ambrosetti, *ArchClass* 11:123–130 (1959).
A. Brelich, *SMSR* 28:113–123 (1957); rejoinder, 1957*b* (below), 24–30; surrejoinder, *SMSR* 29:109–112 (1958).
F. Charlier, *ECl* 25:500–501 (1957).
P.-E. Dumont, *JAOS* 77:143–144 (1957).
A. Ernout, *RPh* 32:151–152 (1958).
P. Grimal, *REA* 59:155–158 (1957); rejoinder, 1957*c* (below), p. 151.
F. Le Roux, *Ogam* 9:332–334 (1957).
M. Leroy, *RBPh* 35:1099–1100 (1957).
J. Loicq, *BAClLg* 6:52–53 (1958).
L. Pepe, *GIF* 10:184 (1957).
G. Redard, *REL* 35:416–423 (1957).
R. Schilling, *Gymnasium* 66:414–415 (1959).

B. Schlerath, *ZDMG* 110:195–198 (1960).
M. van den Bruwaene, *AC* 26:248–249 (1957).

1956*b* "Remarques sur le 'Ius Fetiale,' " *REL* 34:93–108.

1956*c* "Remarques sur les trois premières *regiones caeli* de Martianus Capella," *Hommages à Max Niedermann* (Collection Latomus 23, Brussels), pp. 102–107.

1956*d* "Le *curtus equos* de la fête de Pales et la mutilation de la jument *Viś-palā*," *Eranos* 54:232–245.

1956*e* "Les pas de Kr̥ṣṇa et l'exploit d'Arjuna," *OS* 5:183–188.

1956*f* "L'étude comparée des religions des peuples indo-européens," *PBB(T)* 78:173–180. Rejoinder to Helm, 1955.

1956*g* "Noms mythiques indo-iraniens dans le folklore des Osses," *JA* 244:349–367.

1957*a* "Remarques sur les armes des dieux de 'troisième fonction' chez divers peuples indo-européens," *SMSR* 28:1–10.

1957*b* "Religion indo-européenne: Examen de quelques critiques récentes (John Brough, I; Angelo Brelich)," *RHR* 152:8–30.

1957*c* "Remarques sur *augur, augustus*," *REL* 35:126–151.

1958*d* "La Rígsþula et la structure sociale indo-européenne," *RHR* 154: 1–9.

1958*e* "L'idéologie des trois fonctions dans quelques crises de l'histoire romaine," *Latomus* 17:429–446.

1958*f* "arí, Aryamán, à propos de Paul Thieme, 'arí, Fremder,' " *JA* 245: 67–84.

1958*g* "Métiers et classes fonctionnelles chez divers peuples indo-européens," *AESC* 13:716–724.

1958*h* "Quaestiunculae Indo-Italicae 1–3," *REL* 36:112–131.

1958*i* "L'épopée Narte," *TR* 132 (Dec.):42–55.

1958*j* *L'idéologie tripartie des Indo-européens.* Collection Latomus 31. Brussels.

Reviews and discussions:
F. R. Adrados, *Emerita* 27:396–397 (1959).
P.-E. Dumont, *JAOS* 80:67–68 (1960).
A. Ernout, *RPh* 33:326 (1959).
L. Gerschel, *RHR* 155:239–240 (1959).
———, *Kratylos* 5:32–34 (1960).
P. Grimal, *REA* 61:151–154 (1959).
F. Le Roux, *Ogam* 11:108 (1959).
M. Leroy, *RBPh* 39:457–468 (1961).
W. Pötscher, *Gymnasium* 67:254–255 (1960); rejoinder, 1961*b* (below).
G. Redard, *REL* 36:398–400 (1958).
A. Scherer, *Kratylos* 10:22 (1965).
R. Schilling, *BFS* 38:159 (1959–1960).
A. Taylor, *WF* 20:48–50 (1961).
N. Turcha, *SMSR* 29:253–255 (1958).

M. van den Bruwaene, *AC* 28:488–490 (1959); rejoinder, 1961*b* (below).
M. Walbrecq, *ECl* 27:117 (1959).

1959*a* *Les dieux des Germains: Essai sur la formation de la religion scandinave.* Mythes et religions 38. Paris.
Reviews: P. Chalus, *RSyn* 81:144 (1960).
F. Charlier, *EG* 16:277–278 (1961).
H. Cornelis, *RSPT* 45:279–280 (1961).
F. Le Roux, *Ogam* 11:353 (1959).
C. Lévi-Strauss, *AESC* 17:998–999 (1962).
K. G. Ljungren, *ANF* 75:264 (1960).
M. Simon, *RH* 225:421–422 (1961).
B.-A. Taladoire, *REA* 63:126–127 (1961).
M. Vereno, *Kairos* 5:242 (1963).

1959*b* *Loki.* Trans. Inge Köck. Darmstadt.
Review: J. de Vries, *ZDA* (Anzeiger) 72:1–8 (1960–1961).

1959*c* "Le Rex et les Flamines maiores." In *La Regalità Sacra/The Sacral Kingship* (Studies in the History of Religions IV, Leiden), pp. 407–417. Summary in *Atti dell' VIII Congresso internazionale di storia delle religioni* (Florence, 1956), pp. 118–120.

1959*d* "La transposition des dieux souverains mineurs en héros dans le Mahābhārata," *IIJ* 3:1–16.

1959*e* "L'idéologie tripartie des Indo-européens et la Bible," *Kratylos* 4:97–118. Rejoinder to Brough, 1959.

1959*f* "Remarques comparatives sur le dieu scandinave Heimdallr," *EC* 8:263–283.

1959*g* "Addendum à 'Arí, Aryamán' (*JA*, CCXLVI, p. 67–84)," *JA* 247: 171–173.

1959*h* "Quaestiunculae Indo-Italicae 7: Trois règles de l'Aedes Vestae," *REL* 37:94–101.

1959*i* "Notes sur le bestiaire cosmique de l'Edda et du ṚgVeda," *Mélanges de linguistique et de philologie, Fernand Mossé, in memoriam* (Paris), pp. 104–112.

1960*a* "Carna (Déesses latines et mythes védiques, 5)," *REL* 38:87–98.

1960*b* "Quaestiunculae Indo-Italicae 4–6," *Hommages à Léon Herrmann* (Collection Latomus 44, Brussels), pp. 315–329.

1960*c* "Les trois 'Trésors des ancêtres' dans l'épopée Narte," *RHR* 157: 141–154.

1960*d* "Religion et mythologie préhistoriques des Indo-européens." In *Histoire générale des religions* (2d ed., Paris), I, 375–382. Cf. 1948*e*, above.

1961*a* "Les 'trois fonctions' dans le ṚgVeda et les dieux indiens de Mitani," *BARB* 47:265–298.

1961*b* "L'idéologie tripartie des Indo-européens, MM. Walter Pötscher et Martin van den Bruwaene," *Latomus* 20:524–529.

1961*c* "Quaestiunculae Indo-Italicae 8–10," *Latomus* 20:253–265.

1961*d* "Quaestiunculae Indo-Italicae 11–16," *REL* 39:242–274.

1961*e* "Religion romaine et critique philologique," *REL* 39:87–93.

1961*f* "Høtherus et Balderus," *PBB(T)* 83:259–270.

1961*g* "Primordia civitatis," *RBPh* 39:62–67.

1961*h* Reviews: B. Schlerath, J. de Vries, G. Widengren, *JA* 249:427–433.

1962*a* *De nordiska gudarna: En undersökning av den skandinaviska religionen.* Trans. Åke Ohlmarks. Stockholm.

1962*b* "La société scythique avait-elle des classes fonctionnelles?" *IIJ* 5:187–202.

1962*c* "Les deux Palès (Déesses romaines et mythes védiques, 6)," *REL* 40:109–117.

1963*a* "Quaestiunculae Indo-Italicae 17–18," *REL* 41:87–91.

1963*b* "Le puits de Nechtan," *Celtica* 6:50–61.

1964*a* "Balderiana minora," *Indo-Iranica: Mélanges présentés à Georg Morgenstierne* (Wiesbaden), pp. 67–72.

1964*b* "Remarques sur la stèle archaïque du Forum," *Hommages à Jean Bayet* (Collection Latomus 70, Brussels), pp. 172–179.

1964*c* *Aspekte der Kriegerfunktion bei den Indogermanen.* Trans. Inge Köck. Darmstadt.

1965*a* "A propos de la Plainte de l'Ame du Boeuf (Yasna 29)," *BARB* 51:23–51.

1965*b* "La sabhā dc Yama," *JA* 253:161–165.

1965*c* "Le dieu scandinave Vídarr," *RHR* 168:1–13.

1966 *La religion romaine archaïque.* Bibliothèque historique. Paris.

Reviews:

J. Heurgon, *REL* 44:86–93 (1966).

R. Schilling, *RHR* 172:217–220 (1967); *REA* 70:83–91 (1968).

1968*a* *Mythe et épopée: L'idéologie des trois fonctions dans les épopées des peuples indo-européens.* Bibliothèque des sciences humaines. Paris.

1968*b* "L'aśvamedha du colonel de Polier," *Pratidānam. Indian, Iranian and Indo-European studies presented to F. B. J. Kuiper* (The Hague), pp. 430–435.

1969*a* *Idées romaines.* Bibliothèque des sciences humaines. Paris.

1969*b* *Heur et malheur du guerrier. Aspects mythiques de la fonction guerrière chez les Indo-Européens.* Collection Hier. Paris.

1969*c* "Entretien avec Georges Dumézil," *Nouvelle Ecole* 10:41–44 (Sept.–Oct. 1969).

1960 *Hommages à Georges Dumézil.* Collection Latomus 45. Brussels.

Reviews:

A. Ernout, *RPh* 35:330 (1961).

L. Gerschel, *RHR* 161:255 (1962).

P. Grimal, *REA* 64:136–138 (1962).

G. Piccaluga, *SMSR* 31:160–166 (1960).

H. J. Rose, *CR* 11:304 (1961).

B. Schlerath, *Kratylos* 6:122–127 (1961).

M. van den Bruwaene, *AC* 30:683–685 (1961).

ELIADE, MIRCEA

1948 "Le 'dieu lieur' et le symbolisme des noeuds," *RHR* 134:5–36.

ELIZARENKOVA, T. J.

1968 "Ješče raz o vedijskom boge Varune (Varuṇa)." In *Töid orientalistika alalt I* (Tartu Riikliku Ülikooli Toimetised 201), pp. 113–122.

EL'NICKIJ, L. A.

1948 "Nekotorye problemy istorii skifskoj kul'tury (O knige B. N. Grakova, *Skifi,* Kiev, 1947)," *VDI* 2(24):95–101.

ÉTIEMBLE

1958 "Einstein, Dumézil, Horace et Cuchulainn," *Hygiène des Lettres. III. Savoir et goût* (Paris), pp. 231–258. Originally published in *Temps modernes,* July–Aug., 1950.

FRYE, R. N.

1960 "Georges Dumézil and the translators of the Avesta," *Numen* 7:161–171.

FUGIER, HUGUETTE

1965 "Quarante ans de recherches sur l'idéologie indo-européenne: La méthode de M. Georges Dumézil," *RHPhR* 45:358–374.

GERSCHEL, LUCIEN

1950 "Saliens de Mars et Saliens de Quirinus," *RHR* 138:145–151.

1952 "Structures augurales et tripartition fonctionnelle dans la pensée de l'ancienne Rome," *JPsych* 45:47–78.

1953 "Coriolan," *Hommage à Lucien Febvre* (Paris), II, 33–40.

1956 "Sur un schème trifonctionnel dans une famille de légendes germaniques," *RHR* 150:55–92.

1957 "Georges Dumézil's Comparative Studies in Tales and Traditions," *MF* 7:141–147.

1958 "Varron logicien," *Latomus* 17:65–72.

1960 "Un épisode trifonctionnel dans la saga de Hrólfr Kraki," *Hommages à Georges Dumézil* (Brussels), pp. 104–116.

1962 "La conquête du nombre. Des modalités du compte aux structures de la pensée," *AESC* 17:691–714.

1966 "Couleur et teinture chez divers peuples indo-européens," *AESC* 21:608–631.

GERSHEVITCH, ILYA

1959 Review of Thieme, 1957*b*, and Duchesne-Guillemin, 1958, *BSOAS* 22:154–157. Rejoinder by Dumézil, *ibid.* 22:267 (1959).

GNOLI, GHERARDO

1965 "L'Iran e l'ideologia tripartita," *SMSR* 36:193–210.

GONDA, JAN

1960a "Some Observations on Dumézil's Views of Indo-European Mythology," *Mnemosyne,* ser. 4, 13:1–15.

1960*b* *Die Religionen Indiens. I. Veda und älterer Hinduismus.* Die Religionen der Menschheit 11. Stuttgart.

GOOSSENS, ROGER
1949*a* "Notes de mythologie comparée indo-européenne," *NClio* 1:4–22.
1949*b* "La taupe d'Asklépios et la taupe de Rudra," *Le Flambeau* 32:261–273.

GRANTOVSKIJ, E.
1960 "Indoiranische Kastengliederung bei den Skythen," *PICO* 25. Extra volume 4 of papers presented by the USSR delegation, Moscow.

GRÉGOIRE, HENRI
1949 "Asklépios, le dieu-taupe," *Le Flambeau* 32:22–54.

GRÉGOIRE, HENRI, ROGER GOOSSENS, AND M. MATHIEU
1949 *Asklépios, Apollon Smintheus et Rudra: Études sur le dieu à la taupe et le dieu au rat dans la Grèce et dans l'Inde.* MARB 45.1. Brussels.
Reviews: V. Basanoff, *RBPh* 29:263–268 (1951).
L. Edelstein, *Gnomon* 26:162–168 (1954).
G. Goossens, *AC* 19:527–529 (1950).
P. Guillon, *Archives internationales d'histoire des sciences* 4:243–255 (1951).
———, *Hellénisme contemporain* 5:368–382 (1951).
P.-M. Schuhl. *Revue d'histoire des sciences* 5:192 (1952).

GREIMAS, A.-J.
1963 "La description de la signification et la mythologie comparée," *L'Homme* 3:3.51–66.

HAUGEN, EINAR
1967 "The mythical structure of the ancient Scandinavians: Some thoughts on reading Dumézil," *To Honor Roman Jakobson* (The Hague), pp. 855–868.

HELM, KARL
1955 "Mythologie auf alten und neuen Wegen," *PBB(T)* 77:333–365. Rejoinder by Dumézil, 1956*f*; surrejoinder, *PBB(T)* 78:181 (1956).

HUMBERT, JEAN
1946 "Linguistique et histoire des civilisations," *RHPh* n.v.:309–317.

IVANOV, V. V.
1969 "Zametki o tipologičeskom i sravnitel'no-istoričeskom issledovanii rimskoj i indoevropejskoj mifologii." In *Trudy po znakovym sistemam IV* (Tartu Riikliku Ülikooli Toimetised 236), pp. 44–75.

JACOBI, HERMANN
1893 *Das Râmâyaṇa: Geschichte und Inhalt nebst Concordanz der gedruckten Recensionen.* Bonn. Eng. trans. S. N. Ghosal (Baroda, 1960).

JAKOBSON, ROMAN
1950 "Slavic Mythology." In *Standard Dictionary of Folklore, Mythology and Legend* (New York), pp. 1025–1028.
1969 "The Slavic God Veles" and His Indo-European Cognates," *Studi linguistici in onore di Vittore Pisani* (Brescia), pp. 579–599.

JOHNSEN, GÖSTA
1966 "Varuṇa and Dhr̥tarāṣṭra," *IIJ* 9:245–265.

JUCQUOIS, GUY
1965 "V. sl. *bogatъ*, 'riche', *bogъ*, 'dieu', et apparentés," *Die Sprache* 11:131–135.

KNIPE, DAVID M.
1967 "The Heroic Theft: Myths from Ṛgveda IV and the Ancient Near East," *History of Religions* 6:328–360.

KUIPER, F. B. J.
1961 "Some Observations on Dumézil's Theory (with reference to Prof. Frye's article)," *Numen* 8:34–45.

LAMBRECHTS, PIERRE
1946 "Mars et les Saliens," *Latomus* 5:111–119. Rejoinder by Dumézil, 1948*c*, pp. 169–170.

LAROCHE, EMMANUEL
1960 "Hittite *arawa-* 'libre,'" *Hommages à Georges Dumézil* (Brussels), pp. 124–128.

LATTE, KURT
1960 *Römische Religionsgeschichte.* Handbuch der Altertumswissenschaft 5.4. Munich.
Review: A. Brelich, *SMSR* 32:311–354 (1961).

LE ROUX, FRANÇOISE
1956, 1960 "Notes d'histoire des religions": III, *Ogam* 8.293–299; VII, *Ogam* 12:475–486.
1957 "Le calendrier gaulois de Coligny (Ain) et la fête irlandaise de Samain (*Samonios)," *Ogam* 9:337–342.
1958, 1959 "Taranis: Dieu celtique du ciel et de l'orage," *Ogam* 10:30–39, 11:307–324.
1960*a* "Le dieu celtique aux liens: De l'Ogmios de Lucien à l'Ogmios de Dürer," *Ogam* 12:209–234.
1960*b* "Le Dieu druide et le Druide divin," *Ogam* 12:349–382.
1961*a* *Les Druides.* Mythes et religions. Paris.
1961*b* "Le guerrier borgne et le Druide aveugle: La cécité et la voyance," *Ogam* 13:331–342.
1961*c* "Études sur le festiaire celtique. I. Samain," *Ogam* 13:481–506.

1962*a* "Études sur le festiaire celtique. II. La fête irlandaise de février, Imbolc. III. Beltaine, la fête sacerdotale," *Ogam* 14:174–184.
1962*b* "Études sur le festiaire celtique. IV. Lugnasad ou la fête du roi," *Ogam* 14:343–372.
1963 "Recherches sur les éléments rituels de l'élection royale irlandaise et celtique," *Ogam* 15:123–137, 245–255.
1965 "Aspects de la fonction guerrière chez les Celtes," *Ogam* 17:175–188.
1967 "Introduction générale à l'étude de la tradition celtique," I, *Ogam* 19:269–347.

LINDQUIST, IVAR
1940 *Religiösa runtexter: II. Sparlösa-stenen, ett svenskt runmonument från Karl den Stores tid upptäckt 1937; ett tydningsförslag.* VSLS 24.

LITTLETON, C. SCOTT
1964 "The Comparative Indo-European Mythology of Georges Dumézil," *JFI* 1:147–166.
1966 *The New Comparative Mythology: An Anthropological Assessment of the Theories of Georges Dumézil.* Berkeley and Los Angeles.
Reviews: B. Beck, *American Sociological Review* 33:838–840 (1968).
R. P. Goldman, *JAOS* 89:205–213 (1969); rejoinder, *WF* 29:47–52 (1970).
H. Le Bonniec, *REL* 45:612–613 (1967).
R. Martin, *Latomus* 26:870–873 (1967).
U. Masing, *III Letnjaja škola po vtoričnym modelirujuščim sistemam. Tezisy. Doklady* (Tartu, 1968), pp. 227–248.
E. Polomé, *Die Sprache* 15:190–193 (1969).
R. Rocher, *RBPh* 46:156–158 (1968).
J. F. Szwed, *American Anthropologist* 70:400–401 (1968); rejoinder, *ibid.* 1182.
1967 "Toward a Genetic Model for the Analysis of Ideology: The Indo-European Case," *WF* 26:37–47.
1968 Review: Anne Ross, *Pagan Celtic Britain* (London, 1967), *American Anthropologist* 70:623–624.
1969 "Lévi-Strauss and the 'Kingship in Heaven'," *JFI* 6:70–84.
1970 "Is the 'Kingship in Heaven' Theme Indo-European?" In *Indo-European and Indo-Europeans* (Philadelphia).

LJUNGBERG, HELGE
1947 *Tor: Undersökningar i indoeuropeisk och nordisk religionshistoria.* UUÅ 9.

LOMMEL, HERMANN
1954 "Anahita-Sarasvati," *Asiatica: Festschrift Friedrich Weller* (Leipzig), pp. 405–413.

MARTIN, RENÉ
"Essai d'interprétation économico-sociale de la légende de Romulus," *Latomus* 26:298–315 (1967).

MEILLET, ANTOINE
1907 "Le dieu indo-iranien Mitra," *JA*, ser. 10, 10:143–159.

MERLAT, PIERRE
1960 "Orient, Grèce, Rome, un exemple de syncrétisme? Les 'Castores' dolichéniens." In *Éléments orientaux dans la religion grecque ancienne* (Paris), pp. 77–94.

MOLÉ, MARIJAN
1951 "La structure du premier chapitre du Vidēvdāt," *JA* 239:283–298.
1952, 1953 Le partage du monde dans la tradition iranienne," *JA* 240: 455–463, 241:271–273.
1960 "Deux notes sur le Rāmāyaṇa," *Hommages à Georges Dumézil* (Brussels), pp. 140–150.
1963 *Culte, mythe et cosmologie dans l'Iran ancien: Le problème zoroastrien et la tradition mazdéenne.* Annales du Musée Guimet, Bibliothèque d'études 69. Paris.
1965, *L'Iran ancien.* Religions du monde. Paris.

MONTESI, GIANCARLO
1957 "Uṣāsānaktā: Mitologia vedica della notte," *SMSR* 28:11–52.

OHLMARKS, ÅKE
1963 *Asar, vaner och vidunder.* Stockholm.

ORGOGOZO, JEANINE J.
1949 "L'Hermès des Achéens," *RHR* 136:10–30, 139–179.

PARAIN, BRICE
1956 "Les dieux des Indo-Européens," *NNRF* 4(pt. 3):694–702.

PHILIPPSON, ERNST ALFRED
1962 "Phänomenologie, vergleichende Mythologie und germanische Religionsgeschichte," *PMLA* 77:187–193.

PIGGOTT, STUART
1953 *Prehistoric India to 1000 B.C.* Penguin Books.

POLOMÉ, EDGAR
1953 "L'étymologie du terme germanique **ansuz* 'dieu souverain,'" *EG* 8:36–44.
1954*a* "A propos de la déesse Nerthus," *Latomus* 13:167–200.
1954*b* "La religion germanique primitive, reflet d'une structure sociale," *Le Flambeau* 37:427–463.
1954*c* "Notes critiques sur les concordances germano-celtiques," *Ogam* 6:145–164.

1969 "Some Comments on *Vǫluspá*, Stanzas 17–18." In E. C. Polomé, ed., *Old Norse Literature and Mythology* (Austin), pp. 265–290.

POWELL, T. G. E.
1948 "Celtic Origins: A Stage in the Enquiry," *JRAI* 78:71–79.

PRZYLUSKI, JEAN
1940 "Les confréries des loups-garous dans les sociétés indo-européennes," *RHR* 121:128–145.

PUHVEL, JAAN
1960 "Võrdlev mütoloogia tänapäeval," *Tulimuld* 11:113–120.
1965 "Filles du soleil: Folklore estonien et mythologie indoeuropéenne," *Estonian Poetry and Language: Studies in Honor of Ants Oras* (Stockholm), pp. 167–177.
1968 "Indo-European Prehistory and Myth," *Yearbook of the Estonian Learned Society in America* 4:51–62.
1970 "Mythological Reflections of Indo-European Medicine." In *Indo-European and Indo-Europeans* (Philadelphia).

REES, ALWYN D.
1945 "An Irish Vishnu," *Man* 45:118–119.
1966 "Modern Evaluations of Celtic Narrative Tradition." In *Proceedings of the Second International Congress of Celtic Studies Held in Cardiff 6–13 July, 1963* (Cardiff), pp. 31–61.

REES, ALWYN AND BRINLEY
1961 *Celtic Heritage: Ancient Tradition in Ireland and Wales.* London.

RINGGREN, H., AND ÅKE V. STRÖM
1959 *Die Religionen der Völker.* Stuttgart. German version of *Religionerna i historia och nutid* (2d ed.; Stockholm, 1959).

SCHILLING, ROBERT
1960 "Les Castores romains à la lumière des traditions indo-européennes," *Hommages à Georges Dumézil* (Brussels), pp. 177–192.

SCHRÖDER, FRANZ ROLF
1927 "Ein altirischer Krönungsritus und das indogermanische Rossopfer," *Zeitschrift für celtische Philologie* 16:310–312.
1957 "Indra, Thor und Herakles," *ZDPh* 76:1–41.
1960 "Die Göttin des Urmeeres und ihr männlicher Partner," *PBB(T)* 82:221–264.
1967 "Heimdall," *PBB(T)* 89:1–41.

SIPRIOT, PIERRE
1961 "La religion romaine (Dialogue avec Georges Dumézil)," *TR* 157 (Jan.):66–74.

STRÖM, ÅKE V.

1961 "Das indogermanische Erbe in den Urzeit- und Endzeitschilderungen des Edda-Liedes Völuspá." In *X. Internationaler Kongress für Religionsgeschichte, 11.–17. September 1960 in Marburg/Lahn* (Marburg), pp. 83–84.

TAVADIA, J. C.

1953*a* "Zoroastrian and Pre-Zoroastrian: Apropos the Researches of G. Dumézil," *JRASB* 28:171–186.

1953*b* "From Aryan Mythology to Zoroastrian Theology: A Review of Dumézil's Researches," *ZDMG* 103:344–353.

TAYLOR, ARCHER

1965 " 'What Bird Would You Choose To Be?' A Medieval Tale," *Fabula* 7:97–114.

THIEME, PAUL

1938 *Der Fremdling im Ṛgveda: Eine Studie über die Bedeutung der Worte* ari, arya, aryaman *und* ārya. Abhandlungen für die Kunde des Morgenlandes 23.2. Leipzig.

1952 *Studien zur indogermanischen Wortkunde und Religionsgeschichte.* Sächsische Akademie der Wissenschaften, Berichte über Verhandlungen, Philologisch-historische Klasse 98.5. Berlin.

1957*a* "Vorzarathustrisches bei den Zarathustriern und bei Zarathustra," *ZDMG* 107:67–104.

1957*b* *Mitra and Aryaman. TCAAS* 41:1–96.

1960 "The 'Aryan' Gods of the Mitanni Treaties," *JAOS* 80:301–317.

TOPOROV, V. N.

1961 "Fragment slavjanskoj mifologii," *Akademija Nauk SSSR, Institut slavjanovedenija, Kratkie soobščenija* 30:14–32.

1968 "Parallels to Ancient Indo-Iranian social and mythological concepts," *Pratidānam. Indian, Iranian and Indo-European studies presented to F. B. J. Kuiper* (The Hague), pp. 108–120.

1969 "K rekonstruckcii indoevropejskogo rituala i ritual'no-poetičeskikh formul (na materiale zagovorov)." In *Trudy po znakovym sistemam IV* (Tartu Riikliku Ülikooli Toimetised 236), pp. 9–43.

TURVILLE-PETRE, E. O. G.

1960 "Professor Dumézil and the Literature of Iceland," *Hommages à Georges Dumézil* (Brussels), pp. 209–214.

1964 *Myth and Religion of the North: The Religion of Ancient Scandinavia.* New York and London.

Review: E. Wahlgren, *SS* 36:328–330 (1964).

VERDIÈRE, RAOUL

"Calpus, fils de Numa, et la tripartition fonctionnelle de la société indo-européenne," *AC* 34.425–431 (1965).

VERNANT, JEAN-PIERRE

1960 "Le mythe hésiodique des races: Essai d'analyse structurale," *RHR* 157:21–54 = *Mythe et pensée chez les Grecs* (Paris, 1965), pp. 19–47.

1966 "Le mythe hésiodique des races: Sur un essai de mise au point," *RPh* 40:247–276.

VIAN, FRANCIS

1960*a* "Le mythe de Typhée et le problème de ses origines orientales." In *Éléments orientaux dans la religion grecque ancienne* (Paris), pp. 17–37.

1960*b* "La triade des rois d'Orchomène: Etéoclès, Phlégyas, Minyas," *Hommages à Georges Dumézil* (Brussels), pp. 215–224.

1963 *Les origines de Thèbes.* Études et commentaires 48. Paris.

1968 "La fonction guerrière dans la mythologie grecque." In *Problèmes de la guerre dans la Grèce ancienne* (Paris), pp. 53–68.

WARD, DONALD J.

1965 "The Rescue of Kudrun: A Dioscuric Myth?" *Classica et Mediaevalia* 26:334–353.

1967 "Solar Mythology and Baltic Folksongs," *Folklore International: Essays in Traditional Literature, Belief, and Custom in Honor of Wayland Debs Hand* (Hatboro, Pa.), pp. 233–242.

1968 *The Divine Twins: An Indo-European Myth in Germanic Tradition.* Folklore Studies 19. Berkeley and Los Angeles.

1970 "Kudrun: An Indo-European Mythological Theme?" In *Indo-European and Indo-Europeans* (Philadelphia).

WATKINS, CALVERT

1970 "Studies in Latin and Indo-European Legal Language." In *Indo-European and Indo-Europeans* (Philadelphia).

WIDENGREN, GEO

1960 "La légende royale de l'Iran antique," *Hommages à Georges Dumézil* (Brussels), pp. 225–237.

1961*a* *Iranische Geisteswelt von den Anfängen bis zum Islam.* Baden-Baden.

1961*b* "Salomos vishet och Paris' dom," *Kungar, profeter och harlekiner.* Stockholm. Pp. 36–42.

1965 *Die Religionen Irans.* Die religionen der Menschheit 14. Stuttgart.

1968 *Les religions de l'Iran.* Bibliothèque historique. Paris. French trans. of 1965 above.

WIKANDER, STIG

1938 *Der arische Männerbund: Studien zur indo-iranischen Sprach- und Religionsgeschichte.* Lund.

1941 *Vayu: Texte und Untersuchungen zur indoiranischen Religionsgeschichte.* Teil I. *Texte.* Uppsala.

1947 "Pāṇḍava-sagan och Mahābhāratas mytiska förutsättningar," *RoB* 6:27–39.

1950 "Sur le fonds commun indo-iranien des épopées de la Perse et de l'Inde," *NClio* 1:310–329.

1951 "Hethitiska myter hos greker och perser," *VSLÅ* n.v.: 35–56.

1952*a* "Histoire des Ouranides," *CS* 36:8–17.

1952*b* "Mithra en vieux-perse," *OS* 1:66–68.

1957 "Nakula et Sahadeva," *OS* 6:66–96.

1960*a* "Från Bråvalla till Kurukshetra," *ANF* 75:183–193.

1960*b* "Germanische und indo-iranische Eschatologie," *Kairos* 2:83–88.

1961*a* "Indo-European Eschatology in Myth and Epic." In X. *Internationaler Kongress für Religionsgeschichte, 11.–17. September 1960 in Marburg/Lahn* (Marburg), pp. 139–140.

1961*b* "Indoeuropeisk religion," *RoB* 20:3–13.

1964 "Från indisk djurfabel till isländsk saga," *VSLÅ* n.v.: 89–114.

YOSHIDA, ATSUHIKO

1961, 1962, 1963 "La mythologie japonaise: Essai d'interprétation structurale," *RHR* 160.47–66, 161.25–44, 163.225–248.

1962 "Analyse structurale d'un roman chinois: Le Si Yeou-ki," *AESC* 17:647–662.

1964*a* "Le Punyavantajātaka, analyse structurale d'un Jâtaka," *AESC* 19:685–695.

1964*b* "La structure de l'illustration du bouclier d'Achille," *RBPh* 42:5–15.

1964*c* "Survivances de la tripartition fonctionnelle en Grèce," *RHR* 166:21–38.

1965*a* "Sur quelques coupes de la fable grecque," *REA* 67:31–36.

1965*b* "Piasos noyé, Cléité pendue et le moulin de Cyzique: Essai de mythologie comparée," *RHR* 168:155–164.

1965*c* "Sur quelques figures de la mythologie japonaise," *Acta Orientalia* 29:221–233.

1966 "Le fronton occidental du Temple d'Apollon à Delphes et les trois fonctions," *RBPh* 44:5–11.

1969 "Mythe d'Orion et de Cédalion," *Hommages à Marcel Renard* (Collection Latomus 102, Brussels), II, 828–844.

Index

(The index covers only the text)

AUTHORS

Adam of Bremen, 124, 126, 134, 176–177, 180, 181, 187
Adhamnán, 135–136
Aeschylus, 212, 214–216, 218, 219, 223, 226, 227–228
Amandry, P., 216
Apollodorus, 86–92, 99, 125, 238
Aristotle, 21, 22, 228
Armistead, S., 201

Banning, W., 31
Bartstra, J. S., 31
Bayet, J., 36
Benveniste, E., 5, 96
Betz, W., 61, 81
Bhawe, S., 160
Binchy, D. A., 15
Blau, A., 169
Bloomfield, M., 169
Bodde, D., 35
Brednich, R., 138
Brown, T., 23
Bugge, S., 74, 188

Caesar, 59, 79, 163, 207
Calder, G., 8
Campbell, J., 160
Carnoy, A., 204
Cawasji, J., 206
Chandavarkar, J., 206
Cicero, 127, 203, 210
Clemen, C., 84, 100
Closs, A., 56–57
Collinet, P., 194
Cornelius, F., 195
Darmesteter, J., 204
Davoud-Oghlou, G. A., 42
De Bie, J., 204–205
Defradas, J., 213, 214, 215–216, 217–218
Derolez, R., 59–60, 73
Deubner, L., 227
De Vries, Jan, 35–36, 40, 63, 65, 69, 76–78, 81, 134, 156, 164
Dio Cassius, 163, 199, 207
Diodorus, 20, 22–23, 26–27, 89
Dionysius of Halicarnassus, 91
Dörrie, Heinrich, 24
Dudo of St. Quintin, 131
Dumézil, G., 16, 19, 36, 56, 58–61, 62–63, 64, 66, 67, 73, 76, 78, 79, 93, 119, 120, 123–125, 129, 130–131, 132, 142, 147, 148, 159, 162, 163, 166, 167, 168, 169, 171–172, 193, 194, 197, 199, 203–205, 208, 210, 211, 212, 213, 219, 221, 222, 223, 224, 228, 229, 232–234, 237–238, 242–243, 244, 245
Dumont, P.-E., 160

Eggeling, J., 175, 183, 186
Eliade, M., 56, 57–58
Euhemerus, 19, 20, 23, 24
Eusebius, 20, 23, 100

Fayan, R., 128
Festus, 162
Firdausi, 84, 92, 103, 119
Fontenelle, B. le. B. de, 32
Fontenrose, J., 219
Forrer, E. O., 83
Fowler, M., 188
Frazer, J. G., 71, 89, 90, 186
Friedrich, J., 7
Frisk, H., 87, 235

Furtwängler, A., 198

Geoffrey of Monmouth, 138
Geraldus Cambrensis, 163–164
Gering, H., 5, 65
Gerschel, L., 228, 244
Gobel, J., 46
Goldschmidt, H., 128
Gonda, J., 160
Goossens, R., 197, 220
Gray, L. H., 207
Grégoire, H., 220
Grönbech, V., 55
Grunau, S., 148–149
Güntert, H., 1, 2, 3–4, 5, 7, 57, 61
Güterbock, H. G., 83, 85, 93–94, 95, 96, 97, 99, 100, 102

Hartknoch, Ch., 208
Haugen, E., 3, 224
Helm, K., 60–61
Henssen, G., 139, 141
Herodotus, 32, 35
Hesiod, 85, 86, 88, 89–92, 95, 102, 114, 212, 226, 231–232
Hildebert of Le Mans, 136
Homer, 1–2, 3, 8, 32, 85–86, 87, 96, 133, 214, 218, 230, 231, 232, 233, 234, 236, 237, 240, 241, 245–246
Hübschmann, H., 206–207
Hume, D., 32–33

Ivanov, V. V., 164
Isidore, 8

Jacobus a Voragine, 144
Jacoby, F., 20
Jakobson, R., 16
Janez, S., 87
Jerome, 207
Jordanes, 131

Kirfel, W., 161–162
Klima, O., 207
Koppers, W., 162, 163
Kramer, S. N., 35, 111
Krohn, J., 144
Kuiper, F. B. J., 182
Kuhn, A., 170

Lactantius, 26
Lambert, W. G., 112, 113, 114, 118
Laroche, E., 8
Lattimore, R., 231–232
Lazzeroni, R., 1, 3
Lévi-Strauss, C., 38
Liebermann, F., 42
Littleton, C. S., 19, 36, 62, 208–209, 222, 223
Liungman, W., 71
Livy, 19, 219, 224, 232
Lommel, H., 169
Lucan, 134–135

Malinowski, B., 83, 239
Mannhardt, W., 71
Manuel, F. E., 32
Marie de France, 196
Mathieu, M., 220
Meid, W., 13–14
Meillet, A., 10
Mogk, E., 65, 132
Müller, C. H., 40
Müller, K. O., 35

Neckel, G., 69
Nestor, 149–157
Nilsson, M. P., 221
Nonnos, 86, 92, 93, 99, 120

O'Brien, M. A., 10
O'Clery, M., 136
Oldenberg, H., 161, 183, 186
Orosius, 124, 126, 132
Otten, H., 8

Palmer, L. R., 102
Paulus Diaconus, 162
Pausanias, 69
Pedersen, H., 13
Petersson, H., 108
Philippson, E. A., 61
Philo of Byblos, 84, 100–102, 119
Pindar, 91, 196, 198–199, 215
Pisani, V., 170–171
Pliny the Elder, 124
Plutarch, 91, 162
Polybius, 162
Porphyrius, 100
Prokopios, 124
Puhvel, J., 95, 245

Raglan, Lord, 235
Rank, O., 235
Renel, C., 195
Renou, L., 12, 186
Rodríguez de Almela, D., 201–202
Rooth, A. B., 65
Rose, H. J., 87

Saemund Siggfusson, 84, 106–107
Saint Augustine, 25
Saint Moling, 136–137
Sanjana, D. P., 206

Sastri, P. S., 194
Saxo Grammaticus, 19, 25, 27–29, 31, 32, 37, 65–67, 68, 106, 123, 124, 129, 132, 140–141, 152, 174, 177, 237
Schilling, R., 199
Schippers, J. W., 22, 26
Schrader, O., 207
Schröder, F. R., 64, 70, 72, 73, 76, 159, 163
Snorri Sturluson, 19, 27, 29–31, 32, 34–35, 37, 64, 66, 67, 68, 69–70, 71, 73, 77–79, 84, 106–107, 108, 124, 126
Solmsen, F., 212, 223, 226
Speiser, E. A., 85
Spencer, H., 34
Steiner, G., 85, 119
Stesichorus, 215
Strabo, 134, 207
Susemihl, F., 23

Tacitus, 56, 57, 58, 59, 67, 79, 80, 106, 125–126, 127, 131, 132, 170, 208
Thorpe, B., 42
Thurneysen, R., 10, 13
Tieck, L., 48
Toporov, V. N., 148, 164
Turville-Petre, E. O., 66, 67, 178
Tylor, E. B., 34

Úlfr Uggason, 69, 77

Vallauri, G., 24
V.d. Zeyde, M. H., 31
Van Hamel, A., 178, 179–180, 181
Van Maerlant, J., 30
Van Ossenbeeck, J., 133
Varro, 169, 203, 210
Vergil, 91
Vian, F., 93, 120–121, 218, 221, 227
Virgilius Maro, 8
Von Amira, K., 126

Walcot, P., 110, 112, 113, 114, 118
Ward, D. J., 143, 197, 235, 237
Weber, A., 163
West, M. L., 111
Wikander, S., 19, 63, 84–85, 101, 102–104, 106, 115, 119, 193–195, 197, 235, 242
Wilda, W. E., 44

Xenophanes of Colophon, 21, 22

Yoshida, A., 147–148, 216, 218, 221, 223–224, 230–231, 243, 244–245, 246

Zoroaster, 195

MYTHICAL NAMES

Abzu, 110
Achilles, 71, 230, 231, 232, 237, 238–239, 240–241, 244, 245
Adam, 30
Aedh the Black, 136
Aed Ruad, 166
Aegisthus, 214
Aesir, 29–30, 60–61, 62, 70, 77, 107, 108–109, 166, 168, 224, 226, 232–233
Agamemnon, 213, 214–215, 217, 238, 242, 243, 244
Agdistis, 97–98
Agdos, 97
Agni, 182, 183, 187–188, 189
Ahalyā, 237
Ahura Mazdāh, 195, 235
Aias of Locris, 240, 242
Aias of Salamis, 240, 241
Aidhedh Muirchertaig mac Erca, 137
Aife, 166
Aigipan, 92
Ailill, 76, 167
Alala, 94
Alalu, 94–95, 99, 116
Alcis, 170
Alcmaeon, 215
Amakandu, 113, 116–117
Amalthea, 90
Amphiaraus, 215
Amphion, 196
Amphitryon, 196
Aṃśa, 243
Anāhitā, 165, 168, 205, 210, 221, 228
Ancus Martius, 155
Andromache, 234
Anshar, 110, 111
Anu, 94–96, 97, 99, 100, 110, 114, 116
Aphrodite, 88, 233, 235
Apollo, 165, 213–214, 215, 216, 217, 218, 219–224, 227, 228
Apsu, 99, 110–111
Aranzah, 96
Archon, 228
Areion, 170
Ares, 228
Aria, 144
Ariadne, 231
Arjuna, 153, 156, 157, 235, 239, 240, 241, 242
Armaiti, 205, 210
Aryaman, 63, 155, 221
Ase, 75
Aši Dahāka, 103, 105–106
Asklepios, 165, 220
Askold, 151
Askr, 77
Astydamia, 238
Asuras, 61
Aśvins, 68, 156, 165, 166, 169, 194–195, 196–198, 226, 234, 235
Atar, 195, 235
Athena, 97, 215–216, 220–223, 224, 225, 233
Athenaïs, 228
Atlas, 101
Audhumla, 107

Baal, 101, 109, 113, 117
Badb, 167
Balder, 63–68, 69–82
Bālin, 69
Basileus, 228
Bellerophontes, 170
Bergelmir, 91, 107–108, 117
Bestla, 107
Bhaga, 63, 76, 155
Bhīma, 153, 154, 157, 235, 240–241, 242
Boian, 152
Bör, 107, 109, 116
Bragi, 77
Bress, 225–226
Briseis, 238
Brünhilde, 71
Bruth, 101
Buri, 107, 109, 116

Castor, 198, 199
Castores, 194
Cathubodua, 167
Catualda, 67
Catumerus, 67
Chaos, 84, 86, 107
Chatti, 59, 67, 80–81
Chimaira, 170
Cid, 201–202
Cimbaeth, 166
Clovis, 115
Clytemnestra, 215–215, 222
Conchobar, 166, 167
Corycian Pan, 92
Crunniuc mac Agnomain, 166
Cuchulainn, 166–167
Curiatii, 93, 219
Cybele, 58, 98
Cyclopes, 87, 88, 90

Dagda, 167
Dakṣa, 243
Damkina, 111
Danu, 165
Dārayavahu, 212
Daśaratha, 162

Dasra, 170, 194, 235
Demeter, 89, 90, 170
Despoina, 170
Dhṛtarāṣṭra, 63, 64
Diarmaid, 137
Dias, 228
Dieva dēli, 196, 198
Dievo suneliai, 196, 198
Diomedes, 239, 241, 243
Dionysos, 216
Dioscuri, 69, 165, 170–171, 196, 197–198, 199, 234, 237
Dir, 151
Dithorba, 166
Divó nápāt, 170
Dôn, 165
Draupadī, 165, 168
Draupnir, 66, 78
Duryodhana, 64
Dyauḥ, 119–120, 170, 244

Ea, 98, 99, 110, 111, 112, 114
Edward IV, 128
Eiríkr blóðøx, 77
El, 101–102, 104, 116–117
Electra, 217
Eliun, 100, 102, 116
Embla, 77
Enki, 110, 114
Enlil, 96, 99
Epona, 165
Epopeus, 196
Erichthonios, 97
Erinyes, 214, 215, 217, 220–223, 225, 226, 227
Ériu, 165, 167
Esus, 134
Eumenides, 227–228
Europa, 168–169
Eurystheus, 238
Eve, 30
Eyvindr kelda, 126

Fergus, 76, 167
Feridun, 103, 104–105, 113, 117
Fialarr, 126
Fir Bolg, 9, 10
Fjölnir, 125
Flamen Martialis, 163
Fomorians, 166, 225
Fortuna, 76
Freyja, 224, 233, 237
Freyr, 57, 59, 66, 68, 70, 71, 124, 149, 156, 224, 233
Frigg, 29–30, 65, 70, 79
Frigga, 27–28
Frikko, 176
Frotho, 124

Galarr, 126
Gaṅgā, 119
Gaia, 86, 87–88, 89, 97, 103, 112, 114, 116
Ga'um, 113
Gayomart, 103, 209
Ge, 101
Gelderus, 66
George Duke of Clarence, 128
Gevarus, 65–66
Gilgamesh, 74, 75
Ginnungagap, 107
Glaukos, 125
Grag, 136–137
Gunnhildr, 127

Hadad, 101
Hadding, 124
Hades, 107, 109
Hadingus, 62, 66, 150, 168, 178
Hagen, 71
Hain, 113, 116
Haraldr, 67, 127
Hebat, 99
Hector, 234, 235–237, 239, 241, 245
Heimdallr, 119–120, 244
Hekabe, 235
Hel, 74, 78, 80
Helen, 237
Helgi, 67, 151
Hengist, 199–200
Hephaistias, 228
Hephaistos, 97, 98
Hera, 89, 90, 171, 222, 233, 239
Herakles, 170, 196, 214, 230, 231–232, 237–238, 239, 243
Hercules, 59
Hermes, 90, 92, 101
Hermes Trismegistus, 25
Hermunduri, 59
Hestia, 89, 90
Hodbroddus, 65–66
Hödr, 63–64, 65–66, 67, 69, 71, 73, 75, 76, 77, 81
Horatii, 93, 219
Horatius Cocles, 62
Horsa, 199–200
Hunding, 124, 129
Husheng, 103
Hygieia, 221
Hyrrokkin, 77

Idas, 198
Igor, 149, 151, 153–154, 155, 156, 157
Illuyanka, 120

Indra, 93, 108, 120, 148, 153, 157, 163, 165, 166, 218–219, 221, 235, 237–238, 240–241, 242
Ing, 57
Ingaevones, 59, 156
Ingjaldr illráði, 76
Iole, 238
Iphikles, 196
Iphitos, 238
Irminsūl, 183
Ishtar, 99
Ixion, 171, 223

Jamshid, 101, 103, 104, 105, 116–117
Janus, 244
Jaropolk, 155–156, 157
Juno Seispes, 168
Jupiter, 26, 59, 165
Juturna, 198

Kadmos, 99
Kaiumers, 103
Kalkhas, 243
Kastor, 196, 199, 236–237
Kauravas, 232
Kentauros, 171
Keres, 226
Kingu, 111, 112, 117
Kishar, 110
Kronos, 20, 84, 87, 88, 90, 91, 96, 97, 99, 102, 103, 104, 105, 109, 110, 111, 112, 113, 114, 116–117, 226
Kudrun, 237
Kumarbi, 84, 95–97, 100, 102, 111, 116–117
Kyknos, 170

Lahamu, 110, 111
Lahar, 113, 117
Lahmu, 110, 111
Lailoken, 138
Līber, 81, 82
Lódur, 77, 81, 82
Loki, 63–64, 65, 67, 73–74, 75, 79, 80, 243
Lug, 134, 167, 225–226
Lugaid, 76
Lykomedes, 238
Lynkeus, 198

Macha, 165–167
Maeltne, 225–226
Mag Tured, 62, 225
Mal of the Derevlians, 154, 157
Mannus, 106, 170
Manu, 106, 169–170
Marduk, 96, 108, 110, 111, 112, 113, 117
Mars, 58, 59, 131, 134, 136, 162, 163, 165, 171, 234
Mars Thincsus, 59, 171
Maruts, 221
Matrae, 165
Matres, 165
Matrona, 167
Matronae, 165, 168
Medb, 167
Medusa, 170
Menelaus, 236
Mercurius, 58, 59
Mercury, 124, 135
Merlin, 138
Mimingus, 66
Mit-Othin, 28
Mitra, 148, 150, 152, 153, 156–157, 171, 194, 221, 235, 242–243
Moirai, 226, 227
Mokoš, 165
Mongruad, 166
Morrigu, 167
Mucius Scaevola, 62
Myrddin, 138

Nakula, 193–194, 234, 235–236
Nala, 63
Namuci, 237
Naŋhaithya, 195, 235
Nanna, 65–66, 67, 68, 71
Nāsatya, 148, 170, 194, 195, 235
Nemed mac Agnomain, 166
Nephele, 171
Neptune, 136
Neptūnus, 10
Nerthus, 57–59, 125–126, 168
Nestor, 243, 244
Nike, 221
Ningeshtinna, 113
Nisaba, 113
Njördr, 57, 59, 62–63, 124, 125, 168, 224, 233
Norns, 226

Odin, 27–28, 29–30, 58, 60, 61–62, 64, 65, 66–67, 73, 75–76, 77, 78, 79, 80, 81, 107, 108, 109, 113, 117, 124, 132, 134, 140–142, 151, 177–181, 183, 186, 187, 188–189, 190, 224, 233
Odysseus, 238–239, 243
Oedipus, 38, 93, 235
Okeanos, 114
Óláfr paí, 69
Oleg, 149, 150–153, 154, 155, 156